The North Korean Economy

The
North Korean
Economy

Between Crisis
& Catastrophe

Nicholas Eberstadt

Transaction Publishers
New Brunswick (U.S.A.) and London (U.K.)

This book is printed on acid-free paper that meets the American National Standard for Permanence of Paper for Printed Library Materials.

Library of Congress Catalog Number: 2006044483
ISBN: 978-0-7658-0360-3
Printed in the United States of America

Library of Congress Cataloging-in-Publication Data

Eberstadt, Nick, 1955-
    The North Korean economy : between crisis and catastrophe / Nicholas Eberstadt.
        p. cm.
    Includes bibliographical references and index.
    ISBN 0-7658-0360-7 (cloth : alk. paper)
        1. Korea (North)—Economic conditions. 2. Korea (North)—Economic policy. I. Title.

HC470.2.E255   2006
330.95193—dc22   2006044483

To my beloved children:
Rick, Kate, Izzi, Alexandra

Contents

Acknowledgments

Drawing together as it does almost a decade and a half of work and study, this volume naturally comes to press with an unusually high burden of authorial debts. Only the most acute and pressing among them can be mentioned in this brief space.

All the research presented in the following chapters was undertaken during my tenure at the American Enterprise Institute for Public Policy Research (AEI). AEI has been and remains an extraordinary intellectual haven within the often-troubled waters of contemporary academia. It is my great good fortune to have been allowed to harbor there these many happy years. I would be sorely remiss if I did not also thank the Harvard University Center for Population and Development Studies for its graceful indulgence of my research on North Korean questions during the fondly-remembered years when I was a Visiting Fellow. Both duty and pleasure, furthermore, require an affectionate salute to another wonderful institutional home-away-from-home: the National Bureau of Asian Research, whose abiding encouragement has contributed directly to so much in this book.

Although I alone am responsible for the pages that follow, the findings presented here are in reality the work of many hands. Over the past decade and a half I have enjoyed the help and intellectual company of a veritable all-star team of AEI research assistants and interns. Special thanks are due, in chronological order, to: Jonathan Tombes, Gwendolyn Wilber, David Stetson, Lisa Howie, Heather Dresser, Courtney Myers, Assia Dosseva, Christopher Griffin, and Karla Herdzik. Moving extramurally, I would like to congratulate Jay Philip Nash for his early heroic efforts to fashion this manuscript into a single coherent text, and to applaud Nancy Ackerman of AmadeaEditing warmly for her expert editorial advice during the "arduous march" to completion.

Lest it go unsaid, I should also note my considerable debt to fellow students of contemporary North Korea—from the United States, South Korea, Japan, China, Russia, and other locales. The DPRK is an exceptionally difficult country for outsiders to study. Plausible interpretations of available evidence may lead analysts in very different directions. The prudent student of North Korean affairs is well advised to listen to these discordant and contending assessments. In the pages that follow, I hope it will be apparent that I have valued my colleagues' insights, even on the occasions where I have not been persuaded by their conclusions.

This book would not have been begun, or doubtless completed, but for the kind and generous support of the Korea Foundation. My thanks, and gratitude, go out to the offices of the Korea Foundation for this largesse.

Finally, as always, I wish to thank my family for their love, tolerance, and patience. I have already dedicated a number of books to the indispensable presence in my life, my wife Mary. Now I have the pleasure of dedicating a book to my children, who have enriched their father's life beyond measure.

The dedication is transmitted with great pride and deep affection: and with the hope that they may see a better day dawn over the hapless and tormented land whose plight is the subject of this book.

Preface

This book traces the economic performance—and describes the political economy—of a most unusual country during a most unusual time. The country in question is the Democratic People's Republic of Korea, also known as the DPRK, or North Korea. The period under consideration is the first decade and a half following the "end of the Cold War"—or, to be a bit more clinically precise, following the collapse of the USSR and the concomitant dissolution of the Soviet bloc's arrangements for aid and subsidized trade for fraternal states.

The DPRK was not a Soviet ally—Pyongyang's policy for maximizing its autonomy in those Cold War days was to maneuver Moscow against Beijing—but by the start of the 1990s, North Korea had become dangerously dependent upon Soviet largesse, such as it was. The sudden, unexpected, and total elimination of that support served as the triggering event for the dramas—and tragedies—that followed.

From the partition of the peninsula in the 1940s to this very day, strategy and economic policy in divided Korea have been informed, indeed defined, by the race between the two contending Korean states: the DPRK and the Republic of Korea (also known as ROK or South Korea). For decades, the DPRK seemed to be ahead in that race: as late as the early 1970s, per capita output was believed—by Washington and Seoul—to be higher in the North than in the South. By the start of the 1990s, however, a generation of sustained rapid growth in South Korea had left the North Korean economy lagging behind ever more obviously in an increasingly unequal competition.

With the demise of the USSR, the race between South and North Korean economies entered an entirely new phase, one almost painful to behold. With the Soviet collapse, the economic trajectories of the two Koreas were no longer simply divergent. Their paths were now set in almost diametrically opposite directions. Whereas the South Korean economy continued to enjoy dynamic growth, with erratic annual results, but an impressively high average tempo, North Korea's economy was cast into a steep and terrifying decline.

The post-Cold War performance of the North Korean economy has been nothing short of disastrous. No statistical measure encapsulates that performance so vividly as this single fact: in the 1990s, the DPRK became the first urbanized literate society in human history to suffer famine during peacetime.

Although the magnitude of that famine cannot yet be specified with any precision—for reasons we shall see—it seems all but certain that the toll ran into the hundreds of thousands, and it may have run into the millions.

Yet even as the DPRK descended into mass famine—a dubious and gruesome achievement for any modern industrialized society—Pyongyang was striving to distinguish itself through achievements in the field of mass-destruction weaponry. In 1998, Pyongyang launched a multi-stage ballistic rocket over Japan (the "Taepo Dong"), thereby entering that select club of modern states with demonstrated long-range missile capabilities. In 2005, Pyongyang declared that it possessed "nukes," and indicated that it would not relinquish them "under any circumstances."[1] Thus, at the dawn of the twenty-first century, North Korea qualified as a singularly troubled and troubling country, one that ranked not only among the declining number of contemporary societies seemingly poised permanently on the brink of famine, but also in the handful of countries whose governments claimed to possess nuclear weapons and long-range missiles.

Perverse as this North Korean paradox may appear, it is by no means adventitious. On the contrary, it is the entirely logical consequence of deliberate governmental policies and actions, faithfully reflecting leadership priorities and the carefully considered strategies which devolved from them.

In theory, the task of relieving the desperate privation of the stricken North Korean populace should be almost trivially simple: all that would be required of the masters of this closed and repressed economy is the *cessation* of the manifold costly distortions which they currently insist upon enforcing, so that DPRK policy might move along a more pragmatic and less destructive path. But DPRK policymakers have vetoed this option again and again. According to repeated pronouncements of their state media, they regard the measures routinely adopted these days in other countries to enhance national economic prospects as inimical to their own prospects for regime survival.

According to Pyongyang's official diagnosis, the downfall of Soviet and Eastern European socialism was the consequence of "ideological and cultural infiltration," an insidious bourgeois infection, transmitted by economic and non-economic contact with the outside world. In Pyongyang's telling, such "infiltration" undermined the authority of the dictatorship of the proletariat and eventually brought state-destroying concessions upon all the Warsaw Pact governments. As one official North Korean formulation memorably put it in 1998, just days after Kim Jong Il's formal public accession to the DPRK's "highest office of state":

> We must heighten vigilance against the imperialists' moves to induce us to "reform" and "opening to the outside world." "Reform" and "opening" on their lips are a

honey coated poison. Clear is our stand toward "reform" and "opening." We now have nothing to "reform" and "open." By "reform" and "opening" the imperialists mean to revive capitalism.[2]

In light of such directives, any economic experimentation in the DPRK — and as we shall see, there has been *some* experimentation in North Korea in recent years — could only proceed under strict, indeed forbidding, parameters.

But if the North Korean government is unwilling to acquiesce in regular commercial intercourse in the world economy, how can the regime expect to finance its own survival? Pyongyang's own answers to the question are indicated by the two overarching political slogans that have been unfurled during the Kim Jong Il era: the imperatives of building "a powerful and prosperous state" (*kangsong taeguk*) and "military-first politics" (*songun chongchi*).

A month after the ceremony in which the "Dear Leader" formally acceded to power and in which the banner "powerful and prosperous state" was first publicly waved, North Korean media spelled out the precise meaning of the slogan, explaining that "defense capabilities are a military guarantee for national political independence and the self-reliant economy," and, further, that "the nation can become prosperous only when the barrel of the gun is strong."[3]

More recently, official pronouncements about "military-first politics" elucidated Pyongyang's view of exactly how military might conduces to national wealth:

A country's development and the . . . importance of the military are linked as one . . . . Once we lay the foundations for a powerful self-sustaining national defense industry, we will be able to rejuvenate all economic fields, to include light industry and agriculture and enhance the quality of the people's lives.[4]

One might well wonder how could *any* country's defense sector expect to become "self-sustaining," much less a vehicle for financing the development of other economic sectors, as the North Korean notion of "military-first politics" would have it? That scenario is only conceivable if a country's military expenditures were deployed in such a manner as to generate tangible economic dividends, i.e., to earn net profits. In practice, this can only mean extracting resources from elsewhere, that is to say, from other countries.

Though the DPRK economy is moribund, and its people are afflicted by terrible suffering, Pyongyang's rulers have absolutely no intention of allowing their national situation to be defined as a "humanitarian problem." As they no doubt realize very well, the fate of those national directorates associated with the modern era's "humanitarian emergencies" is seldom enviable. Rather, North Korean leadership sees its fortunes directly tied to its efforts to define the DPRK as a "security problem" for the international community. In the view of North Korea's policymakers, international "protection" payments are now key to the DPRK's survival.

Stated plainly, North Korea's post-Cold War survival strategy is a policy of international military extortion. Loath to embrace the sorts of measures that would predictably revive their stricken economy for fear that such ordinary and unexceptional steps would actually spell doom for their system, North Korea's rulers have concluded instead that it is safer to finance the survival of their state through the international export of strategic insecurity and military menace.

Consequently, the North Korean leadership must today, as a matter of course, generate sufficiently grave international tensions, and present sufficiently credible security threats, to wrest a flow of essentially coerced transfers from threatened neighbors and other international targets in sufficient volume to assure the integrity and continuation of what Pyongyang describes as "our own style of socialism" [*urisik sahoejuui*]. In a very real sense, the North Korean economy has been carefully and intentionally positioned in a realm between crisis and catastrophe.

Judged by its own lights, Pyongyang's predatory post-Cold War economic strategy may actually be working. Indeed, those who command the North Korean state may even deem it a ringing success.

After all, the DPRK, unlike so many other communist regimes, has neither vanished from the face of the earth, nor compromised its claim to unlimited domestic authority through system-altering economic reforms. The terrible famine of the 1990s—a food crisis that unaddressed might have portended an ultimate breakdown of the DPRK's economic structure and the political control apparatus it supported—has for now subsided, albeit conditionally. The North Korean state has managed to unburden itself of the various international obligations and declarations that had heretofore seemingly constrained its prerogative to amass an arsenal of nuclear weapons, and improbable as it may sound, has come to engage South Korea and the Great Powers of the Pacific (China, Japan, Russia, and the United States) in "denuclearization" talks from a position of tactical advantage, with supposed non-proliferation deliberations occurring on a schedule and according to an agenda very largely of Pyongyang's own choosing.

And as the perceived killing potential of the North Korean state has waxed, so has the aggregate level of net foreign resources transmitted to the DPRK through "non-commercial" channels, such as aid payments from concerned neighboring states or state-sponsored criminal activities including drug-smuggling and counterfeiting. As we will document in the following pages, North Korea's balance of trade deficit has soared during the era of *kangsong taeguk* and "military-first politics," and, for the idiosyncratic system they command, DPRK leadership views that deficit not as an indictor of economic weakness, but rather as a proxy for political health.

By any criteria other than the North Korean high command's own cynical and utterly solipsistic calculus, however, the DPRK's stratagem of survival through terror is a political economy of bankruptcy—not least for the hapless and captive DPRK populace. Though the international military extortion program that Pyongyang has been perfecting over the past decade and a half may afford the country's leadership a chance for regime survival—or at least, regime prolongation—it offers their subjects only continuing penury and privation.

As we shall demonstrate in the following pages, North Korea's current political economy does not offer any appreciable scope for broad-based productivity increases for this astonishingly distorted and sadly debilitated economy. Without broad-based improvements in productivity, however, any appreciable, sustained and genuinely self-reliant improvement in living standards is all but impossible. In the absence of productivity improvements, the lot of the North Korean consumer depends—today and over the foreseeable future—upon prospects for subventions from abroad, and the whims of Pyongyang's rulers in allocating them. Under such circumstances, advances in living conditions are likely to be grudging and tentative at best. And they will remain merely provisional, to be erased or even reversed with brutal alacrity as current events dictate. Without fundamental change in the DPRK's political economy, moreover, living standards in the DPRK are currently set, even under the most optimistic of prognoses, to fall ever further behind those in the rest of the Northeast Asian neighborhood—and eventually, behind those of virtually all the rest of East Asia. A sorry outlook for a place that was, one may recall, one of the more industrialized and dynamic spots on the map in continental Asia not so very long ago.

What lies in store for the DPRK and its people? When Chapter 1 was first drafted back in 1993, it was apparent that the regime had foresworn economic reforms worthy of the name, and was reconciled to enduring economic decline, while capitalizing upon the international security dramas it managed to manufacture. In that respect, little has changed over the last decade, and more.

Yet other things *have* changed—including the DPRK's economic capabilities. Unfortunately, many of these changes are for the worse. Information is potential wealth in the modern world. Yet, as we see in Chapter 2, the DPRK, under its policy of suffocating state secrecy and information control, has evidently crippled and blinded the very national statistical apparatus which might otherwise have helped point the way to a more productive and successful economic future.

The economic disasters that awaited North Korea after the Soviet collapse, for their part, have to be understood in terms of the long legacy of policies that had already all but consigned the DPRK to economic failure. Under the slogan of "self-reliance," as we will see in Chapter 3, Pyongyang's abiding allergy to the purchase of foreign capital goods led a largely urbanized nation to invest in a high-cost, low-productivity industrial infrastructure—a fragile and perilous construct that self-evidently could not withstand the shocks it faced with the end of Soviet bloc subsidies and the end of politically-guaranteed Soviet bloc demand for its produce. And Pyongyang adhered to its longstanding slogan of "self reliance" in selective and curious ways. Among these, the apparent stricture, discussed in Chapter 4, that the country spend no more on agricultural products from abroad than foreigners were paying for foodstuffs grown in the DPRK. For a northeast Asian country with a relatively large population, a relatively cold climate and a relatively limited season for crop-growing, this obdurate posture all but sentences the populace to eventual food emergency.

Having won its economic race against the North more or less *nolo contendere*, South Korean governmental circles now focus upon the challenges of an eventual North-South economic reintegration. As Chapter 5 indicates, these challenges are considerable, and growing, precisely in the measure that economic performance in North and South are characterized by a yawning, still-widening gap. Current South Korean policy militates for inter-Korean reconciliation through trade and "economic co-operation," but as Chapter 6 argues, North Korean strictures still largely limit that "co-operation" to one-sided subsidies from South Korean taxpayers to officially designated North Korean recipients.

Is the North Korean economy recovering and advancing today, after its parlous travails of the 1990s? Received wisdom among foreign North Korea-watchers might lean in this direction. But, as is argued in Chapter 7, the distinction between domestic value-added and external subsidy is essential to understanding the performance of the contemporary DPRK economy, and there is scant evidence today that the DPRK economy has turned the corner to self-sustaining economic growth.

"Economic reform" is the perennial mantra for the North Korean people's foreign well-wishers; and not without reason. Chapter 8 attempts to assay the outlines that any movement toward economic reform in the DPRK worthy of the name might assume, It further suggests that no such movement has as yet been visible to the outside world.

The North Korean economy today is so seemingly dysfunctional and unproductive, in relation to its available human resources, that practically *any* change in policy direction would be for the better. As Chapter 9 argues, even "ordinary Stalinism" could be expected to improve the performance, and outlook, for the DPRK economy. A shift away from "military-first politics" might lead to substantial jumps in per capita income—to say nothing about international aid—even under an otherwise unreconstructed socialist regime.

Yet the central fact—to some of us, surprise—about the DPRK is that Pyongyang has maintained its style of governance over the past decade and a half, despite the hostile odds. Chapter 10 attempts to explain how this could have happened. Suffice it to say, the notion that the outside world might organize an economic rescue package for the DPRK would have seemed highly fanciful a decade ago, yet this is exactly what transpired. Many billions of dollars of foreign resources have been transmitted to the North Korean state over the past decade. Those foreign monies have not only financed the continuation of the Kim Jong Il regime, they have also sheltered his economy against domestic and external pressures for reform. As it currently operates, the North Korean economic system can only be sustained through continuing subsidies from abroad. More than they might care to realize, the future of the DPRK lies in the hands of those neighboring states whose official aid and sustenance is helping to keep that dangerous and dysfunctional regime alive.

Notes

1. *Korea Central News Agency (KCNA)*, 2005, 11 February.
2. *KCNA*, 1998, 17 September.
3. *Minju Choson*, 1998, 24 October.
4. *Nodong Sinmun*, 2003, 3 April.

1

Reform, Muddling Through, or Collapse?*

[*Author's Note: This essay was written in June 1993, at the beginning of the first round of the still-ongoing North Korean nuclear crisis. Many momentous changes have occurred in the interim. "Great Leader" Kim Il Sung passed from the earthly scene in 1994, and now serves from beyond as the DPRK's "eternal President", according to the state's 1998 constitution. Many hundreds of thousands of ordinary North Koreans perished as well in the terrible famine that commenced soon after the Great Leader's death—the only peacetime famine to beset a literate and urbanized society in recorded history. The United States would sign an "Agreed Framework" with the DPRK that envisioned a complete denuclearization of North Korea, only to have that document disavowed in 2002 by the North Korean official whose signature appears on it. North Korea launched a multistage ballistic rockets in 1998 and then again in 2006, and declared to possessed nuclear weapons in 2005. A South Korean policy of reconciliation, known originally as "Sunshine", has been in place since 1998, and has provided gradually increasing subsidies and support for the North Korean economy. No less portentously in the view of some observers, the DPRK began in 2002 to implement what was officially termed "measures to improve economic management", steps described in the outside world as "reforms". Yet despite these and many other changes over the intervening years, the dynamics and dilemmas of North Korea's security policies and economic policies today are strikingly similar—it is tempting to say fundamentally similar—to those described here nearly a decade and a half ago. If the past is prologue, this prologue chapter frame the themes, issues, and problems that will recur once and again over the course of this work.]

From its founding in 1948 to the present day, the Democratic People's Republic of Korea (DPRK, or North Korea) has pursued a foreign policy distinct among nations in the modern world for its high and seemingly permanent state of tension. The observation that the DPRK's relations with the international com-

*This chapter originally appeared as an article in *Analysis* 4(3), 1993, published by the National Bureau of Asian Research; it has been revised only slightly for presentation here.

munity are currently in a state of crisis may therefore seem unexceptional. Yet even for a government so accustomed to international confrontation, the level of tension in North Korean external relations today is extraordinary, and has changed only in the devilish details over the past decade.

By comparison with the events that unleashed the Korean War, the ongoing drama of North Korea's quest to develop atomic weaponry appears plodding and civil. For example, North Korea's famous March 1993 announcement of its formal intention to withdraw from the Non-Proliferation Treaty (NPT) came as the culmination of year-long detailed discussions and methodical deliberations involving the Republic of Korea, the United States, the International Atomic Energy Agency (IAEA), and other parties. Since 1993, Pyongyang has actively promoted talks with foreign governments over possible formulae or procedures for defusing the crisis it had ignited. Furthermore, Pyongyang adhered to the letter of international law in acknowledging its obligation to remain a member of the NPT for another 90 days after tendering its withdrawal from the treaty. And in announcing a "temporary suspension" of its NPT withdrawal in June 1993—the day before its scheduled departure from the treaty—North Korea chose continuing discussions over immediate conflict.

However, these forensics cannot conceal the grave situation that has been developing. North Korea's March 1993 NPT announcement—which prefigured Pyongyang's eventual 2003 NPT withdrawal—came in the wake of a series of meetings in which IAEA officials presented evidence that the DPRK, in violation of its duties by that treaty, had not only been producing nuclear materials that could be used for atomic weapons, but had attempted as well to deceive IAEA inspectors about these efforts. The NPT announcement, far from being an isolated sore point, was instead emblematic of a new turn toward international confrontation, even against erstwhile allies, on the part of North Korea.

North Korea's nuclear capability has radically altered the nature of the security threat that Republic of Korea (ROK, or South Korea) and her allies have to consider; it has accelerated an arms race that is already escalating throughout Asia; it has reduced future prospects of dissuading conventionally armed but revisionist states from fulfilling whatever nuclear ambitions they might entertain. In short, international objections to North Korea's atomic quest could not be more solidly grounded. Yet in the commotion these objections have generated, a separate issue, only slightly less troubling, has been obscured. For even if this nuclear crisis were somehow completely resolved today through the ongoing Six-Party Talks or even some other means—indeed, even if the DPRK were to dismantle all existing atomic facilities and nuclear weapons, and forswear nuclear research forever—the unavoidable fact is that the DPRK would still pose an enormous and growing problem to the international community.

Even without nuclear weapons, North Korea possesses a massive and aggressively disposed military machine. In the estimate of the International Institute of Strategic Studies (IISS), this country of slightly more than 22 million people fields the fifth largest army in the world today, with at least 1.1 million men under arms.[1] North Korea's ratio of troops to total population appears to be by far the highest for any country in the post-Cold War era. In fact, it rivals the ratios achieved by the combatant powers of World War II during their drives for total mobilization.[2] Described in the early 1970s in a now-classic study as "perhaps the most highly militarized society in the world today," the DPRK has, in the intervening decades, continued a relentless buildup of its forces and their capabilities.[3]

That the DPRK Korean People's Army (KPA) is poised to inflict terrible destruction upon South Korea is well understood. Less appreciated is the fact that it could do so without invading. For example, forward-deployed KPA artillery have the industrial metropolis of Seoul well within their range. Nor is South Korea the only North Korean neighbor which might hypothetically find itself in harm's way. North Korea's No Dong missile reportedly has a range of 1,000 kilometers.[4] Such population centers as Kyoto, Beijing, and Khabarovsk all lie less than 1,000 kilometers from North Korean territory. This circumstance, in and of itself, has sharpened Russian, Chinese, and Japanese interest in stable and predictable North Korean behavior. Reports from the mid-1990s that the KPA "is capable of producing and employing chemical weapons that virtually all fire-support systems in its inventory could deliver" has intensified their concerns about the predictability of North Korean decisionmaking.[5]

Unfortunately for all of Northeast Asia, this fearsomely armed and tensely coiled state is moving day by day toward a juncture whose outcome is completely unpredictable, but whose results could include instability and turmoil. Pyongyang has lost nearly all of its international allies. The gravitational pull exerted by the peninsular presence of the rival South Korean state dramatically increased with the success of Seoul's experiment in political liberalization. From whence did this crisis arise?

The argument may be advanced that a tense and delicate international posture for North Korea was foreordained, as it would have been for any small country that fiercely maintained its independence in the face of looming hegemons. In deference to that argument, one must concede that the DPRK has indeed suffered for its location. No small country seeking a spot on the map would conceivably, of its own volition, select precisely the place where the spheres of influence for the four Great Powers of the Pacific (Russia, China, Japan, and the United States) happen to collide. But this structural argument neglects an essential point. No matter how star-crossed its geography may be, the fact is that North Korea's current problems with the international community devolve directly from its own policy choices and actions. It is no easy feat to alienate or antagonize *all* the Great Powers in one's vicinity simultaneously, especially as tensions among those Great Powers themselves are on the wane. Yet this is exactly what the DPRK has succeeded in doing.

Paradoxically, to conclude that North Korea's current international problems are in the main of its own making is to perceive some hope for the future. If the DPRK has created the perimeter of tension now surrounding it, the key to a regional, and international, detente lies correspondingly in the hands of the North Korean government. Confidence and stability in North Korea's dealings with other governments can accrue if the DPRK begins to act as if it were a state like any other.

Will the North Korean state emerge from its present international crisis and embark upon a path toward normalcy in its international relations? More specifically, *can* that state, as it is presently constituted, turn the key that would open the door to detente with the rest of the world? One can consider these questions in terms of the demonstrated strengths and capabilities of the existing regime, the pressures facing that state today, and the alternative adjustments to those pressures that would unfold through the mediating mechanism of the North Korean political system.

North Korean Governance

North Korea's particular interpretation of socialism opens the DPRK to easy caricature abroad: the suffocating Father-Son personality cult; the clumsy but obsessive effort to control all information entering, circulating within, and leaving the country; the crude racialism and xenophobia; and the relentless drive to eliminate all private space from daily life present a bizarre and unappealing public face. However, it is easy to misassess—and to underestimate—the strengths of the state that wears the mask.

The capabilities of that government are indirectly indicated by its longevity. The DPRK, after all, is today's oldest standing Communist state. For a less idiosyncratic regime, such a feature of governance would be recognized as trappings of a certain kind of success.

By the criteria of liberal political theory, North Korean governance is a grotesque failure. But those criteria are irrelevant to North Korea's own leadership, which judges its experiment in governance against a very different set of standards. By those standards, a rather different reading of the state's performance can be drawn. For North Korea has succeeded in developing a military force appropriate for a Great Power. It has erected and maintained a truly monolithic political order. No centers of authority exist apart from party and state, and within state and party there is nothing like a challenge to Kim Jong

Il's absolute power. The entire body of North Korea's citizenry, by all external indications, behave as if they are unreservedly loyal to, enthusiastic about, and grateful for the nature of the rule that they experience. Not least importantly, those Communist states which dared to publicly criticize the DPRK's style of socialism have themselves vanished from the stage of history. Given this perspective, North Korean leadership may perhaps be excused if it looks back at the country's record with a certain satisfaction, and if it looks toward today's menacing developments with an unexpected air of confidence.

In and of themselves, economic imbalances and structural distortions in the society they manage do not seem to rattle the North Korean leadership. They have, after all, presided over and intensified these imbalances and distortions for decades. Nevertheless, these imbalances and distortions have reached a point where they should directly worry decision makers in the DPRK, for they now interfere with a prime objective of state—the augmentation of power by the regime.

Central to the dilemma is the KPA itself. This indispensable instrument of North Korean statecraft is valued in proportion to its size, but its size is now an insuperable burden for the economy that must support it. Manpower figures tell the story. By the late 1980s, non-civilian males accounted for fully a fifth of North Korea's men of working ages.[6] Though North Korea's soldiers episodically engage in farming, construction, and the like, they are basically nonproductive workers who must draw sustenance and materiel from other sectors to perform their assigned tasks. Their immediate drag on the economy is substantial. But the growth of the KPA also forestalls economic growth in other ways. Given North Korea's fertility trends and its government policies, there is no more "surplus labor" in the country. To satisfy its thirst for ever more inductees, the army must deprive state enterprises or universities of their recruits. In this institutional competition, the KPA's success in amassing its troop base undercuts training and productivity for the workforce as a whole. It is hardly a coincidence that North Korea's economic troubles began to manifest themselves in the early 1970s, exactly when the current tendency toward military buildup went into its acceleration.

Just as North Korea's military has been abnormally expanded, so its consumer sector has been artificially compressed. Even by Communist standards, North Korea's policies toward the consumer were always severe. By one Western estimate, for example, the share of consumption in the North Korean economy in the 1950s was about twenty percentage points lower than in the Soviet Union.[7] Since then, however, it appears that the share of output claimed by the consumer has been suppressed still further. Today, personal consumption expenditures, for example, are an almost peripheral item in the North Korean economy. Very rough calculations suggest that wages and salaries would amount to no more than 15–25 percent of the nation's output.[8] Moreover, much of the population's consumption package is allocated directly to the household by the state, outside retail channels. While it may seem convenient in the first instance for central planners to disconnect the preferences and desires of consumers from the workings of their planned economy, that separation imposes a variety of economic costs. Such austerity may affect human capital, and thus the potential for augmenting growth. It cannot help but affect the motivation of the workforce. And by decommissioning price signals in the realm of the household—the area where they were most likely to function well, at least under socialism—the North Korean government inadvertently deafened itself to the sounds of its own economy, increasing the chance that waste would not be recognized, or misallocations corrected.

Ever-increasing misallocation and waste, for their part, have been all but ordained by the thrust of North Korean central planning for a full generation. The task of civilian technocrats charged with enhancing the efficiency and productivity of the DPRK national economy seems to have suffered two colossal complications in the early 1970s. First, the State Planning Commission was reportedly deprived of access to information about North Korea's huge and growing military economy, leaving technocrats in the dark about much of the overall economy they were expected to rationalize.[9] Second, the statistical blackout imposed on official DPRK publications and media was apparently accompanied by mounting pressures to politicize and inflate internally circulated production figures. By 1990, statistical officials in the DPRK joked that they were dealing in "rubber statistics."[10] In effect, DPRK leadership, in Wolfgang Stolper's memorable phrase, had been reduced to "planning without facts."[11] This may help to explain why, at a time when it was increasingly hard pressed, the regime embraced so many projects of questionable economic merit but extraordinary reported expense. (According to official sources, for example, the West Sea Gate Lock cost US$4 billion to complete; preparations for the 1989 Thirteenth World Youth Festival, including the necessary facelift for Pyongyang, were said to cost US$4.7 billion.[12])

Finally, the regime's muscular and unceasing activity in indoctrination and information control has strangled scientific and technological innovation in the DPRK. Officially, of course, North Korea has promoted "technical revolution" as a goal of state. It is one of the Three Revolutions explicitly enumerated in the campaign that was set in motion in the early 1970s. But North Korean scientists and intellectuals are expected to achieve their breakthroughs without knowledge of their own, and without discretion or time to learn. All but shut off from international contact and exchange, and shielded from the outside world's information revolution, North Korea has become a research backwater, lagging ever further behind in virtually all fields of inquiry. By the early 1990s, in fact,

North Korea was apparently the only country in Northeast Asia incapable of producing the microchip.[13] Such technological obsolescence not only limits the possibilities for economic development, but increasingly undercuts the effectiveness of a military force that would be exposed to high-precision weapons and other advanced systems.

These policy-induced imbalances and distortions had already set the North Korean economy—the engine ultimately responsible for underwriting state power—on an inauspicious trajectory years ago. By the mid-1980s these cumulative and self-reinforcing difficulties may have helped to bring the national economy to the point of stagnation, or even negative per capita growth.[14] With the collapse of the Soviet empire, North Korea's economic prospects worsened further, as its trade with those countries—heretofore its principal contacts with the world economy—contracted suddenly and dramatically.[15] The North Korean economy endured another significant and adverse turn in its international accounts in January of 1993, when China, which had become, *faute de mieux,* its largest trade partner, insisted on settling its transactions with the DPRK on a hard-currency basis. These jolts and dislocations left the North Korean economy even less capable of self-sustained development and growth.

What must surely be apparent to Pyongyang's leadership—since it is apparent to any outside observers surveying that closed system—is that the North Korean structure at present possesses no self-correcting mechanisms for redressing long-term economic stagnation or decline. In Leninist doctrine, of course, economic factors are but one component of the overall "correlation of forces" between a socialist state and its imperialist adversaries.[16] Nevertheless, the structural inability to forestall relative or absolute economic decline is a serious matter for any Leninist state, insofar as it requires extraordinary countermeasures in non-economic arenas simply to prevent the correlation of forces against competing states from worsening.

How does a regime like the DPRK cope with economic decline? How does it attempt to maintain its overall correlation of forces in the international arena while one of the pillars upon which this correlation rests has visibly eroded? We may consider some of the alternatives at hand, and their implications for the international community, by weighing three possible adjustments to the material pressures facing the North Korean state: reform, "muddling through," or collapse. Let us consider these separately.

Reform

From an economic standpoint, "reform"—which is to say, the moderation of grievous policy-imposed distortions—would seem to be the most obvious strategy for improving the productivity of the North Korean system, and thus ultimately strengthening the sinews of the North Korean state. For more than 20 years, some outside observers have divined indications that North Korea was preparing to embark upon a more pragmatic approach to domestic and international economic policy. In this reading, the initial signals of a turn toward a more moderate path were evidenced in 1984, with the promulgation of the new Joint Venture Law, and the advent of the so-called August 3 campaign to expand consumer goods production by local enterprises.[17] Over the years, students of North Korean affairs have pointed to a number of events that can be interpreted as presaging a relaxation, or shift, in official economic policy.[18] Certain port cities will be accorded the status of special economic zones and presumably exempted from standard North Korean economic governance. A Law on Free Economic and Trade Zones will be ratified. A Tumen development project will be actively promoted, envisioned as involving international financial cooperation with China, Russia, Japan, and even South Korea, and absorbing up to US$30 billion in foreign capital. Negotiations with South Korean *chaebol*[19] will take place to secure inter-Korean trade flows, and to entice investment and technology through long-term project commitments from Seoul. A Foreign Direct Investment Law and the Foreign Exchange Law will be promulgated. Legislation will be passed on rights to underground mineral and natural resources and on foreign technology imports. And so on.

Taken individually or as a whole, these policy decisions and actions incontestably describe a tendency whose impact would be an improvement in economic performance by virtue of restraining the regime's own economically destructive habits and behavior. However, it is one thing to recognize the existence of such tendencies, and another to assess their significance.

The fact of such measures should not occasion surprise. In the face of exigency, Marxist-Leninist regimes have always demonstrated considerable tactical flexibility. Time and again, they have confounded those analysts who predicted that they would be ideologically incapable of embracing seemingly antithetical measures needed for practical purposes or survival. In evaluating North Korea's current reformist tendencies, one must address two questions. First, does the package of reform proposals thus far enunciated offer the possibility of reversing the downslide of the North Korean economy? Second, do these ideological concessions speak to a substantive change of viewpoint of the existing North Korean leadership?

The answer to the first question is relatively straightforward. The reformist measures that have been enacted, promulgated, or discussed are patently inadequate to stem North Korea's ongoing economic deterioration, much less jump-start or rejuvenate its flagging economic system. Like the Joint Venture Law that preceded it, North Korea's more recent forays into reformist international policy are completely halfhearted and neglect to consider the investors they presumably wish to entice. This neglect is not only apparent in DPRK legislation. For a 1991 United Nations Development Program conference arranged to promote the Tumen concept, the DPRK sent a delegation of representatives who were, in the words of one Japanese participant, "pitifully unprepared" for those deliberations.[20]

Even if these reformist policies had been competently crafted, however, they would address issues largely peripheral to the current economic malaise. Consider what these proposals and laws do *not* touch. They avoid completely the subject of military demobilization and conversion of the war industries. They make no provision for increasing the share of consumption in the national economy. They ignore any amendment of property relations for the rural or urban working populations. They do nothing to strengthen market mechanisms within the domestic economy, or to enhance the credibility of the domestic currency. They offer no new avenues for information flows or scientific contacts. They circumvent all questions relating to the government's longstanding default on its international debt obligations. A charitable description of new initiatives, in relation to the problems at hand, would be "tinkering at the margins."

Moreover, however halfhearted and marginal these efforts may by themselves appear, they are countered by policy measures, simultaneously enacted, which press in a completely opposite direction. In April 1992, for example, North Korea promulgated a general wage increase of over 40 percent for the laboring population. In July 1992, it issued a new currency.[21] These two moves may sound innocuous, but they are not. In the context of the chronic scarcity of goods, a general wage increase can only throw the consumer market into still greater disequilibrium, further undermining the role of currency-based transactions and reinforcing the primacy of state-determined allocations of supplies in household well-being. By the same token, currency reform, in the context of a command economy, is an occasion to inventory the savings of the populace, to confiscate assets that cannot properly be accounted for, and to garner leads on participants in the unauthorized underground economy. Unlike the Foreign Direct Investment Law—which essentially remained an offer in search of takers[22]—these restrictive measures have already had an impact on the workings of the North Korean economy.

Inferring the intentions of North Korean leadership in enacting their new regime of reform is not nearly as conclusive as predicting the consequences of the measures embraced. The regime in Pyongyang attempts to keep secret virtually all information about the nation's governance, and state strategy is one of the most tightly guarded secrets of all. Under the best of circumstances outsiders seeking to understand the motivations underlying North Korean policy are left to the "study of semi-esoteric communication"; more often they are simply forced into semiotic exercises.[23] One may note, however, that the North Korean media have reviewed and analyzed the collapse of the Eastern European states, and the downfall of the Soviet Union. They have ascribed these upheavals to precisely the sorts of measures and directions that Western liberals speak of as reforms. As one North Korean official assessment phrased it: ". . . the imperialists . . . have also frantically gone berserk in infiltrating corrupt bourgeois ideology and culture into socialist countries in a bid to inoculate them with the wind of liberalization."[24]

Insofar as North Korean officials give all indications of wishing to avoid rather than share the fates of their erstwhile comrades, one may suspect that Pyongyang is not yet considering a voluntary loosening of control over economy, society, or information.

It may well be that elements in the North Korean leadership hope to have what they view as the best of both worlds: to maintain tight control over their country, and to attract foreign resources at the same time. To date, however, there is little evidence to indicate willingness on the part of the regime to trade any of the former for some of the latter.

Muddling Through

One alternative to policy reform is what Lindblom[25] long ago termed "muddling through"—the attempt to cope through improvisations, without reconsidering basic strategy or readjusting fundamental policies. As a description of North Korean government activity since the onset of the revolutions of 1989, muddling through is clearly superior to policy reform. Yet we should also recognize the shortcomings of this paradigm in modeling recent North Korean behavior. The notion of muddling through, as originally expounded, was meant to pertain to the activities of bureaucracies in Western liberal democracies—organizations not rigidly ideological, not locked in self-defined struggles of national survival, and not immobilized when orders fail to flow down from the top. For all these reasons, the vision of muddling through actually presupposes more flexibility with respect to policy change than North Korea has demonstrated on economic questions in recent years. North Korea's present course of action might just as well be termed "barreling through," for economic policy seems to be informed by a dogged determination to weather the current storm by battening down the hatches and maintaining course.

North Korea's inflexibility in the face of manifest economic decline may, in part, speak to the outlook and experience of its leadership. The generation of Kim Il Sung witnessed much harder times than those his son confronts today. In the early 1950s, after all, Kim Il Sung was living in an underground bunker beneath a ravaged landscape that was under the shifting control of American and Chinese forces. He emerged from that bunker to build the modern North Korean state. That state is like a diving bell, designed to travel safely through a realm whose pressures would crush weaker constructs.

But even the sturdiest diving bells must eventually surface, and it is not clear how North Korea would locate a breathing space on its present economic course. On the contrary, the present direction in economic policy can only lead to the further debilitation of the national economy, and thus ultimately to the debilitation of the KPA as well. On its present direction, then, North Korea can only hope to defend its correlation of forces against the outside world by altering the non-economic elements in the equation.

In the past, one of the elements which might have seemed amenable to alteration was the political stability of the rival South Korean state. Given what once were the fragile foundations of the South Korean polity, it might have been reasonable to hope that patience would be rewarded by a paralyzing crisis in the Republic of Korea, or even its collapse. (It will be remembered that in 1979, South Korea's strongman was assassinated by his own handpicked security chief.) Such an upheaval has become vastly less likely since 1987, when South Korea held its first open, competitive, and reasonably fair mass presidential elections, the first of their kind in the entire history of the Korean people. It has also witnessed signal changes in the capabilities of its political parties, and important new tendencies for cooperation, coalition-building, and consensus-seeking on the part of its politically active groups.[26] To bank on the failing political fortunes of the Republic of Korea would thus seem to be an ever more unrealistic bet. If North Korea is to be rescued from its current predicament, it will not be current economic policies that will offer the escape, nor can the DPRK count on what it calls the "incurable malady" of the South Korean system.[27]

Collapse?

If policy reform is, for whatever reasons, decisively rejected, and if muddling through cannot redress the state's mounting problems, North Korea faces the prospect of an eventual systemic failure or breakdown—a collapse.

North Korean policy has begun to deal explicitly with this contingency. Official thinking on this score is highlighted by the "10-Point Program for the Great Unity of the Whole Nation for the Reunification of the Country," introduced by Kim Il Sung in April 1993. The tenth point in the program deserves special attention. It reads:

> Those who have contributed to the great unity of the nation and to the cause of national reunification should be highly estimated.[28]

Should this proposition appear too abstract, a 1993 DPRK broadcast helped to clarify its meaning. "What is important in appraising people," it explained, "is, above all, to grant special favors to those who have performed feats for the great unity of the nation and the reunification of the country, patriotic mar-

tyrs and their descendants."[29] In effect, Pyongyang is now expressly propos-
ing that a sort of insurance policy be issued to provide for the safety and well-
being of the North Korean leadership and, of course, for "their descendants."

Viewed in the context of the DPRK's 10-Point Program, North Korea's
nuclear program may be seen as having assumed a very specific significance.
That program was begun many decades earlier, at a time when the current circumstances of the North Korean state were not anticipated. Nuclear weaponry,
however, has a way of altering the status and increasing the options of the states
possessing it. It may be seen as an all-purpose instrument of diplomacy, applic-
able to almost any situation by governments wishing to use it. In its current circumstances, North Korea may view the acquisition of nuclear weapons as the
vehicle for extricating it from its current dilemmas.

With nuclear weapons, after all, an unstable North Korea would be a quali-
tatively greater problem for, and threat to, the international community than it
could be today. North Korean leaders might correspondingly calculate that
the international community would feel more compelled to help prevent instability in the DPRK in the years to come, if theirs were a nuclear state. Pyongyang
might even hope that the prospect of nuclear instability in the DPRK could
prompt the international community to help assure North Korea's political
stability—defined as unchallenged rule by the Kim family by those who make
the official definitions—or to offer material assistance to forestall economic
breakdown and its attendant uncertainties. Viewed from this perspective,
nuclear weaponry may look like a promising instrument for helping to maintain
the existing system.

If North Korea does view nuclear weaponry as a sort of insurance policy for
the regime and its leadership, it will be most unlikely to negotiate this oppor-
tunity away. At the same time, if the regime views nuclear weaponry as the
ultimate guarantor of its domestic stability and international security, it is
likely to be all the less interested in experimenting with reforms of its domestic or international policy. The designs and intentions of North Korea's leadership remain well shielded from the outside world. But in attempting to
assess North Korea's options and to decipher its strategy, the international
community should be prepared for the possibility that relations with this most
unusual state will become even more tense in the months and years to come
than they are today.

Conclusions and Implications

North Korea's international relations have always been characterized by a high
degree of tension. In recent years, however, that tension has escalated
markedly. Paradoxically, while relations among Asia's four Great Powers—

China, Japan, Russia, and the United States—have improved in recent decades, North Korea's relations have been worsening with all of them.

International attention today is rightly focused on North Korea's ongoing quest to amass a nuclear arsenal. But decision makers have neglected a subsidiary problem: a *completely* non-nuclear North Korea would still pose significant and growing challenges to security in Northeast Asia. North Korea has a huge army, capabilities in both chemical weaponry and medium-range missiles, and a government whose future is uncertain.

North Korea's political strengths have been underestimated in the past. Proof of those strengths is the DPRK's own longevity. Today it is the world's oldest standing communist state. At the same time, the North Korean economy has suffered from *juche*-style[30] central planning, extraordinary military buildup, and, since 1989, the unexpected loss of aid and trade from erstwhile socialist allies. The correlation of forces on the Korean Peninsula has turned decisively against North Korea.

The North Korean state now faces three alternatives: reform, muddling through, or collapse. There are indications of numerous small attempts by state planners to liberalize the ailing North Korean economy. To date, however, these measures have been peripheral, and completely inadequate to pulling the economy out of its nosedive. There are few signs that North Korean leadership is willing to assume the political risks which a genuine economic reform would entail.

Avoiding reform, North Korea's leadership appears to be attempting to muddle through. They cannot. Their current policies are a recipe for continuing economic decline. Economic decline must eventually weaken their central instrument of power, the Korean People's Army.

Forswearing reform, but doggedly attempting to muddle through, the regime will eventually face the prospect of breakdown or collapse. The North Korean leadership is already dealing with this prospect explicitly in public statements about reunification. It may also view the acquisition of nuclear weaponry as a means of forestalling collapse by forcing the international community to take an interest in a smooth leadership succession, in a functioning North Korean economy, etc. The strategy and intentions of North Korean leadership have always deliberately been kept secret from the outside world. Foreign analysts are left to guess about matters of vital interest to this regime. If, however, North Korean leaders view atomic weaponry as a sort of insurance policy for their regime, they will be most unlikely to negotiate away the possibility of acquiring these, no matter what agreements they may sign. Policymakers must be prepared for the possibility that North Korea will continue to strive to amass an ever-growing nuclear arsenal, even if it gives assurances to the contrary, and must consider the implications of such an outcome.

Notes

1. International Institute of Strategic Studies (IISS), 1992, p. 220; by the IISS assessment, KPA active duty forces totaled 1.132 million in 1991; larger armies were said to be maintained only by the then USSR (3.988 million), China (3.030 million), the United States (1.918 million), and India (1.265 million), that is to say the four most populous countries in the world at the time; the U.S. Defense Intelligence Agency (USDIA) placed North Korea's total active forces at 1.206 million in a 1991 study; see USDIA, 1991, p. 42; Eberstadt and Banister (1991, "Military Buildup . . ." p. 1107) estimated North Korea's non-civilian male population for 1987 at 1.24–1.323 million.

   Interestingly, the most recent numbers suggest that, with a military of 1.106 million men under arms, the DPRK now has the world's fourth largest military (behind China, the United States, and India respectively); see International Institute of Strategic Studies, 2005, pp. 20, 158, 236, 270, and 282.
2. Eberstadt and Banister, 1991, pp. 1110–11.
3. Scalapino and Lee, 1972, p. 919.
4. *FBIS*-EAS, 1992e, p. 23.
5. DIA, 1991, p. 60.
6. Eberstadt and Banister, 1991, p. 93.
7. Fujio Goto. 1990, p. 68.
8. For the calculations, Eberstadt, *Korea Approaches Reunification*, p. 58.
9. Ibid.
10. Personal communications with the author. Pyongyang, 25 May 1990.
11. Stolper, 1966.
12. Personal communication with the author. Pyongyang, 25 May 1990.
13. Koo Bon-hak, 1992, p. 111.
14. Trigubenko, 1991.
15. Moiseyev, 1991.
16. For a "bourgeois" exposition of this concept, see Asparturnian, 1980; for a longer treatment, see Lider, 1986.
17. See the following articles by Hy-Sang Lee, 1988, 1990, and 1992.
18. For one such interpretation, see Merrill, 1993.
19. "*Chaebol*" means "business association" and refers to the large, conglomerate family-controlled firms of South Korea characterized by strong ties with government agencies; there were family-owned enterprises in Korea in the period before 1961 but the particular state-corporate alliance came into being with the regime of Park Chung Hee (1961–1979).
20. Sugimoto, 1992, p. 9.
21. For details, see *FBIS*-EAS, 1992a, p.18; 1992b, p. 16; 1992c, p. 9.
22. According to UNCTAD figures from 1992–93, total foreign direct investment in the DPRK grew from US$572.3 million in 1990 to US$1022.0 million in 2003; see Chang, "Trade and Investment . . ." available at: http://www.stanleyfoundation.org/initiatives/eenk/papers/Lee.pdf.
23. To borrow a phrase from Clippinger, 1981, p. 289.
24. *FBIS*-EAS, 1992d, p. 11.
25. Lindblom, 1959, p. 79–88.
26. For an initial assessment, see Eberstadt, 1992 and 1993a.
27. Eberstadt, 1992, p. 12.

28. *BBC*, 1993.
29. *FBIS*-EAS, 1993, p. 21.
30. *"Juche"* refers to the philosophy of Kim Il Sung, meaning the state-mandated belief that the people, collectively, must be the subject and masters of social revolution; *juche* is often translated (although not by North Korea itself) as "self-reliance."

References

Asparturnian, Vernon V. 1980. "Soviet Global Power and the Correlation of Forces." *Problems of Communism* 29. May–June.

BBC Summary of World Broadcasts. 1993. Rebroadcast from *Korean Central News Agency (KCNA)* as "Kim Il-Sung 10-Point Program of National Reunification Adopted at Assembly." 8 April. FE/1368/C3.

Clippinger, Morgan. 1981. "Kim Chong-Il in the North Korean Mass Media: A Study of Semi-Esoteric Communication." *Asian Survey* 21(3). March.

Eberstadt, Nicholas. 1992. "DPRK: South Korean Economy Termed 'Incurable Malady'." *FBIS: East Asia.* 25 August.

———. 1993a. "Taiwan and South Korea: The 'Democratization' of Outlier States." *World Affairs.* Summer.

———. 1993b. "North Korea: Reform, Muddling Through, or Collapse." *Analysis* 4(3): pp. 5–16. XX

———. 1995. *Korea Approaches Reunification.* Armonk, NY: M.E. Sharpe.

Eberstadt, Nicholas and Judith Banister. 1991. "Military Buildup in the DPRK: Some New Indications from North Korean Data." *Asian Survey* 31(11) pp. 1095–115. November.

Foreign Broadcast Information Service-East Asia (*FBIS*-EAS). 1992a. "Wage Increase Reveals Socialism's 'Superiority'." 25 February.

———. 1992b. "Wage Increase Given in April; State Benefits Noted." 6 April.

———. 1992c. "New Bills Minted, Circulated Beginning 15 July." 15 July.

———. 1992d. "NODONG SINMUN: On Defense of Socialism." 29 July.

———. 1992e. "ROK: DPRK Reportedly Develops 1000 km-range Missile." 24 August.

———. 1993. "Daily Explains Tenth Point in Unity Program." 13 May.

Goto, Fujio. 1990. *Estimates of North Korea's Gross Domestic Product, 1956–1959.* Kyoto: Kyoto Sangyo University Press.

Lee, Chang Jae. 2005. "Trade and Investment in North Korea," Korea Institute for International Economic Policy. Available at: http://www.stanleyfoundation.org/initiatives/eenk/papers/Lee.pdf

Lee, Hy-Sang. 1988. "North Korea's Closed Economy: The Hidden Opening." *Asian Survey* 28(12). December.

———. 1990. "The August 3rd Program of North Korea: A Partial Rollback of Central Planning." *Korea Observer* 21. Winter.

———. 1992. "The Economic Reforms of North Korea: The Strategy of Hidden and Assimilable Reforms." *Korea Observer* 23. Spring.

International Institute of Strategic Studies (IISS).1992. *The Military Balance 1992–93.* London: IISS.

———. 2005. *The Military Balance 2005–06.* London: IISS.

Koo, Bon-hak. 1992. "Political Economy of Self-Reliance: The Case of North Korea. 1961–1990." Unpublished Ph.D. dissertation. University of Cincinnati.

Lider, Julian. 1986. *Correlation of Forces: An Analysis of Marxist-Leninist Concepts.* New York: St Martin's Press.

Lindblom, Charles E. 1959. "The Science of 'Muddling Through.'" *Public Administration Review* 19(2). Spring.

Merrill, John. 1993. "North Korea: Steering Away from the Shoals." *Asian Survey* 33(1). January.

Moiseyev, Valentin. 1991. "DPRK-USSR Trade Patterns." Paper presented at International Symposium on the North Korean Economy; Current Situation and Future Prospects, Seoul, 30 September–1 October 1991.

Morgan. 1981. "Kim Chong-Il in the North Korean Mass Media: A Study of Semi-Esoteric Communication." *Asian Survey* 21(3). March.

Scalapino, Robert A. and Chong-sik Lee. 1972. *Communism in Korea.* Berkeley, CA: University of California Press.

Stolper, Wolfgang F. 1966. *Planning without Facts: Lessons in Resource Allocation from Nigeria's Development.* Cambridge, MA: Harvard University Press.

Sugimoto, Takashi. 1992. "The Dawning of Development of the Tumen River Area." International Institute of Global Peace, Policy Paper 75E. March.

Trigubenko, Marina. 1991. "Industrial Policy in the DPRK." Paper presented at International Symposium on the North Korean Economy: Current Situation and Future Prospects. Seoul, 30 September–1 October 1991.

United States Defense Intelligence Agency. 1991. *"North Korea: The Foundations of Military Strength."* Washington, DC: DIA.

2

"Our Own Style of Statistics": Availability and Reliability of Official Quantitative Data*

Like the country it covers and the government to which it reports, the statistical service of the Democratic People's Republic of Korea (DPRK, or North Korea) remains, from the standpoint of outside observers, largely enveloped in mystery. In the era of the information revolution, the DPRK's release of official statistics is entirely episodic and absolutely minimal, and has been so for over four decades. In an age of globalization, North Korean statistical authorities stand in virtually complete isolation from all international counterparts.

Even the most basic questions about the structure, organization, and performance of the DPRK statistical system cannot be answered by foreign observers with any confidence. We know that the DPRK Central Bureau of Statistics (*Choson Chungang Tonggye Kuk*, or CBS) was established in 1952, under the direct authority of the DPRK State Planning Commission (SPC)—but the precise institutional relationship between those two organizations today is unclear.[1] Originally the CBS was delegated to "collect, analyze, and submit to the government the statistical data necessary for national administration and economic control."[2] But it is no longer self-evident that the CBS enjoys the untrammeled access to all the sectors of the economy that would be required to discharge that function, or other functions it was initially authorized to pursue. No information whatever is available on the size of the CBS, the number of personnel under its jurisdiction, or the training and qualifications of its employees. In fact, over the past generation, as best can be told, there has been no more than a handful of encounters between North Korean statistical officials and persons from the outside world.[3]

---

* This chapter originally appeared as a paper in the *Korean Journal of International Studies*, Volume XXVIII, No. 1, Fall/Winter, 2001; it has been updated for inclusion here.

Modern economies require large amounts of information to carry out their diverse and increasingly complex operations.[4] For policymaking in a centrally planned economy, the need for wide-ranging and reliable information would seem to be especially acute. We do not know how much quantitative data North Korean statistical organs prepare internally for top decision makers in Pyongyang. However, over the past four decades—a period during which North Korean leadership was straining to build a more urbanized and industrialized "independent national economy"—the external supply of official data about social and economic conditions in North Korea dried to a trickle.

In the decade following the Korean War armistice, the DPRK did make a practice of regularly releasing some information on the country's major social and economic trends.[5] Those statistical releases were not exactly torrential, but one should remember that other communist governments at the time were far less forthcoming with statistical data than they would later be. By the early 1960s, though, Pyongyang had begun to impose a strict "statistical blackout" over the entire country—a blackout that continues to this very day.

The success of this longstanding campaign to suppress hard data about the DPRK has been—at least by its own lights—absolutely breathtaking. Unlike any other established Marxist-Leninist state, the DPRK has never, in its 50-plus year history, published a statistical yearbook.[6] The DPRK has not published a *won*-denominated national accounts series for any period of its rule;[7] in fact, it has never published a *won*-denominated estimate of the country's total output.[8] It has never published a detailed price index, and since the mid-1960s has published no price indices at all. It has published almost no information on banking or the monetary situation since the early 1960s. And it has not released even a summary review of its international trade and finance trends for almost four decades.

Even so, the DPRK's statistical embargo has not been absolutely watertight. Tidbits have continued to leak out over the years, and their flow may even have been increasing of late. From time to time over the past generation, North Korea has released reports on physical output for various commodities, on levels of dollar-denominated "national income," indices of intertemporal changes in product, and on other irregularly announced economic soundings. In addition, it has released a certain amount of information on the country's demographic and social situation, most importantly, a relatively recent compendium on the country's "1993 census". Quotation marks should attend the "1993" census because that enumeration was not actually conducted in 1993, but rather in early 1994, with respondents replying to questions about their circumstances as of year-end 1993; needless to say, such a procedure is highly unorthodox. Nor is it the only curious feature of the compendium; in fact, the "1993" census compendium contains such serious internal inconsistencies—and such dramatic inconsistencies with previously reported data from the country's population registration system—that the very integrity of the count itself would seem to come into question. Although these statistical offerings are sparse indeed—vastly more limited than for any other modern country with the DPRK's level of urbanization or educational attainment—sufficient information is at hand that we may attempt not only to describe the official quantitative data that are available, but also to evaluate their quality.

In the following pages we will survey the variety of North Korean statistics currently available to outside observers, and draw inferences about their reliability. And as will be seen, serious questions arise about the accuracy of official quantitative data from the DPRK. Distortions, biases, inconsistency, and irreplicability appear to be pervasive throughout.

The strikingly poor quality of available DPRK quantitative data has direct and inescapable implications for economic policymaking in contemporary North Korea. We will conclude this chapter with a few observations about the bearing of the DPRK statistical system on the country's economic performance, and the implications for North Korean statistical work in the immediate future.

Available DPRK Economic and Social Statistics

Over the past four decades, the CBS has apparently released only two publications of its own.[9] Over this long period, official quantitative data have instead typically been released on three occasions: at regularly scheduled official gatherings (e.g., reports to the Supreme People's Assembly (SPA) on the annual state budget, or the completion of a multi-year economic plan), during visits by foreigners,[10] or on a seemingly ad hoc basis by North Korea's media or supreme leadership.

On the economic ledger, data released includes figures on commodity output, foreign trade, public finance, and national income; on the social ledger, data have been released on such topics as health, labor, and population.[11] We will examine these in turn.

Physical Indicators of Production

In the DPRK's socialist command economy, the planning process necessitates establishment of production targets for a wide variety of agricultural and industrial commodities. Official North Korean communiqués on the end goals of an economic plan sometimes mention performance with respect to key output targets; media reports and pronouncements by the supreme leadership sometimes offer additional figures on the production of specific commodities. Official production targets for a number of major commodities during North Korea's two most recent Seven-Year Plans are presented in Table 2.1.

Table 2.1
DPRK Official Targets vs. Soviet Bloc Estimates of Results:
Key Economic Indicators, 1978–1989

| Indicator (million tons)* | TARGET GOAL | | ACHIEVED RESULT | | |
	2nd 7-Year Plan (1978–84)	3rd 7-Year Plan (1987–93)	1978	1987	1989
Electricity (billion kwh)	56.0	100	23.0	33.0	28.0
Coal	70	120	43	52	51
Iron ore	16	18	11	13	13
Steel	7.4	10.0	3.2	4.2	4.3
Cement	12.0	22.0	7.0	7.8	8.0
Fabrics (million sq. m.)	800	1500	450	535	540
Chemical fertilizers	5.0	7.2	3.4	4.0	3.8
Grain	10.0	15.0	6.8	6.8	6.8
Rice	5.0	7.0	3.9	3.8	4.2
Sea products	3.5	11.0	1.6	2.0	2.1
Meat	—	1.7	0.15	0.19	0.20
Tractors (thousand)	45.0	50.0	24.0	24.5	22.0

*= unless otherwise indicated

Note: plan targets are official; for sources of achieved result estimates see text.

Source: Maretzki, 1991, p. 155.

In principle, it should be a much easier task to keep track of levels of physical production than to estimate levels of aggregate economic output, insofar as the latter calculations for a socialist system beg the issue of valuation and cost in a non-market setting. But according to the estimates also displayed in Table 1, DPRK planning targets over time have grown ever more divorced from the actual or even the feasible levels of local production. According to those particular estimates, for example, electricity output in the DPRK in 1987 was fully 40 percent below the target set for the completion of the second Seven Year Plan set for 1984: yet the third Seven-Year Plan, which began in 1987, raised the official production target by a further 79 percent, so that a true fulfillment of the plan would have required a tripling of electrical power generation in the ensuing seven years!

Those external estimates of actual commodity production, incidentally, were reportedly assembled on a cooperative basis by the staffs of the Council for Mutual Economic Assistance (CMEA) embassies in Pyongyang.[12] Given the once intimate involvement of CMEA countries with particular DPRK state enterprises, which accounted for so much of the output in the heavy industry, we might expect estimates for products from that sector to be especially reliable.

These "enormous discrepancies between plan and reality," according to one North Korea watcher from the former Soviet bloc, are systemic. Maretzki calls them "numerical gymnastics," and asserts that they serve a threefold purpose: "self-deception of the country's economic policymakers; falsification of information for the local populace, and the passion for [regime] credibility overseas."[13]

Whatever their specific purposes, however, those discrepancies are strongly suggestive of an environment of extreme political pressure within the DPRK to create a numerical "reality" that coincides with an officially-imagined ideal. Not surprisingly, that same environment appears to conduce to a broad official tolerance for counterfeit official statistics.

Political incentives for exaggeration, misrepresentation, and distortion of statistical information are, of course, common to all centrally planned economies. Generally speaking, however, the doctoring of data in such systems seems to take place at the level of the enterprise or the region. Central statistical authorities, by contrast, are responsible for validating or correcting those local claims, and providing planners with an accurate representation of actual results.

This is not to say that socialist states make a point of broadcasting unwelcome statistical news. Under socialist governments, however, sensitive or inconvenient data are typically suppressed rather than adulterated: authorities generally attempt to maintain the integrity of the numbers they use, even if these are only circulated internally.[14] Those concerns for the faithfulness of the data, one may note, are grounded in an entirely practical consideration: when socialist planners lose track of the actual situation of the economy they are guiding—as happened during China's Great Leap Forward[15]—disaster beckons.

The DPRK insists that it maintains "our own style of socialism" (*urisik sahoejuii*)—one that purportedly differs fundamentally from "real existing socialism" elsewhere. So, too, Pyongyang seems to compile "our own style of statistics." And in the blunt estimate of an economist from the former Soviet Union with long experience in Pyongyang, the distinction that separates North Korean numbers from the statistics of other socialist countries is that DPRK "official reports falsify the real state of affairs."[16]

If that judgment seems harsh, it would appear to be corroborated by Figure 2.1, which presents North Korea's claimed grain harvests from 1946 to 1997.

For 1984 and 1987, DPRK authorities reported a harvest of 10 million metric tons of grain. However, for 1996 and 1997, the claims were a mere 2.5 million tons and 2.69 million tons, respectively. Such figures would imply a decline of output of 75 percent over the course of nine years (1987–96)—this for a country that was at peace, under continuous governance by a single state,

Figure 2.1

Official DPRK Grain Production, 1946–1997 (million metric tons)

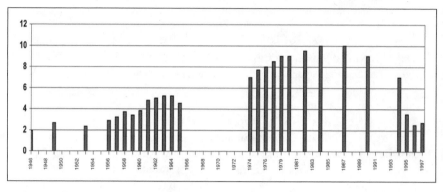

Sources: Chung 1974, pp. 48, 49, 52; Lee, 1994, p. 533; IMF, 1997, p. 10.

and relying upon irrigated agriculture for the cultivation of its major staple cereal during the period in question. They would further imply that the level of grain output in 1997 was lower in the DPRK than it had been 40 years earlier, and that the 1996 harvest was smaller than the harvest in 1949, the first full year of DPRK rule! Since those implications are patently implausible, the figures underlying them cannot be entertained seriously.

To be sure: there is good reason to believe that the DPRK has suffered a genuine decline in agricultural output over the ten year period 1990 to 2000. The figures in Table 2.2, however, clearly do not depict that decline. Rather, they seem to reflect the shifting political imperatives inspiring a government with a procrustean attitude toward statistics.

Before the collapse of the USSR, North Korean leadership was ardently proclaiming the superiority of its version of socialism, and was routinely pulling up numbers to buttress that position. In the mid to late 1990s, by contrast, Pyongyang was canvassing the international community for maximum donations of emergency humanitarian food aid—and thus had developed an interest in making its food situation look as grim as possible.

In other communist economies, as Chung has noted, "Statistics in absolute or physical terms such as the output of major industrial and agricultural commodities and transportation data seem to be far more correct and reliable than those in index numbers."[18] However, for the time being, available official data on physical output for the DPRK cannot be expected to represent the actual level, trend, or even direction of production. Furthermore, if official DPRK data are vulnerable to deliberate misrepresentation for reasons of state—which we

Table 2.2

Officially Claimed vs. Indirectly Estimated DPRK Trade Performance, 1985 (current US$ million)

	Exports	Imports	Balance
Official DPRK figures	6,060	5,620	+440
Indirectly estimated trade by region			
USSR	525	935	−410
CMEA minus USSR	145	37	+108
Japan	159	250	−91
OECD minus Japan	64	83	−19
China	242	260	−18
Third world	95	109	−14
Indirectly estimated total	1,230	1,674	−444
Memorandum item: Claimed total/indirectly estimated total	4.92	3.36	−0.99

Notes:

1. "Indirect estimates" derived from reports of trade partners on merchandise commerce with DPRK; to account for c.i.f. costs, indirectly estimated DPRK "exports" are scaled down from reported trade partner imports by a factor of 1.1; conversely, indirectly estimated DPRK "imports" are scaled up from reported trade partner exports by a factor of 1.1.

2. Figures rounded to nearest US$ million; indirectly estimated trade is based upon official currency exchange rates with US$ in 1985.

Sources: Official DPRK data; Pang, 1987, pp. 150–151; indirect estimates: Eberstadt, unpublished.[17]

may strongly suspect to be the case—that dynamic may itself accentuate observational distortions. For the very figures North Korean authorities may wish to release would also be the numbers most prone to deliberate official adjustments.

It is impossible for outsiders to know whether North Korean statistical authorities submit to policymakers in Pyongyang the same numbers on physical output that are presented to the outside world. Maintaining multiple central ledgers as a matter of course is not an impossible proposition—although it would be a unique, time-consuming, and perhaps also confusing process. If the DPRK's central planners do indeed work with the same numbers on domestic commodity production that their government publicly announces, however, we must recognize that the CBS would no longer be capable of carrying out one of the primary functions for which it was originally established: namely "to conduct statistical investigations concerning the pursuance of economic planning and [to] study the causes for plan failures."[19]

Foreign Trade and Finance

Like other socialist governments, the DPRK treats international commercial and financial activity as a monopoly of the state; in principle, each and every transaction with the outside world is tallied by the state trading company or government institution engaged in the contract. Under such circumstances, it would seem a relatively straightforward matter to tabulate official trends for the DPRK's external economy. Since 1963, however, North Korea has released virtually no data on its international trade and financial performance. The data that have been released, moreover, are at dramatic variance with the results estimated by foreign researchers.

In 1997, for example, North Korean authorities informed a visiting delegation from the International Monetary Fund (IMF) that the country's external debt at "US$3.6 billion plus 2.9 billion rubles."[20] At the Soviet-era official exchange rate of US$1.6 per hard currency ruble, those numbers would imply a total foreign debt of US$8.24 billion. The IMF, by contrast, preferred an estimate of "about US$12 billion . . . which includes the ruble debt converted at what is regarded as a 'reasonable' exchange rate."[21]

While this difference may reflect in part the considerable methodological uncertainties about both the appropriate valuation of the old ruble and the appropriate pricing of the hard currency debt upon which the DPRK had effectively defaulted, we should also recognize that the North Korean authorities at that time did not even agree with their Russian counterparts—who inherited the USSR's international financial assets and liabilities—on the size of Pyongyang's stock of ruble-denominated debt. In 1996, the Russian deputy Prime Minister stated that "North Korea's debt to Russia totals 3.3 billion hard currency rubles."[22]

Determining the volume of trade turnover should be less complex than agreeing upon the value of an outstanding inventory of foreign debt: the former are transactions completed, while the latter, in North Korea's case, are still under active, adversarial negotiation. Nevertheless, the variance between Pyongyang's estimate of its trade volume and outside attempts to reconstruct North Korean trade trends is even greater than the difference between internally- and externally-generated estimates of North Korean foreign debt. This can be seen in Table 2.3.

To the author's knowledge, over the past generation North Korean sources have only reported total trade turnover for a single year, 1985.[23] That source denominated DPRK trade in U.S. dollars, placing exports for the year at US$6.06 billion and imports at US$5.62 billion, for an implied balance of trade surplus of US$440 million. The author's own attempt to estimate North Korean trade turnover on the basis of "mirror statistics" from reporting DPRK trade partners[24] yields a wildly inconsonant result: exports of only US$1.23 billion; imports of just US$1.67 billion; and a balance of trade deficit of about US$440 million.

Table 2.3
Officially Reported DPRK Budget and GNP: 1992–1996
(billion won, current prices)

	YEAR				
	1992	**1993**	**1994**	**1995**	**1996**
Budget Revenue	39.6	40.6	41.6	24.3	20.3
Budget Expenditure	39.3	40.2	41.4	24.2	20.6
GNP	44.8	45.0	31.2	27.5	22.8
Ratio (GNP = 100)					
Budget Revenue	88	90	125	88	89
Budget Expenditure	88	89	125	88	91

Note: GNP converted from U.S. dollars to DPRK won at rate specifically indicated in accompanying table.

Source: IMF, 1997.

The official estimate for total trade turnover is fully four times higher than the estimate based on mirror statistics. The magnitude of the discrepancy differs substantially between imports and exports—a factor of about 3.4 for the former and a factor of 4.9 for the latter. The absolute value of the official and the estimated balance of trade happens to be very close: unfortunately, the two have different signs!

It is not apparent how one can account for the tremendous incongruities witnessed in Table 2.3. Part of the gap between the official and the estimated figures for DPRK trade turnover might be explained by "illicit" commerce—e.g., weaponry, narcotics, and other transactions not identified by trading partners—if DPRK statistical authorities included such business in their official trade ledgers. It seems doubtful that they would, and in any case such traffic would be likely to account for only a small portion of the large differentials illuminated in Table 2.3. North Korea maintains a regimen of multiple exchange rates, with a "commercial" (trade) *won*-dollar rate of 2.15:1 and an "official" (essentially ceremonial) rate of about 1:1. Revaluing *won*-denominated import and export volumes in accordance with the official rather than the commercial rate would tremendously inflate the calculated value of foreign trade. But even that questionable technique would still leave a disparity of over US$5 billion between the officially claimed and the indirectly estimated trade turnover, a disparity equal to nearly half the claimed trade turnover itself. The author, indeed, has been unable to devise any method or approach to reconcile these to contrasting sets of trade figures—or to replicate the officially claimed North Korean results.

One can only guess whether North Korean policymakers utilize the same international trade and finance figures for decision making that they have provided to foreigners. If they have, we may surmise that they would have been seriously misinformed about the DPRK's international economic performance. Indeed, they would have been under the impression that North Korea's trade is far more robust, its balance of payments situation much healthier, and its foreign debt burden less worrisome than any indirectly gathered information on these trends would have suggested.

State Budget Revenues and Expenditures

For several decades after the onset of North Korea's official statistical blackout, the report on the state budget—read annually at the SPA every spring, and summarized in the DPRK media—was one of the few regularly released bits of data on social or economic conditions in the DPRK. By the early 1990s, it was the only regular release of official DPRK data whatsoever. After Kim Il Sung's death in July 1994, the SPA did not meet for over four years. In April 1999, a report on the 1998 budget was delivered to the SPA[25]—but final figures for the budgets for 1994–97 were not broadcast. In 1997, DPRK authorities did provide a visiting IMF group with state revenue and expenditure totals for the missing years 1994–96, but not for calendar year 1997. Thus, as of now, not even one continuous statistical series on postwar social or economic trends in the DPRK is available in the outside world. The budgetary data that have been released, moreover, include obvious anomalies that raise as yet unanswerable questions about the limited data on public finance and national output that Pyongyang has officially disclosed.

By the identities of national income accounting, a country's government budget cannot exceed its national output. According to the data transmitted to the IMF, however, North Korea managed to overcome that definitional constraint in 1994, when both state revenues and state expenditures reportedly exceeded the country's GDP by fully 25 percent (see Table 2.3).

At a minimum, this impossible "accomplishment" indicates that North Korea's budget data and national accounts data were prepared entirely independently of one another, without even so much as a check for internal coherence. Something about the nature of current statistical work in the DPRK may also be revealed by the fact that such a glaring irregularity was not detected, and corrected, before these data were transmitted to the IMF. But exactly how, in actual practice, did DPRK statistical authorities arrive at this particular erroneous calculation?

We cannot know the answer, but a variety of methodological missteps and procedural problems suggest themselves. One obvious issue could be completeness of coverage in the two data series: for example, if a substantial share of the country's economic activity were excluded from the national account ledgers, it would be possible to generate numbers whereby the budget numerator seemingly exceeded the national output denominator.

Completeness of coverage, however, is an issue not solely begged by that denominator. There are reasons as well to wonder whether the DPRK's state budget encompasses the entire scope of governmental expenditures and revenues.

The DPRK is an extraordinarily militarized state. That reality is officially acknowledged. Indeed, in 1976, Kim Il Sung declared that "of all the socialist states, ours shoulders the heaviest military burden. . . ."[26] Yet according to official North Korean budget reports, the share of defense spending in North Korea's state budget fell precipitously in the early 1970s, from over 31 percent in 1971 to 15.4 percent in 1973. For over two decades thereafter, it reportedly remained around or below that level, reaching an official nadir of below 12 percent in the early 1990s, and registering an official 14.6 percent for 1998.

By longstanding practice, many socialist states—and some non-socialist ones as well—under-reported their defense budgets by hiding particular kinds of military spending within other, ostensibly "civilian" budget categories.[27] That accounting subterfuge, however, typically seems to have left overall state budget totals accurate and intact. The suspicion that Pyongyang may, by contrast, have entirely exempted large amounts of its military spending from its reported totals for the budget arises because North Korean authorities did just that for other reported statistical totals.

Between 1970 and 1975, during the same years that North Korea reported the great drop in its "military burden," DPRK population statistics ceased registering total population, and began instead only to enumerate civilian population.[28] According to a CBS representative with whom the author conversed in Pyongyang in May 1990, North Korean statistical authorities at that date simply did not have access to data about the size of the country's armed forces.[29]

Ironically, Pyongyang's decision to extract military personnel from the country's population registration system enabled foreign researchers to reconstruct trends in non-civilian male population for the late 1970s and 1980s. Those estimates suggested that the directive excluding North Korean soldiers from counted population totals was followed by an immediate and dramatic buildup of military manpower (Table 2.4), to the point where, by 1986, North Korea would have had the highest ratio of armed forces to population of any country in the world (Table 2.5).

By those same estimates, as of 1986, fully one out of five North Korean men between the ages of 16 and 54 would have been serving in the military.[30] If officially reported defense expenditures had absorbed over 30 percent of DPRK state spending back in 1970—when by some outside estimates only about a tenth of the men in that same age group would have been under arms[31]—the share should presumably have been still higher in 1986, ceteris

Table 2.4
Estimates of Males Not Reported: DPRK, 1975–1987 (in thousands)

Date Year-end	Reconstructed Total Male Population	Reported Male Population	Total Males Missing	Missing in Ages 16–54
1975	8,147	7,433	714	NA
1980	8,918	8,009	909	NA
1982	9,234	8,194	1,040	NA
1985	9,737	8,607	1,130	NA
1986	9,912	8,710	1,202	1,201
1987	10,090	8,841	1,249	NA

Notes: The reported totals are for the civilian male population of North Korea. The missing males constitute our estimate of the size of the male military population of the DPRK. NA means not available.

Source: Eberstadt and Banister, 1991, p. 1104.

Table 2.5
Military Mobilization, Estimated 1986 Percent of Population in Armed Forces, North Korea and "Top Ten" Other Countries by Source of Estimate

	SOURCE		
Country	Ranked by IISS	Country	Ranked by ACDA
North Korea	6.0*	North Korea	6.0*
Iraq	5.5	Iraq	4.9
Syria	3.5	Israel	4.3
Israel	3.4	Syria	3.7
United Arab Emirates	3.1	Jordan	3.2
Jordan	2.6	Qatar	3.0
Nicaragua	2.2	Cuba	2.9
Singapore	2.1	United Arab Emirates	2.6
Taiwan	2.1	Nicaragua	2.3
Greece	2.0	Oman	2.2
Qatar	2.0	Singapore	2.2

Notes: Estimate for North Korea refers to year-end 1986. Estimates for other countries refer to midyear 1986. IISS estimates refer to active duty military manpower, and ACDA estimates refer to armed forces.

*Eberstadt and Banister estimate.

Sources: Derived from U.S. Arms Control and Disarmament Agency, 1987, Table 1, pp. 27–28; International Institute for Strategic Studies, 1987, pp. 15–127, Tables 30 and A–1. Eberstadt and Banister, 1992, p. 94.

paribus. Yet, as shown in Figure 2.2, North Korea's 1986 budget claimed that only 14.1 percent of state expenditures had been devoted to defense!

Thus, North Korea's state budget was by then masking a large portion of the country's military spending, perhaps even the great majority of it. But exactly how? Outsiders can only guess. It is possible that these quantities were entirely concealed within the reported budget.

Alternatively, it is possible that the country's military authorities were routinely denying information on defense spending to state budgeters, just as they were routinely withholding data on military manpower from the CBS. Under other socialist systems, such seemingly "Bonapartist" tendencies might be difficult to imagine. But then again, in other socialist systems the military services are carefully subordinated both to the Party and the highest organs of the State, whereas under the current DPRK constitution the "highest post of state" is that of Chairman of the National Defense Commission.[32] And considering the enormity of the North Korean military effort, the withholding of data on the military from DPRK statistical authorities could only stand to impress severe and far-reaching distortions upon their work.

Per Capita "National Income" and National Output Data

As we can already see, there is no reason to invest any great confidence in official DPRK claims about per capita national income or national output. Reliable calculations of those quantities presuppose accurate assessment of physical pro-

Figure 2.2

Reported Defense Expenditures as a Percentage of

Overall Budget Expenditures, DPRK, 1958–1998

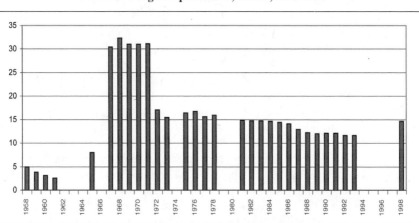

Sources: For 1958–93: Hwang (1993), pp. 150–151; for 1998: *KCNA*, 4 July 1999.

duction—hardly a given in North Korea today. They further require complete-ness of coverage of economic activity. But completeness of coverage may be compromised in the DPRK today, both by North Korean authorities as a matter of principle, and also as a practical matter by the rumored rise of an unofficial "second economy."[33]

To complicate matters further, the virtually complete absence of price series for North Korea makes interpretation of any reported national income or output numbers an exercise in conjecture. And even if all these problems were some-how resolved, there would remain the question of international comparability, for, despite heroic efforts to square the circle—most memorably by Bergson (1961)—there is no single technique by which to represent unambiguously the output of centrally planned economies in a market-style framework, insofar as it is impossible to offer a common unit of valuation for systems with such fundamentally different approaches to pricing and resource allocation.[34]

Nevertheless, we must note that Pyongyang has made available some data on its per capita national income and per capita national output. Although North Korea has never published a *won*-denominated national accounts series, it has announced or implied (through reported intertemporal ratios) figures about per capita national income and national output for various benchmark years. Those figures are presented in Table 2.6.

Before 1989, all DPRK official figures on national income or output were pre-sumably prepared in accordance with the socialist countries' national accounts schema, the System of Material Product Balances (SMPB); per capita national income (*kukmin soduk*) is thus presumed to indicate per capita net material prod-uct. For the years 1989 to 1995, Pyongyang has also released some numbers for what is explicitly termed per capita GNP, that is, calculations that should therefore have been prepared in accordance with the market-oriented national accounts framework, the System of National Accounts (SNA). In addition, in 1997, North Korea transmitted to the IMF some figures on "gross domestic product" by broad sector for the period 1992–96[35] but the transmission did not include the population data that would be necessary for computations of per capita output.

The per capita national income series is marked by a major discontinuity: it is denominated in *won* for 1946 to 1974, but in US dollars for 1979 to 1991. Fortunately, that discontinuity reveals the method utilized in calculating the lat-ter numbers: to go by DPRK data for the year 1987, annual reported net mater-ial product in *won* was divided by the reported (i.e., civilian) year-end popula-tion and then converted into dollars at the most favorable of the DPRK's multiple exchange rates.[36] Unfortunately, the approach revealed is fundamen-tally flawed. And while uncovering the approach may permit us to reconstruct an implicit *won*-denominated national income series for the DPRK for 1946 to 1991, the trends and levels that it might indicate per se can tell us almost noth-ing about the actual evolution of the DPRK macro-economy.

Table 2.6
Official DPRK Reports of Per Capita "National Income" for Various Years, 1946–1995

Year	National Income Per Capita	Source
1946	64.44 Won	"1967 national income is nine times bigger than that of 1946" in DPRK Central Yearbook, 1980
1949	131.82 Won	"1967 national income is 4.4 times bigger than that of 1949" in DPRK Central Yearbook, 1980
1962	416.67 Won	"1966 national income is 1.2 times bigger than that of 1962" in DPRK Central Yearbook, 1968
1966	500 Won	The Fourth Supreme People's Committee Meeting, 16 December 1967
1967	580 Won	Choson Central Broadcasting, 17 September 1979
1970	605.73 Won	"1970 national income is 9.4 times bigger than that of 1946" in DPRK Central Yearbook, 1974
1974	1,029.75 Won	"1974 national income is 1.7 times bigger than that of 1970" in DPRK Central Yearbook, 1976
1979	1,920 USD	Kim Il Sung's New Year's Message, 1 January 1980
1982	2,200 USD	Kim Woo-joung, Deputy Director of External Cultural Committee interview, 12 September 1993
1986	2,400 USD	Bang Whan-Joo, "Chosun Gaekwan-DPRK Country Book," 1988
1987	2,400 USD	Lee Myung-soh, Professor at the Social Science Academy
1988	2,530 USD	New York Times, quoted from DPRK newspaper, July 1989
1989	2,580 USD	Author's meeting with DPRK CBS representatives, 25 May 1990
1989	798* USD	DPRK submission to United Nations, October 1992
1990	911* USD	DPRK submission to the United Nations, May 1997
1991	2,460 USD	Kim Jung-woo, Deputy Director of DPRK External Economic Committee, interview in *Yonhap*, 24 February 1992
1995	719* USD	Kim Jung-woo, in address to a conference in Washington, DC, April 1996
1995	239* USD	DPRK submission to the United Nations, May 1997

Notes: *= GNP per capita

Sources: Koh, 1999; Kim, 1997; Eberstadt meeting with DPRK CBS representatives, 1990.

Adding to the muddle is the utter discordance between the recent per capita national income and per capita GNP figures—and indeed between the per capita GNP figures themselves. For the year 1989, for example, one has three completely different official observations: a per capita national income of US$2,580; a per capita GNP of US$798; and another per capita GNP of US$911.

It is quite simply impossible to reconcile these figures. We may guess that national income and GNP were converted into dollars at rather different exchange rates. But applying the commercial rather than the official rate to the national income datum would still result in a per capita level of US$1,200—a level far higher than the alternate per capita GNPs for the same year. Net material product, however, excludes "nonproductive" services, which are encompassed within the conception of gross national product—and thus, by definition, the former must always be smaller than the latter. How the DPRK's computed net material product manages to exceed its GNP remains an unanswered mystery.

The DPRK's per capita GNP numbers, for their part, present their own as yet unanswerable mysteries. Depending upon which figures one uses, one can conclude either that per capita GNP declined by only 11 percent between 1989 and 1995, or that it dropped by over 70 percent![37] To make matters worse, the gross domestic product data transmitted to the IMF, in conjunction with totals from the 1993 population census, imply a per capita GDP for 1993 of US$987. Assuming Pyongyang's net factor income from abroad in 1993 to be negligible, that figure would seem to indicate a distinct improvement in DPRK per capita output between 1989 and 1993![38]

The severe inconsistencies between North Korea's few recent figures on per capita national income and national output would seem to pose the question of whether DPRK authorities maintain multiple, conflicting accounts of their country's aggregate economic performance, and, if so, whether any series among them can offer a credible impression of the country's overall economic performance. If policymakers in Pyongyang rely upon the same numbers that the DPRK has furnished the outside world, they will currently be unable to determine either the level, or the tempo, or even the direction of change in national income and output on the basis of the numbers themselves.

Social Statistics

On the whole, the DPRK's social statistics seem to provide outsiders with a potentially more accurate representation of conditions in North Korea than do the county's official economic statistics. Three factors may explain characteristic differences in utility between these two categories of statistics. First, the DPRK's social statistics are primarily demographic; thus, the trends they chart must conform to the simple and inalterable arithmetic rules of demographic change. Inconsistencies and contradictions are much easier to detect in demographic data than in economic data, and proposed corrections require less surmise. Second, social-demographic statistics are intrinsically easier to compile and tabulate than economic data, and thus less subject to honest misrepresentation by technicians with limited qualifications or training. Third, because the North Korean government's priorities (and political campaigns) have weighed heavily toward economic rather than purely social achievements, official pressure for political adjustments of social statistics has been correspondingly milder. Even so, available DPRK social statistics are by no means free of limitations.

Health and Mortality Data

From the 1945 partition until its 1993 census, North Korea's demographic statistics were generated exclusively by the country's vital registration system and its population registration system. Those systems apparently produced detailed mortality data. Only a tiny portion of those data is now available to outsiders[39]—but the data available permit a relatively robust reconstruction of DPRK mortality trends, and through those trends, a reflection of health conditions in the country. Those reconstructed DPRK mortality trends allow us to evaluate the quality of official North Korean mortality data.

Unlike some DPRK economic data, no obviously spurious or doctored numbers stand out in the available official data on mortality. On the other hand, mortality registration in North Korea appeared to be incomplete through at least the late 1980s. Incomplete registration of vital events is quite common in low-income countries—although it may surprise some that it should also be characteristic under a state that strives for such total scrutiny over the lives of its citizenry.

In 1960, according to reconstructed trends, North Korea's vital statistics system was missing about 37 percent of the deaths in the country, and was still missing around 28 percent as late as 1970. The situation had improved by 1986, but an estimated 12 percent of the country's total deaths were still unaccounted for in that year. Not surprisingly, under-reporting of infant mortality was particularly pronounced: an estimated two thirds or more of the deaths of infants under one year of age were not picked up by the DPRK's vital registration system.[40]

The corollary of under-reporting mortality was the over-estimation of life expectancy. DPRK sources put the country's overall life expectancy at birth at 73.0 years for 1976—almost a decade higher than reconstructed trends suggested. For 1986, the official claim was 74.3 years—closer to the reconstructed estimate, but still over six and a half years above it. Though exaggerated, those official claims appear to have resulted from an honest albeit unsophisticated use of standard demographic techniques rather than any deliberate effort to manipulate data.

Since the official acknowledgement in 1995 of a food emergency in the DPRK, the death toll exacted by the ongoing hunger crisis has been a question of pressing international humanitarian concern. Although Pyongyang has accepted hundreds of millions of dollars in relief aid from the international community (including millions of tons of food donations) to combat its hunger problem, it has steadfastly refused to divulge the detailed mortality data that would specify the dimensions of the problem itself.

In May 1999, an official with the DPRK Flood Rehabilitation Committee announced that the crude death rate for the total population had jumped from 6.8 per thousand in 1995 to 9.3 per thousand in 1998;[41] positing a DPRK population of over 20 million, those numbers would imply, very roughly, "excess mortality" of about 50,000 in calendar year 1998.

Those numbers, however, look completely inconsistent with the figures previously provided to a team from the U.S. Centers for Disease Control and Prevention (CDC) in 1997, which was told that "[f]rom 1994 to 1996, overall crude mortality for children [under] 5 years increased from 31 per 1,000 to 58 per 1,000."[42]

According to the 1993 census compendium, North Korea's crude death rate for children under five in 1993 was only about 5.4 per thousand. A jump to a level of 31 per thousand in 1994 would, ceteris paribus, imply an annual increase in deaths for this age group alone of something like 50,000, and of something like 100,000 for calendar year 1996.[43]Indeed, a jump in mortality for children under five years of age of the magnitude reported would by itself, all other things being equal, have been sufficient to push North Korea's 1994 total crude death rate up to about 8 per thousand—far above the 6.8 rate subsequently claimed for 1995. And an upsurge of child mortality of the magnitudes indicated would likely be accompanied by an increase in death rates among adults as well.[44]

If the child mortality data provided to the CDC were relatively accurate, the crude death rates later offered by the DPRK Flood Rehabilitation Committee could only correspondingly be underestimates of the country's true mortality levels—possibly, quite substantial underestimates. Such under-reporting—if it did indeed occur—could be due to growing incompleteness of mortality coverage, that is to say, to a significant and progressive breakdown of the vital registration system. Alternatively, it could speak to the emergence of the mortality rate as a politically sensitive indicator—and thus a number subject to recalculation for purely political reasons. Note, however, that those two potential sources of distortion are not mutually exclusive.

Labor Force and Employment

Over the years the DPRK has occasionally released bits of data bearing upon the distribution of economically active manpower. The 1993 census augmented that information. Tremendous gaps, to be sure, remain in DPRK employment data, and basic definitional and methodological questions still must be answered about those data that have been released—not the least of these regarding the extent of coverage of workers in the military industries. Even so, the statistical picture of North Korea's disposition of its able-bodied manpower seems to have come into slightly sharper focus. In fact, this may be the only area in which the North Korean statistical situation has improved in recent years.

For the period from 1946 to 1993, Pyongyang has reported on the changing distribution of the North Korean labor force using an essentially tripartite classification scheme: the economically active were categorized as "farmers," "workers," or "office workers." By those definitions, North Korea reportedly experienced a phenomenal structural transformation over the course of its socialist construction, whereby between 1946 and 1993, the share of workers in the North Korean labor force leapt by over 50 percentage points, so that workers accounted for over five-eighths of the country's enumerated labor force by the early 1990s.

Unfortunately, this employment typology is a class-based schema—not a categorization according to economic activity. By the somewhat tortured taxonomy employed in Table 2.7, a laborer who services tractors in a repair shop in an agricultural cooperative counts as a farmer, whereas a field hand raising crops for a state enterprise counts as a worker.

For the first time ever, the 1993 census provides numbers on North Korea's labor force distribution by industrial sector. Though the categories listed do not immediately square with the conventional groupings outlined by the International Standard Industrial Classification of all Economic Activities (ISIC), they nevertheless offer a different and perhaps more reliable impression of DPRK manpower distribution.

Whereas, for example, over 63 percent of North Korea's economically active population was classed as workers by the census, the share of the enumerated workforce in manufacturing and construction—the two "productive" non-agricultural sectors of the economy recognized in the socialist typology—is 42 percent, a gap of over 20 percentage points!

Table 2.7
Reported Distribution of DPRK Population by Employment Category, 1946–1993

Year	Farmer/Agricultural Cooperative Member	Worker	Office Worker	Other
1946	74.1	12.5	6.2	7.2
1949	69.6	19.0	7.0	4.4
1953	66.9	21.2	8.5	3.9
1956	56.6	27.3	13.6	2.5
1960	44.4	38.3	13.7	3.6
1963	42.8	40.1	15.1	1.9
1986	25.9	56.3	17.0	0.9
1987	25.3	57.0	16.8	0.9
1993	23.5	63.1	13.4	—

Sources: For 1946–63: Chung, 1974, pp. 146–147; for 1986–87: Eberstadt and Banister, 1992, p. 83; for 1993: DPRK CBS, p. 508.

Table 2.8
Distribution of DPRK Labor Force, 1993

Sector	Total (1,000s)	Percent
Overall labor force	11,004	100
Manufacturing	4,118	37.4
Farming	3,381	30.7
Construction	464	4.2
Transport and communication	402	3.7
State farms	251	2.3
Commerce	509	4.6
Education, culture, health	844	7.7
Others	1,305	9.4

Source: Derived from DPRK CBS, 1995.

Almost as striking, the proportion of the labor force reported to be actually engaged in farming or working on state farms is nearly ten percentage points higher than the proportion defined as farmers on the basis of class status. Indeed, the proportion of the workforce reportedly in the farm and state farm sectors in the 1993 census was substantially higher than the percentage of farmers in the labor force back in 1986 (Figure 2.3). Obviously, we cannot yet estimate changes over time in the sectoral distribution of manpower in the DPRK economy—but we can be quite sure that the available, class-based labor data do not provide an accurate indication of those trends.

For the first time, the 1993 census permits direct calculations of labor force participation rates for the DPRK. The (presumably civilian) workforce enu-

Figure 2.3
Reported Percentage of Labor Force in Primary Sector DPRK, 1986–1993

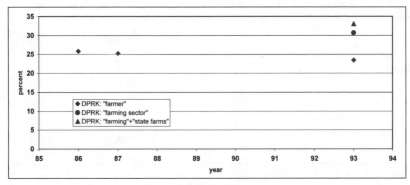

Sources: Eberstadt and Banister, 1992; DPRK CBS, 1993.

merated amounts to fully 76 percent of the (presumably civilian) population 16 years of age or older for whom age data were presented; if military personnel were counted along with what the DPRK census terms the "labor population," the calculated ratio would presumably be even higher.[45]

Even for a communist state, the DPRK appears to have an extremely high level of labor force participation, as Table 2.9 demonstrates.[46]

The data seem to ratify the widespread perception of the DPRK as an extraordinarily mobilized society—but they also beg the question of how "work" is being defined in North Korea. For, as Table 2.10 illustrates, labor force participation rates implied for a number of cohorts looks to be almost impossibly high.

Among men between the ages of 35 and 49, for example, the ratio approaches 99 percent. Yet some middle-aged men suffer from disabilities, chronic illnesses (such as tuberculosis), and other incapacitating conditions in every society, and in North Korea that incidence of functional incapacitation is likely to

Table 2.9
Labor Force Participation Rates for North and South Korea and Selected Other Countries, Various Years (percent)

Country (Year, Age Group)	Total	Male	Female
North Korea, excluding army			
(1993, 16+)	76.0	84.6	68.9
South Korea (1995, 15+)	62.0	76.5	48.3
Communist States			
Czechoslovakia (1980, 15+)	67.8	75.5	60.8
East Germany (1981, 15+)	67.5	76.2	60.0
Hungary (1980, 15+)	60.5	71.9	50.2
Cuba (1981, 15+)	53.4	72.8	33.8
China (1982, 15+)	78.7	86.5	75.0
Vietnam (1989, 15+)	77.3	81.6	73.6
Asian NICs			
Hong Kong (1995, 15+)	62.8	77.3	48.0
Taiwan (1989, 15+)	60.4	74.8	45.4
Singapore (1995, 15+)	64.3	78.4	50.0
Developed Market Economies			
Germany (1995, 15+)	58.5	69.7	48.2
Japan (1995, 15+)	63.4	77.6	50.0
Switzerland (1995, 15+)	55.0	64.0	46.4
United States (1995, 16+)	66.6	75.0	58.0

Sources: Derived from DPRK CBS, 1993; ROK NSO, 1995; ROK NSO, 1996; ROC Executive Yuan, 1990; all others, ILO, various editions.

Table 2.10
Reported Labor Force Participation Rates
by Age and Sex, 1993 (percent)

Age	Male	Female	Total
16–19	62.5	66.3	64.6
20–24	90.9	92.7	91.8
25–29	89.0	86.8	87.8
30–34	95.9	87.0	91.4
35–39	98.5	89.4	93.9
40–44	98.8	91.1	94.9
45–49	98.6	91.1	94.7
50–54	97.8	86.5	93.6
55–59	95.9	16.3	52.8
60+	16.5	4.1	8.4

Source: Derived from DPRK CBS, 1995, pp. 505, 517.

be rather higher than the official data on labor force participation would imply.[47] Though this may not ultimately prove to be their greatest defect, it would thus appear that DPRK manpower data currently include persons incapable of productive work in the rosters of the active labor force.

The "1993 Census": A Falsified Count?

In terms of absolute volume, the 500-plus page compendium on the DPRK's "1993" census—evidently, the first such population count since partition—ranks as the most massive statistical release in North Korean history. The census also offers a level of detail never previously provided in any DPRK statistical transmission. But from the standpoint of statistical openness, transparency, and reliability, the document does not constitute an unqualified advance.

As noted earlier, the 1993 census appears in quotation marks because it was not actually conducted in 1993, but in early 1994, and is characterized by such serious internal inconsistencies, that its integrity is open to question.

The first evident problem with the 1993 census is the reported sex ratio for the country. In 1953—after the terrible losses incurred in the Korean War—the DPRK's sex ratio was 88.3 males per 100 females, according to population registration data. Thereafter, as would be normally expected in a period of recovery, the reported sex ratio gradually rose. In 1970, it was reportedly 95.1.

North Korea's sex ratio should have risen still further during the subsequent 23 years. Only a major war or some other equally momentous perturbation could have forestalled that anticipated equalization.[48] Yet, as seen in Figure 2.4,

Figure 2.4
Reported DPRK Sex Ratio: 1953–1993 (males per 100 females)

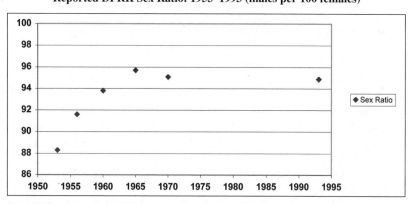

Note: 1993 sex ratio from DPRK census; all others from DPRK population registration data.
Sources: Eberstadt and Banister, 1992, p. 32; DPRK CBS, 1995, p. 3.

the "1993" census put the sex ratio for the country's entire population at 94.9, slightly lower than the ratio the population registration system had recorded for the year 1970!

To be sure, the population registration data do not look entirely free of error: the sex ratio for 1965 in particular looks strangely high. But unless the DPRK population registration system was systematically and severely over-counting men between the Korean armistice and 1970, North Korea's reported sex ratio in its population census was far too low, implying that some hundreds of thousands of men in the country were uncounted in "1993."

However, it is not only the number of men counted in the 1993 census that looks strangely low. The total figure for women looks curiously low as well. The contradiction is first apparent when one compares reported figures for growth of total female population in North Korea with data from the vital registration system.

In the 1970s and 1980s, as already noted, North Korea's population registration system counted only civilians. But since only small numbers of women are thought to have served in the DPRK's armed forces, those data should not have been significantly affected by national security demands. The population registration data depict a gradual slowdown in both the relative and the absolute growth of North Korea's female population between 1970 and 1987, with annual increments declining from about 212,000 in the early 1970s to about 165,000 a year in the mid-to-late 1980s, and the pace of growth dropping from about 2.7 percent to about 1.6 percent a year.

Thereafter, the growth of the female population appears to have fallen suddenly. To go by 1987 registration figures and the 1993 census, the growth of North Korea's female population abruptly slowed to under 0.5 percent per annum, with implied annual increments down to about 53,000 a year.

In principle, a deceleration of that magnitude is not suspicious, but it must square with other data on population change. This one does not. Since North Korea's net migration rate is essentially zero, the growth of female population should track very closely with the country's rate of natural increase (birth rates minus death rates). But according to official DPRK vital statistics, North Korea's annual rate of natural increase in the mid-to-late 1980s was about 1.7 to 1.8 percent. And in 1993, according to the data in the census compendium, the rate of natural increase would have been about 1.4 to 1.5 percent per year.

For a variety of technical reasons, reconstructions of DPRK vital trends would result in calculated rates of natural increase lower—but only slightly lower—than the ones reported. In the absence of any reasons for positing severe demographic shocks in North Korea between 1987 and 1993, the average rate of natural increase for the period should closely approximate an interpolation from the two endpoints. Yet such interpolations for 1987–93 cannot be reconciled with the rates of increase implied by Table 2.11. The same holds true for absolute totals. According to the raw data in the census compendium, the natural increase for North Korea's female population in 1993 alone exceeded 150,000, whereas the total six-year rise in female population implied by the 1987 registration data and the 1993 census is about 370,000.

Again, it is quite likely that data from both the population registration system and the vital statistics system are subject to error. But unless those errors were systematic and increasing over time—that is, unless those two systems were increasingly recording nonexistent women and phantom births—the census count of North Korea's female population would look inexplicably low.

Table 2.11
DPRK Reported Female Population, 1970–1993 (thousands)

Year	Population	Increase per annum	Growth rate per annum
1970	7,492		
1975	8,533	212	2.68%
1980	9,289	147	1.65%
1985	10,185	179	1.86%
1987	10,515	165	1.61%
1993	10,884	53	0.49%

Note: 1970–87 data from population registration system; 1993 data from census.

Sources: Eberstadt and Banister, 1992, p. 32; DPRK CBS, 1995, p. 3.

Questions about the accuracy of the 1993 census count of North Korea's female population are compounded by the extreme disparity between reconstructed estimates of female life expectancy at birth and the implicit survival ratio of girls and young women. Indirect estimates of mortality for the DPRK[49] suggest steady and fairly rapid improvements since the end of the Korean War, with female life expectancy at birth in excess of 70 years in the late 1980s and the early 1990s.

But implicit survival ratios for younger North Korean females can also be calculated on the basis of the 1993 census and the DPRK population age structure data divulged for year-end 1986.[50] The year-end 1986 age structure disaggregated the population 16 years of age and under into five discrete groups. In conjunction with the age data afforded by the 1993 census, implicit survival ratios for the years 1986–93 can thus be obtained for five groups of girls and women between the ages of seven and 23 as of year-end 1993.

The survival ratios implied by these data are extraordinarily low—that is to say, they would be consonant with practically catastrophic levels of mortality. "Model life tables" make the point. Mapped against either the UN's "Far Eastern Pattern" or "General Pattern" mortality schedules, for example, the implicit 1986–93 survival ratio for girls aged 8–10 at the time of the census, if accurate, would be characteristic of a society with a life expectancy at birth of under 45 years. For girls 11–12 years of age at the time of the census, the implicit survival ratio—if accurate—would accord with a "model" life expectancy at birth of well under 30 years.[51] Since such mortality schedules are intrinsically impossible to countenance—and furthermore inconsistent with all other data we have that bears upon North Korean mortality patterns in the late Kim Il Sung era—the implicit survival ratios in Table 2.13 amount to additional evidence of a pervasive undercount of younger females in the 1993 census.[52]

Table 2.12
Indirectly Estimated Expectation of Life at Birth
for Females in the DPRK, 1970–1993 (years)

Year	Life expectancy
1970	62.2
1975	66.3
1980	69.0
1985	70.4
1993	73.9

Notes: 1993 estimates derived from 1993 census; earlier estimate based upon population registration data; annual estimates for 1970–1985 are interpolated from series.

Sources: For 1970–1985: Eberstadt and Banister, 1992, pp. 108–109; for 1993: Banister and West, 1997, p. 4.

Table 2.13
DPRK Implicit Survival Ratios for Females:
1986 Population Registration Data and 1993 Census Data

Birth Cohort	Age in 1993	1986 Total	1993 Total	Implicit Survival Ratio
1986	7	188,877	182,833	0.968
1983–85	8–10	591,046	532,288	0.901
1982–83	11–12	452,365	347,825	0.769
1972–81	13–22	2,164,644	1,805,809	0.834
1971	23	279,817	226,904	0.811

Sources: Eberstadt and Banister, 1992; DPRK CBS, 1995.

How can we account for these striking and profound irregularities? Without recourse to the original DPRK population registration and census data, it is impossible to render a conclusive assessment. At this juncture, however, a conjecture worth entertaining is that North Korean authorities may have deliberately misreported the returns from the 1993 census in an effort to conceal the true size of the country's military population.

Like China's recent censuses, North Korea reports one figure for overall national male and female population, but then presents geographic breakdowns for the country's male and female population that add up to a smaller total than the countrywide number. The difference between the two totals, by implication, is the DPRK's military population.[53] The census provides a detailed age structure for what is implicitly the country's civilian population, but no age structure data for the presumed military cohorts. And for the entire national population, the only sex ratio that can be derived is the relationship between males and females of all ages.

In the 1993 census, the gap between countrywide and regionally aggregated population totals amounted to just under 700,000 persons: about 652,000 men and 39,000 women. That is a much lower total than the 1.25 million non-civilian men at year-end 1987 suggested by earlier reconstructions of DPRK demographic data.[54]

If North Korean authorities wished to disguise, and reduce, the size of their military force in the 1993 population count, they would have to take account of the technique that had permitted outside observers in the past to derive their own independent estimates of DPRK defense manpower from the country's demographic data. The technique utilized in those earlier reconstructions of North Korean non-civilian male manpower relied crucially upon the sex ratio for the DPRK civilian population: the lower the reports of the latter, the greater the estimate of the former. To thwart that technique, one could attempt to inflate the reported civilian sex ratio. But one would have to do so in a manner that would not invite detection through the creation of other glaring internal inconsistencies in the reported demographic data.

One relatively simple approach achieves these diverse objectives. To minimize the chances of outside discovery of a major underreporting of military male manpower, one could understate the true number of men under arms, while also undercounting the female civilian population, and scaling down actual reported female population totals for every age cohort, so that the resultant civilian sex ratios looked less extreme. As it happens, the three major anomalies in the 1993 census described above—the apparent undercount of total male population, the apparent undercount of total female population, and the apparent undercount of girls and younger women—could all be explained by official embrace of the approach just described.

It is premature, of course, to assert that North Korea's 1993 census was officially and systematically falsified. It is a fact that no government has ever before engaged in such wholesale demographic deception. Even if Pyongyang were to attempt to undertake such an exercise, it is by no means clear who could carry it out, or how—practically and administratively—they would proceed. For now, it will suffice to observe that deliberate misreporting would be the most parsimonious explanation for the different problems we have identified in the 1993 census data—and that the release of doctored data would hardly constitute a departure from standard practice for contemporary North Korean authorities.

Concluding Observations

In 1974, Joseph Sang-hoon Chung, in his classic study of the North Korean economy, offered this qualified assessment of available official statistics from the DPRK:

> Published data seem to be by and large internally consistent relative to certain obvious mathematical and technical relationships existing among different variables. Several consistency tests performed on industrial output data seem to bear out this point. To be sure, internal consistency is not the same as statistical accuracy.[55]

A quarter century later, a distinctly less optimistic appraisal is warranted. For now internal inconsistency is the hallmark of the few official quantitative data that the DPRK does divulge. The overall credibility of available North Korean statistics today can currently only be described as low, and, as we have seen, not a few statistical claims in recent decades appear to be utterly fantastical. The official statistical blackout that has suppressed the issue of quantitative information has evidently also severely suppressed both the standards of statistical work in the DPRK and the very capabilities of the North Korean statistical system.

Under half a century of DPRK governance, North Korean statistical capabilities have been shaped by conflicting pressures. On the one hand, the country's highest authorities have avowed that accurate statistical returns were—as an early official slogan put it—"the Necessary Condition for the Development of the People's Economy."[56] No less a commentator than Kim Il Sung instructed that "it is essential to have accurate statistics for the country as a whole, for each ministry, and for each factory and enterprise under the ministries."[57] On the other hand, Kim Il Sung himself also warned that "the [DPRK] statistics bureau is an important agency of state secrets."[58] Correspondingly, statistical work was also to be governed by national security considerations, as those were interpreted by Pyongyang. Over the course of DPRK rule, those national security considerations have weighed ever more heavily upon the North Korean statistical apparatus, with entirely predictable consequences for the quality of statistical work. Indeed, today it is far from clear that the DPRK CBS is even in a position to prepare a comprehensive and accurate description of socio-economic trends in North Korea. And even if separate, special internal ledgers were actually being prepared for confidential perusal by the country's top leadership, one can only wonder how the DPRK's highest circles could possibly glean a precise and detailed impression of economic performance and social conditions in the country they command from the information at their disposal.

In 1974, Chung expected that the highest authorities in the DPRK would strive to maintain the integrity of their statistical system because "[p]utting out false information regarding the economy will mislead the planning process and . . . create general chaos."[59] On the first score, he has been proven wrong; on the second, however, he seems to have been chillingly prescient. For, although we lack precise figures on its real situation, it is no secret that North Korea's economy is in grave condition today.

North Korea's present economic straits, of course, have many causes. In this venue, we may note that North Korea's manifest and mounting economic failure is inextricably related to the failure of its statistical system. In a command economy, "planning without numbers" (to borrow a phrase from Wolfgang Stolper) can only invite tremendous economic losses. And the more ambitious the plan, the more monumental the costs. Moreover, when economic disaster strikes, a lack of reliable information can only impede the effort to chart a course toward economic recovery, by concealing the impact of destructive policies and practices, impairing efforts to optimize or prioritize, and limiting the careful consideration of alternative paths and strategies.

There are some indications that North Korean authorities have at last come to recognize the threat that the current disarray within the DPRK's statistical apparatus poses to their socialist economic system, and may now regard the improvement of the country's statistical capabilities as a matter of some urgency. In April 1999, the SPA passed a new Law on People's Economic Plans.[60] Most of the language of that law reaffirmed the (presumably existing) authority of the socialist state to control and direct the operations of the national economy. However, many of the articles in this law concerned the collecting, transmitting, and processing of accurate economic and social data to statistical authorities, and from statistical authorities to policymakers. Article 12 of that law specifically states, "A people's economic plan cannot be formulated without basic information."

Whether socialist command planning of the style envisioned in this new law will be adequate to the task of sparking economic revival in the DPRK, of course, remains to be seen. We may confidently venture, however, that North Korea's economic rehabilitation cannot occur without a rehabilitation of the North Korean statistical system.

A rehabilitation of the DPRK's statistical system, for its part, cannot occur without a decisive rejection of the atmosphere of internal secrecy and external isolation in which statistical work has been conducted over the past many decades. Irrespective of whether North Korean leadership intends to cleave to its strict and classical variant of command socialism or to entertain a move toward greater market orientation, the statistical system upon which it relies stands in need of a thoroughgoing overhaul and a wholesale retraining of personnel. Technical assistance from abroad and international cooperation with foreign specialists are the obvious avenues for beginning such a process in earnest. Such contacts, however, would embark the North Korean system, however implicitly, on a path toward greater openness and transparency. To date, DPRK authorities have vigilantly and explicitly opposed precisely those tendencies as inimical to the integrity of "our own style of socialism."

From the standpoint of North Korean leadership, it would seem, profound perils lie not only in the decay of the country's statistical capabilities—but also in their prospective recovery. It remains to be seen how North Korean policy will attempt to resolve this thorny contradiction.

Update 2006: DPRK Statistics in the New Century

In the seven years since the preceding analysis was prepared, a number of significant developments within the DPRK would appear to have heightened the importance of timely and accurate North Korean statistical data for policymakers in Pyongyang.

To begin, North Korea's halting but gradual development of economic ties with South Korea (discussed in greater detail in Chapter 6) would seem to militate in favor of greater availability and reliability of statistical information about the DPRK. Simply put, foreign investors hate risk, and lack of information—in and of itself—constitutes a serious risk for prospective business partners from abroad. Hardly less important, Pyongyang's July 2002 "economic management improvement measures" (discussed in greater detail in Chapter

10)—moves often described outside North Korea as "economic reforms"— have further raised the salience of generating reliable quantitative information for North Korean economic performance. The July 2002 measures effected both a limited remonetization of the consumer sector and a limited emergence of sanctioned domestic market activity, and market responses can be neither efficient nor terribly effective in a data vacuum.

In principle, North Korean leadership has formally embraced the rehabilitation of the country's statistical capability as an official priority in the Kim Jong Il era. In the years since Kim Jong Il's September 1998 accession to "the highest post of state," DPRK directives have repeatedly identified and affirmed the urgency of strengthening statistical capabilities, and have explicitly linked this objective to the overarching national goal of creating a "powerful and prosperous state" (*kang-song taeguk*). As North Korea's leading economic journal instructed in 2003:

> Only by ensuring the party spirit and the quality of scientific accuracy and objectiv-ity, and of timeliness in statistical work is it possible to perform statistical work in the interests of the party and revolution . . . To that end, every loop in the system of the state statistics agencies has to be strengthened and its role elevated. . . .

Without careful use of accurate statistics, it ominously warned,

> it will be impossible to expect any improvement to be made in the nation's economic work.[61]

To judge by available evidence, however, these pronouncements amount to little more than lip service as yet. In the period since September 1998, the North Korean government has released precious little in the way of new economic or social data.[62] Those few data that have been released, moreover, appear to be highly problematic from the standpoint of internal consistency, reliability, and faithfulness, as a brief overview may demonstrate.

Errors, Internal Inconsistencies, Implausible Results

Table 2.14 highlights official data on demographic and economic trends DPRK over the 1990–2000 period.

These numbers were not released directly by Pyongyang, but instead were published in, of all places, a United Nations Environment Programme (UNEP) report on environmental conditions in North Korea, prepared in 2003 with the assistance of the DPRK government, and with access to information from the DPRK Central Statistical Bureau.[63]

On the demographic side, problems are immediately apparent even with these basic annual population totals. The figure for 1990 is identical to the fig-ure for 1991, and the study indicates two alternative totals for the year 1994, with the same for the year 1996. These official demographic figures, moreover, indicate a steep reduction in national population between 1994 and 1995 (that

Table 2.14
DPRK Central Statistics Bureau Reports or Implicit Estimates for North
Korean Population and GDP: 1990–2000

Year	Population (million)	GDP (US$ billion)	GDP Per Capita (US$)	Previously Reported DPRK "national income" Per Capita (US$)	Agriculture as Percent of GDP	Implied Agricultural output Per Capita (US$)
1990	20.96			2460		
1991	20.96					
1992	21.086	20.875	990		21.8	216
1993	21.213					
1994	21.51/ 21.359	15.421	772		20.9	161
1995	21.21			(719) (239)		
1996	22.114/ 21.966	10.588	482		14.7	71
1997						
1998	22.34	10.273	460			
1999						
2000	22.996	11.156	485			

Note: Figures in italics are implicit, derived from other reported data; figures in parentheses are contrasting officially reported numbers for same year.

Sources: UNEP, 2003, pp. 15, 16, 41, 42, 56; Table 2.6 in this chapter.

is to say, for the period before Pyongyang's international emergency appeal for humanitarian relief) while implying positive population growth during the years 1996–98 (i.e., during the depths of the famine).[64]

As for the economic data, figures on North Korean GDP between 1992 and 1998 are given in current US dollars, and indicate a fall of over half in those six years! While there is little doubt North Korea's economy was in dire straits during this period, the magnitude of the calculated decline looks highly questionable. Even in the wake of China's disastrous Great Leap Forward, GDP in current domestic prices dropped by far less (e.g., about 20 percent).[65] While the overall decline in GDP may seem suspicious, some of the proposed sectoral reductions look practically impossible. The DPRK statistics, indeed, indicate that the share of agriculture in DPRK output contracted between 1992 and 1996 from about 22 percent down to 15 percent, implying that per capita agricultural output over those four years had plummeted by over two-thirds. In the darkest days of the great Maoist famine, per capita agricultural output is believed to have fallen by less than 30 percent.[66] Without in any way diminishing the catastrophic suffering the North Korean population endured over the course of the 1990s, we can observe that these official numbers cannot be regarded as an accurate macro-economic depiction of the tragedy.

Nor do the few newly released tidbits on trade present a plausible portrait of the country's trade performance in the 1990s.[67] As we shall see in Chapter 3, the "mirror statistics" of DPRK trade for those years, developed from the reports of North Korea's international trade partners, document much higher levels of purchases from abroad than those acknowledged by Pyongyang. Those same mirror statistics point to a chronic and pronounced North Korean balance of trade deficit with the outside world.

Even if these new statistical offerings were faithfully compiled, computed and reproduced, the calculations are on their very face characterized by fundamental inaccuracies, calling into question whether Pyongyang is currently capable of tracking even the most basic social and economic trends in North Korea with any precision.

Statistics Deliberately Doctored?

Although Pyongyang has accepted hundreds of millions of dollars of food aid from the international community since its initial emergency appeal for assistance in 1995, the North Korean government has been strikingly unresponsive to the requests from foreign relief organizations for basic information about the dimensions of the local food crisis—information that could, among other things, assist in the mobilization of international resources for the stricken in North Korea, and improve the effectiveness of interventions intended to save lives.

In 2003, however, the DPRK did consent to provide UNICEF and the World Food Programme (WFP) with its own assessment of the nutritional situation in the country, based on a survey conducted by the DPRK Central Bureau of Statistics in 2002.[68] The release of these data was, not unreasonably, regarded as an important event in international relief circles, and the numbers reported were widely discussed. The bulk of the assessment seemed to suggest that the nutritional status of North Korean children, while still precarious, had nonetheless improved markedly since the previous 1998 nutritional survey sanctioned by Pyongyang. The data were commonly interpreted in international humanitarian circles as evidence that food aid to North Korea had "worked," but that more was still needed, so that international food assistance should continue—a conclusion that could hardly have displeased the government that prepared and provided it.[69]

Yet the credibility of the entire study was called into question by its claims about the incidence of "low birthweight" in the DPRK. Those claims are reprinted in Table 2.15.

Table 2.15

Reported Incidence of Low Birthweight in DPRK and Selected Provinces or Major Cities: 2000–2002 (percent)

Area	LBW (percent)
Pyongyang	4.8
Nampo	6.3
Kaesong	8.0
N. Hamgyong Prov.	8.0
N. Hwanghae Prov.	8.5
N. Phyongan Prov.	6.6
Ryanggang Prov.	8.5
S. Hamgoyng Prov.	6.4
S. Hwanghae Prov.	5.7
S. Phyongan Prov.	5.7
Total DPRK	6.7

Note: "Low birthweight" refers to live birth of babies under 2500 grams; data reported from survey conducted by DPRK CBS.

Source: DPRK CBS, 2002, p. 24.

Low birthweight incidence—the proportion of babies born at under 2,500 grams (about 5.5 pounds)—is a statistical indicators used to judge the health and nutritional status of the infants in any given population.[70] The DPRK 2002 assessment reported that the incidence of low birthweight (LBW) for the 2,500 North Korean children under two years of age in its survey was 6.7 percent.

How would the claimed LBW profile look against the profile in other contemporary societies? Table 2.16 presents the comparison.

First, North Korea claims to have a better (i.e. lower) LBW incidence than that of the United States, lower, even, than the reported LBW for American non-Hispanic whites. The DPRK claim is also lower than the LBW for Asian-Americans. North Korea's claimed LBW would put it on par with the European Union average, and ahead of such EU states as Austria, France, and Britain. Moreover, North Korea's LBW claim would give it a better profile than Singapore—continental Asia's most prosperous and highly developed state.

The North Korean authors of the 2002 assessment do not shy away from the apparent implications of these LBW numbers:

The birthweights reported by the [North Korean] mothers are impressively good. The overall [LBW] rate of only 6.7% is better than that of 7.7% reported for England and Wales in 1996, and the rate reported for Pyongyang of 4.8% puts it on part [sic] with Denmark, with one of the best low birthweight rates reported by any nation.[71]

Table 2.16
Low Birthweight (LBW) in International Perspective:
DPRK Claims for 2000/2001 vs. Recent Incidences of LBW
from Selected Other Countries

Country/Year	LBW (percent)
DPRK (2000/2002)	6.7
USA (2003)	
All races	7.9
Non-Hispanic white	7.0
Asian-Pacific islanders	7.8
European Union (pre-accession, 2000)	6.7
Austria (2004)	6.8
Spain (2000)	6.9
Portugal (2001)	7.1
France (1999)	7.3
United Kingdom (2000)	7.5
Greece (2000)	8.1
Selected Asian Countries	
Singapore (2000)	8
Malaysia (1998)	10
Philippines (2000)	20
Sri Lanka (2000)	22

Note: "Low birthweight" refers to live birth of babies under 2500 grams.
Sources: Table 15; WHO, "European Health For All Database"; WHO, 2004.

But the inferences are preposterous. No country just emerging from famine could be expected to have an OECD-style LBW profile—much less an incidence of LBW more favorable than that of Singapore! The reasons are purely biological, as it is well established in the medical and nutritional literature that poorly-fed mothers predictably bear smaller and lighter babies.[72] For these reasons, North Korea's expected LBW incidence might (optimistically) be likened to those of such low-income, relatively low-mortality, societies as the Philippines and Sri Lanka—but the estimated LBW incidences in those countries were roughly three times as high as the levels North Korea was claiming for itself. While recognizing that the 2002 assessment introduced an element of methodological bias that would have pushed North Korea's reported LBW artificially downward in any case,[73] we must also recognize odds that a random sample of 2,500 contemporary North Korean infants and toddlers would generate an LBW profile on par with the globe's most affluent societies for what they are: namely, impossibly small.

Wherefore, then, such biologically bizarre results? The simplest explanation for these anomalous and indeed outlandish claims is that they were political inventions rather than genuine statistical returns.

Of course, without access to the raw data behind the 2002 nutritional assessment—foreigners were frozen out of the actual processes of survey design, interview compilation, and primary data analysis—it is impossible for outsiders to know what actually happened there. But those who would wish to disprove the contention that Pyongyang has taken to manipulating the statistical data that modulates its interface with foreign aid-dispensing organizations face some fairly imposing forensics.

Index Number Problems

Adjusting for price changes is always something of a challenge for statistical authorities—and especially for those in centrally planned economies. The difficulty is that there is no single obvious "best" method for deflating series over time under the best of circumstances—and adjusting for price changes under conditions of command/control and ration/shortage are far from ideal circumstances.

Whatever else they may have accomplished, the "economic management improvement measures" of July 2002 ushered in explosive changes in DPRK price levels. By slashing the official exchange rate against the dollar from about 2.1:1 to around 150:1, by raising nominal wages by a factor of ten or more, and by letting the price for formerly controlled commodities fluctuate under supply-demand pressure, the stage was set for a huge upward surge in nominal price levels. For statistical authorities, this price explosion posed at least two practical problems: 1) determining accurately the actual dimensions of changes in price levels; and 2) determining the real, inflation-adjusted, trends of economic activity in the domestic economy.

Official reports on the DPRK state budget make the point. Between the years of 2001 and 2004, according to official DPRK pronouncements, state expenditures rose from 21.7 billion *won* to about 349 billion *won*[74]—an increase of over 16-fold. Over those same years, according to various statements by the North Korean government, real budgetary expenditures were estimated to have increased by more than 24 percent—a tempo of expansion that would qualify as decidedly vigorous for any national economy.[75]

But is this calculated result correct? The problems facing official statisticians in the DPRK in the quest for accuracy, as we have seen, are monumental. And if the true average rate of price change for the DPRK over that period were just slightly higher than the statistical authorities were calculating—say, 8 percent per month, as opposed to the 7.4 percent per month presumed in the DPRK budget statements—the true growth in real expenditures would have been not robust (8+ percent per year), but instead only marginal (0.2 percent per year). Similar problems obtain with other official DPRK economic claims under conditions of rapid price change. In 2003, for example, the government asserted that gross industrial output had soared by 12 percent during the year 2002.[76] Yet a relatively small adjustment in the DPRK's (unpublished) implicit price deflator for calendar year 2002—the year in which wages were suddenly raised by a factor of ten or more—could easily have reduced that claimed surge to zero growth, or even to a real decline.

Rapid changes in North Korean price levels have evidently continued since the enactment of the July 2002 measures.[77] It would thus seem safe to say that the index problem is inherently an even more nettlesome challenge for North Korean statistical authorities today than it has been for decades—maybe since the early post-Korean War era. But just how competently can Pyongyang's official statistical workers compute price deflators today? Indeed, is the North Korean government even capable of measuring inflation as accurately today as it could do half a century ago? The question has profound implications for North Korean policymakers, and the answer to it is not self-evidently affirmative.

In summary, in terms of availability, timeliness or accuracy, there is scant evidence of *any* improvement in DPRK statistical output over the years since September 1998, when Kim Jong Il formally assumed state power. Far from strengthening, Pyongyang's few irregular releases of official numbers in recent years suggest that North Korea's capabilities for generating comprehensive and reliable statistical data may actually still be deteriorating. Improbable as this may seem, considering the state of affairs in the late 1990s, with respect to official North Korean data, the gap between requirements and supplies still seems to be widening. This cannot augur well for the national economic performance.

Notes

1. In the 1950s and early 1960s, publications from the CBS specifically identified it as "DPRK State Planning Commission, Central Bureau of Statistics" (DPRK CBS, 1961) whereas in the 1980s and 1990s it was described simply as the "DPRK Central Bureau of Statistics" (DPRK CBS 1983 and 1995); that semantic difference may or may not be important; it should be recalled, however, that the formal structure of the North Korean state, as indicated by the DPRK constitution and other documents, has undergone important transformations over the past four decades.
2. Chung, 1974, Appendix B.
3. In 1990 in Pyongyang, the author was privileged to enjoy a discussion of more than three hours with representatives of the DPRK CBS about statistical work in North Korea; between 1989 and 1995, specialists from the United Nations Population Fund (UNFPA) met with CBS officials on several occasions, regarding the

UNFPA's technical assistance in the preparation, conduct, and completion of the DPRK's 1993 census; insofar as North Korean authorities reportedly relied upon data processing facilities in China for some of their work on the 1993 census, one may infer that CBS personnel had some interaction with Chinese counterparts; those latter presumed contacts—and any others—remain only surmise, and have not been documented.

4. See Eberstadt, 1995.
5. Cf. DPRK CBS 1961; Chung, 1974.
6. The closest thing to a statistical yearbook that the DPRK has ever published is probably DPRK CBS 1961, a work which appeared almost 40 years ago.
7. The DPRK did provide a 1997 IMF delegation with some summary, dollar-denominated numbers purportedly representing sectoral output for 1992–96 (IMF, 1997); in 1997 it also provided a few macro-economic time-series numbers on per capita GNP to the United Nations (Kim, 1997, p. 575)
8. On a single occasion, the DPRK revealed a won-denominated national output number to outsiders: in 1989, the UNFPA was furnished with a figure for North Korea's "GNI" for 1987 (Eberstadt and Banister, 1992, p. 7).
9. DPRK CBS, 1983 and 1993.
10. See also Eberstadt and Banister, 1992 and IMF, 1997.
11. Some observations and returns have been announced for categories additional to those just enumerated (e.g., transportation, wages, educational enrollment, and medical care); but this chapter offers only a general survey of available DPRK statistical materials—not an exhaustive inventory of every available item.
12. Interview with Hans Maretzki, Potsdam, Germany, May 1993.
13. Maretzki, 1991, p. 154.
14. Li, 1962; Grossman, 1963; Chung, 1974; Blum, 1994.
15. Cf. Becker, 1998.
16. Trigubenko, 1991, p. 2.
17. This unpublished electronic database, updated regularly by the author, reconstructs trends of North Korean export and import performance from the early 1960s onwards; it is derived from sources including the UN International Commercial Merchandise Trade Database (COMTRADE), official Chinese, South Korean, and Russian data on their economic relations with the DPRK, and reports by the former Soviet government on its commercial exchanges with DPRK.
18. Chung, 1974, p. 171.
19. Chung, 1974, Appendix B.
20. IMF, 1997, p. 13.
21. Ibid., pp. 13–14.
22. *FBIS*-EAS-1996-0413.
23. Pang, 1987, pp. 150–151[0].
24. These estimates draw upon mirror statistics reported by the USSR, China, and the countries participating in the UN International Commodity Trade Database, valuing trade in current U.S. dollars at official exchange rates and adjusting results to account for presumed c.i.f. costs; for more details, see Eberstadt, 1998 and Eberstadt et al., 1995.
    Other efforts to derive North Korean trade patterns from mirror statistics have been undertaken by JETO in Japan and KOTRA and the Ministry of National Unification in the ROK; although there are some differences between these various estimates, they track very closely.

25. For details, see the account in *The People's Korea*, available at: http://www.korea-np.co.jp/pk/090th_issue/99041407.htm.
26. Kim Il Sung, vol. 31, p. 76.
27. Eberstadt and Tombes, 2000.
28. Eberstadt and Banister, 1991 and 1992.
29. So much for the DPRK CBS's original mandate to "unify and standardize the statistical computational system"! Chung, 1974, Appendix B.
30. Eberstadt and Banister, 1992, p. 93.
31. Derived from Eberstadt and Banister, 1991 and 1992.
32. See *People's Korea*, 1998.
33. On the latter, see Chun, 1998.
34. See Rosefielde and Pfouts, 1995; Eberstadt and Tombes, 2000.
35. IMF, 1997.
36. Dividing the DPRK's 1987 reported national income of 47.02 billion won by its reported 1987 year-end population of 19.346 million yields a value of 2,430 won per capita; the DPRK's official exchange rate with the U.S. dollar was then 1:1; the DPRK reported per capita national income figure of US$2,400 for 1987 is very close to that total, perhaps identical to it—given the proclivity of DPRK commentators for rounding numbers off.
37. The DPRK national income datum for 1987, in combination with the gross domestic product numbers transmitted to the IMF, imply a nominal decline of 62 percent for North Korea's net material product between 1987 and 1995; if the country's population was larger in 1995 than it was eight years earlier, this would imply an even greater decline in per capita net material product, with 1995 net material product calculated by combining reported dollar-denominated output for agriculture, industry, and construction, and converting the total into won at the commercial exchange rate; it is difficult to surmise just what this calculated decline should be taken to signify: in relative magnitude, after all, this would be roughly twice as large as the drop in calculated Chinese net material product in the aftermath of the Great Leap Forward!

    Among other things, the North Korean total raises issues about price trends and changes in the completeness of coverage of economic activity, perhaps with respect to both economic sectors and geographic regions.
38. The anomalies in the DPRK national accounts data, alas, do not end here; the data transmitted to the IMF, for example, report a dollar-denominated drop in agricultural output between 1994 and 1996 of about 26 percent; but DPRK authorities also told the IMF team that grain harvests fell by over 64 percent—from 7 million tons to 2.5 million tons—during those same two years (IMF, 1997, pp. 10, 17); even positing tremendous price gyrations, it is not clear how trend differences of such a magnitude could be reconciled.
39. See Eberstadt and Banister, 1992.
40. Preliminary analysis of the DPRK's "1993" census compendium—which included relatively detailed data on reported deaths as well as total reported population for calendar year 1993—implied that the North Korean vital registration system was still missing a little more than 10 percent of the country's total deaths (Banister and West, 1997).
41. Watts, 1999.
42. U.S. CDC, 1997, p. 564.
43. The actual absolute increase in 0–4 mortality for 1994 and 1996, however, would likely be lower because all other things would *not* be equal; for one thing, birth rates

typically fall off during extreme hunger crises, and thus the total size of the DPRK's 1994–96 new birth cohorts would likely have been smaller than for the years immediately preceding; for another, mortality rates of the magnitude indicated would themselves be a factor in reducing the size of the 0–4 cohort over the 1994–96 period.

44. In ordinary model life tables, crude death rates for children under five years of age of the level reported for DPRK for 1994 would correspond with life expectancies at birth in the mid-to-upper 40s; the level reported for 1996 would be consonant with model life table life expectancies at birth in the 1930s (derived from United Nations, 1982); though mortality schedules created by sudden nutritional crises may differ somewhat from the high mortality patterns predicted by model life tables, the fact remains that such high crude death rates for children are suggestive of low levels of life expectancy and high levels of mortality for the population as a whole.

45. Age data were not provided for almost 700,000 persons in the 1993 census. The implication is that those were military personnel.

46. The labor force participation rates of China and Vietnam may look comparable to the DPRK's in Table 9, but in predominantly agrarian societies active labor force participation is very often overestimated.

47. To say nothing of the DPRK's data on disability. The DPRK 1993 census counts 57,833 "disabled persons" out of an officially designated working-age population of just over 12 million; that works out to an incidence of officially certified disability among men 16–60 and women 16–55 of just under 5 per 1,000, suggesting a very strict definition of disability.

48. Eberstadt and Banister, 1992; demographic projections based on reconstructed DPRK population data from the late 1980s and earlier had suggested that North Korea's sex ratio around year-end 1993 might be about 98 males per 100 females.

49. Eberstadt and Banister, 1992; Banister and West, 1997.

50. Eberstadt and Banister, 1992, pp. 38–41; the groupings reported in the 1986 age structure were idiosyncratic, and covered only the civilian population; presumably, though, very few North Korean girls aged 16 or younger were outside the civilian population in 1986.

51. Derived from United Nations, 1982.

52. Note that this does not exclude the possibility of an overcount of young girls in the reported age structure for year-end 1986 from the population registration system.

53. China's censuses have been explicit about their adoption of that procedure.

54. See Eberstadt and Banister, 1991 and 1992.

55. Chung, 1974, p. 171.

56. Ibid, p. 170.

57. Kim Il Sung, *Selected Works*, vol. I, p. 359.

58. Ibid, vol. 24, cited in Koh, 1999.

59. Chung, 1974, p. 171.

60. For the text of that law, see *The People's Korea*, 1999.

61. *FBIS*-EAS-2003-1031.

62. That fact by itself is noteworthy, not least because it raises questions about the regime's intentions with respect to economic reform; it is important to remember that, regardless of time or place, the relaxation, liberalization, or reform of economic policy under a communist government has always been accompanied by an increase in the release of previously secret state data on social conditions and economic performance; there are, as of this writing, no historical examples to the contrary.

63. UNEP, 2003.

64. Far more plausible would seem the current United States Census Bureau (USCB) projection for that period, which conjectures that total DPRK population rose by almost half a million in the 1993–95 period, but declined by 200,000 between 1996 and 1999. USCB, International Data Base, available at http://www.census.gov/ipc/www/idbagg.html.
65. PRC, 2002, Table 3-1; calculations for 1959–62 period.
66. Ibid., Tables 3-1 and 3-3; calculations based upon comparable domestic prices for the 1959–61 period.
67. These newly released data report that annual exports and imports were consistently identical: at US$962 million in 1992, US$896 million in 1994, and US$756 million in 1996; UNEP, 2003, p. 16.
68. DPRK CBS, 2002.
69. Thus, in the words of James T. Morris, Executive Director of the WFP, on the North Korean food situation in February 2003, before the U.S. Senate Foreign Relations Committee:

    There is one bright spot. The nutrition survey by UNICEF, WFP and the Government of North Korea released last week showed some marked improvement in nutritional indicators for children, but they are still alarming by WHO standards and a breakdown in food deliveries could mean we lose the ground we have gained. The hard work of WFP and dedicated NGOs has had an impact. Morris, 2003, p. 4.

70. Public health specialists have long recognized that infants below this birthweight threshold have much higher odds of dying in the first year of life than those above it, and that the incidence of low birthweight in a society tends to be increased by poverty and nutritional stresses with predictable regularity; for a classic treatment, see Bergner and Susser, 1970, pp. 946–66.
71. DPRK CBS, 2002, p. 45.
72. For a summary of these findings, see Shetty and James, 1994.
73. That is to say: by surveying only mothers of surviving children, the 2002 assessment by design excluded infants who would have perished in their first two years of life—a group whose LBW incidence would likely have been much higher.
74. *BBC*, 2003; *FBIS*-EAS, 2005 (13 April).
75. Calculation derived from various official reports on DPRK state budget.
76. *BBC*, 2003.
77. Sustained high inflation in North Korea is indicated by the fact that the fact that the reported informal exchange rates for the DPRK *won* against the dollar has dropped from about 150:1 in July 2002 to well over 2000:1 by 2005; see *inter alia* Salmon, 2005, p. A16.

References

Banister, Judith and Loraine A. West. "A Re-assessment of DPRK Demographic Trends, Using 1993 Census Data." Washington DC: US Bureau of the Census, International Programs Center. 21 May 1997. Unpublished paper.
Becker, Jasper. 1997. *Hungry Ghosts: Mao's Secret Famine.* New York: Basic Books.
Bergner, L. and M.W. Susser. 1970. "Low birth weight and prenatal nutrition: an interpretative review." *Pediatrics* 46(6):946–66. December.

Bergson, Abram. 1961. *The National Income of Soviet Russia Since 1928.* Cambridge, MA: Harvard University Press.

Blum, Alain. 1994. *Naitre vivre et mourir en URSS: 1917–1991.* Paris : A. Michel.

British Broadcasting Corporation (BBC) Worldwide Monitoring International Reports. 2003. "Text of North Korea's 2003 State Budget Report at Assembly Session." 28 March.

Chun, Hong-Tack. 1998. "The Second Economy in North Korea." Seoul: Korea Development Institute. May. Unpublished Paper.

Chung, Joseph Sang-hoon. *The North Korean Economy: Structure and Development.* Stanford, CA: Hoover Institution Press.

DPRK Central Bureau of Statistics (DPRK CBS). 1961. Statistical Returns of the National Economy of the DPRK, 1946–1960. Pyongyang: Foreign Languages Publishing House.

———. 1983. The Health Statistics of the Democratic People's Republic of Korea. Pyongyang: DPRK CBS.

———. 1995. Tabulation on the Population Census of the Democratic People's Republic of Korea (31 December 1993). Pyongyang: DPRK CBS.

———. 2002. *Report on the DPRK Nutrition Assessment: 2002.* Pyongyang: DPRK CBS. November. Available at: http://www.unicef.org/dprk/nutrition_assessment.pdf

Eberstadt, Nicholas. 1995. *The Tyranny of Numbers: Mismeasurement and Misrule.* Washington, DC: American Enterprise Institute.

———. 1998. "The DPRK's International Trade In Capital Goods, 1970–1995: Indications From 'Mirror Statistics.'" *Journal of East Asian Affairs* 12(1):165–223. Seoul.

———. 2001. "'Our Own Style of Statistics': Availability and Reliability of Official Quantitative Data for the Democratic People's Republic of Korea." *The Korean Journal of International Studies* XXVIII(1): 27–76. Fall/Winter.

———. North Korea International Commodity Trade DataBase. Unpublished.

Eberstadt, Nicholas and Judith Banister. 1991. "Military Buildup in the DPRK: Some New Indications from North Korean Data." *Asian Survey* 31(11):1095–1115.

———. 1992. *The Population of North Korea.* Berkeley, CA: University of California Institute of East Asian Studies.

Eberstadt, Nicholas, Marc Rubin, and Albina Tretyakova. 1995. "The Collapse of Soviet and Russian Trade with the DPRK, 1989–1993." *The Korean Journal of National Reunification* 4:87–104.

Eberstadt, Nicholas and Jonathan Tombes, eds. 2000. *Comparing the Soviet and the American Economies.* Washington, DC: AEI Press.

Foreign Broadcast Information Service (FBIS-EAS) (electronic version). Various issues.

———. 1996. Reprinted from *Choson Ilbo* as "ROK: Russian Deputy Prime Minister on DPRK Visit." 15 April.

———. 1996-0413. Reprinted interview with Vitaly Ignatenko from *Choson Ilbo* as "ROK: Russian Deputy Prime Minister on DPRK Visit." 13 April.

———. 2003-1031. Reprinted from *Kyongje Yongu* as "DPRK Economic Journal Stresses 'Superiority' of 'Unified' Statistical System." 24 November.

———. 2005 (13 April). Reprinted from KCNS as "DPRK Radio Carries Finance Minister's Report at 3rd Session of 11th SPA 11 Apr." No. 200504131477. 1_055104c0b6022e13.

Grossman, Gregory. 1963. "Soviet Concern with Reliability." In Harry G. Schaffer, ed. *The Soviet Economy.* New York: Appleton-Century-Crofts. pp. 10–15.

Hwang, Eui-Gak. 1993. *The Korean Economies: A Comparison of North and South.* New York: Oxford University Press.

International Institute for Strategic Studies. 1986. *Military Balance 1986–87.* London: IISS.

International Labor Office. Various Years. *Yearbook of International Labor Statistics.* Geneva: ILO.

International Monetary Fund. 1997. "Democratic People's Republic of Korea: Fact-Finding Report." IMF Asia and Pacific Department. 12 November 12. Unpublished paper.

Kim, Il Sung. Various editions. *Selected Works.* Pyongyang: Foreign Languages Publishing House.

Kim, Philip Wonhyuk. 1997. "North Korea's Food Crisis." *Korea and World Affairs* 21(4):568–585.

Koh, Il-dong. 1999. "Realities and Issues of Economic Statistics in North Korea." (in Korean). Seoul: Korea Development Institute. June. Unpublished paper.

Korea Central News Agency (KCNA). Various issues.

Lee, Hy-sang. 1994. "Supply and Demand for Grains in North Korea: A Historical Movement Model for 1996–1993." *Korea and World Affairs* 18(3):509–552.

Li, Choh-ming. 1962. *The Statistical System of Communist China.* Berkeley: University of California Press.

Maretzki, Hans. 1991. *Kim-ismus in Nordkorea.* Boeblingen, Germany: Anita Tykve Verlag.

Morris, James T. 2003. Testimony at Hearing before the Committee on Foreign Relations, US House of Representatives [sic]on "The State of the World Report on Hunger, From Africa to North Korea." 25 February. Available at: http://foreign.senate.gov/testimony/2003/MorrisTestimony030225.pdf

Pang, Hwan Ju. 1987. *Korean Review.* Pyongyang: Foreign Languages Publishing House.

The People's Korea. Various issues. Available at: http://www.korea-np.co.jp/pk/

———. 1998. "General Secretary Kim Jong Il Elected State Head—Constitution Altered." 7 September. Available at: http://www.korea-np.co.jp/pk/72nd_issue/98120206.htm

———. 1999. Law on People's Economic Plans. 21 April. Available at: http://www.korea-np.co.jp/pk/091st_issue/99042105.htm

People's Republic of China (PRC). 2002. *China Statistical Yearbook 2002.* Beijing: National Bureau of Statistics.

Republic of China (ROC) Executive Yuan. 1990. *Republic of China Statistical Yearbook 1990.* Taipei: Bureau of Budget and Accounting.

Republic of Korea (ROK) National Statistics Office. 1995. *Social Indicators in Korea 1995.* Seoul: NSO.

———. 1996. *Korea Statistical Yearbook 1996.* Seoul: NSO.

Rosefielde, Stephen and Ralph W. Pfouts. 1995. "Neoclassical Norms and the Valuation of National Product in the Soviet Union and its Post-communist Successor States." *Journal of Comparative Economics* 21(3):375–389.

Salmon, Andrew. 2005. "Capitalist economy rises stealthly [sic] in North Korea." *Washington Times.* 21 October.

Shetty, P.S. and W.P.T. James. 1994. "Body mass index − A measure of chronic energy deficiency in adults." *FAO Food and Nutrition Paper 56.* Rome: Food and Nutrition Organization.

Trigubenko, Marina. 1991. "Industry of the DPRK: Specific Features of the Industrial Policy, Sectoral Structure, and Prospects." Paper presented at the International Symposium on the North Korean Economy: Current Situation and Future Prospects. Seoul: Korea Development Institute and Korea Economic Daily, 30 September–1 October.

United Nations Department of International Economic and Social Affairs. 1982. *Model Life Tables for Developing Countries*. New York: United Nations.

———. Environment Programme (UNEP). 2003. *DPR Korea: State of the Environment, 2003*. Bangkok: UNEP. Available at: http://www.unep.org/PDF/DPRK_SOE_Report.pdf

United States Arms Control and Disarmament Agency. 1988. World Military Expenditures and Arms Transfers 1988. Washington: ACDA.

———. Census Bureau (USCB). International Data Base. Available at: http://www.census.gov/ipc/www/idbagg.html

———. Centers for Disease Control and Prevention. 1997. "Status of Public Health: Democratic People's Republic of Korea, April 1997." *Morbidity and Mortality Weekly Report* 46(24):561–65. June.

Watts, Jonathan. 1999. "A Starving Nation." *The Lancet* 353(9166): 1773. 22 May.

World Health Organization (WHO). "European Health For All Database." Available at: http://data.euro.who.int/hfadb

———. 2004. *Low Birthweight: Country, Regional and Global Estimates*. Geneva: WHO. Available at: http://www.who.int/reproductive-health/publications/low_birthweight/low_birthweight_estimates.pdf

3

International Trade in Capital Goods, 1970–1995: Indications from "Mirror Statistics"*

[*Author's Note: The next two chapters rely heavily upon "mirror statistics"—data on foreign trade trends reconstructed through trading partners' reports on international sales and purchases—to assess aspects of North Korean economic performance that could not otherwise be analyzed quantitatively, owing to the regime's extraordinary and still continuing statistical secrecy. This chapter focuses on what such "mirror statistics" can reveal about North Korea's trade in capital goods—and by extension, on the DPRK's policies and performance with respect to industrial and infrastructural development. The following chapter analyzes DPRK trade in food, energy and transport in search of further insights into the workings of the North Korean economy. Although both of these chapters use the same tools and techniques, relying as they commonly do on "mirror statistics" for an aperture into the North Korean economy, their focus is sufficiently different to warrant two distinct and separate treatments.*]

As students of North Korean affairs are all too well aware, precious few sources of quantitative data are available by which to assess the economic performance of the Democratic People's Republic of Korea (DPRK, or North Korea). With the death of Kim Il Sung in 1994 and the subsequent four-year postponement of the Supreme People's Assembly (SPA)—at whose gatherings annual state revenue and expenditure figures had customarily been released—virtually the last official statistical series on the North Korean economy were interrupted.

*This study, originally published in the *Journal of East Asian Affairs* XII(1) 1998, was initially prepared under the auspices of a National Bureau of Asian Research (NBR) project on North Korean Economic Stability; the author wishes to thank Jonathan Tombes for his painstaking and meticulous work on the UN Trade Database used herein; in addition, he wishes to thank William Newcomb, Marcus Noland, Dwight Perkins, Marc Rubin, and Peter Rimmer for their valuable comments and helpful criticisms of an earlier draft of this study; the opinions expressed are those of the author.

There is one area, however, in which meaningful and detailed information on North Korea's economic trends continues to be collected regularly. These are so-called "mirror statistics": the commodity import and export data reported by North Korea's trading partners. These numbers provide a basis by which to assess both the current state and the development over time of one consequential component of the North Korean economy—its external merchandise trade sector—and in addition offer a window through which to observe, and draw inferences about, the condition of the DPRK domestic economy.

This study is a preliminary effort to utilize mirror statistics to analyze the economic performance of the DPRK within a narrowly delimited area, and to draw broader inferences about the performance of its economy. In the following pages, we will examine the North Korean international trade in "capital goods"—that is to say, machinery, equipment, and the manufactured parts utilized as capital stock in the production process.

Imports of capital goods are incorporated into, and augment, a country's industrial base, i.e., its endowment of fixed reproducible capital. Capital goods exports, for their part, presuppose a requisite measure of industrial organization, technological attainment, and labor force skill on the part of the country that produces and sells them. Quantifying North Korea's actual record of capital goods imports and exports, correspondingly, may not only afford us a clearer view of this commerce per se, but may also shed light on patterns of output, trends of development—and as it happens in this case, dimensions of crisis—within the overall DPRK economy.

This chapter consists of five sections: the first briefly reviews the literature on patterns of capital goods trade in the process of industrialization and economic development. The second offers some background on the history of the DPRK as a capital goods importer and exporter. The third outlines the method by which we reconstruct North Korea's capital goods trade from mirror statistics, and discusses some of the issues and problems inherent in this exercise. The fourth presents our main findings, and considers what these findings may reveal about North Korean industrial performance and economic development over the past generation. A final section offers some concluding observations.

Patterns of Capital Goods Trade in Modern Economic Development: An Abbreviated Survey

To inquire about the role of the capital goods trade in economic development is to expose oneself, if only implicitly, to two central issues in economics: the role of capital in development, and the role of trade. These open upon a profound and often troublesome theoretical terrain.[1] For our limited purposes, it may suffice to focus upon the empirical research on the subject, and what it has indicated about past and current relationships between the international trade in capital goods, on the one hand, and industrialization and economic development, on the other.

Detailed quantitative studies on the relationship between trade and international industrialization may have commenced during World War II with the work of Hilgert (1945). Subsequent postwar milestones included the contributions of Maizels (1963) and Kuznets (1961 and 1966). These studies documented a general positive association, both internationally and within given countries over time, between the trade ratio and the level of per capita output. These studies also pointed to a tendency for the composition of trade to change with industrialization: generally speaking, the more industrialized a country became, the greater the share of machinery and transportation equipment in both its exports *and* imports.[2] Maizels further noted that, historically, machinery imports appeared to be strongly associated with economic growth in both industrialized and less industrial countries.[3]

Quantitative research on patterns of development adopted more sophisticated econometric techniques over the course of the 1960s, 1970s and early 1980s, thanks in large measure to the work of Hollis Chenery, his students, and his World Bank colleagues.[4] Unfortunately, the thrust of that research—with its strong concentration on issues in development planning—meant that the developmental significance of changing patterns of international trade was not examined in any great detail in their corpus of studies.[5] Over just the past decade, however, a number of new studies have helped illuminate the relationship between capital goods trade and the process of modern economic development.

One careful "structuralist" study, for example, has examined patterns of trade for developing countries between the early 1960s and the early 1980s.[6] It noted considerable unexplained differences across countries and across time with respect to the shares in GDP of imports or exports of electrical and mechanical goods (a fair proxy for capital goods). Nevertheless, it also identified some strong general tendencies. For example, the share in GDP of both imports and exports of capital equipment were positively associated with per capita GNP. The ratio of capital goods imports to GDP tended to be lower for more populous countries, and greater if either domestic capacity utilization or real effective exchange rates were measured as being high. The share of capital equipment exports to GDP, for its part, tracked positively with trends in the absolute size of the OECD economies—which offered the prime markets for such produce.

In two major recent studies, researchers using econometric techniques have argued that investment in capital goods is not simply *associated* with higher levels of productivity and per capita output in modern economies, but is actually a *causative factor* in contemporary economic growth, and helps to account for differences in national economic performance. The first, using data for

61 non-communist developed and less-developed countries, concluded that "nations which invested heavily in equipment relative to other nations at the same stage of development enjoyed rapid growth over 1960–85."[7] It further concluded that each additional percentage point of GDP invested in equipment would be predicted to increase the tempo of growth in output per worker by about a third of a point per year, and speculated that the *social* rate of return on such physical investment might commonly exceed 30 percent per year in developing countries.[8]

These results pertained to investment in all capital equipment, rather than imported capital goods *per se*. A subsequent study, however, examined the relationship between capital goods imports and economic growth in over 60 contemporary less-developed countries between 1960 and 1985. Its findings "implie[d] that an increase of 0.1 in the ratio of imports in [overall machinery and equipment] investment le[d] to an increase in the growth of per capita income of 0.3 percent per year."[9] The study further stated that "imported capital goods increase growth directly by enhancing the productivity of capital . . . [I]mported capital goods have much higher productivity than [developing countries'] domestically-produced capital goods . . . [B]y switching a portion of GDP devoted to the purchase of domestic capital goods to the importation of cheap foreign capital goods, countries can grow faster. . . . [T]rade distortions that restrict the importation of capital goods hurt the economy in the long run."[10]

The "distortions that restrict" capital goods imports by less developed countries, of course, are not solely the consequence of deliberately formulated trade and development policies: they can equally be the unintended but inexorable outcome of other official policies and practices, or result from external economic shocks for which policy adjustments do not fully compensate. Economies with poor records of meeting their external debt obligations may be more prone to all of three sorts of restrictions. Quantitative research by Hentschel has recently demonstrated that international debt problems can compromise productivity and growth by their impact on (among many other things) an affected economy's capital goods imports.[11]

Reviewing trade and national accounts data for the 1970s and 1980s, Hentschel identified a strong tendency among less developed countries for the share of capital goods within imports of capital goods to fall after the onset of debt crisis; the share of foreign equipment and machinery within gross domestic capital formation also tended to decline during these episodes. (By contrast, no such tendencies were observed in creditworthy developing economies even during periods of external economic shock, and even if their ratios of international debt to GDP or debt service payments to export revenues were relatively high.) "Growth prospects" for such "problem debtor countries," Hentschel suggested, were "quite endangered in the medium to longer run" not only by "reduced levels of capital formation, but also [by] the changing composition of these investments,"[12] insofar as his estimates indicated marginal productivity to be typically higher for imported capital equipment than for domestically manufactured machinery.[13]

North Korea, of course, maintains a centrally planned economy;[14] the logic and dynamics of its economic performance may thus be expected to differ in key respects from those observed in market-oriented economies, whether more- or less-developed. Nevertheless, many of the relationships revealed through empirical research on the relationship between capital goods trade and industrial development in non-communist economies might be expected to bear upon North Korean economic development patterns and potentialities as well.

The DPRK's Capital Goods Trade: Some Historical Background

The DPRK's officially promoted doctrine of *juche* (roughly, "self-reliance") was formally unveiled shortly after the ceasefire in the Korean War. Despite its autarkical connotation, North Korean economic policymakers have always looked to other countries for aid and materiel in their quest to build an independent national economy.

North Korea's industrial base—of limited size and capabilities at the start of the 1950s—was utterly devastated by the Korean War. Rapid postwar recovery and development could only be achieved by means of relatively massive imports of capital goods from abroad. To this end, Pyongyang succeeded in securing sizeable inflows of machinery and equipment through a network of aid agreements with fraternal communist states.[15] During this period, the USSR, China, and the countries of Council for Mutual Economic Assistance (CMEA) Europe provided not only essentially free machinery and equipment to North Korea, but in many instances built entire industrial enterprises.[16]

From the 1953 armistice through the mid-1960s, China and the Soviet bloc were virtually the only sources of foreign capital equipment for North Korea. Yet for a variety of reasons—including the Sino-Soviet rift, the economic crisis in China that followed the Great Leap Forward, Pyongyang's apparent decision to decline CMEA membership in 1962,[17] and the deterioration of Sino-DPRK relations during the Cultural Revolution—North Korea's aid and trade relationships with its socialist patrons became progressively less secure, and more problematic over the course of the 1960s.

Pyongyang's policymakers responded to their changing environment by moving toward economic relations with non-communist countries, cautiously at first, but with seeming abandon just a few years later. In the early 1970s, North Korea executed a strategic turn toward Japan and other OECD countries[18] for capital goods. A surge of western equipment imports, including whole factories made in the OECD, proceeded on hard currency credit until North Korea fell into arrears on the loans which were financing these purchases in the mid-1970s.[19] Precisely why this debt problem so quickly overtook North Korea's western equipment import program is still a matter of debate. However, some observers noted that the DPRK had also neglected to make timely payments on its many ruble-denominated loans from the USSR.[20] In any case, Pyongyang took an unusually aggressive stance against its western creditors in rescheduling negotiations, and from the late 1970s on remained in virtual default on its hard currency debts. The DPRK's international commerce was thus largely reduced to counterbarter with hard currency countries, and constrained within the non-convertible currency area by the same political considerations that the shift toward western markets had been intended to circumvent.

The hard currency debt problems of the mid-1970s did not, of course, put an end to Pyongyang's desire to acquire capital goods from abroad, nor completely undermine its ability to procure them. It did, however, substantially complicate the task. In theory, the DPRK had five options to accumulate additional foreign capital equipment: 1) it could run a balance of trade surplus on intermediate and consumption goods in the international marketplace; 2) it could secure international loans for desired capital goods imports; 3) it could negotiate export credits from the countries selling the prospective machinery and equipment; 4) it could attract foreign investors, who would themselves provide the capital goods; and 5) it could establish or revitalize political ties with foreign powers who would provide the DPRK with capital equipment on a concessional basis.

For whatever reasons, North Korean commercial policy seems always to have rejected the first option. The second option was basically precluded by the state's defiant posture on debt repayments, as was the third option—insofar as both private and public export credits must take measure of the creditworthiness of the partner to whom goods stand to be exported. By the process of elimination, North Korea was thus left with the fourth and fifth options at the start of the 1980s.

Pyongyang grasped for both of them. In 1984, the DPRK promulgated a Joint Venture Law intended to attract foreign (i.e., Western) capital and technology.[21] That same year, the DPRK began negotiations for an economic cooperation agreement with the USSR for the years 1986–90;[22] this arrangement seems to have envisioned a sharp and continuing increase in Soviet aid, and was apparently informed by a warming of Soviet-North Korean political relations between Leonid Brezhnev's death in late 1982 and Kim Il Sung's state visit to Moscow in the summer of 1984.

Though initially promising, neither of these initiatives proved durable. Given North Korea's "business climate," the 1984 Joint Venture Law attracted few foreign investors: nearly all the deals eventually contracted were signed with pro-Pyongyang, ethnic Korean residents from Japan[23] and by the early 1990s these joint ventures achieved an estimated total capitalization of only about US$150 million.[24] For their part, after growing briskly throughout the second half of the 1980s, Soviet subsidies to North Korea collapsed with the final crisis and liquidation of the Soviet state.[25]

Even before the demise of the Soviet Union, it was apparent that North Korea's economy was seized by malaise. The Soviet breakup, however, precipitated acute additional problems for the DPRK, among them, the problem of achieving the volume of capital goods imports scheduled for delivery from its heretofore principal, and now defunct, trade partner.

Still in virtual default on its western debts, Pyongyang attempted in the early 1990s to attract additional western capital goods through a succession of new foreign investment codes. The response of the international business community, however, was skeptical, and commitments were apparently minimal.[26] Concessional transfers of capital equipment from foreign governments have likewise apparently been minimal since the Soviet collapse, the nuclear drama of the mid-1990s evidently having dissipated whatever interest Seoul, Tokyo, or Washington might otherwise have shown for such a project.[27] And Beijing, operating under calculations of its own, has proved to be a more hardnosed patron for an increasingly distressed North Korean regime.[28] It is worth noting that the DPRK made no appreciable adjustments to this approach despite the dire economic circumstances of the mid- and late 1990s.

Although North Korea today is tentatively exporting its own domestically manufactured capital equipment, the country remains structurally a net capital goods importer. North Korean authorities have yet to devise a workable formula for securing adequate inflows of the capital equipment their economy requires.

Although external assessments of the economic performance of this extraordinarily secretive state remain problematic, it is universally acknowledged that the 1990s was a decade of steady and dramatic economic decline in the DPRK. The emergence of a prolonged food crisis in North Korea—acknowledged by DPRK authorities from the spring of 1995—was the first official confirmation of such suspicions.

Reconstructing North Korea's Capital Goods Trade: Methodology and Limitations

To reconstruct North Korea's capital goods trade, it was necessary first to reconstruct North Korea's overall trade patterns. Our approach, and the problems encountered, can be succinctly described.

Assembling the Data Series

At least four distinct sources of mirror statistics currently exist, reflecting separate components of North Korea's international merchandise trade.

The first, and by far the most comprehensive, is the *United Nations International Commodity Trade Statistics Database*, which is maintained and regularly updated by the UN Statistical Office.[29] Yet, as it happens, three countries that have been, at varying junctures, among North Korea's most important trading partners have reported to the UN only intermittently—or not at all—on their commerce with the DPRK: the USSR/Russia, China, and South Korea.

Under both Soviet rule and Russian Federation governance, Moscow has simply never reported into this system. China, for its part, began releasing detailed figures on its international commercial activities in the calendar year 1982, but only as of 1987 regularly forwarded such data to the UN Statistical Office. Finally, the Republic of Korea legally insists that its trade with the North is domestic rather than international in nature, and thus, on principle, omits data on North-South trade from its foreign trade reports.

Fortunately, each of these three governments publishes detailed—if at times idiosyncratic—breakdowns for their merchandise trade with the DPRK. Moscow's data appear in the official series *Vneshnaya Torgovlya SSSR* and *Vneshneekonomicheskie Sviazi Rossiiskoi Federatsii*; the breakdowns for China are in Beijing's *Customs Statistics Yearbook*, and those for South Korea can be found in the South Korean Unification Ministry's *Wolgan Nambuk Kyoryu Hyomnyok Tonghyang*. These serve as our second, third, and fourth data sources, respectively, in reconstructing overall patterns of North Korean foreign trade from mirror statistics.

Our exercise begins with the *United Nations International Commodity Trade Statistics Database*.[30] We gathered UN mirror statistics on North Korean trade for the years 1970 to 1995; that is, from the eve of the DPRK's first OECD capital equipment import spree to the most recent year for which the UN Database afforded broad country coverage at the time of first writing.[31] The UN Trade Database provides breakdowns of trade transactions according to four different coding schema.[32] We selected revision 1 of the Standard International Trade Classification (SITC), because it offered the broadest country coverage available.[33] Unfortunately, the SITC, rev. 1 schema excludes an item which happens to be vitally important in North Korean trade: non-monetary gold. We therefore obtained a separate series for UN mirror statistics on North Korea's reported international gold trade, drawn from SITC, rev. 2 data.[34]

Adding Soviet/Russian, Chinese, and South Korean mirror statistics to this database turned out to be a fairly straightforward task. Thanks to painstaking work at the International Programs Center of the U.S. Census Bureau, officially reported Soviet and Russian trade with the DPRK for the years 1972–95 had already been converted from the CMEA's Standard Foreign Trade Classification (SFTC) to SITC, rev. 1 at a 2-digit level of disaggregation.[35] IPC had also already analyzed Chinese data on DPRK trade for the missing years 1982–86, and converted them from the Harmonized System (HS) in which they were originally reported into SITC, rev. 1 at the 2-digit level.[36] And since North-South trade in Korea to date has entailed a rather limited list of commodities and manufactured products, matching these with the SITC, rev. 1 schema for the years 1989–95 was not difficult.

Combining these data series, of course, required a common basis for valuation. By convention, the transactions reported in the *UN International Commodity Trade Statistics Database* are valued in current U.S. dollars, converting transactions conducted in other currencies into dollars at the current official exchange rate. Chinese and South Korean trade with North Korea is likewise officially reported in current U.S. dollars. Soviet trade data, however, were always officially denominated in rubles. Soviet-DPRK trade flows were therefore converted from current rubles to current dollars on the basis of current official exchange rates.

A final overall adjustment to the data series estimated charges for cost, insurance, and freight (c.i.f.) on North Korean trade. The prevailing UN practice is to limit free-on-board (f.o.b.) valuation to home country exports, while recording home country imports on a c.i.f. basis.[37] Since DPRK imports are proxied in our data by reported exports to North Korea (always recorded f.o.b.), some correction for c.i.f. seemed appropriate. In the absence of any specific knowledge about these costs, the general rule of thumb used by the International Monetary Fund (IMF) was adopted, and f.o.b. exports were scaled up by an additional ten percent to account for those expenses. Conversely, to produce a proxy for DPRK exports, imports from North Korea were divided by a factor of 1.1 to remove the charges presumably associated with c.i.f.[38]

Defining "Capital Goods"

To reconstruct the capital goods trade from this combined data series on DPRK global commerce, a fixed and detailed definition of capital goods was needed. The United Nations Statistical Office provides such guidelines in its occasional studies on *Classification By Broad Economic Categories* (BEC), which translate SITC and HS categories into economic groupings within the System of National Accounts (SNA) framework. Since our study utilized the SITC, rev. 1 schema for classifying international goods and services, we used the corresponding BEC handbook.[39]

BEC offers a definition for capital goods down to a 5-digit level of SITC product disaggregation. For the USSR and Russia, however, and for China 1982–86, only a 2-digit SITC breakdown was available. Furthermore, a number of countries in the UN *International Commodity Trade Database* reported their trade figures at less than 5-digit disaggregation for at least some years (Czechoslovakia, Hungary, India, and Pakistan among them).

To cope with these data limitations, we had to build a capital goods series on the basis of 2-digit SITC categories. In doing so, we selected categories which seemed to conform most closely to the conception of capital goods as this is generally understood, and which also encompassed most of the 5-digit products defined as capital goods by BEC.

In this study, our "capital goods" is therefore composed of the five following 2-digit SITC, rev. 1 categories:

SITC 69 ("Manufactures of metal");

SITC 71 ("Machinery, other than electric");

SITC 72 ("Electrical machinery, apparatus, and appliances");

SITC 86 ("Professional, scientific, and controlling instruments; photographic and optical goods; watches and clocks");

SITC 89 ("Miscellaneous manufactured articles, not elsewhere specified (n.e.s.)").

Unavoidably, our categorization is arbitrary and imperfect. Some items defined by BEC as capital goods—for example, SITC 629.4: "Transmission, conveyor, or elevator-belting of rubber"—are not included; conversely, some of the goods which are included—e.g., SITC 719.4: "Domestic appliances, non-electrical"— are defined by BEC as consumer durables rather than capital goods.

Working at a 2-digit level of definition for capital goods, misclassification of at least some products will be inevitable. But as we shall see, initial sensitivity checks indicate that these systematic errors represent a minor rather than a major problem in this study, insofar as these do not appear to bias calculated trends to any significant degree.

Problems with Our Mirror Statistics

In addition to the taxonomic problems just described, five other practical or theoretical difficulties should be explicitly identified.

The first concerns country coverage. Although the data series developed for this study includes over 130 countries, there are some gaps. Taiwan, for example, is one of the world's major trading economies, but it is purposely excluded from the UN's trade accounts. Moreover, some of the countries which are included in the UN trade database report only episodically. Of the six Eastern European members of the CMEA, for example, only Hungary provides an uninterrupted series for 1970–89, while Iran and Iraq, which have often been important commercial partners for North Korea, ceased reporting trade statistics to the UN completely in 1978.

Second, there is the problem of spurious data on North Korean trade in the UN database. Errors of coding, whether by the transmitting government or the UN compiling unit, are evident in various entries. In 1994, for example, the UN database purports that Mexico was importing and exporting hundreds of millions of dollars worth of goods to the DPRK; closer inspection suggests that coders had somehow confused "North Korea" and "South Korea." Similarly, Saudi Arabia reports a vigorous commerce with the DPRK in the 1970s and early 1980s, but these figures also apparently mistake North Korea for the South.[40] In the 1990s, moreover, according to the UN datatape, Sikkim reports a trade with North Korea that tops US$30 million in exports in some years; lacking specific information about DPRK-Sikkimese relations, these observations are taken *prima facie* to be spurious. Data from Saudi Arabia and Sikkim have been entirely expunged from our adjusted series, as have the data for Mexico for 1994 and 1995. There may well be other spurious entries in the database which have not yet been detected.

Third, our mirror statistics database for North Korea does not include all of the represented trading partners' commercial activities with the DPRK, even for the years in which trade figures are submitted. Certain illicit transactions are likely to go unreported: among them, weapons traffic, narcotics, and the smuggling of other contraband.[41] In some cases—most importantly, the USSR/Russia— mirror statistics do seem to reflect at least some large portion of the two countries' weapons trade.[42] Elsewhere, however, it is much less certain that special transactions have been recorded in officially reported statistics, and such activities may account for a rather higher proportion of external commerce for North Korea than for most contemporary economies.

Fourth, there is an entire set of issues related to valuation of transactions from nonconvertible currencies into dollars. The "trade ruble," in which so much of North Korea's commerce was denominated during the decades under consideration, was not in any meaningful sense a currency, but rather an accounting unit.[43] Yet in this database, trade transactions reported by communist states are converted into dollar values on the basis of officially established prices and official exchange rates. This procedure clearly biases calculated totals upwards, probably by different magnitudes according to the non-convertible currency, the year, and the product. Valuation of capital goods imports by North Korea from the non-convertible currency countries may be especially problematic. Treml has demonstrated that Soviet machinery and equipment sold at a substantial discount in international (i.e., hard currency) markets, when compared with corresponding products manufactured in OECD countries.[44] These price differentials reflected purchasers' assessments of discrepancies in quality and reliability between Soviet and western capital goods. No similar mechanisms exist assessing the DPRK-USSR trade in capital goods, or for the DPRK's capital goods trade with China and Eastern European countries in the years before hard currency terms of settlement were introduced.

Finally, as Oskar Morgenstern noted more than a generation ago, there is a fundamental question of the intrinsic reliability of mirror statistics for representing trade patterns.[45] Substantial discrepancies in reported trade flows between trading partners often occur; viz., the major and systematic differences today between Washington's and Beijing's statistics on U.S.-China trade.[46] Although it is often possible to reconcile such conflicting trade accounts methodologically—that is, by comparing the definitions and approaches used by the two partners in compiling their own trade statistics—methodological concordance does not always eliminate these discrepancies. In using mirror statistics to proxy North Korean trade, we have no independent basis for standardizing or correcting any methodological or empirical peculiarities which may be embedded in a given trade partner's accounts.

Coverage and Sensitivity

The conundrum surrounding mirror statistics and the valuation of products from non-market economies in market economies prices and currencies cannot be resolved in this study. On a practical level, however, our data series *can* be checked for the completeness of its global coverage, and for the reliability of its necessarily inexact definition of capital goods. Initial tests on both of these scores are encouraging.

To examine the extent of under-coverage in our series, we compared our computed global DPRK export and import totals against those in what is arguably the most exhaustive and comprehensive treatment to date of North Korean foreign trade: the 1991 dissertation by Choi Soo-young on the topic.[47] As shown in Figures 3.1a and 3.1b, the differences between these estimated

Figure 3.1a

Completeness of Coverage: Choi (less Saudi Arabia) vs. Eberstadt

Total DPRK Imports, 1972–1988

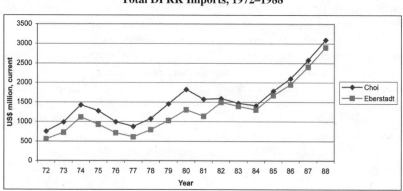

Sources: Choi, 1991 and Eberstadt, unpublished.

Figure 3.1b

Completeness of Coverage: Choi (less Saudi Arabia) vs. Eberstadt

Total DPRK Exports, 1972–1988

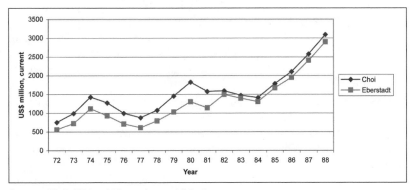

Sources: Choi, 1991 and Eberstadt, unpublished.

global trade totals for North Korea and our calculated totals are contrasted for the period from 1972 to 1988, the last year included in Choi's study.

Our calculated totals are typically lower than Choi's—in a few instances (e.g., 1980 DPRK exports), quite substantially lower. For 1982 to 1988, however, our DPRK import series is very close to his. The same is true for our DPRK export series.

Most of the discrepancy between Choi's series (as adjusted) and our own revolves around DPRK-China trade: our detailed data series includes observations for China only from 1982 onwards, whereas Choi reports aggregated totals for these exports and imports from 1950 through 1988. However, China is not the only source of discrepancy: there are nontrivial inconsistencies in our two series for the DPRK exports to Japan, other OECD countries, and Eastern Europe, especially for the period 1978–80.

Nonetheless, the very close correspondence between Choi's trade turnover estimates and our own for the later years of Choi's series suggests that our trade database can provide not only detailed but also quite complete coverage of North Korean trade patterns for the years 1982 to 1995—a period during which North Korea's economic stresses became more evident and acute. Our data series should be able to represent quantitatively the trade shocks during this period, and the changes in composition and direction of North Korean external merchandise commerce. But even in the years 1972–81, for which the coverage of our series is less complete, the close correlation between movements in Choi's adjusted series and our own suggests that our calculations may faithfully represent North Korea's overall import and export trends for the years in question.[48]

And what of our somewhat Procrustean definition of capital goods? To test its reliability, we used Japan to compare results of our approach, which aggregates the five 2-digit SITC product groupings that principally characterized capital equipment with an aggregation of all items defined as capital goods by BEC at the SITC 5-digit level. (Figure 3.2.)

Generally speaking, our crude definition of capital goods produces somewhat higher—i.e., up to 30 percent—estimates than are derived from strict adherence to the BEC-SITC concordance. Changes in the two capital goods series, however, correspond extremely well.[49] Our capital goods series, in sum, appears to generate robust trends, although its estimated absolute values for North Korean capital equipment imports and exports should probably be treated as upper boundaries rather than central estimates.

The mirror statistics that form the backbone of this study, as we have demonstrated, are by no means problem-free. They are, however, distinctly more informative than the alternative, if that means reliance upon North Korea's officially released trade data. Handled with appropriate care, they can be a useful quantitative tool for the study of North Korea's economy.

Calculated Results and Their Implications

In the following pages, we present our estimates of trends and regional composition of North Korea's international capital equipment trade. We should emphasize that our calculations are denominated in current dollars. In other

Figure 3.2

Estimated DPRK Capital Goods Imports from Japan: 2-Digit Eberstadt Approximation vs. 5-digit Aggregation, 1970–1995

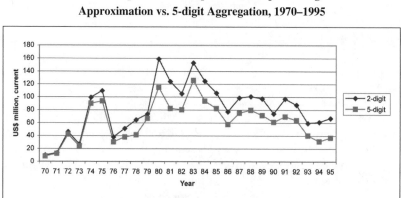

Sources: Choi, 1991 and Eberstadt, unpublished.

words, we have not deflated the nominal values from our time series to indicate the "real" levels and trends for this commerce in constant prices. We have eschewed such corrections, not because we deem that task immaterial, but rather because we see it as insurmountable. Given North Korea's international trade patterns and our decision to denominate global DPRK trade in U.S. dollars, a reliable index for scaling current Soviet rubles into constant dollars would be essential for that exercise. But none exists, nor, in fact, is likely to be devised. Therefore, we must make do with a series calculated in current dollars against current prices at current exchange rates, recognizing the distortions that inexorably intrude upon these calculated trends.

Figures 3.3 and 3.4 present the calculated values and regional composition of North Korean capital goods trade, as defined above, for the period 1970–95. A number of trends represented in this series deserve comment.

Between 1972 and 1995, according to our data series, the DPRK imported a total of about US$6.8 billion in capital goods, or an average of about US$280 million a year. Capital goods exports, for their part, totaled an estimated US$2 billion between 1972 and 1995, averaging US$85 million a year.

For the entire period and in current prices, North Korean capital goods from USSR/Russia amounted to US$2.26 billion, while imports from Japan came to about US$2 billion. The remainder of the OECD[50] supplied about US$1.6 billion in machinery and equipment. Eastern European reporters included in the database provided a total of about US$330 million. China, for the years it reported, supplied about US$375 million, and "third world" countries—as the rest of the countries reporting are categorized in our schema—nearly US$130 million. Stated slightly differently, the DPRK imported an estimated total of about US$3.7 billion in machinery and equipment (in nominal terms) from

Figure 3.3
Estimated DPRK Capital Goods Exports by Destination, 1972–1995

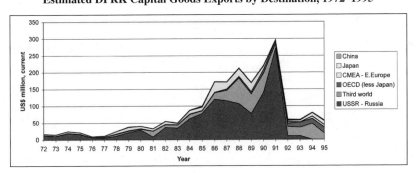

Sources: Choi, 1991 and Eberstadt, unpublished.

Figure 3.4

Estimated DPRK Capital Goods Imports by Source, 1972–1995

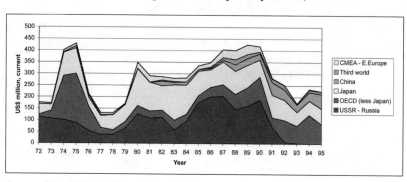

Sources: Choi, 1991 and Eberstadt, unpublished.

western industrial countries, and an estimated US$3 billion from fraternal socialist states (again in nominal terms) between 1972 and 1995.

Of total DPRK capital goods exports between 1972 and 1995, about US$1.2 billion went to USSR/Russia. Third world countries obtained about US$410 million and Eastern European countries received about US$225 million. Reported capital goods exports to OECD countries (minus Japan) came to just under US$100 million. Over the period under consideration, such exports to Japan and China were negligible.

The estimated current dollar value and regional distribution of North Korea's capital goods trade has oscillated over the past generation. Between 1972 and 1979, capital equipment imports averaged about US$230 million a year. Between 1980 and 1990, they averaged about US$350 million a year. Between 1991 and 1995, they again averaged about US$230 million a year. In the 1970s, the DPRK was obtaining about three-fifths of its capital goods (nominal value) from OECD countries (including Japan), and about two-fifths from the Soviet bloc. Between 1980 and 1990, OECD and CMEA were roughly equal capital goods sources for the DPRK, each supplying just under half of total measured imports. In the early 1990s, however, capital goods shipments from the former Soviet bloc plunged to barely 7 percent of North Korea's total. The OECD group accounted for over two-thirds of North Korea's capital equipment imports in those years. China also emerged as a source for these goods, supplying about one fifth of the DPRK's total.

With respect to capital goods exports, measured totals rose from an average of about US$20 million a year in 1972–79 to about US$120 million for 1980–90, falling to about US$110 million a year for 1991–95. (For 1992–95, those exports averaged only about US$65 million a year.) In the 1970s, the Soviet bloc was the destination for roughly nine-tenths of all identified North Korean capital goods exports; for the 1980s, that share declined to about three-fourths, and it fell to about half for the former Soviet bloc area for the early 1990s. (The shift is more dramatic if we consider the period from the end of the Soviet Union onward: for 1992–95, only 8 percent of North Korea's capital equipment exports went to Russia and Eastern Europe.) Third world countries obtained a minimal fraction of North Korea's modest capital goods exports in the 1970s, but absorbed about a fifth of these in the 1980s and about a fourth in the early 1990s. (In 1992–95, the third world accounted for about half of North Korea's machinery and equipment exports; the OECD countries also procured some limited volumes of North Korean capital goods.)

Several distinct phases or episodes in North Korea's capital goods trade show up in our calculated totals. The ill-fated import spree for western equipment and machinery shows up clearly in mirror statistics, although it is concentrated in the years 1974–76 rather than slightly earlier, as other commentary puts it.[51] Between 1974 and 1976, according to our figures, North Korea imported just over US$750 million in capital goods from the industrialized West; for 1972–76, those purchases amounted to nearly US$870 million.

After that import binge, the overall nominal value of North Korean capital goods imports slumped; it has stagnated—or worse—ever since. The year 1975, in fact, appears to have been the high-water mark for DPRK imports of machinery and equipment from abroad, as, to this day, according to our calculated totals, North Korea has not reattained that value of capital goods imports, *even in nominal terms.*

As we indicated earlier, 1984 was a moment of truth for DPRK policy in capital goods trade: both the Joint Venture Law and the preparations for the 1986–90 Soviet-DPRK economic cooperation agreement were entered into at that time. If it was intended to attract western capital equipment, the Joint Venture Law appears to have been an abject failure. In the five years immediately after the Joint Venture Law was promulgated, DPRK imports of capital goods from the OECD countries were actually lower than in the five years before the law was passed. The new arrangements with the Soviet Union look to have been more successful: by our calculations, Pyongyang's capital equipment imports from Moscow were almost $400 million higher in the second half of the 1980s than they had been in the first half.

But as might be expected, the crisis of Soviet Bloc communism brought crisis to the North Korean capital goods commerce as well. In the four years 1988–91, our data indicates that the DPRK obtained nearly US$675 million in machinery and equipment from the USSR and CMEA Europe. Over the following four years, Russia and Eastern Europe are reported to have shipped North Korea *only* US$14 million of such products. North Korea was not successful to any visible degree in locating substitute suppliers for these vanished fraternal states. Between 1988 and 1991, according to our database, non-Soviet bloc countries (including China) provided the DPRK with about US$850 million in capital goods. In the years 1992–95 those same countries provided North Korea with about US$870 million in capital equipment—in other words, barely more than they were shipping to Pyongyang during the final years of Soviet rule. In all, the estimated nominal value of DPRK capital equipments imports was over 40 percent lower in 1992–95 than it had been during the preceding period.

As we have already explained above, it is impossible to derive a reliable inflation-adjusted time series for North Korean capital goods imports or exports. That being said, there is, nonetheless, strong reason to believe that the real volume of capital equipment acquired by the DPRK has been on a steady downward trend since the early 1970s.

Between the 1970s and the 1980s, the average annual nominal value of North Korean capital goods imports as calculated here rose by almost 50 percent. Over that same period, however, the price index for exports of goods and services from the hard currency region rose more: by over 60 percent for United States, and over 75 percent for the entire OECD group.[52] Between the 1970s and the 1980s, moreover, the share of Soviet bloc produce in North Korean capital goods imports increased substantially, and as we have already mentioned, there is reason to think that our current dollar series tends to overvalue these goods in particular. It is plausible, then, to expect that real annual levels of capital goods imports were actually lower for North Korea in the 1980s than they had been in the 1970s. And, even taking into account all the unavoidable imprecisions of the comparison, real annual import levels of foreign machinery, equipment, and allied parts were surely lower in the 1990s than they were in the 1980s.

The real level of DPRK capital equipment exports, on the other hand, very likely rose between the 1970s and the 1980s: the roughly sixfold current dollar value increase in annual export revenues from these products is dramatic enough to support that presumption. But even the nominal value of Pyongyang's capital goods is estimated to have dropped between the 1980s and the 1990s. In 1992–95, in fact, the average annual *nominal* value of North Korean capital goods exports was slightly less than the corresponding estimated totals a decade earlier. If a real North Korean export index were available, it would likely show that capital goods exports slumped deeply in the 1990s.

North Korea's apparent long-term decline in real volumes of capital goods imports was not due solely to the regime's failure to achieve sustained expansion of its foreign trade. The stagnation and decline of DPRK capital equipment imports was also due to anomalous but long-term changes in import composition. Our estimates for capital goods imports as a percentage of total North Korean imports are presented in Figure 3.5.

Figure 3.5
Capital Goods Imports Estimated as a Percentage
of Total DPRK Merchandise Imports, 1972–1995

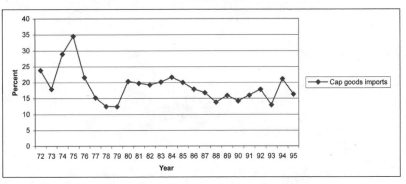

Sources: Choi, 1991 and Eberstadt, unpublished.

While there is volatility in the series, a strong secular trend is also evident: over the past generation, the share of North Korean imports devoted to machinery and equipment has been gradually declining. According to our calculations, the share of capital goods in DPRK imports hit its peak in 1975—during the unsustainable splurge in western plants and equipment—and has dropped dramatically since then. We should note, however, that the proportion of capital goods within DPRK imports was substantially lower in the 1980s and the 1990s than it had been in 1972—before the western capital goods import campaign was in full swing. We may also note that the trade policy decisions of 1984—the Joint Venture Law and the move toward "better" economic relations with the USSR—did absolutely nothing to raise the share of capital goods in North Korea's imports. Insofar as the North Korean leadership enjoyed at least some latitude in crafting the 1986–90 Soviet-DPRK economic cooperation agreement, this suggests that the "distortions that restrict importation of capital goods," in Lee's fateful phrase, derived in this instance from deliberate choices by policymakers in Pyongyang.

As shown in Figure 3.6, the composition of North Korean exports brings additional information to bear.

Between 1972 and 1983, capital goods exports accounted for a measurable, but negligible, fraction of overall exports—generally less than 5 percent. With the 1986–90 economic cooperation agreement with Moscow, the share of capital goods within exports jumped to the 10–15 percent range. After an exceptional year in 1991—when capital goods exports spiked to over 25 percent[53]—the ratio fell back to an average of about 7 percent for 1992–95—a little lower than it

Figure 3.6
Capital Goods Exports Estimated as a Percentage
of Total DPRK Merchandise Exports, 1972–1995

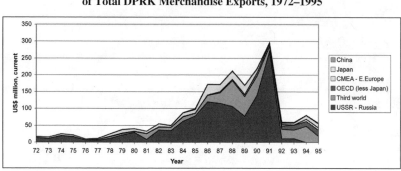

Sources: Choi, 1991 and Eberstadt, North Korea International Commercial Trade Data Base, unpublished.

had been in 1984. Evidently, apart from guaranteed purchases by the Soviet state, the North Korean industrial base was not—and is not yet—capable of producing much machinery or equipment that foreign customers would wish to pay for.

Figures 3.5 and 3.6 present a paradox: why should a contemporary economy whose ability to export marketable capital equipment is so apparently limited simultaneously evidence not only a likely long-term decline in real levels of capital goods imports, but also a long-run reduction in the share of capital goods within its given assortment of imports?

In considering this question, we should attempt to place North Korea's calculated patterns of capital goods trade in international perspective. Table 3.1 provides some of this background, by comparing the estimated share in turnover and per capita volume of the international capital goods trade for North Korea, with the international trade in "machinery and transportation equipment" for selected communist and non-communist countries and regions.[54] All figures are calculated in terms of current dollars, based on current official exchange rates, for reasons already explained.

As Table 3.1 illustrates vividly, North Korea's patterns of capital good commerce, and its attendant development path, differed starkly over the past generation not only from those of the developing regions, but also from those of the rest of the communist world. Whereas the share of imports devoted to capital equipment purchases gradually increased during the 1970s, 1980s, and 1990s in nearly all other places, it declined in North Korea.

Given its relatively small population, North Korea's absolute volume of capital goods imports was already strikingly low in the 1970s for a socialist economy:

Table 3.1
DPRK Capital Goods Trade in International Perspective

Country/Region	Capital Goods as a Proportion of Trade			Capital Goods Trade per Person		
	Percent			Current US$ Value		
Imports	1970s	1980s	Early 1990s	1970s	1980s	Early 1990s
USSR	35.9	37.1	—	45	18	—
CMEA Europe	35.7[1]	31.7[2]	—	175[1]	303[2]	—
Cuba	26.6	31.7	21.0	97	237	77
China	21.8[3]	28.6	37.8	2[3]	10	28
DPRK	20.9[4]	18.5	16.4	14[4]	18	12
ROK	28.8	30.2	35.1	68	238	774
Developing economies	27.4	32.1	46.5[5]	27	57	114[5]
Exports	1970s	1980s	Early 1990s	1970s	1980s	Early 1990s
USSR	18.4	14.6	—	24	49	—
CMEA Europe	42.3[1]	46.7[2]	—	192[1]	455[2]	—
Cuba	Negl.	Negl.	Negl.	Negl.	Negl.	Negl.
China	3.7[3]	3.3	13.9	Negl.[3]	2	11
DPRK	2.9[4]	7.6	11.1	1[4]	6	6
ROK	14.8	32.3	45.0	32	294	922
Developing countries	4.8	12.8	27.4[5]	4	23	67[5]

Notes: [1] = 1970, 73–79; [2] = 1980–88; [3] = 1970, 75–79; [4] = 1972–79; [5] = 1990–94; trade volumes estimated in current US$ at official exchange rates, imports CIF (except developing economies), exports FOB "Developing economies" defined per UN taxonomy (less China); per capita trade volumes calculated according to 1975, 1985, 1990/95 pop.

Sources: For Cuba and USSR: USCIA, Handbook . . .; for Eastern Europe: USCIA, Handbook . . .; for ROK: Korea Statistical Yearbook; for developing countries: United Nations, 1995; population derived from United Nations, 1990.

at an estimated US$14 per person, it was less than one-seventh of the Cuban level, and barely a twelfth of the level estimated in Soviet bloc Europe. By the 1980s, these gaps had widened still further. Cuba was importing an estimated 13 times as much capital equipment as North Korea on a per capita basis; Eastern Europe, over 18 times as much. By the 1990s even China—with its internal market of 1.2 billion people—was importing three times as much capital equipment on a per capita basis as North Korea, a country of only some 20 million.

The contrast with non-socialist countries is similar. With the exception of China, for the developing regions as a whole, estimated per capita imports of capital equipment were nearly twice as high as for the DPRK in the 1970s, over three times as high in the 1980s, and about 12 times as high in the 1990s. As for South Korea, the per capita volume of the ROK's capital equipment imports was about five times as high as North Korea's in the 1970s and over 80 times as high in the early 1990s.

North Korea's persistent—and by the benchmarks in Table 3.1—ever more glaring tendency to underinvest in foreign capital goods augured ill for the country's industrial development. The consequences of this tendency are predictable, and are reflected in our figures on DPRK export performance.

In the 1970s, capital equipment accounted for roughly the same low share of overall exports for the DPRK as for Maoist China or the collectivity of third world countries. During the 1980s and 1990s, however, the share of machinery and equipment in the exports of both the non-communist third world and China rose faster and more steadily than in North Korea. By the end of the Cold War, North Korea's structure of exports was decidedly less industrialized than either China's or that of the non-communist developing areas as a whole. In absolute volume, North Korea's per capita exports of capital goods for 1990–95 were only about half as high as China's; they were less than one-seventh the average for non-communist third world countries, and less than one-hundredth that of South Korea.[55]

Further international perspective on the DPRK's pattern of capital equipment trade may be seen in Figures 3.7, 3.8a and 3.8b.

Figure 3.7

Capital Goods Imports in Highly-Indebted Economies:
DPRK vs. Selected LDCs, ca. 1970–1985/95

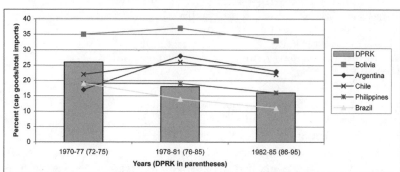

Notes: For 1982–85, Bolivia and Brazil = 1982–84; Philippines = 1982–86.
Sources: For DPRK, Choi, 1991 and Eberstadt, unpublished; for others, see Hentschel, 1989, p. 85.

Figure 3.8a

Capital Goods Imports During (8-yr) Periods of Economic Crises: Estimated Absolute Value for China, Cuba, DPRK

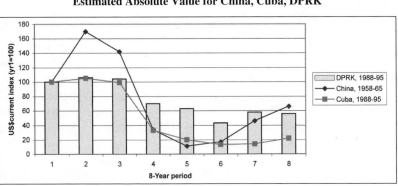

Sources: Choi, 1991 and Eberstadt, unpublished.

Among contemporary less developed economies, as we have seen, international debt payment problems have typically depressed the share of capital goods within imports. North Korea is also a debt problem country. As Figure 3.7 underscores, however, the drop in the ratio of capital goods imports to total imports has been far more severe for North Korea since the advent of its international debt problems than for other countries during their debt crises. And

Figure 3.8b

Capital Goods Imports During (8-yr) Periods of Economic Crises: Estimated Percentage for China, Cuba, DPRK

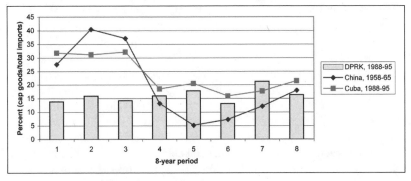

Sources: Choi, 1991 and Eberstadt, unpublished.

whereas reductions in the ratio of capital goods imports to total imports have typically been temporary occurrences in other debt-stressed countries, the phenomenon has been enduring—and intensifying—in North Korea.

North Korea today is not only a country experiencing continuing debt payment problems, but is a communist system under severe economic stress.[56] Figures 3.8a and 3.8b compare capital equipment trade patterns for North Korea in recent years with those of two communist economies during phases of economic crisis: China 1958–65 and Cuba 1988–95. There are elements of similarity among the three cases: in each instance, for example, the absolute volume of capital equipment imports fell sharply. However, unlike China after the Great Leap Forward or Cuba after the cutoff of Soviet aid, North Korea's ratio of capital goods imports to total imports did not plummet with the onset of its recent economic troubles. Moreover the absolute decline in machinery and equipment imports in North Korea, while steep, was nonetheless much less extreme than in contemporary Cuba, or in China during its years of food crisis. Although North Korea's economy may well be in crisis today, its import patterns appear to be less subject to exigency than those of other Communist systems during their periods of extreme difficulty.

A prolonged restriction on capital goods imports would be expected to affect economic performance adversely under almost any circumstances. In practice, North Korea's restrictive approach to the importation of capital goods may have been even more costly than might otherwise have been expected. For although North Korea continued to accumulate a growing inventory of foreign capital equipment during the 1980s and 1990s, Pyongyang apparently chose to skimp on the repair and maintenance of those potentially productive assets. This much is suggested by Figures 3.9 and 3.10, which track estimated trends in North Korean purchases of capital equipment parts and accessories from western industrial countries between 1980 and 1995.[57]

These purchases declined steadily: from US$65 million for 1980–84 to US$60 million for 1985–89, and US$46 million for 1990–94. (It should be remembered that these numbers are nominal values; applying the appropriate deflators, the real declines would appear correspondingly steeper.) This gradual downturn in parts and accessories purchases is not explained solely by unfavorable overall hard currency import trends: for imports of parts and accessories also decline *as a proportion of capital goods imports* during the years in question. Why North Korean policymakers should have so stinted on the upkeep of their foreign capital stock is not clear;[58] the implications for the utilization and productivity of that capital stock are unambiguously negative.

Reliable official data on the volume and composition of North Korean production are famously unavailable. Mirror statistics on North Korean trade, however, may help us assess trends in the overall industrial output of the

Figure 3.9

DPRK Imports of Parts and Accessories (BEC 42)

from OECD and Japan, 1980–1995

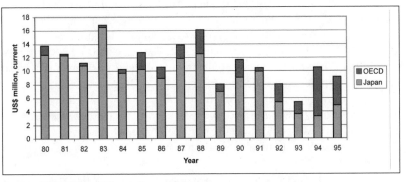

Sources: Choi, 1991 and Eberstadt, unpublished.

Figure 3.10

Parts and Accessories Imports from OECD Estimated

as a Percentage of Capital Imports from OECD, 1980–1995

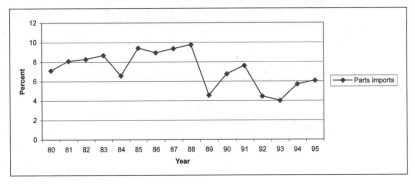

Sources: Choi, 1991 and Eberstadt, unpublished.

DPRK. For in the North Korean economy, industrial infrastructure happens to support production of a number of goods that are not only broadly representative of light and heavy manufacture within the economy, but also designated as export items. These goods include iron and steel products, cement, magnesite, gold, and textiles and clothing. By estimating export trends for these critical commodities,[59] we may attempt to draw broader inferences about the performance of the DPRK economy. Figures 3.11a to 3.11e provide calculations for the total global nominal dollar value of these North Korean industrial export items between 1972 and 1995.[60]

Cement is a traditional staple in the North Korean export sector. In 1978, total measured cement exports increased significantly, as new facilities came on line, established in part through previous capital good imports. Between 1979 and 1988, cement exports fluctuated between an estimated US$110 million and US$190 million, with no clear sign of trend; presumably, a fixed capacity was producing for a domestic market and an export market. After 1988, however, cement exports declined, dropping by a third between 1988 and 1990.[61] Then between 1990 and 1991, they fell by another 88 percent, to US$14 million. Although cement exports rose somewhat between 1991 and 1995, in 1995 they were still almost 80 percent below their nominal dollar level from 1988.

Iron and steel exports seem to tell a similar story. Around the mid-1970s, it would appear, new capacity in this sector came on line. Thereafter, the nominal value of iron and steel exports fluctuated without apparent trend for about a decade, increasing sharply once again between 1984 and 1987. The increase in iron and steel exports, however, was not sustained. Between 1987 and 1990—in other words, *before* the traumas induced by the Soviet trade shock— the nominal value of iron and steel exports dropped by an estimated 30 percent. It fell by almost two-thirds between 1990 and 1991. In 1995 estimated iron and steel exports were barely half their 1991 level, and less than a sixth of their 1987 level.

Figure 3.11a
DPRK Export Performance: Steel, 1984–1995

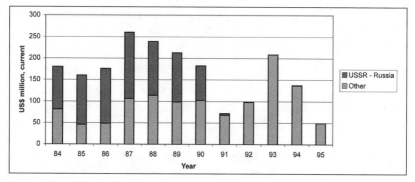

Sources: Choi, 1991 and Eberstadt, unpublished.

Figure 3.11b

DPRK Export Performance: Cement, 1982–1995

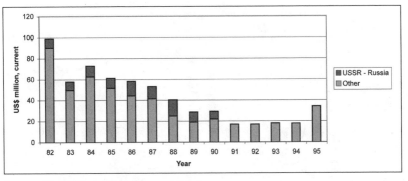

Sources: Choi, 1991 and Eberstadt, unpublished.

Until 1980, North Korea was not an appreciable exporter of textiles and clothing. In the early 1980s, again apparently as new facilities came on line, textile and clothing output increased. In the late 1980s and early 1990s, thanks to cooperative agreements with the USSR,[62] textile exports virtually boomed: in 1988–90, these averaged over US$500 million a year in nominal dollars at official exchange rates. With the demise of the Soviet Union, however, that newly built textile capacity apparently could not be effectively utilized. Despite the attempt to develop a "processing on commission" clothing industry, the DPRK's textile and clothing exports in 1992–95 averaged under US$200 million a year—sixty percent lower than the calculated level for 1988–90.

Then there are the reported exports of mineral products, magnesite and gold. Magnesite exports appear to have stagnated between 1979 and 1992, and to have declined thereafter. However, price trends for the commodity could strongly affect this series. As for gold, reported sales have fluctuated without a strong evident trend since the early 1980s. Annual measured sales in the 1990s, however, appear to have been lower in the 1990s than in the previous decade. Measured export revenues from gold will, of course, be affected by international price trends, decisions about inventory sales, and unreported transactions secured by payment in bullion. Taken together, however, export trends for gold and magnesite would seem suggestive of stagnation and decline in the DPRK's mining sector.

The faltering export performance underscored in Figures 3.11a–3.11e should not be attributed solely to deterioration of the capital stock in the particular sectors under consideration. A number of other constraints—including shortages of intermediate products—are also likely reflected. But shortages of intermediate

Figure 3.11c
DPRK Export Performance: Textiles, 1980–1995

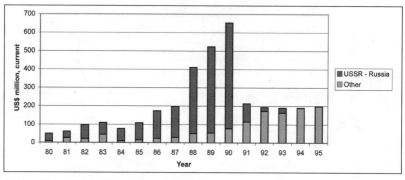

Sources: Choi, 1991 and Eberstadt, unpublished.

inputs may themselves speak to deterioration of capital stock in other sectors,[63] and to that extent reflect broader problems in the DPRK industrial infrastructure.

Concluding Observations

Mirror statistics on capital goods and associated data for exports of selected manufactures corroborate and further document an industrial slump in North Korea which commenced around 1991. By 1995, it had apparently not yet bot-

Figure 3.11d
DPRK Export Performance: Magnesite, 1980–1995

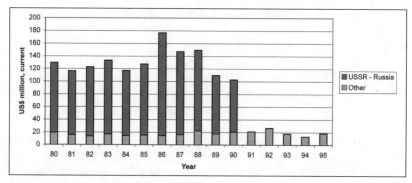

Sources: Choi, 1991 and Eberstadt, unpublished.

Figure 3.11e
DPRK Export Performance: Gold, 1978–1995

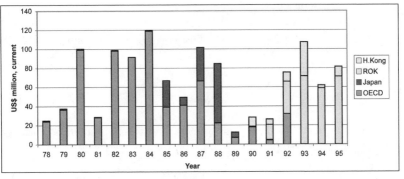

Sources: Choi, 1991 and Eberstadt, unpublished.

tomed out. But as we have seen, the deep troubles afflicting the North Korean industrial system did not suddenly burst forth with the collapse of the USSR. Our data, instead, strongly suggest that North Korea's industrial infrastructure was under severe pressure, and perhaps even in decline, well *before* the crisis of Soviet bloc communism. North Korea's capital goods trade appears to have figured directly in this gradually gathering economic crisis.

For over two decades, North Korea appears to have devoted remarkably few resources to the acquisition and installation of modern international capital equipment. In so doing, the DPRK has stood athwart the general patterns of modern industrial development. But in violating these general tendencies, Pyongyang did not establish a new development path. Instead, the consequences of this pattern of underinvestment were grimly predictable. In this respect, North Korea is now reaping what it has sown.

Or, to be more precise: what its policymakers have sown. For North Korea's paradoxical capital goods trade trends over the past generation appear to reflect a purposeful design. North Korea's anomalous and increasingly distorted patterns of capital equipment trade would indeed seem difficult to maintain if they were not shaped by a strong and abiding policy.

If reducing the role of foreign machinery and equipment in the North Korean industrial base had been a key objective of Pyongyang's economic policy, the paradoxes of North Korea's capital goods trade over the past generation could largely be explained. By this criterion, in fact, a considerable measure of success might have been achieved. Even at the height of the import binge during the 1970s, the proportion of the DPRK's imported capital goods within gross domestic capital formation (GDCF) looks to have been low by any international benchmark.[64] By the 1980s and 1990s, the ratio of capital goods imports to GDCF in the North Korean economy may have been among the lowest on earth.

Ironically, Pyongyang's determined quest to build an independent socialist economy appears to have succeeded, but its success has brought the country to a point where it is desperately—indeed, structurally—dependent on the largesse of outsiders.

Notes

1. For example: as the continuing intensity of the discussion known as the "Cambridge controversy" underscores, even the definition and measurement of "capital" remains contentious; from the standpoint of pure theory, the problem of assaying the influence of international trade on production and distribution can seem almost as unsettling, not least because this commerce involves export and import of "capital"; for a concise and masterful exposition of some of these unsettled issues, see Blaug, 1985.
2. For example, Maizels (1963, p. 174) calculated that the share of machinery and transport equipment in imports between 1899 and 1959 rose from 10 percent to 35 percent for "industrial countries," from 11 percent to 50 percent for "semi-industrial countries," and from 17 percent to 39 percent for the "rest of world"; such results also led Maizels and others to conclude that the composition of trade across countries at any given point in time was affected by a number of other important factors, among them, the size of the country's domestic market and the difference between domestic and international relative price structures.
3. Maizels, 1963, p. 181.
4. Chenery, 1971 and 1979; Chenery and Syrquin, 1975; Chenery et al., 1986.
5. An exception to the generalization may be found in Kobo et al., 1986.
6. McCarthy et al., 1987.
7. De Long et al., 1991, p. 453.
8. These results are further developed in De Long and Bradford (1992), and De Long et al. (1992, and 1993).
9. Lee, 1995, p. 105.
10. Ibid., pp. 105–106 and 109.
11. Hentschel, 1989, 1992a, and 1992b.
12. Hentschel, 1989, p. 88.
13. For some "problem debtor" developing countries, in fact, Hentschel (1992a) calculated the marginal productivity of domestic capital to be negative!
14. Considerable quantitative research on patterns of development in the various communist economies has been published; in addition, much literature exists on the changing composition of trade for these economies; unfortunately, fundamental measurement and valuation problems critically limit the comparability of economic structure and performance in such socialist systems with capitalist counterparts; the lengthy exegesis needed to present those results reliably and in context would clearly be inappropriate for this abbreviated survey.
15. As one Soviet source notes, North Korean official statistics once reckoned aid and credits from the socialist camp to the DPRK to have accounted for fully three-

fourths of all capital investment in the DPRK between 1954 and 1960; see Smirnov, 1984, p. 37.

16. See Choi (1991), Chung (1974), Ginsburgs (1982), Kim (1979 and 1987), Mueller (1964), Mikheyev (1989), and van Ree (1989).

17. Details on this incident remain scanty. See Kaser, 1967, pp. 94–95.

18. Not, however, including the United States; legislation severely restricting American commerce with the DPRK had been enacted only days into the Korean War; those strictures were continued and even intensified over the next several decades.

19. Choi, 1991.

20. Ginsburgs, 1982; van Ree, 1989.

21. Choi, 1991; Namkoong, 1995; Noland, 1996.

22. The Intergovernmental Agreement on Mutual Goods Deliveries and Payments for 1986–1990, as it was formally known, was technically signed on February 26, 1986; see Zhukov, 1986, p. 16; but the groundwork for this agreement was laid earlier; as Soviet specialists noted in the late 1980s, "Soviet-[North] Korean cooperation received a significant impetus from the 1984 visit to the USSR by Kim Il Sung"; see Mikheyev, 1989, p. 69.

23. Of the 116 "Foreign Invested Enterprises" established in the DPRK between 1985 and 1993 listed in a study by Namkoong (1995), the investing partner is identified as Japan in 104 cases; see Namkoong 1995, pp. 478–481.

24. Namkoong, 1995, p. 468; socialist Vietnam's performance with joint ventures provides a telling contrast: between 1988 and 1993, it attracted nearly US$7.5 billion in direct foreign investment; see Namkoong, 1995, p. 471.

25. Eberstadt et al., 1995.

26. Namkoong, 1995 and 1996; Noland, 1996.

27. It is true, of course, that Washington and Pyongyang signed an Agreed Framework in 1994, a document which envisions foreign construction and financing of two nuclear reactors in the DPRK as the North Korean government meets a schedule of reciprocal actions; the ultimate cost of these plants—which will clearly count as capital equipment—has been estimated at well over US$4 billion; but at first writing—nearly three years after the initialing of the Framework document—construction had yet to get underway on these enterprises.

28. Eberstadt et al., 1995.

29. United Nations, 1997; the database begins with the year 1962, and contains at least some transmitted information from over 170 countries.

30. On the basis of two special requests, the UN Statistical Office prepared a diskette containing the details of registered commodity transactions with North Korea according to its reporting trading partners for use in this study.

31. Although the UN Trade Database continues to report international transactions attributed to the DPRK, since the mid-1990s the quality of these data have become increasingly problematic, due, in the main, to an increasing confusion on the part of international reporters; it seems that "North Korean" transactions in the database are, in fact, *South Korean* transactions misreported; disentangling and correctly identifying these thousands of transactions is an onerous and forbidding proposition; for the 1995–2005 period, this book relies instead on trade estimates from South Korea's KOTRA, China's *Customs Statistics Yearbook*, and the ROK Ministry of Unification.

32. SITC, rev. 1; SITC, rev. 2; SITC, rev. 3, and the Harmonized System (HS).

33. In any given year between 1970 and 1995, between 90 and 133 countries around the world provided the UN Statistical Office with SITC, rev. 1 trade data.
34. SITC, rev. 2 was not adopted until 1976; accordingly mirror statistics on DPRK gold trade are not available for 1970 to 1975 within the UN trade database; thereafter, information on gold transactions is derived from reports issued by 40 to 101 countries, depending on the specific year.
35. For details, see Eberstadt et al. (1995) and Rubin (1996).
36. Harbaugh et al., 1995.
37. "c.i.f." stands for "cost, insurance and freight," and refers to the difference in price between the actual purchase of merchandise in a foreign country and the ultimate expense of bringing the merchandise to the importing country; f.o.b. (free-on-board) can refer to either the buyer or the seller, depending on which is responsible for and claims ownership of goods while they are in transit; the UN recommends using the f.o.b. method for exports and recording import values on both an f.o.b. and c.i.f. basis; not all countries adhere to this guideline when it comes to companion f.o.b. valuations of imports.
38. The one exception here was for Moscow's reported imports from Pyongyang in the years before 1990; during that period, it was Soviet practice to record all imports on an f.o.b. basis; DPRK exports, as mirrored by Soviet imports, were left unadjusted, because no c.i.f. charges would have been applied to these trade flows by Goskomstat, and home country exports should, according to Western convention, be valued f.o.b.
39. United Nations, 1971b.
40. According to the UN datatape, North Korea exported several hundred million dollars worth of merchandise to Saudi Arabia between 1974 and 1982; the evidence supporting the hypothesis that this commerce was in fact a coding error, while not conclusive, is nonetheless compelling; during the years in question, Riyadh and Pyongyang had neither established diplomatic representation nor concluded trade protocols; moreover, during this period of ostensible Saudi-DPRK commerce, the combined "North Korean" and South Korean import figures recorded by Saudi Arabia track very closely with the export totals reported by Seoul for goods destined for Riyadh.
41. Eberstadt et al., 1995; Eberstadt, 1996.
42. Eberstadt et al., 1995.
43. Or as Zwass put it, "The transferable ruble takes on all monetary functions—but not the function of an international currency"; see Zwass, 1988, p. 60.
44. Treml, 1981.
45. Morgenstern, 1963.
46. West, 1995.
47. Choi, 1991; because Choi includes figures on Saudi-DPRK trade in his series which we believe to be spurious, we have adjusted his series accordingly.
48. Moreover, since sales of capital goods appear to have played only a relatively minor role in China's trade with North Korea in the years before the Soviet collapse, the omission of China from our series from 1972 to 1981 may not have a substantial impact on completeness of coverage of North Korea's capital goods trade.
49. The R-square for the OLS regression is 0.94.
50. Minus Turkey, and, in later years, Mexico and South Korea.
51. This discrepancy could possibly be explained in terms of differences between dates of contracted purchase and dates of recorded shipment; see Choi (1991) and Kim (1979).

52. Derived from OECD (1996, p. 142) on the basis of unweighted average of annual price levels for 1970–79 and 1980–89; one may note that the price level for Japanese exports rose by much less than for other OECD countries—only about 20 percent between the 1970s and the 1980s; on the other hand, Japanese currency also appreciated much more sharply against the dollar: the dollar-yen exchange rate was about 30 percent higher in the 1970s than the 1980s; thus our generalization holds for Japan as well as the rest of North Korea's OECD trading partners.

53. The overwhelming bulk of that commerce—over 90 percent, in nominal dollars value—was a one-time-only shipment of machinery and equipment to Moscow; we can surmise that this was a transaction of exigency, responding to the Soviet Union's insistence that from January 1, 1991 onwards, its trade with North Korea be settled on hard currency terms; further research will be required to determine just what kinds of capital equipment North Korea shipped to the USSR in that unusual year; Soviet statistical sources, however, never fully detailed their capital goods trade with the DPRK; in the 1990 edition of *Vneshnaya Torgovlya*, for example, products identified under "Machinery, Equipment and Transport Means" account for only two thirds of the stated value of that commerce; for more details on the Moscow-Pyongyang capital goods trade from Soviet sources, see Zhukov (1987), Mikheyev (1989), and Trigubenko et al. (1994).

54. That is to say, SITC 7; the most significant difference between this broad category and the definition of capital goods used in this study might appear to be that SITC 7 includes—whereas we exclude—motor vehicles in general, and passenger automobiles in particular; but we include several groupings of manufactured products which do not fall under SITC 7—SITC 69, SITC 86, and SITC 89 (rev. 1).

How much does this difference of coverage affect our calculated results? One indication may be found in the 1994 edition of the United Nations' *International Trade Statistics Yearbook;* according to that volume, global trade in "machinery and transportation equipment" (SITC 7) totaled about US$1.4 trillion in 1993; the products encompassed within our definition of capital goods, by contrast, amounted to somewhat over US$1.5 trillion; the different definitions for capital goods might conceivably result in substantial contrasts in calculated totals for certain countries in certain years; however, on the basis of preliminary sensitivity tests, we assume that the results in Table 3.1 are not strongly biased by differences of product coverage; to the extent that such biases occur, they may tend to *over- rather than understate* the DPRK's output of traded capital goods.

55. We should recall that these DPRK averages for the 1990s include the extraordinary and non-recurrent shipments of machinery and equipment to the USSR in 1990 and 1991; the contrasts would be even greater had we compared the period since 1992.

56. Eberstadt, 1997.

57. For these calculations, aggregated reported purchases of all SITC items defined as "parts and accessories" with the capital goods category detailed in BEC (United Nations, 1971); because the OECD countries in our database report transactions at a 5-digit level of detail, we could estimate reported totals.

58. While this trend may seem lacking in economic logic, there may be administrative logic to it; given North Korea's approach to commercial contract relationships, for example, it may seem easier to North Korean policymakers to attract new capital equipment from new trade partners than to obtain replacement equipment from countries that have had the experience of doing business with the DPRK.

59. Since the mid-1980s, these five product groups have accounted for nearly half of North Korea's estimated exports in our data series.

60. A word about method is in order here: our series on North Korean gold exports is somewhat problematic, insofar as the USSR/Russia database does not yet include time series data for them; with respect to the other export products, however, coverage is fairly straightforward and classification issues are minimal.

    Clothing and textiles, for example, are each given their own 2-digit categories within the SITC schema (SITC 65: "Textile yarn, fabrics, made-up articles and related products"; SITC 84: "Clothing"); the same is true for iron and steel products (SITC 67: "Iron and steel").

    Cement is coded as SITC 661; we extracted values for DPRK cements exports from our database wherever 3-digit SITC breakdowns were available, and elsewhere used SITC 66 ("Non-metallic mineral manufactures").

    Magnesite is referred to in SITC 276.24; reported international purchases of DPRK magnesite could be extracted from the UN database for countries conforming to the convention of 5-digit trade coding, but not for others; consequently, to capture North Korean magnesite exports to those other countries—most significantly, the USSR and Russia—we used the broader SITC 27 grouping ("Crude fertilizers and crude minerals"); although magnesite may have been the major item traded within that category, our procedure biases both the computed levels and trends to some degree.

61. Possibly, this drop reflected increased domestic demand: special construction projects underway in 1988 included the West Sea Lock Gate and the renovations in Pyongyang for the 1989 World Youth Festival; however, those projects were completed by 1990, and thus could not account for the estimated drop in cement exports for that year.

62. The USSR supplied the capital goods and intermediate products: see Mikheyev (1989), Trigubenko et al. (1994) and Eberstadt et al. (1995).

63. For example, lack of electricity may betoken problems with the capital stock in the power sector.

64. This point can be made despite the paucity of reliable data about North Korean economic activity; several sources have hazarded estimates for North Korean GNP in current dollars for the year 1975; these range from US$9.4 billion (ROK National Unification Board, 1988, p. 21), to about US$10 billion (USCIA, 1978, p. 4) to US$11.9–US$25.0 billion (Hwang, 1993, p. 220); if these numbers are taken to indicate a plausible range of possibilities, and if gross domestic investment is assumed to have accounted for no less than 25 percent of GNP, then GDCF calculations for North Korea for 1975 would result in numbers in the range of US$2.35–US$6.25 billion; since our estimated figure for 1975 DPRK capital goods imports was just under US$430 million, these calculations would imply an upper number of 18.3 percent for the ratio of capital equipments imports to GCDF—and a lower figure of 6.9 percent; such ratios would be unusually low for a relatively small, relatively low-income economy; indeed, even the upper end of that range would be fairly low for a problem debtor country; for the comparisons see Hentschel, 1989 and 1992b; since 1975, the ratio of capital goods imports to GDCF would be presumed to have dropped substantially in North Korea.

References

Blaug, Mark. 1985. *Economic Theory in Retrospect*. New York: Cambridge University Press.

Chenery, Hollis, ed. 1971. *Studies in Development Planning*. Cambridge, MA: Harvard University Press.

Chenery, Hollis. 1979. *Structural Change and Development Policy*. New York: Oxford University Press.

Chenery, Hollis and Moises Syrquin. 1975. *Patterns of Development 1950–1970*. New York: Oxford University Press.

Chenery, Hollis. 1986. Sherman Robinson and Moises Syrquin, *Industrialization and Growth: A Comparative Study*. New York: Oxford University Press.

Choi, Soo-young. 1991. "Foreign Trade of North Korea, 1946–1988: Structure and Performance." Unpublished Doctoral Dissertation, Northeastern University.

Chung, Joseph Sang-hoon. 1974. *The North Korean Economy: Structure and Development*. Stanford, CA: Hoover Institution Press.

De Long, J. Bradford. 1992. "Productivity Growth and Machinery Investment: A Long-Run Look, 1870–1980." *Journal of Economic History* 52(2):307–324.

De Long, J. Bradford, and Lawrence H Summers. 1991. "Equipment Investment and Economic Growth." *Quarterly Journal of Economics* 106(2):445–502.

———. 1992. "Equipment Investment and Economic Growth: How Strong is the Nexus?" *Brookings Papers on Economic Activity* 2:157–199.

———. 1993. "How Strongly Do Developing Economies Benefit from Equipment Investment?" *Journal of Monetary Economics* 32(3):395–415.

Eberstadt, Nicholas. 1996. "Financial Transfers from Japan to North Korea: Estimating the Unreported Flows." *Asian Survey* 36(5):523–542.

———. 1997. "The DPRK as an Economic System Under Severe Multiple Stresses: Analogies and Lessons from the Historic and Recent Past." *Communist Economies and Economic Transformation* 9(2).

———. 1998. The DPRK's International Trade in Capital Goods, 1970–1995: Indications from "Mirror Statistics." *Journal of East Asian Affairs* XII(1). Winter/Spring.

———. North Korea International Commercial Trade Data Base, unpublished.

Eberstadt, Nicholas, Marc Rubin, and Albina Tretyakova. 1995. "The Collapse of Soviet and Russian Trade with the DPRK, 1989–1993: Impact and Implications." *Korean Journal of National Reunification* 4:87–104.

Eberstadt, Nicholas, Christina W. Harbaugh, Marc Rubin, and Loraine A. West 1995. "China's Trade with the DPRK, 1990–1994: Pyongyang's Thrifty New Patron," *Korea and World Affairs* 19(4):665–685.

Eckstein, Alexander. 1966. *Communist China's Economic Growth and Foreign Trade*. New York: McGraw Hill.

Ginsburgs, George. 1982. "Soviet Development Grants and Aid to North Korea, 1945–1980." *Asia Pacific Community* (Tokyo) 18:42–63.

Harbaugh, Christina W., Marc Rubin, and Loraine A. West. 1995. "China's Trade with the DPRK, 1950–1994." Washington, DC: U.S. Bureau of the Census, International Programs Center. March. Unpublished.

Hentschel, Jesko. 1989. "The Changing Composition of Imports of Highly Indebted Countries." *Economia Internazionale* 42(1–2):79–89.

————. 1992a. "A Note on the Relationship between Imports and Growth." *Weltwirtschaftliches Archiv* 128(2):339–345.

————. 1992b. *Imports and Growth in Highly Indebted Countries: An Empirical Study.* New York: Springer Verlag.

Hilgert, Folke. 1945. *Industrialization and Foreign Trade.* Geneva: League of Nations.

Hwang, Eui-gak. 1993. *The Korean Economies: A Comparison of North and South.* New York: Oxford University Press.

Kaser, Michael. 1967. *COMECON: Integration Problems of the Planned Economy.* London: Oxford University Press.

Kim, Youn-soo, ed. 1979. *The Economy of the Korean Democratic People's Republic, 1945–1977.* Kiel: German Korea-Studies Group.

Kim, Youn-soo. 1987. "The Foreign Trade of North Korea with European CMEA Countries." *Korea and World Affairs* 11(4):785–803.

Kobo, Yuji, Jaime de Melo, and Sherman Robinson. 1986. "Trade Strategies and Growth Episodes." Chenery, Hollis. 1986. Sherman Robinson and Moises Syrquin, *Industrialization and Growth: A Comparative Study.* New York: Oxford University Press.

Kuznets, Simon. 1961. "Quantitative Aspects of the Economic Growth of Nations IX. Level and Structure of Foreign Trade: Comparisons for Recent Years." *Economic Development and Cultural Change* 13(1):1–106, Part 2.

————. 1966. Simon, *Modern Economic Growth: Rate, Structure, and Spread.* New Haven: Yale University Press.

Lee, Jong-Wha. 1995. "Capital Goods Imports and Long-Run Growth." *Journal of Development Economics* 48(1):91–110.

Maizels, Alfred. 1963. *Industrial Growth and World Trade.* Cambridge, UK: Cambridge University Press.

McCarthy, F. Desmond, Lance Taylor, and Cyrus Talati. 1987. "Trade Patterns in Developing Countries, 1964–1982." *Journal of Development Economics* 27(1–2):5–39.

Mikheyev, V. 1989. "The DPRK's Regional Economic Relations." *Far Eastern Affairs* (Moscow) 2:66–75.

Morgenstern, Oskar. 1963. *On the Accuracy of Economic Observations.* Princeton, NJ: Princeton University Press.

Mueller, Kurt. 1964. *The Foreign Aid Programs of the Soviet Bloc and Communist China: An Analysis.* New York: Walker And Company.

Namkoong, Young. 1995. "An Analysis of North Korea's Policy to Attract Foreign Capital: Management and Achievement." *Korea and World Affairs* 19(3):459–481.

————. 1996. "Trends and Prospects of the North Korean Economy." *Korea and World Affairs* 20(2):219–235.

Noland, Marcus. 1996. "The North Korean Economy." *Joint US-Korean Academic Studies* 5:128–174.

Organisation for Economic Co-operation and Development. 1996. *National Accounts 1960–1995: Main Aggregates 1.* Paris: OECD.

People's Republic of China (PRC) State Statistical Bureau. 1995. *China Statistical Yearbook 1995.* Beijing: China Statistical Publishing House.

————. Various years. *Customs Statistics Yearbook.* Hong Kong: Economic Information & Agency.

Republic of Korea National Statistics Office. Various years. *Korea Statistical Yearbook.* Seoul: NSO.

————. National Unification Board. 1988. *The Economies of South and North Korea.* Seoul: NUB.

————. (ROK MOU) Various issues. *Wolgan Nambuk Kyoryu Hyomnyok Tonghyang.* Seoul: Unification Ministry

Rubin, Marc. 1996. "North Korea's Trade with the USSR and Russia, 1972– 1995." Washington, DC: U.S. Bureau of the Census, International Programs Center. November. Unpublished.

Smirnov, V. 1984. "Development of Foreign Economic Ties of the Democratic People's Republic of Korea." *Far Eastern Affairs* (Moscow) 4:36–45.

Treml, Vladimir and G. Treml. 1981. "The Inferior Quality of Soviet Machinery as Reflected in Export Prices." *Journal Of Comparative Economics* 5(2):200–221.

Trigubenko, Marina, Georgi Toloraya and Alexander Mansurov. 1994. "DPRK: First Mixed Enterprises." *Far Eastern Affairs* (Moscow) 3:21–34.

Union of Soviet Socialist Republics. Various years. *Vneshnaya Torgovlya SSSR..* Moscow: Goskomstat.

————. Various years. *Vneshneekonomicheskie Sviazi Rossiiskoi Federatsii.* Moscow: Goskomstat.

United Nations. 1971a. *Trade Database: Classification of Commodities by Industrial Origin.* Series M, no. 43, rev. 1. New York.

————. 1971b. *Trade Database: Classification by Broad Economic Categories.* Series M, no. 53. New York.

————. 1997. International Commodity Trade Statistics Database. Specially Requested Diskette. Processed.

————. 1990. *World Population Prospects.* New York.

————. 1995. *International Trade Statistics Yearbook 1994.* New York: United Nations, 1995.

United States Central Intelligence Agency, *China, International Trade.* Washington, DC: USCIA National Foreign Assessment Center, various editions.

————. Various Years. *Handbook of International Economic Statistics.* Washington, DC: CIA Directorate of Intelligence.

————. 1978. "Korea: The Economic Race between the North and the South." Research Memorandum 78-10008. Washington, DC: USCIA National Foreign Assessment Center.

Usack, A.H. and R.E. Batsavage. 1972. "The International Trade of the People's Republic of China," in US Congress Joint Economic Committee, *The People's Republic of China: An Economic Assessment.* Washington, DC: Government Printing Office.

van Ree, Erik. 1989. "The Limits of Juche: North Korea's Dependence on Soviet Industrial Aid, 1953–76." *Journal of Communist Studies* 5(1):50–73.

West, Loraine A. 1995. "Reconciling China's Trade Statistics." Washington, DC: U.S. Bureau of the Census, International Programs Center. January. Unpublished.

Zhukov, Nikita. 1986. "USSR-DPRK: The Course for Broader Cooperation." *Foreign Trade* (Moscow) 111:15–17.

Zwass, Adam. 1988. *Der Rat fuer gegenseitige Wirtschaftshilfe 1949 bis 1987.* Vienna: Springer Verlag.

4

Interlocking Crises in Food, Energy, and Transport Equipment: Indications from "Mirror Statistics"*

For over two generations—more precisely, since the early 1960s—analysis of the performance of the economy of the Democratic People's Republic of Korea (DPRK, or North Korea) has been severely limited by a prolonged and strictly administered "statistical blackout." Even by comparison with other deliberately closed societies in the modern era, the duration and extent of the DPRK's embargo on socioeconomic information is arguably unparalleled. At this juncture, in fact, not a single official data series relating to any aspect of the country's economic performance is being regularly released.

Given the extraordinary success, by its own lights, of Pyongyang's campaign to suppress domestically collected information on its national economy, virtually the only new North Korean data regularly available concern the DPRK's international commerce, and come from reports by trade partners: figures known in the jargon as "mirror statistics." While these numbers are not without their limitations, they nonetheless can provide a basis by which to assess both the current state and the development over time of one consequential component of the North Korean economy: its external merchandise trade sector, and in addition offer an aperture through which to observe, and draw inferences about, broader conditions within the DPRK domestic economy.[1]

This chapter examines the DPRK's trade trends in three sectors of strategic significance to the entire North Korean economy: food, energy, and transport.

*This study, originally published in March 1998 in *Asian Survey* 38(3), was prepared as part of a project on North Korean Economic Stability directed by the National Bureau of Asian Research (NBR); the author wishes to thank Jonathan B. Tombes for his heroic labors in processing data from the UN International Commodity Trade Database, and Marc Rubin of the U.S. Census Bureau for helpful advice on the finer points of Soviet and Russian trade statistics; the views expressed are those of the author.

To judge by official pronouncements, the very highest authorities in Pyongyang have long viewed these three sectors as potential "bottlenecks," in which unresolved problems might seriously jeopardize performance in the rest of the DPRK economy. Nearly 40 years ago, for example, Kim Il Sung personally highlighted the troubles of the country's transportation infrastructure, and expounded on the broad consequences of that contemporary "strain on transport."[2] On various occasions in the 1970s and 1980s, the late Great Leader continued to identify transport as the *primary* problem facing the DPRK economy.[3] By the same token, over the past 20 years both Kim Il Sung and Kim Jong Il publicly declaimed about the broad ramifications of not "solv[ing] the fuel and power problems successfully." (In Kim Jong Il's ominous 1982 formulation, having to "depend on others" for fuel "is as good as leaving one's economic lifeline in the hands of others."[4] In addition, "the food problem" has been a perennial concern of North Korean policy for obvious—officially acknowledged—reasons.

The severe and apparently continuing downturn that has gripped North Korea's economy since 1989 has evidently intensified the pressures on each of these critical sectors. The most dramatic impact has been felt in the food sector, prompting Pyongyang in 1995 to issue its unprecedented, and still continuing, international appeal for food aid.[5] Yet in a complex, modern economy— and the DPRK economy still assuredly qualifies as one of these—difficulties witnessed in any one sector cannot be understood in isolation. North Korea's current agricultural troubles, for example, have probably been compounded materially by energy shortages, on the one hand, and transport system problems on the other. Furthermore, the linkages between these three sectors suggest that problems in one area are unlikely to be resolved, and may not even be significantly relieved, without tangible progress in the other two.

For all of Pyongyang's rhetoric about "economic self-reliance," North Korea's patterns of international trade bear directly on the performance of the country's food, transport, and energy systems. In the following pages we will attempt to use mirror statistics to indicate some of the dimensions and origins of North Korea's current problems in transportation, food, and energy. We will also examine those numbers for what they may reveal about North Korean policy in each of these three arguably critical economic areas. We will conclude with some speculations about the prospects for the DPRK's food, energy, and transport sectors in the period ahead.

Method

The methodology utilized in assembling the data series on DPRK international merchandise trade from which these sectoral figures are drawn has been described in detail in Chapter 3. Briefly, mirror statistics on North Korean trade from the United Nations' International Commodity Trade Database for the years 1970–95,[6] and from official Soviet trade yearbooks for 1972–95,[7] have been compiled in accordance with the SITC, rev. 1 schema, valued in current dollars according to current official exchange rates, and adjusted for presumed c.i.f. charges.[8] Mirror statistics for Chinese-DPRK trade for the period 1982–95 have been added to the data series in the same manner.[9] As reported by the Ministry of Unification of the Republic of Korea (ROK, or South Korea), the data on the officially sanctioned inter-Korean trade that commenced in 1988 offer the final component necessary for reconstructing DPRK trade patterns from partner mirror statistics for the period 1972–95.[10]

Because mirror statistics are notorious for reporting errors, the assembled data were checked for questionable entries. A few major transactions deemed to be spurious *prima facie* were stricken from the database.[11] We expected, however, that the data series would still contain additional, undetected misclassifications. As we shall see, that expectation appears to be amply justified.

Our analysis of sectoral trade patterns in this chapter follows the same taxonomy outlined in SITC, rev. 1; for food trade, we use the broad, one-digit category 0 ("Food and Live Animals") found in SITC, rev. 1; for energy, we use the corresponding broad, one-digit category 3 ("Mineral Fuels, Lubricants and Related Materials"); for motor vehicles, we use the two-digit category 73 ("Transport Equipment").

Results

Transport Equipment

Reported trends in import and export of transport equipment over the years 1982–95 are summarized in Figures 4.1 and 4.2. These figures cannot measure any China-DPRK trade in transport equipment before 1982, the first year for which Beijing offers detailed breakdowns of its international trade. Between 1972 and 1981, however, that particular component of Chinese-North Korean commerce was probably negligible. More importantly, we should remember that Figures 4.1 and 4.2 likely reflect only North Korea's purchases and sales of *non-military* vehicles. Soviet mirror statistics typically did not itemize the military component within overall exports, and virtually none of the DPRK's other trade partners detail defense industry transactions with Pyongyang through trade accounts.

In the 24-year period illustrated in Figure 4.1, North Korea is reported to have imported just over an estimated US$2 billion in transport equipment, in nominal dollars and at current official exchange rates. Over half of the computed nominal value of DPRK transport equipment imports originated in the erstwhile Soviet bloc territories (48 percent USSR/Russia; 7 percent Euro-

Figure 4.1

DPRK Imports of Transport Equipment by Source, 1972–1995

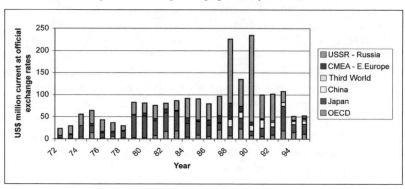

Source: Eberstadt, unpublished.

Figure 4.2

DPRK Exports of Transport Equipment by Destination, 1972–1995

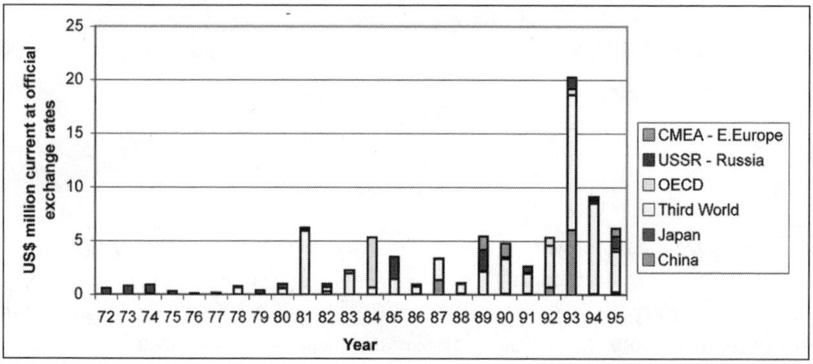

Source: Eberstadt, unpublished.

pean CMEA/Eastern Europe). Roughly two-fifths of the computed nominal value of these products came from OECD countries[12] (29 percent from Japan, 10 percent from Germany and other OECD members). The remainder—just 6 percent of the computed nominal total—was shipped from China or "third world" venues. Although inter-Korean trade officially commenced in the late 1980s and had achieved a cumulative turnover that was approaching US$1 billion by 1995, reported South Korean transport equipment exports to the DPRK during the period under consideration were inconsequential.

Between 1972 and 1995, the DPRK's commercial transport equipment exports, as reflected in mirror statistics, totaled only US$178 million—an average of less than US$8 million a year. Even this sum, however, would appear to be an overestimate. Fully a third of the computed nominal value of North Korea's overall transport equipment exports during the years in question derives from a single transaction: a reported sale to India in 1992 of US$59 million of "Ships and boats, non-war." This is almost certainly a miscoding of a *South* Korean sale: after Japan, South Korea was the world's second largest merchant vessel exporter in 1992. Given that the reported US$59 million transaction was for a single ship, moreover, North Korea would seem a most unlikely supplier. It is not even clear that the DPRK has dry docks large enough to manufacture a ship of that size!

Of the remaining US$119 million in aggregate exports of transport merchandise, nearly a third—US$37 million—reportedly accrued from product shipments to the Soviet Union in the calendar year 1990, according to U.S. Census Bureau reconstructions of Soviet-North Korean trade. Inspection of the original data from the USSR's trade yearbook for 1990, however, strongly suggests that this "sale" is actually a computational error that somehow crept into the Census Bureau data files.[13]

Apart from the likely spurious reported boat sale to India and that highly suspicious once-only burst of transport equipment shipments to Moscow, the North Korean transport equipment sales identified through mirror statistics averaged a trivial US$3.4 million per year. Evidently, North Korea's "independent national economy" never really developed the capability to manufacture non-military motor vehicles that could be sold abroad.

North Korea's reported imports of civilian transport equipment averaged an estimated US$86 million a year between 1972 and 1995, in terms of nominal dollars and at official exchange rates. That average, however, masks notable oscillations. Between 1972 and 1980, the nominal value of imported transport equipment averaged under US$50 million per year. Between 1981 and 1990, it averaged about US$120 million a year. For the years 1991–95, they averaged a little over US$80 million a year. Mirror statistics thus indicate that in the early 1990s, even in nominal terms, DPRK imports of transport equipment were 35 percent lower than they had been over the decade 1981-90, and were fully 60 percent lower than in 1988–90 (the period of peak transport equipment imports).

Mirror statistics offer some indications about the composition of North Korea's motor vehicle imports. The UN Trade Database, for example, registers roughly US$1.07 billion in such sales and shipments for the years 1972–95. Of this total, buses were identified as accounting for US$46 million, railway vehicles for US$67 million, autos for US$193 million, and lorries and trucks for US$365 million. (The remaining US$400 million included products not dis-aggregated, such as spare parts and allied equipment, and imports of such products as ships, aircraft, and motorcycles. The reported composition of civilian transport equipment imports from the Soviet Union and Russia looks only slightly different. Over half of that commerce is estimated to have consisted of trucks and spare parts for trucks. Another third was accounted for by airplanes and aviation equipment. The remainder consisted of automobiles, rail vehicles, and ships.

Mirror statistics also offer some insight into the physical quantities of non-military transport equipment which North Korea may have imported. Between 1972 and 1995, according to the UN trade tapes, the DPRK's identifiable imports of railway equipment totaled just under 5,500 tons. The tapes similarly identify imports of just under 13,300 foreign automobiles. However, some auto imports in that series are measured in terms of tonnage. If we assume the same ratio of cost to sales as for transactions where vehicles were enumerated, this would make for an additional 17,500 car imports, for a total of 30,800 imported cars. Using the same sorts of benchmarks, we would estimate that the DPRK imported a total of about 2,300 buses and about 25,000 trucks in the period between 1972 and 1995.

Soviet and Russian trade yearbooks identify a total of 115 locomotives, about 10,800 automobiles, and about 19,200 trucks sent to North Korea between 1972 and 1995. Idiosyncratically, though, Soviet trade yearbooks neglect to report the number of trucks shipped to DPRK between 1977 and 1985, offering instead only the ruble value of those goods. Prorating the reported value of that commerce against the implicit ruble cost per truck for North Korea for the years 1972–76 would suggest that no more 2,300 trucks were sent to Pyongyang between 1977 and 1985.[14] This would make for a total of no more than 21,500 imported Soviet and Russian trucks for the entire period.

To go by the data and clues from mirror statistics, North Korea would appear to have imported a non-military total of roughly 41,500 automobiles, roughly 46,500 trucks, roughly 2,300 buses, some 115 locomotives, and an additional 5,500 tons of railway equipment in the period between 1972 and 1995. What would such totals signify? One impression easily gained from them is that the conveyance capabilities of the DPRK's economy during the past generation were distinctly—perhaps extraordinarily—limited.

Although railways reportedly form the backbone of the DPRK's transport system, for example,[15] identified imports of non-Soviet railway equipment averaged less than 250 tons a year—barely a ton of such equipment for every 100,000 persons in the country. North Korea did import additional rail equipment from the USSR—but that extra amount works out to fewer than five locomotives a year on average for the period under review!

Ratios for imported road transport equipment look equally constrained. Even if every one of the cars, trucks, and buses identified or estimated through mirror statistics were still in running order, there would be only one such vehicle for every 250 persons in the country. If we further presume that imported autos were almost exclusively used by a tiny, privileged stratum, as many press reports have indicated, the ratio of the general population to imported buses or trucks would come to almost 500 to one!

These computed ratios, of course, take no account of the DPRK's domestically produced rolling stock. But the DPRK's capacities in these areas are not thought to be great.[16] It is true that North Korea imported some civilian transport equipment that went un-itemized within our mirror statistics, and very likely additional amounts that went undetected by them. Yet when all these factors are taken into account, they do not alter the picture suggested by the mirror statistics themselves: namely, an economy severely beset by what Kim Il Sung once described as a "strain on transport."

That "strain" may be better appreciated when placed in international perspective. Mirror statistics do not, unfortunately, allow us to estimate the size of North Korea's road fleets. However, one US government source has offered the estimate of 264,000 total vehicles in use in the DPRK in 1990, including military trucks and jeeps.[17] If this estimate is correct—and the number itself would seem broadly consistent with the indications we have just gleaned from mirror statistics—North Korea's ratio of road vehicles to general population around 1990 would have ranked among the very lowest of any communist state. In Eastern Europe, for example, the ratio of vehicles to population around 1989–90 would have been ten times higher than in the DPRK. For the USSR as whole, that ratio would have been well over three times North Korea's—and for subsidiary Soviet Republics, the disparity would have been even greater. Even contemporary Cuba would have had four times as many road vehicles per capita as the DPRK. Only China would have had a ratio lower than North Korea's—but whereas China was predominantly rural and agricultural in 1990, the DPRK was largely urbanized and industrialized.[18] North Korea's strikingly low estimated ratio of automotive vehicles to population may have been shaped by security considerations—overarching apprehension, for example, that enhancing personal mobility would complicate the tasks of state control—but security considerations presumably cut both ways. For as Kim Il Sung had noted in 1968, "properly building up motor roads acquires great importance from the viewpoint of national defense."[19]

Additional perspective on North Korea's patterns of transport equipment purchases may be had by comparing the DPRK not just with the communist world, but with the world as a whole. Between 1972 and 1995, according to UN trade data, the nominal value of global purchases of transport equipment of all kinds jumped from US$38 billion to over US$500 billion. Per capita global imports of these goods (*not* adjusted for inflation) increased by a factor of nine.[20] By contrast, between 1972 and 1995, North Korea's nominal imports of transport equipment barely doubled, and per capita imports—again in nominal terms—were up by barely 50 percent. Owing to the difficulties of converting current rubles into constant dollars, we cannot calculate the "real" change in imports over time for the DPRK. Even so, it seems quite possible that North Korea's level of motor transport imports may have been lower in the mid-1990s than they had been in the early 1970s.

Mirror statistics have previously been used to detail a chronic and severe underinvestment by North Korea in foreign machinery and equipment—capital goods that can substantially improve the productivity of a country's capital stock.[21] They seem to reflect an analogous pattern of chronic and severe underinvestment with respect to foreign transport equipment. Between the early 1970s and the mid-1990s, a revolution in transportation capabilities has swept the world. To judge by mirror statistics, however, that revolution bypassed North Korea. In fact, one may infer from the absolute decline in the nominal value of North Korean transportation imports in the early 1990s and from the recent reports of North Korean sales for scrap metal of what had been motor vehicles[22] that within the DPRK today, a transportation system already under-mechanized and stretched thin is now afflicted by positive decay.[23]

Food

Overall trends in North Korea's reported commerce in foodstuffs are outlined in Figures 4.3 and 4.4. These figures necessarily exclude the Chinese-North

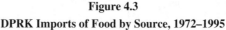

Figure 4.3
DPRK Imports of Food by Source, 1972–1995

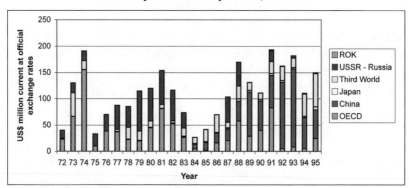

Source: Eberstadt, unpublished.

Figure 4.4
DPRK Exports of Food by Destination, 1972–1995

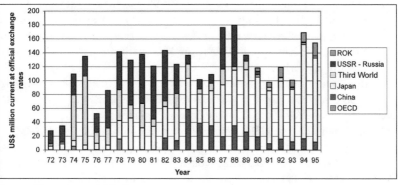

Source: Eberstadt, unpublished.

Korean food trade before 1982. There is reason to believe, however, that
North Korea's commerce in foods with Beijing in the 1970s and early 1980s
accounted for only a small fraction of the Sino-DPRK trade turnover[24] and
thus did not figure significantly in North Korea's overall food trade in that
period.

Mirror statistics indicate that North Korea imported about US$2.7 billion in
foodstuffs (excluding beverages, which SITC classifies separately) between
1972 and 1995. The nominal dollar value of DPRK food exports for those same
years is very close to that total: US$2.8 billion. This appears to be virtually
the only sector in which DPRK's long-term exports and imports are in rough
balance, and for which annual trade surpluses have been registered on a fairly
regular basis. We will later return to this striking point.

For the years 1972–95, DPRK reported food imports averaged about
US$110 million a year. Valued in current dollars at official exchange rates,
roughly a third (34 percent) of North Korea's food imports originated from
the OECD grouping (though Japan's contribution here was minor); China
accounted for about a quarter (26 percent); and the USSR/Russia and the third
world accounted for almost all of the remainder—23 percent and 17 percent,
respectively. (South Korea began to record commercial exports of food to
DPRK in 1991, but by 1995 the cumulative total was only US$3 million.)

The regional composition of the DPRK's reported food imports has shifted
over time. In the 1970s, OECD countries were North Korea's prime source of
food imports. According to mirror statistics, since the early 1990s, China has
served as North Korea's major food supplier.

North Korean food imports identified through mirror statistics averaged US$97 million a year between 1972 and 1979, US$100 million a year in 1981–90, and about US$160 million a year for 1991–95. For reasons previously mentioned, devising a deflator for this series is problematic. Even so, this relatively modest long-term increase in nominal import values would seem to raise the possibility that the real level of DPRK food purchases from abroad may have been lower in the early 1990s than it was in the 1970s.

North Korea's food exports between 1972 and 1995 averaged about US$115 million a year. North Korea's principal overseas purchaser was Japan, which accounted for about 44 percent of the nominal total for the entire period. (Purchases by the rest of the OECD grouping were insignificant.) The USSR/Russia accounted for just over a quarter (26 percent) of identified North Korean food exports, third world countries, about a sixth (16 percent), and China, about one-eighth (11 percent). Between 1989 and 1995, South Korea's purchases of North Korean foodstuffs totaled roughly US$70 million.

In the 1970s, third world countries, in particular, Indonesia, Malaysia, and Singapore, appear to have been the principal purchasers of North Korean foodstuffs. In the early 1980s, the Soviet Union served as the DPRK's main market for food exports. Since the mid-1980s, Japan has been North Korea's major partner for food exports. In fact, Japan accounted for well over half of all North Korean food sales every year between 1988 and 1995.

Like North Korean exports as a whole, the DPRK's overseas foods sales seem to have risen somewhat during the 1980s, and to have dropped since the final crisis of Soviet socialism. Between the 1970s and the 1980s, the nominal value of food exports rose, from an average of about US$95 million a year in 1972–80 to about US$135 million a year for 1981–90. It then fell in the 1990s to an average of about US$128 million a year for 1991–95. If a deflator for this trade were available—which it is not—we might well discover that real levels of food exports were lower in the 1990s than they had been not only in the 1980s, but in the 1970s as well.

Mirror statistics detail some pronounced changes in the commodity makeup of the North Korean food trade—particularly among exports. In the 1970s (1972–80), exports of cereals accounted for about 70 percent of North Korean foodstuff exports. By the 1990s (1991–95), cereals accounted for less than 1 percent of North Korea's food sales abroad. Over the intervening years, such items as seafood and mushrooms assumed a much more prominent place among North Korea's limited offering of foodstuffs available for sale overseas.

This circumscribed transformation of food export structure conforms to an economic logic: "low-cost" calorie foodstuffs were gradually being replaced by "high-cost" calorie exports. From such behavior, one can discern a tactic of "caloric arbitrage," that is, of trading agricultural commodities in such a way as to obtain a maximum nutritive value from the commerce in food products.

Mirror statistics permit us to track not only trends in North Korea's overall food trade, but also its commerce in foodgrains. Between 1972 and 1995, North Korea's trade partners recorded an estimated US$2.2 billion in commercial grain shipments to Pyongyang, or an average of about US$90 million a year. OECD countries (minus Japan) accounted for about two-fifths (39 percent) of the nominal value of these shipments; the Soviet Union, over a quarter (26 percent); China, a little over a fifth (22 percent), and third world countries (principally Thailand) about one-eighth (13 percent). The nominal value of reported cereal imports has remained relatively steady, averaging about US$90 million in the 1970s, US$85 million in the 1980s, and just over US$100 million in the early 1990s.

Reported North Korean cereal exports, for their part, totaled under US$1 billion (US$933 million) between 1972 and 1995. In the 1970s, the annual average amounted to US$65 million. By the 1980s, it had fallen to US$35 million a year. By the early 1990s, cereal exports had essentially ceased, averaging under US$1 million a year. While the drop-off in cereal exports in the 1990s looks particularly sudden, and could therefore be consonant with certain types of economic or agricultural shocks, we should also recognize that the decline in DPRK foodgrain exports was a phenomenon gradually in the making over the course of several decades, and that such a trend could reflect a great many factors besides mounting nutritional distress.

Mirror statistics detail the physical quantities involved in the DPRK's international commerce in cereal products over the years 1985–95, the period in which both Moscow and Beijing reported on the tonnage of their grain trade with North Korea. In the decade 1985–94, North Korea's net imports of cereal products reportedly totaled about 6 million tons, or an average of about 600,000 tons per year. While currently available information is insufficient to construct reliable "food balance sheets" for the DPRK,[25] rough arithmetic suggests that the average nutritive value of North Korea's net cereal imports during that period would have exceeded 300 calories per person per day.[26] By this crude measure, it would appear that net grain imports could have comprised a consequential portion of overall dietary energy for the North Korean population in the decade before Pyongyang's first emergency appeal for food aid.

Several aspects of North Korea's international cereal commerce, as reflected in mirror statistics, deserve special comment.

First, within the North Korean cereal import ledger, a bifurcated purchasing pattern is evident. On the one hand, the overwhelming bulk of cereal imports in any given year is accounted for by a relatively small number of transactions, typically exceeding 50,000 tons apiece. On the other hand, cereal deals in any given year are typified by a large number of small-volume sales—purchases of less than 20 tons of a particular product, and sometimes only a ton or two. These small-volume transactions generally appear to be delicacies or luxury items: "bread or biscuits," "cakes or pastries," even "diet infant cereal preparations." Although such a structure of purchases could be explained in various ways, it clearly would be consistent with a two-tier food procurement system, in which one set of decisions pertained to food supplies for the population as a whole, and another decision-making apparatus secured provisions for a small, but distinctly better-fed, elite circle.

Second, mirror statistics indicate that North Korea experienced an abrupt fall-off in cereal imports in the year 1994. For 1987–93, identified cereal imports totaled just under 5.7 million metric tons, or an average of about 800,000 metric tons per year. In 1994, by contrast, identified foodgrain imports averaged only 335,000 metric tons per year. The immediate cause of this dramatic drop was apparently a change in Chinese grain shipment patterns. In 1992 and 1993—that is to say, immediately after the collapse of the USSR—Chinese grain shipments to North Korea reportedly averaged nearly 800,000 tons. In 1994, they fell to under 280,000 tons. It is striking that reports of a North Korean food crisis which began to circulate in the international media in early 1995[27] should have followed so closely upon this drop-off in grain shipments from the country then serving as North Korea's principal cereal supplier. While these particulars open themselves to a number of somewhat different interpretations, they would certainly be consistent with the hypothesis that a proximate factor precipitating the current, officially acknowledged, DPRK "food problem" was China's reluctance to continue to finance major grain shipments to North Korea on "friendship" terms in 1994, the year of Kim Il Sung's death, and Kim Jong Il's presumptive accession to supreme power.

Finally, one should note that trends in the DPRK's balance of trade for cereals diverge sharply from those for its overall balance of trade in foodstuffs. The DPRK's foodgrain trade has shown a surplus in only three of the 24 years under consideration here, and over the 1980s and 1990s the nominal value of the average annual deficit has been gradually rising. As we have already seen, though, North Korea's overall trade in foods registered a slight cumulative nominal dollar *surplus* between 1972 and 1995. Moreover, net food trade surpluses were apparently registered in 15 of those 24 years—including the pre-crisis year 1994, and even the year 1995, which witnessed North Korea's first international appeal for humanitarian aid!

As it happens, the balance of trade pattern revealed by mirror statistics for North Korea's food products is utterly different from that of its non-food commodities. As shown in Figure 4.5, North Korea maintained a slight nominal cumulative surplus in its food trade—an estimated average of US$5 million a

Figure 4.5

DPRK Balance of Trade, Food vs. Non-food, 1972–1995

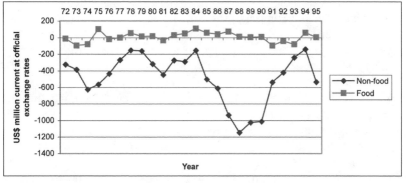

Source: Eberstadt, unpublished.

year. By contrast, between 1972 and 1995, Pyongyang appears to have run a deficit in its non-food accounts year in and year out: a deficit averaging over US$450 million a year in nominal dollars, and equaling fully two-fifths of its non-food exports for the period as a whole.

Such a dramatic contrast within North Korean trade accounts likely would not have persisted for so long unless it were somehow set deeply in policy. But what kind of policy choices (or priorities) could result in such a pattern? Without precluding other possibilities, we may note that the pattern is consistent with one particularly intriguing hypothesis: namely, that North Korea's food trade, unlike its trade of other merchandise, has been abidingly subject to a relatively strict administrative standard of financial self-sufficiency. Reviewing North Korea's food trade record, one might easily get the impression that North Korean trade authorities have operated on the understanding that they generally should spend no more on the purchase of foreign foodstuffs than foreigners were paying for North Korean food products. Such an approach, moreover, would appear quite consonant with Kim Jong Il's formulation about the importance of "solving the problem of food *on one's own through successful farming*" (emphasis added).[28]

If our interpretation here is correct, the DPRK would hardly be the only modern state to embrace some variant of a "food self-sufficiency" policy. In many parts of the world, food self-sufficiency continues to be an emotive, deeply-felt, and broadly supported political objective—particularly in East Asia, where *most* of the region's governments have adopted expensive measures to limit their dependence upon foreign food supplies.[29] It appears to be the case, furthermore, that DPRK trading officials have developed sophisticated tactics of caloric arbitrage in support of their ostensible food trade "strategy." Yet when all is said and done, the economic strategy itself suggested by DPRK's international food trade appears to be extraordinarily misguided.

Contemporary North Korea is an urbanized, industrialized country with a high ratio of population to arable land and a relatively short growing season. The DPRK's comparative advantage in international trade almost certainly does *not* lie in agriculture—any more than that of Japan or South Korea, and perhaps even less so. Yet, despite the protectionist colorations of their respective agricultural policies, Japan and South Korea both run substantial food trade deficits with the outside world, in effect financing their continuing industrialization with the help of cheap food from abroad.[30] By contrast, by maximizing its imports of intermediate and manufactured goods and minimizing its food trade deficit, North Korea looks as if it is attempting to use industry to finance the development of its domestic agriculture. This would be tantamount to an *anti*-industrialization policy! Such a paradoxical posture—all the more so for a state that has always accorded urgency to rapid industrial growth—hints at the enormous economic costs that may already have been exacted by North Korea's food trade strategy.

We must recognize that any portrait of the DPRK's international trade in foodstuffs and cereals which relies on the mirror statistics of its trading partners will have shortcomings. Today, one of the most important of these may be that the mirror statistics we have assembled pertain only to purportedly *commercial* flows, whereas North Korea has recently emerged as a major recipient of bilateral and international food *aid*.

The phenomenon is highlighted by Figure 4.6. By comparison with estimates from the FAO and the USDA, our mirror statistics appear to have tracked North Korea's foodgrain imports quite well between 1985 and 1994. However, in 1995 our mirror statistics suddenly produce much lower estimates than either the Food and Agriculture Organization (FAO) or the U.S. Department of Agriculture (USDA). The discrepancy is apparently due to the 650,000 in rice aid provided that year by Japan and South Korea, but not included within those countries' *trade* accounts.

At first glance, solving the food problem through flows of humanitarian aid from abroad would hardly seem to conform with Kim Il Sung's or Kim Jong Il's guidance on the subject. On the other hand, such an approach could possibly be squared by DPRK administrators with pre-existing food policy directives—if we have assessed those correctly.

Concessional food aid, after all, imposes no additional burdens upon the DPRK's foreign exchange account allocated to the food trade. Insofar as North Korea apparently sold slightly more food abroad in 1995 than it *paid for*, the

Figure 4.6
DPRK Cereal Imports, 1985–1995: FAO, Eberstadt, USDA

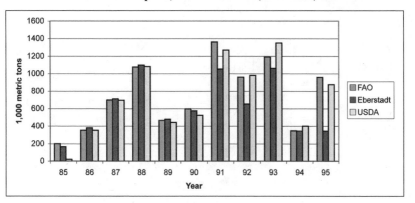

Sources: For FAO: UN FAO; for USDA: US FASC; for Eberstadt: Eberstadt, unpublished.

argument could be made that the DPRK was still *technically* self-sufficient in food in that crisis year!

We are, of course, speculating here, as this thinking may or may not reflect the actual internal logic of DPRK food policy. If it does reflect that internal logic, however, we should recognize that North Korea's recent turn toward utilizing food supplied for free by international aid organizations would represent not so much a departure from its food trade policies of the previous generation as a continuation of them. Indeed, the turn to international food aid could even be described as a tactic permitting their preservation.[31]

Energy

North Korea's reported patterns of energy trade are illustrated in Figures 4.7 through 4.9. Between 1972 and 1995, the nominal dollar value of reported energy product shipments into North Korea amounted to about US$6.3 billion, or about US$260 million a year. Over 95 percent of these identified flows originated in the USSR/Russia and in China for the period as a whole. After the collapse of Soviet-DPRK trade, China remained as the only self-identified source of North Korean foreign energy supplies of any significance, accounting for nearly 90 percent of total identified DPRK energy imports.

Although China was probably a major source of energy supplies for North Korea in the period before 1982, Beijing only began providing detailed breakdowns of her international trade that year. For this reason, it is possible to

Figure 4.7

DPRK Imports of Energy by Source, 1972–1995

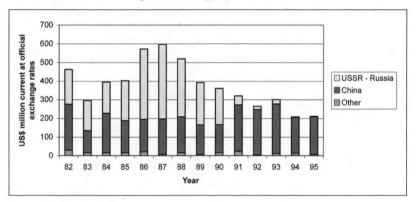

Source: Eberstadt, unpublished.

Figure 4.8

DPRK Energy Exports by Destination, 1972–1995

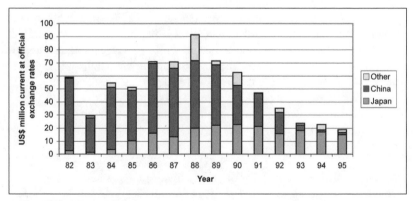

Source: Eberstadt, unpublished.

obtain a relatively complete picture of North Korea's international energy trade through only by using mirror statistics for the years 1982–95. Those data, however, depict a massive disruption in DPRK energy supplies, brought on by the final crisis of the Soviet state. Between 1982 and 1990, North Korea's estimated energy imports averaged almost US$450 million a year. For 1991–95, they averaged about US$250 million a year—two-fifths less, in nominal dol-

Figure 4.9
DPRK Balance of Trade in Energy, 1982–1995

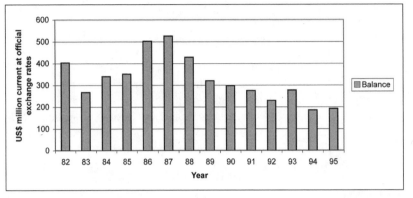

Source: Eberstadt, unpublished.

lar terms. The highpoint for North Korean energy imports, in nominal dollar terms, was apparently the period 1986–88, when these flows exceeded US$560 million a year. Against that benchmark, the nominal value of reported energy imports in the early 1990s was down by over one-half.

North Korea's reported energy exports for 1972–95 totaled US$742 million: an average of about US$30 million a year for the period as a whole, and about US$50 million a year for 1982–95 (the years in which energy trade with China are reported). Roughly three-fifths (61 percent) of the nominal value of North Korean energy exports went to China. Just under a third (31 percent) went to Japan. Between 1982 and 1990, DPRK energy exports, as identified, averaged about US$63 million a year. For 1991–95 they averaged under US$30 million a year.

North Korea's identified balance-of-trade deficit with respect to energy products has declined substantially since the collapse of the USSR. In the years 1982–90, North Korea managed to "achieve" a balance-of-trade deficit in energy products with its reporting trade partners which averaged about US$380 million a year. In 1991–95, that balance-of-trade deficit was estimated at about US$230 million—a nominal drop of two-fifths.

Perhaps counterintuitively, the implications for North Korea of the narrowing trade deficit illustrated in Figure 4.9 are adverse. As a country entirely dependent upon foreign supplies for some of the fuels it must use domestically, the trends in Figure 4.9 depict a sudden sharp squeeze on North Korea's "economic lifeline," to paraphrase Kim Jong Il. Yet there is also a measure of ambiguity in it, because Figure 4.9 reflects the net current dollar value for a variety of energy products, and because the cost of those energy products have been influenced both by the fluctuations of prices on the international fuel markets and the idiosyncracies of friendship pricing mechanisms.

A more precise impression of the economic impact of the DPRK's energy trade problems would be conveyed by examining trends in physical supply of fuel, disaggregating by distinct types of energy products. As it happens, mirror statistics permit us to track, with whatever degree of accuracy, the metric tonnage of coal, coke, oil, and refined oil products that North Korea's trade partners were selling, and purchasing from, Pyongyang during the decade 1986–1995.[32] (See Figures 4.10–4.12.)

According to our mirror statistics, North Korea's imports of crude oil and petroleum products in 1994–95 averaged 1 million tons a year—less than half the 2.2 million tons a year reported in 1986–87. The collapse in identified petro-product imports is due principally to the collapse of Soviet/Russian shipments, which plummeted from 1,000,000 tons in 1986 to a mere 19,000 tons in 1995. Significantly, though, China's reported oil and oil product exports to North Korea also declined over that decade, albeit only gradually.

Reported imports of coking coal (coke) appear to have fallen even more steeply: from about 330,000 tons in 1986 to under 100,000 tons in 1995. In the mid and late 1980s, the USSR had been North Korea's main supplier of coke. But in 1989, the Soviet Union's coke exports to the DPRK began to drop, and with the dissolution of the USSR, coke shipments by Moscow to Pyongyang effectively ceased.

Figure 4.10
DPRK Imports of Oil and Oil Products, 1986–1995

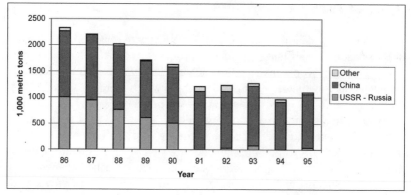

Source: Eberstadt, unpublished.

Figure 4.11
DPRK Imports of Coking Coal: 1986–1995

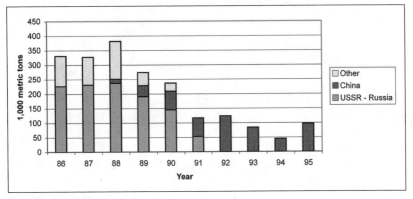

Source: Eberstadt, unpublished.

Figure 4.12
DPRK Trade in Coal: 1986–1995

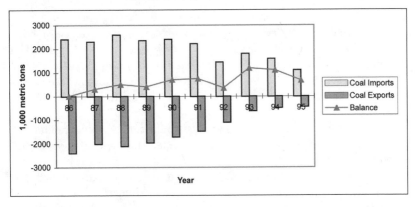

Source: Eberstadt, unpublished.

Trends in North Korea's coal trade are more complex, and perhaps more unexpected. In the 1980s, North Korea was reportedly importing about 2.4 million tons of coal a year (mainly from China). By 1995, its coal imports were reportedly down to 1.1 million tons. But North Korea was also a coal *exporter* over this period. In fact, in 1986 the DPRK reportedly *exported* about 2.4 million tons of coal.[33] Between 1986 and 1995, however, North Korea dramatically slashed its coal exports, almost all of which had been heading to China. By 1995, its coal exports totaled barely 400,000 tons. Consequently, North Korea's net imports of coal appear actually to have *risen* during its recent economic slump, Whereas these averaged under 400,000 tons a year between 1986 and 1990, they averaged over 750,000 tons in the years 1991–1995!

Figures 4.10 to 4.12 provide hints of possibly differentiated economic consequences from North Korea's various shortages of foreign fuels. The drop in petro-product imports, for example, would obviously constrain the use of petroleum powered motors—e.g., the road transport system. Less obviously, it would also limit the possibility of producing some petroleum-intensive agricultural inputs, such as fertilizer and pesticides. A drop in the availability of coking coal, used principally in metallurgy, could create bottlenecks for North Korea's iron and steel industries, and thus for other sectors whose demand for iron and steel is high.

On the other hand, North Korea's coal trade trends would not appear to augur especially ill for the DPRK economy. For one thing, net imports of coal appear to have risen between the 1980s and the 1990s. For another, North Korea's trade in coal is thought to be quite small in relation to its level of domestic coal production.[34]

If foreign observers are correct, the current troubles with North Korea's coal supplies relate less to the country's trade in coal *per se* than to sharp drops in its own coal output. The fall-off in North Korea's coal production, however, may itself be caused in part by other energy shortages, such as a lack of diesel fuel for mining equipment, to cite one possible example. In short, it is possible that constraints imposed by North Korea's fuel trade may have an economic impact entirely out of proportion to their size in a notional DPRK "energy balance sheet."

Although it has, of course, reaffirmed the familiar call for a more careful husbanding of energy resources within its "independent national economy,"[35] much of Pyongyang's effort in recent years to solve the fuel and power problems successfully seems to have focused instead on the international arena, more specifically, on negotiations with foreign governments for concessional supplies of coal and oil. By outward indications, the DPRK's diplomats have pursued that objective with considerable skill, and no small success. For example, according to press accounts in the summer of 1996, Beijing agreed to provide North Korea with annual shipments of 1.3 million tons of oil and 2.5 million tons of coal for the next five years—all *gratis*.[36] Further, under the terms of the Agreed Framework it signed with Washington in October 1994, North Korea obtained heavy crude oil *free of charge* through the Korean Peninsula Energy Development Organization (KEDO). As Pyongyang itself has pointed out, "the U.S. and KEDO . . . delivered a total of 650,000 tons of heavy oil" to

North Korea in the two years immediately subsequent to the signing of that document.[37] And under the terms of that accord, Pyongyang stood to gain additional amounts of free oil—up to 500,000 a year—until the reactors under construction in North Korea by KEDO became operational. But the Agreed Framework largely broke down in 2003, cutting off the DPRK's free supply of oil[38] and KEDO itself was officially disbanded in June 2006.[39]

If these reports about Chinese commitments had proved accurate, and if the KEDO schedules had actually been fulfilled, North Korea's "energy aid diplomacy" would have managed effectively to reverse the sharp drop-off in foreign fuel which seems to have been so damaging to the DPRK economy in the early 1990s. Yet even if North Korea's quest for energy aid had been completely successful, it would only have provided a limited measure of relief to an already badly battered economic system. Taken together, after all, the supplies of Chinese fuel and the deliveries by KEDO would not quite have brought the DPRK's levels of coal, coke, and petro-product imports back to the *status quo ante* of the late 1980s, a time at which the DPRK economy may already have begun to stagnate, if not actually decline.[40]

Concluding Observations

The mirror statistics assembled here cannot speak to many of the pressing questions foreign observers are currently raising about North Korea's food, energy, and transport sectors. For example, mirror statistics can tell us nothing about the manner in which the DPRK transportation sector divides its resources between the competing claims of military and civilian customers. They can provide no specific insight into the current utilization levels of specific energy-intensive factories, much less various branches of North Korean industry. Perhaps most importantly at this particular time, they can offer us no concrete impressions of the severity of the country's hunger problem.

Yet these mirror statistics do offer a relatively detailed, and internally consistent, glimpse of conditions within the North Korean economy in each of these areas. What they reveal is arresting: the North Korean economy has been in the grip of a tightening vise since at least the mid-1980s—by some indications, perhaps even earlier. That vise, however, is of Pyongyang's own design. The pressures now afflicting North Korean transport, energy, and food can be seen through mirror statistics to derive in large measure from official policies— policies distinctively formulated, and unremittingly implemented.

North Korea's current transport problem, for example, looks to be the entirely predictable culmination of a full generation of stubborn skimping on investment in the country's motor vehicle capabilities. Similarly, the DPRK's long and determined embrace of a particularly eccentric version of food self-sufficiency would appear to have all but guaranteed that the North Korean people would eventually face a food crisis. North Korea's current shortages of imported fuels, for their part, are inextricably linked to a defining and characteristic of North Korea's policy of economic self-reliance, that is, its exceptionally weak performance over the past quarter century in generating export revenues. After all, the immediate reason that North Korea's current and acute energy and food troubles should be "problems" at all is simply that the DPRK's extraordinarily limited capability precludes it from purchasing the imports it now so desperately needs, even though those requirements appear modest by any contemporary international measure.

At the moment, as we have seen, Pyongyang appears to be pursuing an "aid-based" solution to its food and energy crises. For the DPRK's leadership, such an approach to domestic economic problems is surely a familiar one. In fact, for nearly half a century North Korean external policy has steadily worked at extracting concessional resources from Big Powers, often with masterful results.

The current aid-oriented approach to North Korea's food and fuel problems can be critiqued as pure temporizing, as the pursuit of mere tactical remedies for deep-seated structural problems, or as an attempted substitute for a more thoroughgoing overhaul of the state's economic policies. Yet, from the vantage point of North Korea's leadership, this may be the real allure of the current approach.

Contemporary North Korea's "mendicant" method of dealing with its conjoint economic crises, one may note, is eerily reminiscent of South Korea's "aid-maximizing" gambits in an earlier era.[41] South Korea, of course, decisively rejected that approach as inimical to its long-term economic development, but not until a military coup had replaced a governing circle that was steeped in the art of aid maximization, and tremendously confident of its talents in that domain. Whether North Korea can embrace a fundamentally new international economic orientation without a new cast of economic policymakers remains to be seen.

Notes

1. "Mirror statistics" have been used routinely over the course of this century to assess the economic performance of states which deliberately restricted outside access to data on local economic conditions; in earlier generations, for example, specialists relied heavily upon such mirror statistics in analyzing the economies of Stalin's USSR and Mao's China; for the DPRK, two the early western attempts to reconstruct and analyze trade patterns through mirror statistics were made by Chung Joseph Sang-hoon (1974) and Kim Youn-Soo (1979); perhaps the most comprehensive analysis of DPRK mirror statistics to date may be that by Choi Soo-young (1991); Soviet and Russian analysts also seem to have used mirror statistics to follow North Korean economic affairs, and perhaps the most interesting of these studies is by Natalya Bazhanova (1993).

2. Kim, Il Sung, 1968, 250–275.
3. Chung, 1983, p. 178.
4. Kim, Jong Il, 1982, p. 47.
5. For contemporary accounts of Pyongyang's initial 1995 appeal for emergency humanitarian relief, see Reid (1995), p. A22, Kristof (1995), p. 16, and Sullivan (1995), p. A16.
6. United Nations, 1997.
7. USSR Ministry of Foreign Economic Relations.
8. Rubin, 1996.
9. Harbaugh et al., 1995.
10. Republic of Korea Ministry of National Unification.
11. Most importantly, reports by the Riyadh government of a thriving Saudi-DPRK commerce between 1974 and 1982, and reports by the Mexican government of a booming Mexican-DPRK trade in 1994 and 1995.
12. Some semantic confusion may attend our use of the term "OECD members." For example, the Republic of Korea joined OECD in 1996, as did Hungary and Poland; the Czech Republic joined in 1995, Mexico in 1994, and Turkey has been in the OECD since its inception in 1961; we should emphasize that we are *not* referring to *any* of these countries when we speak of OECD members in this chapter.

    In our taxonomy, Turkey and Mexico are included in the "third world"; Hungary, Poland, the Czech Republic (and its predecessor state) are included within "European CMEA/Eastern Europe," while South Korea's trade with the North is dealt with as a special and separate ledger item; when we speak of OECD members in this study, we are really referring to the earlier OECD membership roster-and then only to the "advanced Western" countries within it: i.e., Japan plus North America, Western Europe, Australia, and New Zealand.
13. See USSR, 1990, p. 224; the only itemized North Korean export of "transport vehicles and equipment" to the USSR that year was for "ships and ship equipment," valued at just under 3 million rubles-barely US$5 million at official exchange rates at the time.
14. If the nominal ruble price of trucks exported to the DPRK rose between 1977–85 and 1972–76, the total would have been correspondingly lower.
15. Namkoong, 1995, pp. 1–43; an interesting description of DPRK transportation infrastructure may also be found in Kim, 1997, pp. 121–133.
16. North Korea produces no non-military automobiles to speak of; its capabilities for producing buses and trucks are thought by foreign governments never to have exceeded 20,000 a year (see USCIA, 1990 ed., p. 140); DPRK also reportedly produces locomotives and rail cars for domestic use, but not in large quantities.
17. For North Korean estimates, see Chung, 1994, p. 147; for Chinese estimates, PRC State Statistical Bureau, 1995, p. 480; other estimates are derived from United Nations, 1994, tables 8 and 62.
18. Eberstadt and Banister, 1992.
19. Kim, 1972, p. 271, footnote 3.
20. For DPRK estimates, see Chapter 3 on DPRK international trade in capital goods; global figures are derived from United Nations *International Trade Statistics Yearbook*, various editions.
21. See Chapter 3, footnote 14.
22. For example, *FBIS*-EAS-1997-176.

23. Some reports in the late 1990s suggested that Pyongyang was considering what would have amounted to major new expenditures on foreign transport equipment to relieve the squeeze on its international transportation system; for example, rumors in the Russian press talked of a possible North Korean purchase of ten large Soviet passenger jets at an implied cost of over US$250 million; see *FBIS*-SOV-1997-337; that talk, however, was never followed by action.

24. Choi, 1991, pp. 227–232, footnote 2.

25. For some heroic labors toward this goal, see Lee, Hy-Sang. (1994) and Smith (1997).

26. Very roughly: if we assume that net imports amounted to 0.6 million tons per year, that North Korea's population averaged 20 million a year, and that each gram of grain contained 4 kcal of nutritive energy, we arrive at a figure of 120,000 kcal/person/year of food energy through net grain imports-or about 330 kcal/person/day.

27. See, for example, *FBIS*-EAS-1995-049, -1995-079, and -1995-081, and Schmetzer, 1995, p. 8.

28. Kim 1982, p. 47, footnote 5.

29. See Timmer, 1993.

30. Between 1992 and 1995, the Republic of Korea's annual food trade deficit averaged US$2.4 billion a year, while that of Japan averaged US$22.7 billion a year; derived from United Nations, 1995.

31. One recent DPRK commentary would appear to provide some corroboration for our speculations about Pyongyang's view of the role of food aid in relation to overall DPRK agricultural policy; the broadcast in question severely criticized a USDA official who had reportedly argued that "the only way for North Korea to solve the food problem is to stop efforts for self-sustenance in food"; the reaction is worth quoting at some length: "Our food shortage . . . has nothing to do with the efforts for self-sustenance in food. Self-sustenance is a just agricultural policy pursued by the Workers' Party of Korea consistently. By this policy, our agriculture has developed to be an independent domain capable of fully supplying the people with food. *Self-sustenance . . ., which is one of the two mainstays of the independent national economy, is the only way of solving the food problem*" (emphasis added); *FBIS*-EAS-1997-179.

32. How accurate are the trends outlined in Figures 10 to 12? One way to gauge their accuracy is by comparing them against estimates from other sources; JETO (the quasi-official Japan Trade Research Organization) has prepared estimates of North Korean coal and coke imports for the years 1989–92; see Lee, Chong-sik, 1994, pp. 6–12; our estimates for those same years track closely, but are actually slightly higher in each instance, suggesting perhaps that we have achieved somewhat more complete coverage; estimates of DPRK oil imports for 1986–95, for their part, have been published by both the International Energy Agency (IEA) and the ROK National Unification Board (NUB); see International Energy Agency, 1997, and Smith, 1997, footnote 27; our estimates of DPRK oil imports are consistently higher than the corresponding figures published by the IEA; on the other hand, the NUB estimates are always higher than ours, and not infrequently much higher; for example, for the period 1987–90 the discrepancy amounts to over one million tons a year; almost all of that discrepancy involves purported oil shipments by Middle Eastern states (principally, Iran) which do not provide detailed data on their international commerce; the results from these "sensitivity checks" seem quite plausible at face value; given the inherent differences between the international coal trade and

the international oil trade, it would be reasonable to expect our data on North Korea's coal and coke imports to be the more complete; on the other hand, if the NUB's estimates are roughly accurate, the drop in DPRK oil imports between the mid-1980s and the mid-1990s would be even more pronounced than our Figure 4.10 suggests.

33. According to Chung (1994, footnote 19), North Korea imports mainly bituminous coal and exports mainly anthracite coal.
34. Chang, 1994; von Hippel and Hayes,1997; if correct, conjectural calculations would suggest that North Korea's coal-based energy supply in 1996 was 45 percent lower than in 1990, and that seven-eighths of that reduction was due to the drop in domestic coal production; even if these "estimates" are not excessively precise, their broad implications are probably sound.
35. See, inter alia, *FBIS*-EAS-1996-041.
36. *FBIS*-EAS-1996-139.
37. *FBIS*-TAC-1996 (21 November).
38. For details, see Medeiros, 1995, p. 29.
39. Lee, 2006.
40. For details, see Eberstadt, 1995.
41. For a poignant reminder of that era in South Korea, see Pyong, 1964.

References

Bazhanova, Natalya Ye. 1993. *Vneschneekonomicheskie Sviaze KNDR* (Tr. Foreign Economic Relations of the DPRK). Moscow: Nauka.

Chang, Yong-sik. 1994. *Pukhan ui Enoji Kyongje*. (Tr. *North Korea's Energy Economy*.) Seoul: Korea Development Institute.

Choi, Soo-young. 1991. "North Korean Trade 1946–1988: Structure and Performance." Northeastern University, Unpublished doctoral dissertation.

Chung, Joseph S. 1974. *The North Korean Economy: Structure and Development*. Stanford, CA: Hoover Institution Press.

———. 1994. "The Economy." Andrea Matles Savada, ed. *North Korea: A Country Study*. Washington, DC: Library of Congress, Federal Research Division.

———. 1983. "Economic Planning in North Korea." In Robert A. Scalapino and Jun-yop Kim, eds. *North Korea Today: Strategic Issues*. Berkeley, CA: University of California Institute of East Asian Studies.

Eberstadt, Nicholas. 1993. North Korea's Interlocked Economic Crises: Some Indications from "Mirror Statistics." *Analysis* 4(3), September 1993.

———. 1995. *Korea Approaches Reunification*. Armonk, NY: M.E. Sharpe.

———. 1997. "The DPRK as an Economic System Under Severe Multiple Stresses: Analogies and Lessons from the Historic and Recent Past." *Communist Economies and Economic Transformation* 9(2).

———. North Korea International Commercial Trade Data Base, unpublished.

Eberstadt, Nicholas and Judith Banister. 1992. *The Population of North Korea*. Berkeley, CA: University of California Institute of East Asian Studies.

FBIS-East Asia (EAS) 1995-081. (14 November): reprint from *Choson Ilbo*, 27 April 1995, p. 3, translated as "'Serious' Food Shortage in North Korea Revealed."

——— 1995-079. (14 November): reprint from *Chungang Ilbo*, 24 April 1995, p. 10, translated as "Daily Speculates on DPRK 'Food Crisis.'"

———— 1995-049. (18 November): reprint from *Sankei Shimbun*, 10 March 1995, p. 1, translated as "LDP Studying Plan to Send Rice to DPRK."

———— 1996-041. (2 March): reprint from *Nodong Sinmun* 26 January 1996, p. 3, translated as "DPRK Treatise on Values of Increased Production, Conservation."

———— 1996-139. (18 July): reprint from *Yonhap*, 18 July 1996, reprinted as "ROK: PRC Agrees to Grain, Oil, Coal Aid to DPRK For 5 Years."

———— 1997-176. (27 June): reprint from *The Korea Herald*, 26 June 1997, as "South Korea: MNU Reports ROK Import Of DPRK Scrap Steel Increased In May."

———— 1997-179. (1 July): reprint of KCNA Pyongyang, broadcast 28 June 1997, as "North Korea: KCNA Criticizes Comments of U.S. Agricultural Expert."

FBIS-SOV-1997-337. (12 December): reprint from Interfax, 2 December 1997.

FBIS-TAC. 1996 (21 November): reprint from Pyongyang KCNA broadcast, 1 November 1996, as "DPRK: U.S. Affirms Heavy Oil Delivery Despite Outside Influence."

Harbaugh, Christina W., Marc Rubin and Loraine A. West. 1995. "China's Trade with the DPRK, 1950–1994." Washington, DC: U.S. Bureau of the Census, International Programs Center, March. Unpublished;

International Energy Agency. 1997. *Energy Statistics and Balances of Non-OECD Countries*. Paris: OECD/AEI. Various editions.

Kim Chong-min. 1997. "North Korea: Defector Describes Military Roads." Translation from *Pukhan*, November. FBIS-East Asia-97-364. 1 January 1998.

Kim, Il Sung. 1972. "On Relieving the Strain on Transport." Speech delivered 16 November 1968. Reprinted in *Selected Works* 5. Pyongyang: Foreign Languages Publishing House.

Kim, Jong Il. 1982. *On the Juche Idea*. Pyongyang: Foreign Languages Publishing House.

Kim, Youn-Soo, ed. 1977. *The Economy of the Korean Democratic People's Republic, 1945–1977*. Kiel: German Korea Studies Group.

Kristof, Nicholas D. 1995. "Korean Rice Aid is Largely Feeding Tensions." *New York Times*. 20 August.

Lee, Chong-sik. 1994. "The Political Economy of North Korea." NBR *Analysis* 5(2).

Lee, Hy-Sang. 1994. "Supply and Demand for Grains in North Korea: A Historical Movement Model for 1966–1993." *Korea and World Affairs* 18(3):509–52.

Lee, Joo-hee. 2006. "KEDO ends reactor project in N. Korea." *Korea Herald*. 2 June.

Medeiros, Evan S. 1995. "KEDO Takes First Steps to Fulfill Nuclear Accord with North Korea." *Arms Control Today* 25(7).

Namkoong, Young. 1995. "A Comparative Study on North and South Korean Economic Capability." *Journal of East Asian Affairs* 9(1):1–43.

People's Republic of China (PRC) State Statistical Bureau. 1995. *China Statistical Yearbook 1995*. Beijing: China Statistical Publishing House.

Pyong, Choon Hahm. 1964. "Korea's 'Mendicant Mentality'? A Criticism of US Policy." *Foreign Affairs* 43(1).

Reid, T.R. 1995. "North Koreans Ask Japan for Emergency Rice." *Washington Post*. 27 May.

Republic of Korea Ministry of National Unification (ROK MOU). Various issues. *Nambuk Kyoryu Hyomnyok Tonghyang* (Tr. Monthly North-South Exchange and Cooperation Trends). Seoul.

Rubin, Marc. 1996. "North Korea's Trade with the USSR and Russia, 1972–1995." Washington, DC: U.S. Bureau of the Census, International Programs Center. November. Unpublished.

Schmetzer, Uli. 1995. "Acute Food Shortage Pinches N. Koreans." *Chicago Tribune*. 27 May.

Smith, Heather. 1997. "The North Korean Economy: Collapse, Stasis, or Reform?" Canberra: Australian National University, Research School of Pacific and Asian Studies. February. Unpublished.

Sullivan, Kevin. 1995. "North Korea Makes Rare Plea After Floods Devastate Country." *Washington Post*. 22 September. p. A16.

Timmer, C. Peter. 1993. "Rural Bias in the East and South-East Asian Rice Economy: Indonesia in Comparative Perspective." *Journal of Development Studies* 29(4): 149–76.

United Nations. 1994. *UN Statistical Yearbook 1994*. New York: UN Department for Economic and Social Information and Policy Analysis, Statistical Division.

———. 1995. *International Trade Statistics Yearbook 1995*. New York: UN Department for Social Information and Policy Analysis, Statistical Division.

———. Various years. *International Trade Statistics Yearbook*. New York: UN Department for Social Information and Policy Analysis, Statistical Division.

———. 1997. International Commodity Trade Statistics Database. Specially Requested Diskette. Processed 1997.

———. Statistical Database. New York: UN FAO.

United States Central Intelligence Agency. 1990. *Handbook of International Economic Statistics*. Washington, DC: CIA.

———. Foreign Agricultural Service Commodities and Products database (US FASC). Available at: http://www.fas.usda.gov/data.asp

USSR Ministry of Foreign Economic Relations. Various editions. *Vneshnaya Torgovlya SSSR* (Tr. Foreign Trade of the USSR). Moscow. Goskomstat.

———. 1990. Various editions. *Vneshnie Ekonomicheskie Sviazi SSSR* (Tr. Foreign Economic Relations of the USSR). Moscow: Goskomstat

Von Hippel, David F. and Peter Hayes. 1997. "DPRK Energy Sector: Current Status and Scenarios for 2000 and 2005." Berkeley, CA: Nautilus Institute for Security and Sustainable Development. September. Unpublished.

5

Socioeconomic Development in Divided Korea: A Tale of Two "Strategies"*

Reunification has been a cherished and abiding goal for many Koreans on both sides of the "demilitarized zone" that separates them. The milestone June 2000 summit in Pyongyang between then President Kim Dae Jung of the Republic of Korea (ROK, or South Korea) and chief Kim Jong Il of the Democratic People's Republic of Korea (DPRK, or North Korea)—the first meeting between the top leaders of divided Korea since the peninsula's partition in August 1945—revived these hopes and gave them dramatic stimulus. In the afterglow of this conciliatory get-together between heads of state—still officially at war—there was extensive speculation in East Asia—and especially in South Korea—about the sorts of diplomatic formulas that might permit North and South Korea to move toward a peace treaty to finally end the Korean War, and thereafter, to deepen the economic and political integration that would finally culminate in peaceful and voluntary reunification. But if one is to contemplate the prospect of an eventual Korean unification, one must consider not only the policies and negotiating frameworks that might one day bring the Korean people back together, but also the disparities in socioeconomic development that separate them today.

Indeed, to even approach discussion of an eventual reintegration or reunification of the two Koreas in a practical fashion, it is absolutely essential to have some sense of the starting points for this prospective journey. We need to know concretely, in other words, about social and economic conditions in both parts of Korea, so that we may have some presentiment of the magnitude and nature

---

*This chapter was originally presented on 23 June 2000 as a paper at the conference "Constitutional, Legal and Economic Preparations for Korean Unification," sponsored by the Korean Economic Research Institute and the Yonsei University Institute for Korean Unification Studies, Seoul, Republic of Korea; a somewhat abridged version appeared in *Asian Survey* XL(6), in 2000.

of the gaps that will have to be bridged and the adjustments that will have to be accommodated, in order for the divided nation to congeal.

Alas, it is extraordinarily difficult today to offer a reliable socioeconomic comparison of North and South Korea. The reason, quite simply, is that North Korean conditions are not readily or easily quantified. Two problems, one general, the other quite particular, account for this.

The general problem is the dilemma of valuing output produced by a Soviet-type economy (STE)[1] in market terms. Although Western economists developed a variety of techniques and devices for representing the results from centrally-planned economies in a market-style framework,[2] none of these attempts could solve the conundrum of how to offer a common unit of measurement for systems with such fundamentally different approaches to pricing and resource allocation.[3]

This basic methodological predicament has continually confounded attempts to place the performance of communist economies in comparative international perspective. During the Cold War, the U.S. government devoted considerable resources to its effort to describe and measure trends in the Soviet economy. In fact, that undertaking may well have been the largest social science research project ever mounted.[4] Yet despite the great financial and intellectual investment in that project, its findings in retrospect appear in a number of respects to have been seriously off the mark. Such indicators as output per capita, levels of per capita consumption, and rates of economic growth may have been consistently overestimated. (An analogous overestimation of a communist system's economic performance can be seen in the case of the German Democratic Republic, the severity of whose economic troubles only became generally apparent to Western specialists after the 1989 breach of the Berlin Wall.)[5]

The second and more particular problem is the remarkable dearth of reliable social and economic information about North Korea today. Since the early 1960s, the government of the DPRK has steadily enforced a strict "statistical blackout" on conditions within that country. The North Korean state's campaign to suppress all such information is reminiscent of earlier campaigns in Stalin's USSR and Mao's China, but Pyongyang's campaign has lasted far longer than those of any communist precursor.

Closed though they were before the downfall of their communist governments, Soviet bloc countries in the 1980s nonetheless regularly published a variety of statistical compendia.[6] By contrast, the DPRK has *never* published an official statistical compendium of any sort on a regular basis![7] To make matters worse, some of the few data the DPRK has released have clearly been deliberately distorted or falsified. In fact, the actual ability of the DPRK Central Bureau of Statistics to compile and prepare accurate data remains as yet an open question.[8] Under such circumstances, the question of "what we know and how we know it" figures centrally in any assessment of North Korean social and economic conditions. In the case of North Korea, we cannot simply take "data" as given. Although a number of institutions—most importantly, the Central Intelligence Agency (CIA) in the United States and the ROK Ministry of National Unification (formerly MNU, now MOU), the Korea Development Institute (KDI) and the Bank of Korea (BOK)—analyze and attempt to quantify North Korea's economic performance, the quality and reliability of their estimates are inescapably limited by the general and particular problems to which we have already alluded.[9]

If we are to attempt a meaningful comparison of socioeconomic conditions in North and South Korea, and at the same time avoid the pitfalls of false precision, we must search indicators that are both inherently reliable and subject to a minimum of interpretive ambiguity. Two kinds of data suggest themselves for our purposes. The first are demographic data collected by the DPRK Central Bureau of Statistics;[10] these bear directly upon social conditions, and can shed some light on economic conditions as well. The second are so-called "mirror statistics" on North Korea's foreign trade, as reported by the DPRK's trading partners. These quantify a consequential component of the North Korean economy (the external sector) and in addition provide a window on the domestic DPRK economy.[11]

Some additional, and intriguing, bits of statistical data pertaining to North Korea's socioeconomic situation have also become available over the course of the late 1990s. These include data that DPRK officials provided to the International Monetary Fund (IMF) on trends in national economic output and the national budget,[12] and results of an independent nutritional survey conducted in the DPRK under the auspices of the UN World Food Programme (WFP), UNICEF and the European Union (EU) in late 1998.[13] A number of questions may be raised about these figures, even upon initial inspection, but they are, nevertheless, worth reviewing. The data given to the IMG represents the first official report of North Korean national accounts data in a Western-style framework. The WFP nutritional survey provides a clearer impression of the impact of the terrible hunger crisis that apparently erupted in the DPRK in the mid-1990s.

Population

The starting point for a socioeconomic comparison of divided Korea is population size and composition. Table 1 presents some basic indicators on this, drawn from South Korea's statistical system and from the North Korean population census for year end 1993.[14]

According to official data for 1993, the DPRK's population was about 21 million, while that of South Korea, by contrast, was roughly 44 million.

(Thus, whereas the ratio of West to East Germans at the moment of unification was about 4:1, the ratio of South to North Koreans is roughly 2:1.) South Korea looks to be much more densely populated than North Korea, and also appears to have a significantly higher ratio of males to females in its population—possibly due, in part, to the lingering effects of the Korean War, in which the North suffered even more severely than the South.

In Germany in the mid-1990s, the median population age was about 40.[15] To judge by Table 5.1, in the mid-1990s South Korea's population was much younger, with a median age of about 31. The population of North Korea was younger still, with a median age officially represented at just under 27. Children under 15 years of age accounted for a higher share of the total population in the DPRK than the ROK. For the population 65 years of age or more, the share was slightly larger in the South than in the North. People between the ages of 15 and 65—sometimes described as the "economically active cohort"—accounted for a somewhat greater share of the total population in South Korea than in North Korea in the early 1990s.

According to official data, household size averaged about 4.7 persons in the DPRK in the early 1990s. In South Korea, it averaged about 3.3. (By way of comparison, average household size in Germany was under 2.3 in the early 1990s.[16]) In general, smaller household size reflects 1) lower fertility levels and

Table 5.1
Comparative Demographic Indicators from Official Data: DPRK and ROK, 1993

	DPRK	ROK
Population (millions)	21.2	44.2
Area (thousands sq. km.)	122.8	99.3
Population density (persons per sq. km.)	173	445
Sex ratio (males per 100 females)	94.9	101.3
Median age (years)	27	31[1]
Population aged 0–14 (percent)	27.9	23.2[1]
Population aged 15–64 (percent)	66.6	70.7[1]
Population aged 65 and older (percent)	5.5	6.1[1]
Crude birth rate (births per 1,000 pop.)	19.9	16.5
Crude death rate (deaths per 1,000 pop.)	4.9	5.5
Rate of natural increase (per 1,000 pop.)	13.9	11.1
Average household size (persons)	4.7	3.3[1]

Notes: DPRK census data are for year-end 1993; ROK census data are for midyear. [1] = 1995.

Sources: Derived from DPRK CBS, 1995; ROK NSO, *Social Indicators in Korea 1995*; ROK NSO, 1996.

2) the increased ability or disposition of persons to live alone, in independent one-person households. Evidently, these "modern" trends affect South Korea rather more strongly than North Korea.

In both North and South Korea, population growth in the early 1990s was due entirely to natural increase, that is, the excess of births over deaths. According to official data, the rate of natural increase in 1993 was slightly higher in the DPRK than in the ROK (1.4 percent a year vs. 1.1 percent a year). Between the early 1960s and the early 1990s, both Koreas had made the transition from high- to low-fertility regimens. In the early 1960s, the total fertility rate (births per woman per lifetime, or TFR) was about six in both North and South Korea. South Korea's fertility level has been below replacement since the mid-1980s, and is currently about 1.7.[17] As for the DPRK, by 1993, to judge by census data, North Korea's TFR was down to about 2.2—just barely above replacement.

As it happens, the relatively detailed data for North Korea that are highlighted in Table 5.1 describe the country immediately before a fateful demographic shock. About a year and a half after the official North Korean population census, Pyongyang announced that the country had been beset by severe food shortages, and launched an official appeal for emergency humanitarian food aid.[18] That appeal, in various guises, continues to this writing, suggesting that a desperate affliction still stalks the country. As mentioned earlier in Chapter 2, as of this writing, it is impossible to provide an accurate assessment of the demographic impact of North Korea's nutritional problems, despite the millions of tons of emergency food assistance given to North Korea since 1995 by international relief agencies, Pyongyang has refuses to provide those same agencies with the detailed official demographic data that could help to specify the precise dimensions of this humanitarian crisis.

If North Korea's ongoing food crisis were sufficiently dire, it could by now have affected both the size and the composition of the DPRK's population. For one thing, serious food shortages usually depress local fertility sharply. (In the years immediately following the Great Leap Forward, for example, fertility levels in China are thought to have dropped by half or more.[19]) Furthermore, hunger crises typically exact a disproportionate mortality toll upon the old and the very young. Finally, famine-like situations can induce large movements of people, even in the face of hardship and repression, as occurred in late 1999, when it was reported that many North Koreans—perhaps as many as several hundred thousand—had crossed into China to forage and seek sustenance.[20]

Thus, due to the ongoing food crisis, North Korea's population profile at the end of the 1990s may well have looked rather different from the outlines projected for it earlier in the decade. For example, demographic projections before the food crisis anticipated an increase in DPRK population of over 3 million persons (of about 15 percent) between midyear 1990 and midyear 1998.[21] The 10th DPRK Supreme People's Assembly (SPA), however, impaneled exactly the same number of delegates (687) for its September 1998 deliberations as had been inducted for the 9th SPA in April 1990. Since the DPRK constitution stipulates that one SPA delegate is required for every 30,000 population, these SPA delegate totals might seem to imply that the country's population was no larger in 1998 than it had been eight years earlier.[22]

Of course, this is only speculation, as the stagnant vote total might equally well have had an entirely different, internal, non-demographic rationale. Suffice it simply to observe that the advent of the hunger crises has suddenly, and grimly, broadened the range of plausible population profiles for contemporary North Korea, and only new information from Pyongyang will permit a reliable narrowing of that range.

Mortality and Health

A population's health is intrinsically important for both personal and humanitarian reasons. Health levels also reflect living standards, and may provide clues to the potential of a population for productive economic activity.

Perhaps the single clearest measure of population health is its expectation of life at birth. Estimates for life expectancy for North and South Korea are presented in Table 5.2. (Note that these estimates are based upon reconstructions

Table 5.2

Estimated Life Expectancy at Birth for DPRK and ROK: 1955–1985

	DPRK			ROK		
	Both Sexes	Male	Female	Both Sexes	Male	Female
1955–60	NA	NA	NA	49.6	46.9	52.5
1960	49.0	46.0	52.1	NA	NA	NA
1960–65	51.9	48.9	55.0	50.7	48.1	53.5
1970–75	61.3	58.2	64.6	NA	NA	NA
1978–79	65.2	62.1	68.4	NA	62.7	69.1
1980	65.7	62.7	69.0	64.9	63.2	68.8
1985	67.2	64.1	70.4	NA	64.9	71.3

NA = Not available

Notes: For North Korea, the life expectancy estimates given for 1960–1965 are 1963 estimates; for 1970–1975, 1973 estimates, and for 1978–79, 1979 estimates.

Source: Eberstadt and Banister, 1992, p. 48.

of population data from the two countries, rather than simply upon the claims of their governments.)

According to these estimates, both North and South Korea enjoyed rapid health progress over the decades between the end of the Korean War and the mid-1980s. Even more striking, perhaps, is the similarity of both the levels and the pace of increase in life expectancy in the two Koreas: over this long period, male and female life expectancy at birth in North and South Korea remained essentially indistinguishable from one another. When one considers the very different development paths embraced by the two contending regimes, and the fact that contact between the two populations was virtually nonexistent over those years, the result looks even more remarkable.

Preliminary analysis of the North Korean 1993 census would imply a life expectancy at birth for males of about 68 years, and for females of about 74 years. That would have been just below South Korea's levels, where the respective figures were estimated at 68 and 76 in 1991.[23]

Not surprisingly, divided Korea's overall life expectancy would have been lower—on average, roughly five years lower—than that of united Germany, where overall life expectancy for males and females in 1993–95 was estimated at 73 and 79, respectively. What may come as more of a surprise, however, is that the estimated differentials in life-span between the two parts of just-reunited Germany look to be wider than the contemporaneous gap in still-divided Korea. According to demographic reconstructions, in the early 1990s, expectation of life at birth for males was less than one year higher in South Korea than in the North. In Germany, by contrast, life expectancy for men was about three years higher in the West than in the East.[24] Given the generally-presumed close correspondence between health and living standards (or productivity), and the widely-held perception that disparities both in living standards and in productivity were greater in divided Korea in the early 1990s than they had been in Germany before *die Wende*, the ostensible parity in life expectancy in the two Koreas in the early 1990s presents us with a seeming empirical paradox, one which remains to be explained.

Since the early 1990s, steady improvements in life expectancy have been recorded in the ROK. According to the South Korean National Statistical Office (NSO), overall expectation of life at birth by 1997 had reached 70.6 years for males and 78.1 years for females.[25] By contrast, North Korea's life expectancy has undoubtedly declined with the upsurge of mortality consequent to its ongoing food crisis. But it is unclear just how much it has dropped. Guesses about the toll of "excess mortality" exacted by the food crisis in the 1995–98 period vary by more than an order of magnitude: from the South Korean NSO's proposed figure of 270,000 to the three-million-plus numbers asserted by some other sources.[26]

The scale of the retrogressions in life expectancy that may have been suffered, of course, depends directly upon the scale of excess mortality. According to the NSO's conjectures, life expectancy in North Korea would have fallen by about four years between 1993 and 1998. By contrast, the projections offered by the US Bureau of the Census, which hypothesize excess deaths of over 1.1 million for the 1995–98 period,[27] imply a conditional DPRK life expectancy of about 51 for the year 1998; this which would, in turn, imply a drop of 20 years over the course of the 1990s. Though we cannot estimate the current level of life expectancy for North Korea with any precision, it is safe to assume that the gap in survival chances between North and South Korea has never before been as wide as it has been over the past several years.

In the wake of other 20th century catastrophes involving sudden and massive loss of life (viz., China's 1959–62 famine and the Korean War), life expectancy typically rebounded rapidly. Once North Korea's food crisis comes to an end, we might expect life expectancy to rise quickly toward its former levels. Unfortunately, however, there is reason to think that the DPRK's hunger problem may have a more enduring impact on the health of the North Korean populace. In late 1998, the European Union, UNICEF and the UN World Food Programme conducted a nutritional survey in the DPRK, measuring heights and weights for an ostensibly random sample of boys and girls.[28] Without downplaying the long odds of actually implementing a truly random survey under the DPRK's auspices, the results of that exercise were striking—and deeply troubling.

By comparison with data from other contemporary surveys, North Korea's children would appear to suffer a far higher incidence of acute malnutrition ("wasting") than children from any country in Eastern Asia—or, for that matter, any population in the Indian sub-continent.

But North Korean children also reported an extremely high incidence of "stunting," that is, unusually low height-for-age, a condition consonant with serious long-term malnutrition. Note that the reported prevalence of child stunting in Table 5.3 is significantly greater in North Korea than in such low-income, high-illiteracy settings as Laos or Cambodia, and is indeed higher than the contemporary estimates for either Pakistan or Bangladesh. These data, furthermore, suggest that North Korea's hunger problem did not suddenly begin with Pyongyang's official public acknowledgement of a food emergency in the summer of 1995, but rather predated the announced crisis by a considerable stretch of time.

The current differentials in nutrition and health separating children in contemporary North and South Korea are suggested by Figures 5.1 and 5.2, which compare data on the heights and weights of 7-year-old boys.

The data for South Korea come from the annual measurements for school-children of the ROK Ministry of Education. And since primary schooling has been essentially universal in South Korea since the mid-1960s, those figures are

Table 5.3
Indicators of Malnutrition in Children Under 5 Years: Anthropometric Survey Data for DPRK and Other Asian Countries

COUNTRY	YEAR	NUTRITIONAL MEASURE (PERCENTAGE)		
		Severe Underweight	Moderate/Severe Wasting	Moderate/Severe Stunting
Cambodia	1990–95	7	8	38
China	1990–95	3	4	32
Indonesia	1990–95	8	13	42
Laos	1990–95	12	11	47
Malaysia	1990–95	1	ND	ND
Mongolia	1990–95	ND	2	26
Myanmar	1990–95	16	8	45
Philippines	1990–95	5	8	33
Thailand	1990–95	4	6	22
Vietnam	1990–95	11	12	47
Bangladesh	1990–95	21	18	55
India	1990–95	21	18	52
Nepal	1990–95	16	11	48
Pakistan	1990–95	13	9	50
Sri Lanka	1990–95	7	16	24
DPRK	*1998*	*32[1]*	*19*	*57*

Note: [1] = Under 7 Years of Age   ND= No Data

Sources: World Food Programme, 1999; UNICEF.

likely to be quite representative. For North Korea, the data are more problematic. There we draw upon a purportedly random sample for a single year, conducted by foreign organizations in the DPRK who were granted only grudging and limited cooperation by local authorities, and who consequently were only able to measure a total of 102 seven-year-old boys for their survey. Therefore, although we cannot invest too much confidence in the exact figures recorded and computed on the North Korean side of the ledger, the results are arresting.

By the late 1990s, to go by Figure 5.1, the average (mean) seven-year-old boy in South Korea may have been as much as 20 centimeters taller than North Korean seven-year-old boys. Moreover, if these DPRK data are even roughly accurate, South Korean boys this age were far taller three decades ago than North Korean boys are today. Anthropometric data for earlier periods in Korean history are more episodic and less comprehensive. Nevertheless, to go by a 1953 biometric study which included over 600 South Korean seven-year-old boys, the DPRK boys surveyed in the late 1990s would have been distinctly

Figure 5.1
Mean Reported Height of Seven-Year-Old Boys:
ROK (1965–1997) and DPRK (1998)

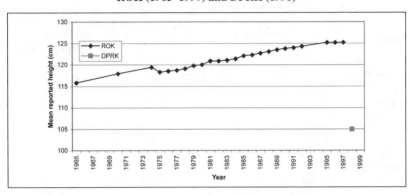

Note: Data for ROK refer to the country's entire cohort of enrolled seven-year-olds; for North Korea, the survey's sample size for seven-year-old boys was n = 102.

Sources: For ROK: ROK NSO, *Social Indicators in Korea*, 1985 edition, p. 214; 1990 edition, p. 206; 1993 edition, p. 178; 1997 edition, pp. 266–267; 1998 edition, pp. 270–271; for DPRK: WFP, 1998–99, raw data kindly provided by the WFP at the request of the author.

shorter than their ROK counterparts from the Korean War era. Indeed, if we can take anthropometric data for Korea for the 1913–22 period as reliable, contemporary North Korean boys may actually be somewhat smaller than their predecessors in the Japanese colonial era, roughly 80 years earlier.[29]

Figure 5.2 seems to tell a similar story. If these data are reliable, North Korean seven-year-old boys would have weighed nearly 10 kilograms less than their South Korean counterparts around 1997–98. That is to say, at present, a seven-year-old South Korean boy would weigh roughly *two-thirds more* than a North Korean boy of the same age. To judge by those data, furthermore, South Korean boys were not nearly as light even 35 years ago as North Korean boys are today. More serious than that, available survey data would suggest that seven-year-old boys in colonial Korea[30] were heavier than seven year old North Korean boys eight decades later.

The data in Table 5.3 and Figures 5.1 and 5.2 are evocative. In starkly physical terms, they suggest that the health status of the North Korean population differs dramatically from that of South Korea today—likely more than ever before. These differences, furthermore, imply diminished or constrained capacities for the North Korean populace, and such constraints are inherently subject to only gradual relaxation over time.

Figure 5.2
Mean Reported Weight of Seven-Year-Old Boys:
ROK (1965–1997) and DPRK (1998)

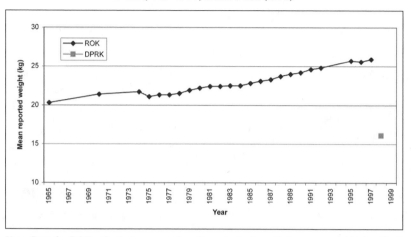

Note: Data for ROK refer to the country's entire cohort of enrolled seven-year-olds; for North Korea, the survey's sample size for seven-year-old boys was n = 102.

Sources: For ROK: ROK NSO, *Social Indicators in Korea*, 1985 edition, p. 216; 1990 edition, p. 208; 1993 edition, p. 180; 1997 edition, pp. 266–267; 1998 edition, pp. 270–271; for DPRK: WFP, 1998–99, raw data kindly provided by the WFP at the request of the author.

Urbanization

The level and pace of urbanization provides some indications of a country's social and economic development. Data on urbanization in North and South Korea are presented in Figure 5.3. According to these figures, both North and South Korea have made the transition from a predominantly rural to a predominantly urban way of life.

North Korea's level of urbanization appears to have been higher than South Korea's for some time after the Korean War, but the DPRK seems to have been surpassed by the ROK during the 1970s. Since then the pace of urbanization has continued to be brisk in South Korea, whereas it appears to have stagnated in the North. These trends may be read as a commentary on overall development patterns in the two Koreas. One must caution, however, that the slow pace of urbanization in North Korea over the past two decades could also reflect non-economic factors, such as policies to disperse population for security or military reasons.

Figure 5.3
Urbanization in the DPRK and ROK, 1955–1995

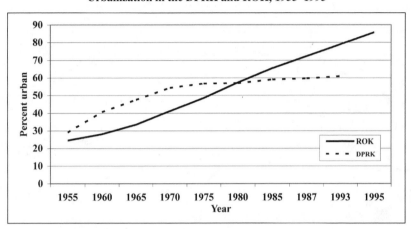

Notes: For South Korea, urban areas are defined as administrative cities with an urban population of 50,000 or more; the definition of the urban population in North Korea has not been published.

Sources: For ROK, see ROK NSO, *Social Indicators in Korea,* various editions; ROK NSO, *Korea Statistical Yearbook,* various editions; for DPRK, Eberstadt and Banister, 1992.

It is possible that Figure 5.3 exaggerates North Korea's urbanization in comparison with that of South Korea, as the definition of "urban area" in North Korea appears to be both undemanding and exceptionally elastic. Consequently, many places which would not qualify as urban in the ROK may be counted as urban in the DPRK. One hint to this effect: whereas almost 60 percent of North Korea's population was defined as urban in 1987, only 37 percent of North Koreans at the time lived in cities of 100,000 or more. In South Korea, well over half of the entire populace lived in such cities in 1985. Thus, whereas only one in six urban South Koreans at that time lived in cities of less than 100,000, fully 3 out of 8 "urban" North Koreans did so.

Militarization

As mentioned in Chapter 1, the DPRK maintains an exceptionally, indeed, extraordinarily, militarized society and economy. Indications of just how militarized North Korea has become can be found in estimates of military manpower.

Throughout the 1970s, 1980s, and 1990s, South Korea maintained a relatively stable number of men under arms. North Korea, by contrast, appears to have pursued a steady military buildup during the 1970s and 1980s. By the late 1980s, even though South Korea was fielding one of the world's largest armies, North Korea, with a population only half as large, was apparently billeting twice as many soldiers. By those numbers, North Korea would look to have been the most militarized country in the world at that time, with over 6 percent of its total population in the armed forces—a fraction similar to that of the United States in 1943—and fully a fifth of the country's men between the ages of 16 and 55 in the barracks.[31]

Just how large the North Korean armed forces are today is not clear. Pyongyang's 1993 census can be interpreted as indicating a military strength of just under 700,000. On the other hand, inconsistencies within that census—and between that census and earlier DPRK population registration data—are consistent with a proposition that hundreds of thousands of additional men of military age were deliberately overlooked in the 1993 count.

Even if the lower, officially released, figure turned out to be close to the mark, North Korea today would be a country shouldering a tremendously heavy military burden. Moreover, it is entirely possible that North Korea's degree of militarization may actually have *risen* over the past decade. Such an outcome could have been assured, in fact, simply by a more rapid tempo of economic decline in the DPRK's civilian sector than in its military sector. Given the adamant and explicit commitment of the North Korean government to augmenting its military power,[32] that possibility should not be regarded as fantastical. Unfortunately, for the time being all attempts to estimate the actual level of "military burden" for the DPRK economy amount to little more than pure guesswork.

If the two Koreas do eventually enter into a peaceful reintegration, there would be scope for a vast "build-down" of military forces on the peninsula. This would be especially true for North Korea, where a very substantial proportion of the population of "economically active age" could be released to other pursuits. As a consequence, most of the presumably high fraction of North Korea's capital stock currently devoted to supporting the military industries would have to be converted, or simply scrapped.

Labor Force

With the release of the 1993 DPRK census, more information than ever before is available on the North Korean workforce. These data, to be sure, are not without ambiguity. While one assumes that the figures include workers in the country's extensive military-industrial sector, for example, the census does not spell this out. Such ambiguities notwithstanding, the census numbers provide insights into both social arrangements and patterns of development, and can be contrasted with the corresponding data from South Korea.

Figure 5.4

Inferred and Reported Military Manpower in the DPRK and ROK, 1975–1995

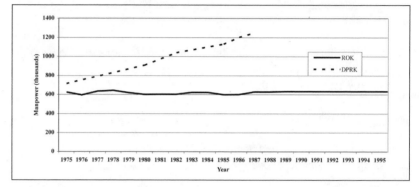

Note: Military manpower for ROK as reported; military manpower for DPRK inferred from estimates of non-civilian male population based on demographic reconstructions.

Sources: For ROK, IISS, various editions; for DPRK, Eberstadt and Banister, 1992.

According to the figures in Table 5.4, North Korea's overall labor force in 1993 was slightly more than half as large as that of South Korea in 1995. Both workforces had made the transition from a primarily agricultural to a primarily non-agricultural pattern of employment. That said, the distribution of the labor force among economic sectors nevertheless looks strikingly different in the two Koreas.

Table 5.4

Distribution of Labor Force: DPRK 1993 vs. ROK 1995

	DPRK		ROK	
	Total (1,000s)	Percent	Total (1,000s)	Percent
Overall labor force	11,004	100	20,377	100
Manufacturing	4,118	37.4	4,773	23.4
Farming	3,381	30.7	2,551	12.5
Construction	464	4.2	1,896	9.3
Transport and communication	402	3.7	1,068	5.2
State farms	251	2.3	—	—
Commerce	509	4.6	3,763	18.4
Education, culture, and health	844	7.7	1,312	6.4
Other	1,305	9.4	5,014	24.8

Sources: Derived from DPRK CBS, 1995 and ROK NSO, *Korea Statistical Yearbook 1996.*

Not surprisingly, "commerce" absorbs much less of the North Korean than the South Korean workforce (5 percent vs. 18 percent). More unexpected is the finding that North Korea devotes a rather smaller share of its manpower to construction than does South Korea (4 percent vs. 9 percent), a reflection, perhaps, of the fact that by the early 1990s the troubled DPRK economy was simply not undertaking many new building projects.

As we saw in Chapter 2 (Table 2.9), in keeping with its traditional emphasis on development of industry (especially heavy industry), "manufacturing" absorbs more North Korean manpower than any other sector. On the other hand, "farming" also accounts for well over 30 percent of North Korea's employment, whereas it represents less than 13 percent in South Korea. Even for a communist society, North Korea's degree of labor force mobilization appears to be remarkably high. Note further that these North Korean rates ostensibly pertain to the *civilian* population only. If military manpower were taken into account, the rate for "mobilized adult manpower" would be still higher—perhaps even historically unparalleled.

Clearly, a peaceful reintegration of the two Koreas would portend vast, possibly wrenching, changes for the North Korean labor market. If, as a very crude first approximation, we hypothesize that North Korean labor force participation rates were made to match those currently seen in the Korean South, over two million North Korean "workers" would immediately be redundant. (Posit massive military demobilization and that total quickly approaches three million—out of a total adult population of about 15 million, and a total economically (or militarily) active population of about 12 million.)

But even these large numbers might underestimate the scale of labor force displacement, because at South Korean participation and distributional patterns, there would be only a little over a million "farmers" in the North (as opposed to the 3.6 million registered in the 1993 census), and only a little over two million workers in the manufacturing sector (as opposed to the 4 million plus reported by North Korea in 1993). Simply conforming to South Korea's sectoral employment patterns and labor force participation rates would imply that virtually half of North Korea's workers would have to find new jobs or leave the workforce altogether—even more than half, if one envisions significant military demobilization and considers soldiers as "employees."

Few available data pertain to the economic potential of today's North Korean workers. The health and education of a workforce bear directly upon its capacity to produce. As already noted, we still lack reliable current figures relating to the health of the North Korean populace. And while it would be helpful to know something about the educational background of the North Korean labor force, the DPRK's population count, in contradistinction with most contemporary population censuses, evidently did not gather *any* information on educational attainment![33]

Although information on the potential productivity of North Korea's workers is all but nonexistent, the DPRK's labor force distribution patterns provide hints about overall productivity levels, and trends, in that economy. Figure 5.5, for example, contrasts trends in employment in the "primary sector" (e.g., farming, forestry and fishing) in North and South Korea in the 1980s and 1990s.

In 1993, "farming" occupied about a third of North Korea's workforce. Accounting for forestry and fishing (as does South Korea in its figures on "primary sector" workers) would presumably raise that fraction still further for North Korea.

Despite the robust international patterns that have been identified here, a strict and mechanistic correspondence between sectoral employment patterns and per capita output should obviously not be expected.[34] Nonetheless, it is interesting to note that the last time "primary sector" activities occupied 35 percent or more of South Korea's workforce was in the late 1970s—when per capita output in the ROK was roughly only a quarter as high as it is today. We may further note that the displacement of manpower out of agriculture appears to have been much more rapid in South Korea than in North Korea during the 1980s and 1990s (to judge at least by the DPRK's reported figures on the share in its workforce of "farmers," a class category, not an occupational category. These findings are consistent with the propositions that 1) even before the

Figure 5.5

Reported Percentage of Labor Force in Primary Sector

DPRK vs. ROK, ca. 1986–1995

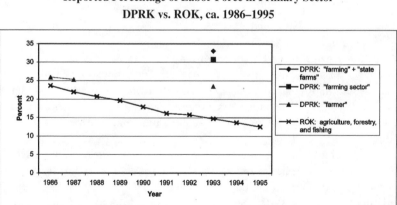

Sources: For ROK, ROK NSO *Social Indicators in Korea*, various editions; for DPRK, Eberstadt and Banister, 1992 and DPRK CBS, 1995.

DPRK's food emergency, the level of material attainment was much higher in the South than in the North; and 2) the pace of development has been markedly higher in the South than in the North for at least a generation—that is, since well before the DPRK's post-Cold War economic troubles.

Foreign Trade and Domestic Economic Infrastructure

Mirror statistics for North Korea and reported trade data for South Korea permit comparison of the two Korean economies in a number of meaningful ways—characteristic limitations of mirror statistics notwithstanding.[35] The following estimates on trade turnover for North and South Korea are given in current U.S. dollars, *not* real, inflation-adjusted dollars, for a variety of technical reasons.[36]

Figures 5.6 and 5.7 contrast overall trade trends in North and South Korea between 1972 and 1997.

Over those two decades, the nominal value of South Korea's trade turnover exploded, jumping by a factor of almost 70 to reach US$136 billion in exports and US$144 billion in imports in 1997. Even after adjusting for rises in the international price level, South Korea's trade expansion over this period was

Figure 5.6
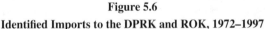
Identified Imports to the DPRK and ROK, 1972–1997

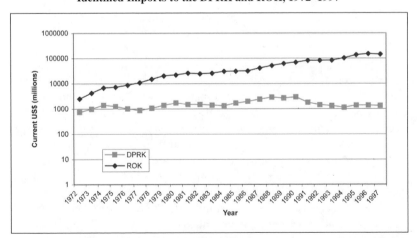

Note: Imports measured or estimated c.i.f.; method for estimating DPRK imports is explained in the source.

Sources: For ROK, IMF, 1975; IMF, 1997b, and IMF, 1999; for DPRK data 1970–1995, see Eberstadt, 1998, pp. 165–223; for DPRK data 1996–1997, see Eberstadt, 1999b, Chapter 5.

Figure 5.7
Identified Exports from the DPRK and ROK, 1972–1997

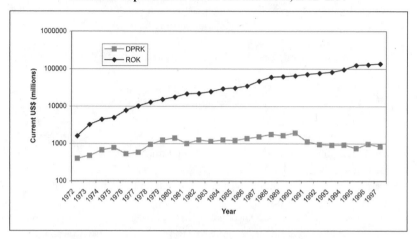

Note: Exports measured or estimated f.o.b.; method for estimating DPRK exports explained in source.

Sources: For ROK, IMF, 1975, IMF, 1997b, and IMF, 1999; for DPRK data 1970–95, see Eberstadt, 1998; for DPRK data 1996–1997, see Eberstadt, 1999, Chapter 5.

extraordinary, with a real increase in trade volume for the ROK over this interval of probably over 20-fold,[37] indicating that real per capita imports and exports may have risen by something like a factor of 15.

The ROK's approach to trade and the international economy—a strategy described as "export orientation" in current economic literature[38]—was central to the country's great successes in economic development over the past three and a half decades. The determination to participate in, and compete in, the world economy opened the ROK to dynamizing pressures and opportunities, and played a major role in the amazingly rapid economic transformation that South Korea has experienced over the past generation and a half. (Though the economic shocks and adjustments South Korea suffered in the wake of its late 1997 international liquidity crisis have certainly reminded those who needed reminding that ROK material performance over the past generation was no "miracle," the short, deep recession of 1998–99 neither erased the tremendous gains that the country accrued under its export orientation policies, nor cast serious doubt on the soundness of that outward-looking approach.)

In addition to dramatically expanding its aggregate trade volume, South Korea's trade composition has progressively shifted. Agricultural commodities and labor-intensive wares have steadily given way to complex manufactured goods and technology-intensive products. This was especially evident in the ROK's export sector. In 1972, machinery and equipment (category "7" in the SITC taxonomy) accounted for less than 11 percent of South Korea's merchandise exports. By 1997, that fraction had jumped to 50 percent. This dramatic shift in the composition of South Korean exports reflected the dramatic underlying structural changes in the economy generating those exports.

North Korea's trade patterns tell a very different tale. In 1972—with a population roughly half the size of South Korea's—the value of the DPRK's estimated merchandise trade turnover was about 27 percent of South Korea's, and by 1997 had plummeted to less than one percent of the ROK level. That decisive and overwhelming tilt in trade performance on the Korean peninsula spoke not only to South Korea's great successes in international commerce, but to jarring North Korean failures. If South Korea's achievements in expanding trade volume over the quarter century between 1972 and 1997 rank among the world's very best, North Korea's trade performance over that period ranks among the very poorest.

In quantitative terms, aggregate identified North Korean trade turnover rose by just 88 percent between 1972 and 1997 *in nominal dollars*. (By way of comparison, nominal trade turnover for the world as a whole is estimated to have increased by almost 1,300 percent over this same interim; and even the economically troubled African continent registered a nominal increase of about 650 percent over those same years.[39]) Although North Korea's total population in 1997 is still a matter of some uncertainty, it is clear that the DPRK's population in 1997 was significantly higher than it had been in 1972. Consequently, North Korea's nominal per capita growth in trade turnover would have been even lower than this. Given the prominence of transactions in non-convertible currencies in North Korea's trade ledgers through the end of the Cold War, and the problems of converting current Soviet trade rubles into constant US dollars, we cannot offer a precise estimate for the trends in North Korea's real trade volume between 1972 and 1997. However, if we *were* to adjust North Korea's estimated current dollar trade series against the U.S. producer price index, we could calculate an implied decline in trade turnover of about 40 percent between 1972 and 1997, and an implied drop in per capita trade turnover on the order of 55–62 percent.[40]

In all, then, the proposition that North Korea's real per capita trade volume declined substantially between 1972 and 1997 looks like a fairly safe one. A substantial decline in real per capita exports and imports over a 25-year period would, in turn, have major implications for our understanding of the long-term performance of the North Korean economy. It would indicate either a significant turn towards autarky during the period in question, or a notable decline in output per person during the years under consideration—or, within fairly broad parameters, the possibility of *both* increased autarky and decreased per capita output.

North Korea's trade performance, like all other aspects of its economic performance, has suffered sharply since the end of the Cold War and the collapse of the state's Soviet bloc benefactors. But it would be unwise to exaggerate the DPRK's trade performance even during its "Golden Age" of economic growth, from the late 1950s through the early 1970s.

In nominal dollar terms, identified North Korean trade turnover reached its apogee (just under US$5 billion) in 1990. That would have made for a nominal 330 percent rise over 1972. Such a record hardly qualifies as a distinctive achievement. Over those same years, beleaguered Africa registered a 425 percent increase.[41] That nominal DPRK trade increase, in any case, would have amounted to only about 210 percent on a per capita basis, and if deflated by the US producer price index, would have implied a "real" per capita increase in trade turnover of under 10 percent! Any (slight) gain in real per capita North Korean trade volume during this "heyday" of North Korean international commerce, furthermore, could not be attributed to DPRK performance in competitive global markets. Instead, in purely arithmetic terms, it must be *entirely* ascribed to the growth of Soviet-DPRK commerce between 1984 and 1990—and that was a commerce willed into existence by political figures in Moscow during the 1980s after Leonid Brezhnev's death. When Moscow's political will to subsidize that traffic evaporated, the commerce evaporated as well. North Korea's trade policies, in short, were not designed to be economically self-sustaining, and in the event have, indeed, proved to be fatefully unsustainable.

North Korea's bleak economic performance over the generation between 1972 and 1997 is underscored not only by trends in the aggregate volume of its international trade, but also by the composition of this trade. Unlike South Korea's steadily shifting export structure, North Korea's export patterns (as reflected by mirror statistics) were basically stuck in the same makeup between the early 1970s and the late 1990s. Over this period, identified (i.e., civilian-sector) exports consisted principally of extracted minerals (gold, magnesite), relatively simple manufactured goods (steel, cement, and later textiles[42]), and agricultural goods (rice and marine products). Exporting limited quantities of such merchandise, of course, hardly requires much technical attainment. And unlike other developing countries with largely urbanized populations and predominantly nonagricultural workforces, the DPRK, as explained in Chapter 3, evidently failed to develop any appreciable capability to export machinery and equipment. According to reports by its trading partners, capital goods would have accounted for less than 8 percent of North Korea's international merchandise sales in 1995—scarcely more than the negligible 4 percent recorded a quarter century earlier.[43] The long-term stasis in the structure of North Korean exports (as reflected in mirror statistics) looks to be entirely consistent with the proposition that the North Korean economy has been beset by a pronounced technological stagnation for at least a generation.

Trade data and mirror statistics can provide further, and somewhat more specific, insights into the state of a country's economic infrastructure. Figures 5.8 and 5.9, for example, trace aggregated trends in imports and exports of machinery and capital goods in the two Koreas. These figures attest to the continuing modernization of the ROK capital stock through the import of productivity-enhancing foreign machinery. As South Korea developed, machinery imports came to account for an ever-greater fraction of overall ROK imports (roughly half the total by the mid-1990s).

In North Korea, on the other hand, 1975 looks to have been the high-water mark for capital goods imports, even in nominal terms. If trends could be measured in real terms, capital equipment imports may well have trended down-

Figure 5.8
Identified Imports of Capital Goods and Machinery
to the DPRK and ROK, 1972–1997

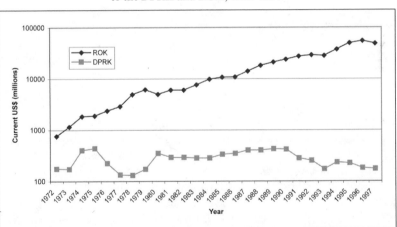

Note: Imports measured or estimated c.i.f.; method for estimating DPRK imports and exports is explained in source; for DPRK, "capital goods" are defined to include SITC 69, 71, 72, 86, and 89; for ROK, machinery and transport equipment covers all SITC 7; for further details on methodology, see sources.

Sources: For ROK, UN *International Trade Statistics Yearbook*, various editions, and ROK NSO, 1998; for DPRK data 1970–1995, see Eberstadt, 1998, pp. 165–223; for DPRK data 1996–1997, see Eberstadt, 1999, Chapter 5.

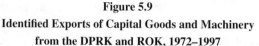

Figure 5.9

**Identified Exports of Capital Goods and Machinery
from the DPRK and ROK, 1972–1997**

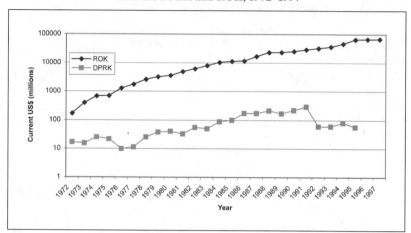

Note: Exports measured or estimated f.o.b.; method for estimating DPRK imports and exports is explained in source; for DPRK, "capital goods" are defined to include SITC 69, 71, 72, 86, and 89; for ROK, machinery and transport equipment covers all SITC 7; for further details on methodology, see source.

Sources: For ROK, UN *International Trade Statistics Yearbook*, various editions; and ROK NSO, 1998; for DPRK, see Eberstadt, 1998, pp. 165–223.

ward through the 1970s, 1980s, and 1990s. No less significant, the share of capital goods within DPRK imports appears to have declined progressively over these same decades. As a result of those longstanding patterns—and, presumably, the policy directives that created them—North Korea today surely has one of the lowest proportions of foreign machinery in its overall capital stock of any modern country. Thus, paradoxically, despite the seeming fetish of the DPRK leadership for "investment," *effective* investment in industrial infrastructure—and thus potential for industrial production—has been severely constrained by the regime's own policies.

North Korea's marked allergy to capital investment on the basis of imported foreign machinery appears to have been unique even among communist economies, let alone market-oriented economies. One consequence of this allergy has been the aforementioned inability to generate exports of machinery or capital goods. On a per capita basis, North Korea's level of such exports is probably lower today than it was a decade ago—possibly even two decades ago.[44]

Also important to note is the conspicuous lack of investment in "transport equipment" revealed by DPRK mirror statistics. Based on those numbers, it would appear that the DPRK has been seriously underinvesting in means of transport for the better part of the past generation. The revolution in transportation that has swept up the rest of the world, to go by these data, has bypassed the DPRK. To judge by the clues from mirror statistics, North Korea's transportation and communications infrastructures today are probably woefully underdeveloped.

As discussed in detail in Chapter 4, over the past decade several major economic studies have detailed the relationship between investment in capital equipment—including imported capital goods—and economic growth.[45] These studies indicate that capital goods imports can serve as a critical means to reduce production costs and improve productivity in any country's domestic economic infrastructure. Outward-oriented trade policies and heavy investment in foreign machinery and equipment have made for a complete transformation of South Korea's economic infrastructure over the past generation, and in the process have facilitated rapid, sustained economic growth, and permitted the country to approach Western levels of productivity.[46] North Korea's stringently enacted trade regimen, for its part, was set on almost diametrically opposite objectives, that is to say, avoiding integration with the world economy and minimizing imports of foreign capital goods. The results of Pyongyang's policies were entirely predictable—and economically adverse. To infer from available data, North Korea seems to have constructed a high-cost, low-productivity industrial infrastructure—and a fragile one at that. Pyongyang's longstanding quest for economic "self-reliance" may have succeeded in building the envisioned "independent national economy" for the DPRK—but that assiduously-created "independent" economy is presently incapable of supporting its own populace, and is thus structurally dependent upon the largesse of foreign governments for sustenance.

National Output

With the 1997 IMF "fact finding mission" to the DPRK, official figures have been transmitted by Pyongyang to the outside world concerning the country's national accounts and patterns of aggregate economic output.

Enormous unresolved questions weigh upon these disclosures. It is not clear, for example, if these numbers are meant to include the military economy or not. No price deflators were offered. Presentation of output in terms of US dollars is, to say the least, a highly problematic proposition, and it is by no means self-evident that the DPRK would be capable of measuring value-added in its economy under the best of circumstances. Nevertheless, despite all these serious and unresolved problems with these data, it may still be worthwhile to compare reported recent patterns of output in North and South Korea.

If we were to give credence to the numbers in Table 5.5, aggregate GDP in 1993 would have been about 16 times larger in the ROK than in the DPRK. Per capita output would have been about eight times higher in the South than in the North. By those same numbers, agricultural output in the South would have been "only" three times higher than in the North—a curiously small difference, considering that 1) the population of the South was twice as large as that of the North, 2) farm output in the South is valued at nearly twice world (inter-national) prices, and 3) the North in 1993 was only months away from pub-licly declaring a severe food shortage and seeking international emergency food aid on a humanitarian basis. In other sectors, reported gaps are vastly greater, such as the recorded differences ranging from roughly 20-to-1 to nearly 40-to-1—numbers which, if trusted, would imply differences of per capita output of roughly 10-to-1 to 20-to-1.

We have no way of testing, or replicating, these DPRK national accounts fig-ures. It would be highly unwise to harness those statistics to any exacting pur-poses. Suffice it to say that these figures tally with the prevailing assumption—supported by a variety of data not drawn upon in Table 5.7—that per capita out-put has been dramatically higher in South than in North Korea for some con-siderable time.

Table 5.5
Official Data on GDP and its Composition: DPRK and ROK, 1993

	DPRK	ROK	Ratio
GDP (current US$ million)	20,935	333,022	16:1
GDP per capita	990	7,600	7.7:1
Sectoral output (current US$ million)			
Agriculture	8,227	23,978	2.9:1
Industry	4,689	89,916	19.2:1
Construction	1,256	46,290	36.9:1
Other	6,762	173,504	25.7:1
Sectoral output (percent)			
Agriculture	39.3	7.0	0.18:1
Industry	22.4	27.0	1.2:1
Construction	6.0	13.9	2.3:1
Other	39.3	52.1	1.6:1

Note: US$ values calculated on the basis of official exchange rates.

Sources: For ROK derived from ROK NSO, 1996; for DPRK, IMF, 1997a and DPRK CBS, 1995.

Concluding Observations

Given the imprecision of any statistical comparison of contemporary North and South Korea, curiosity must be tempered by caution. False precision will not serve our aims. Yet when all is said and done, our search for numbers about the North's social and economic circumstances may be said to reinforce, and indeed to enhance, a number of prevailing impressions about divided Korea.

Available data affirm the common perception that the DPRK economy has been, and continues to be, extraordinarily militarized, structurally distorted, and sheltered from interaction with world markets. They also illustrate a most peculiar "development path" for North Korea since the 1953 Korean War ceasefire, a parabolic trajectory, in which rapid structural change and material progress gradually gives way to a period of stagnation, and thereafter to severe decay and decline. As best as can be told from available data, that phase of decay and decline has not yet abated for the DPRK. On the contrary, to judge by available empirical evidence, North Korea is currently suffering from economic and social retrogression so pervasive and so serious that we may properly talk about a systemic failure in the contemporary DPRK.

Of all post-World War II national "development experiences," there may be no country other than the DPRK in which such palpable early material successes were followed by such extreme and prolonged material failure. Attempting to explain the dynamics of North Korea's long-term performance would take us far afield.[47] For the purposes at hand, it may suffice simply to emphasize that the North Korean development strategy has proved to be manifestly unsustainable, and remains utterly unworkable today.

The long-gathering failure of the North Korean economic system is, very largely, responsible for the developmental gap that separates North and South Korea today. Per capita output is now obviously far lower in North than in South Korea, although it is impossible to say just how great that differential may be. By any relevant quantifiable measure—e.g., international trade volume, output of physical goods—that gap looks to have been widening over the past decade. As long as the current DPRK regime remains in power and cleaves to its traditional political economy, we may anticipate that the difference in per capita output between North and South will widen still further.

For most of the history of divided Korea, our few available indicators of human resource development pointed to remarkable similarities between circumstances in the North and the South. In particular, estimates of life expectancy at birth for the ROK and the DPRK were essentially indistinguishable for the 1960s, the 1970s and even the 1980s—that is, even after a yawning divide in economic productivity is generally thought to have opened between the two societies.

Over the past decade, unfortunately, an additional gap in "human development" between the two Koreas has made itself glaringly evident. The ongoing food crisis in North Korea is only the most alarming illustration of that gap. Although we lack precise figures, it is apparent that trends in life expectancy at birth have been moving in opposite directions over the past decade in the two Koreas. Furthermore, available anthropometric data strongly suggest that North Korean and South Korean children, though identical in heritage and ethnicity, are now strikingly different in their very height and weight. Such significant differences in weight and stature may well indicate that other meaningful differences in "human capital formation" now distinguish the North Korean from the South Korean populace.

Our attempt to provide a quantitative comparison of socioeconomic conditions in the two Koreas points to the enormity of the challenges that lie in store in the event of a reunification. As a first order approximation, it may be the case that North Korea's entire capital stock would be next to worthless in open, competitive, market conditions. And it is hardly unreasonable, in the light of the data we have reviewed, to imagine that most North Korean workers would have to find new occupations if their system were exposed to systematic market forces.

Yet daunting as these potential adjustments may appear, it is possible that they would pale next to the human resource problems to which we have alluded. In the final analysis, the DPRK's legacy to a united Korea will be the human potential it contributes to the venture.

Given the proper institutional framework and enlightened governmental policies, rapid recovery and sustained development can be elicited in settings where economic infrastructure has been utterly destroyed and labor markets thoroughly disrupted, but where human capital has been largely preserved—viz., postwar Japan and West Germany. But even under auspicious institutional and policy environments, the prospects and scope for recovery and development will depend critically upon the available human resources.

At the moment, we know amazingly little about the quality of human resources in the DPRK. While North Korea has a highly—indeed, extraordinarily—mobilized adult workforce, the capabilities of that population have not been adequately surveyed at this time. Virtually no data are available about the educational attainment of the populace. Such data as we do have regarding mortality and health, however, seem to mark out ominous tendencies.

As we know, under certain auspices, policy regimens can be changed very rapidly. Given particular political conditions, institutional frameworks can also be swiftly reconfigured. But human resources cannot be altered so summarily. Their augmentation and development can only take place over historical periods of time.

As we consider a possible Korean reunification, it is essential to think about optimal institutional arrangements and government policies. But it is also important to recognize that the pace of economic recovery and development for the population of the North will also depend upon their levels of human resources—quantities whose dimensions are largely uncharted, and which lie beyond the immediate influence of policymakers.

Notes

1. For useful background on the STE, see Winiecki, 1988, and Kornai, 1992.
2. Perhaps the most important is that of Bergson, 1961.
3. For an elaboration on this argument, see Rosefielde and Pfouts, 1995, pp. 375–89.
4. A point originally made in Eberstadt, 1995, in the chapter "The CIA's Assessment of the Soviet Economy," pp. 136–149; for a measured defense of the results of that research effort, however, see Maddison, 1998, pp. 307–323.
5. There is an enormous literature bearing on the reassessment of the GDR's economy; for a sense of this literature, see Schneider, 1990, Bryson and Melzer, 1991, Kuhrt, 1996, and Kopstein, 1997.
6. For example, BRD, 1997.
7. Indeed, the only regular official statistical series of any kind bearing on the performance of North Korean economy—the annual report on state budgetary revenues and expenditures—was interrupted by the four year (1995–1998) suspension, in the wake of Kim Il Sung's death, of the DPRK Supreme People's Assembly (SPA), the forum at which those figures were traditionally announced.
8. For an extended analysis of the quality of Pyongyang's statistical releases, see Chapter 2.
9. To the extent that those institutions rely upon privileged or classified information in their assessment of North Korea's performance, we are confronted with additional issues regarding the replicability of results.
10. In 1989, the DPRK transmitted some demographic information to the United Nations Population Fund (UNFPA) to meet conditions for possible UNFPA technical assistance with an upcoming population census; those data are analyzed in detail in Eberstadt and Banister, 1992; North Korea eventually held a population census—evidently, the first-ever in the history of the regime—in early 1994, focused on the situation as of year-end 1993; for more details, see DPRK CBS, 1995; results from this census were formally published in 1995, and became available in the West in 1997; for a more in-depth discussion of the 1993 census, see Chapter 2.
11. Mirror statistics on the North Korean economy used in this chapter are drawn from the UN International Commodity Trade Database, and from Soviet/Russian, Chinese, and South Korean statistical compendia on their trade with the DPRK; for more details, see Eberstadt, 1999a.
12. International Monetary Fund, 1997a.
13. World Food Programme, 1999.
14. There are some notable problems with the DPRK 1993 census data; most importantly, internal inconsistencies—and inconsistencies between the 1993 census and earlier DPRK population registration data—suggest that the 1993 population may substantially understate North Korea's true population.

15. The figure is for the year 1995; derived from BRD, 1997, p. 62.
16. BRD, 1997, p. 65.
17. One noteworthy feature of South Korea's recent fertility patterns has been the coincidence of strong son preference and sub-replacement fertility; for more than a decade, South Korea's newborns have been distinguished by unnaturally high "sex ratios"—up to 120 boys for every 100 girls; the eventual consequence of this pattern, as some researchers have noted, may be a "marriage crisis"; in other words, other things being equal, by 2015 there will be 25 percent more young South Korean men of marriageable age than young South Korean women who could marry them; see Park and Cho, 1995, pp. 59–84.
18. See Sullivan, 1995, p. A16.
19. See Banister, 1987.
20. *FBIS*-EAS-1999-1019.
21. See Eberstadt and Banister, 1992, p. 105.
22. For further discussion, see Eberstadt, 2001.
23. United Nations, 1997, p. 145.
24. BRD, 1997, p. 76.
25. *FBIS*-EAS-1999-0803.
26. For a report on the NSO estimate, see *FBIS*-EAS-1999-0827; for various sources placing the North Korean famine toll at around 3 million or more, see *FBIS*-EAS-1998-131; *FBIS*-EAS-1999-0313; *FBIS*-EAS-1999-0216.
27. Calculation provided to the author by the International Programs Center, US Bureau of the Census, based on unpublished data.
28. Summary results of the survey are reported in World Food Programme, 1999.
29. For the data on the 1953 ROK and the 1913–22 Korea anthropometric studies cited here, see Yun, 1987, Chapter 3, section 2.
30. The colonial period covers the years from 1910 to 1945.
31. For more details, see Eberstadt and Banister, 1992, pp. 86–97.
32. For a fuller description of North Korean military policy in the context of its economic development, see the first two chapters of Eberstadt, 1999.
33. In an earlier study, Eberstadt and Banister (1992) showed that by the 1980s, North Korea's episodically released numbers on school enrollments would have been consistent with near-universal primary school education, with relatively high rates of secondary school enrollment, and with quite a high proportion of adults with some post-secondary education; these ratios, of course, tell us nothing about the quality or content of the education obtained; the 1993 North Korean census did provide information on the distribution of so-called "technicians and specialists" within the workforce, but that certification looked to be decidedly non-educational in nature; whereas the highest incidence of post-secondary education would have been expected among persons in their late 20s, the proportion of "technicians and specialists" is by far the highest for workers over 60 years of age.
34. See, for example, Syrquin and Chenery, 1989.
35. On the general characteristics of mirror statistics, see Morgenstern, 1963, Chapter IX; an additional complication in North Korea's case is the relatively large share of DPRK international commerce in illicit goods (weaponry, narcotics, and the like) which ordinarily do not show up in trade partners' official export or import accounts.
36. Most important among these: the absence of any reliable index for converting current Soviet rubles (in which much of North Korea's trade was denominated) into constant U.S. dollars.

37. Series deflated against U.S. producer price index, as reported in U.S. Bureau of the Census, 1998, p. 487.
38. For expositions on the dynamics of "export orientation" by some of its prominent proponents, see the following: Balassa, 1989), pp. 3–55; Krueger, 1990, pp. 108–112; Lal, 1993, pp. 169–97.
39. Derived from IMF, 1998, pp. 126–131. Note that the figures for Africa refer only to 1972–96, and therefore somewhat understate the nominal expansion of trade for the continent.
40. Presuming midyear 1997 populations of 21 million and 24 million, respectively.
41. IMF, 1998, pp. 126–131.
42. Under the DPRK's last 5-year economic agreement with the USSR, a North Korean apparel industry was stimulated by Soviet design; clothing and textiles—mainly, Moscow-bound—came to account for a substantial share of North Korea's overall exports; with the end of the USSR, however, North Korea's textile and clothing exports entered into a slump, from which they have not yet recovered; for further discussion, see Eberstadt, 1999, Chapter 5.
43. We should note that somewhat different definitions of "capital goods" and "machinery and equipment" are being used for North Korean and South Korean merchandise trade; in practice, these definitional differences affect calculated results only slightly, and have no bearing whatever on the broad trends described in this section; it is worth noting, however, that North Korean mirror statistics cover only the commerce its partners voluntarily report; exports of North Korean military hardware, for instance, almost never show up in such numbers; thus, mirror statistics may not fully represent the technological capabilities of the DPRK.
44. See Chapter 3, Table 1.
45. See De Long and Summers (1991) and Lee (1995).
46. In 1998—a year of acute recession in the ROK—South Korea's per capita GNP, measured in PPP dollars, was placed by the World Bank at 42 percent of the US level, 58 percent of the German level, and 94 percent of the Greek level; World Bank, 1999, pp. 230–231.
47. One attempt to illuminate those dynamics, however, may be found in my recent study, *The End of North Korea* (1999b).

References

Balassa, Bela, ed.1989. *Policy Choices for the 1990s.* New York: New York University Press.
Banister, Judith. 1987. *China's Changing Population.* Stanford, CA: Stanford University Press.
Bergson, Abram. 1961. *The Real National Income of Soviet Russia since 1928.* Cambridge, MA: Harvard University Press.
Bundesrepublik Deutschland (BRD). 1997. *Statistiches Jahrbuch für die Bundesrepublik Deutschland 1997* (Tr. Statistical Yearbook of the Federal Republic of Germany). Statistisches Bundesamt. Stuttgart: Metzler-Poeschel Verlag.
Bryson, Philip J. and Manfred Melzer. 1991. *The End of the East German Economy.* New York: St. Martin's Press.
De Long, J. Bradford and Lawrence H. Summers. 1991. "Equipment Investment and Economic Growth." *Quarterly Journal of Economics* 106(3):445–502.

DPRK Central Bureau of Statistics (DPRK CBS). 1995. *Tabulation of the Population Census of the Democratic People's Republic of Korea.* Pyongyang: DPRK Central Bureau of Statistics.

Eberstadt, Nicholas. 1995. *The Tyranny of Numbers: Mismeasurement and Misrule.* Washington, DC: AEI Press.

———. 1998. "The DPRK's International Trade in Capital Goods, 1970–1995: Indications from 'Mirror Statistics.'" *Journal of East Asian Affairs* XII(1):165–223. Winter/Spring.

———. 1999a. "Self-Reliance and Economic Decline: DPRK's Trade in Capital Goods, 1975–1995." *Problems of Post-Communism* 46(1):1–13.

———. 1999b. *The End of North Korea.* Washington, DC: AEI Press.

———. 2000. "Disparities in Socioeconomic Development in Divided Korea: Indications and Implications. *Asian Survey* XL(6):867–93.

———. 2001. "Development, Structure and Performance of the DPRK Economy: Empirical Indications." Laurence J. Lau and Chang-ho Yoon, eds., *North Korea in Transition: Developmental Potential and Social Infrastructure.* Stanford, CA: Stanford University Press.

Eberstadt, Nicholas and Judith Banister. 1992. *The Population of North Korea.* Berkeley, CA: University of California Institute of East Asian Studies.

FBIS-EAS-1998-131. (11 May 1998) reprinted from *Korea Times* (Internet version), translated as "South Korea: Around 3 Million Reportedly Die of Famine in DPRK."

——— -1999-0216. (16 February 1999) reprinted from *Yonhap* translated as "DPRK Report Says Population Reduced by 3 Million."

——— -1999-0313. (13 March 1999) reprinted from *Yonhap* translated as "Hwang: Over 3 Million People Died of Starvation in DPRK."

——— -1999-0803. (3 August 1999). "Average Life Expectancy in ROK 71 for Men, 78 for Women."

——— -1999-0827. (27 August 1999). Reprinted from *Yonhap,* translated as "DPRK Population Estimated at 22.08 Million."

——— -99-1019. (18 October 1999); reprint from *Chungang Ilbo* (Internet version), translated as "Active Government Role for DPRK Defectors Urged."

International Institute for Strategic Studies. Various editions. *The Military Balance.* London: IISS.

International Labour Organisation. Various years. *Yearbook of Labour Statistics.*

International Monetary Fund. 1975. *International Financial Statistics.* July.

———. 1997a. "Democratic People's Republic of Korea, Fact Finding Report." Washington, DC: IMF Asia and Pacific Department. 12 November. Unpublished.

———. 1997b. *International Financial Statistics Yearbook 1997.* Washington, DC: IMF.

———. 1998. *International Financial Statistics Yearbook 1998.* Washington, DC: IMF.

———. 1999. *International Financial Statistics.* November (CD-ROM).

International Programs Center. Various years. US Bureau of the Census. Unpublished data.

Kopstein, Jeffrey. 1997. *The Politics of Economic Decline in East Germany, 1945–1989.* (Chapel Hill, NC: University Of North Carolina Press.

Kornai, Janos. 1992. *The Socialist System: The Political Economy of Communism.* Princeton, NJ: Princeton University Press.

Krueger, Anne O. 1990. "Asian Trade and Growth Lessons." *American Economic Review* 80(2):108–112.

Kuhrt, Eberhard, ed. 1996. *Die Wirtschaftliche und Oekologishe Situation der DDR in den Achtziger Jahren*. Opladen, Germany: Leske and Budrich.

Lal, Deepak. 1993. "Foreign Trade Regimes and Economic Growth in Developing Countries." Deepak Lal, ed., *The Repressed Economy: Causes, Consequences, Reform*. Brookfield, VT: Ashgate. 169–97.

Lee, Jong-wha. 1995. "Capital Goods Imports and Long-Run Growth." *Journal of Development Economics* 48(1):91–110.

Maddison, Angus. 1998. "Measuring the Performance of a Communist Command Economy: An Assessment of the CIA Estimates for the USSR." *Review of Income and Wealth* 44(3):307–323.

Morgenstern, Oskar. 1963. *On the Accuracy of Economic Observations.*.Princeton, NJ: Princeton University Press.

Park, Chai Bin and Nam Hoon Cho. 1995. "Consequence of Son Preference in a Low Fertility Society: Imbalance of the Sex Ratio at Birth in Korea." *Population And Development Review* 21(1):59–84.

Republic of China (ROC). 1990. *Statistical Yearbook of the Republic of China 1990*. Taipei: Directorate General of Budget, Accounting, and Statistics, Executive Yuan.

Republic of Korea National Statistical Office (ROK NSO). Various years. *Social Indicators in Korea*. Seoul.

———. Various years. *Korea Statistical Yearbook*. Seoul.

Rosefielde, Steven and Ralph W. Pfouts. 1995. "Neoclassical Norms and the Valuation of National Product in the Soviet Union and its Postcommunist Successor States." *Journal of Comparative Economics* 21(3):375–89.

Schneider, Gernot. 1990. *Wirtschaftswunder DDR: Anspruch Und Realitaet* (Tr. The East German Economic Miracle: Claim and Reality). Cologne: Bund Verlag.

Sullivan, Kevin. 1995. "North Korea Makes Rare Plea After Floods Devastate Country." *Washington Post*. 22 September 1995. p. A16.

Syrquin, Moishe and Hollis B. Chenery. 1989. *Patterns of Development: 1950 to 1983*. Washington, DC: World Bank.

UNICEF. "At a Glance: Korea, Democratic People's Republic of." Electronic database. Available at: http://www.unicef.org/infobycountry/korea_statistics.html

United Nations. 1997. *Demographic Yearbook 1995*. New York: United Nations.

United States Bureau of the Census. 1998. *Statistical Abstract of the United States 1998*. Washington, DC: Government Printing Office.

Winiecki, Jan. 1988. *The Distorted World Of Soviet-Type Economies*. Pittsburgh, PA: University Of Pittsburgh Press.

World Bank. 1999. *World Development Report 1999–2000*. New York: Oxford University Press.

World Food Programme. 1999. *Nutritional Survey of the Democratic People's Republic of Korea*. Rome: WFP.

———. 1998–1999. *Nutritional Survey of the Democratic People's Republic of Korea*. Rome: WFP.

Yun, Nam-sik. 1987. *Hangugin ui Ch'ewi*. (Tr. South Korean Physique). Seoul: Ehwa Women's University Press.

6

Prospects for Inter-Korean Economic Cooperation in the "Sunshine" Era*

For the first four decades of inter-Korea relations, the question of devising a workable approach to economic cooperation between the two Koreas would have been nothing more than a fascinating but purely abstract intellectual exercise. The same can hardly be said today: at this writing, inter-Korean trade has been underway for nearly eighteen years, and many billions of dollars of merchandise has been shipped from one half of the Korean peninsula to the other.

The factor that has invested the question of inter-Korean economic cooperation with topicality and practical interest, of course, is the government of the Democratic People's Republic of Korea (DPRK, or North Korea)—more specifically, Pyongyang's apparently evolving attitude toward economic interactions with the Republic of Korea (ROK, or South Korea). Over time, through fits and starts, the DPRK evidenced a greater willingness to pursue concrete measures for promoting and sustaining economic intercourse with the Republic of Korea—so that the economic ties linking North and South today are both broader and deeper than at any previous juncture in the tormented history of the divided peninsula. In South Korea and elsewhere, proponents assert that this expansion of economic linkages between the two Koreas is a consequence of the "Sunshine" policies they favor: that is to say, the official ROK approach toward the North since 1998 that has gone by a number of different names ("Sunshine," "Engagement," "Peace and Prosperity"), but has, under two successive South Korean presidents, consistently emphasized the principles of reconciliation, financial generosity, and postponing reunification.

Indirect trade between the two Koreas commenced officially in 1988—thirty-five years after the cease-fire in the Korean War. Over the following

---

*This chapter was originally published in Korea and World Affairs XXIV(4), winter, pp. 537–572; it has been updated for inclusion here.

decade, Pyongyang tolerated a gradually rising volume of economic transactions, but never really granted the process a seal of official approval. (In late 1991, Pyongyang and Seoul did sign a "North-South Joint Agreement on Reconciliation, Nonaggression, and Cooperation and Exchange," which called for "economic cooperation and exchange . . . and joint investment for the coordinated and balanced development of the national economy and for the promotion of the well-being of the whole nation."[1] But the agreement was lifeless from the outset, for all intents and purposes strangled at birth by its northern signatory.)

The North's reluctance to formalize and legitimize an economic relationship with the South has deep doctrinal roots. The charter of the DPRK's ruling Worker's Party of Korea (WPK),[2] for example, stipulates that the "present task of the WPK is to secure the complete victory of socialism in the [DPRK] and . . . the revolutionary goals of national liberation and people's democracy in the entire area of the country. . .,"[3] i.e., including South Korea. Given the programmatic commitment of the WPK to "establishing a communist society throughout the entire country"[4]—meaning the South—the proposition of economic cooperation with South Korean authorities would seem decidedly problematic. But in 1998—three years into the country's officially acknowledged food emergency, and in a phase of DPRK socialism that authorities termed the "Arduous March," and with the advent of the Sunshine era in the South—Pyongyang's official posture toward economic cooperation with the ROK began to change perceptibly.

In that year, North Korean authorities created the North Korean National Economic Cooperation Federation (NECF) for inter-Korean transactions. With Kim Jong Il's public blessing, the group negotiated a billion-dollar, multi-year deal with South Korea's Chung Ju-yung, founder of the Hyundai business group, whereby Hyundai would ferry tourists from South Korea to North Korea's scenic seaside Kumgang Mountain area. Even then, Pyongyang's acquiescence in the specific deal was meant to be something less than an endorsement of inter-Korean cooperation *per se*. To emphasize the fact that the DPRK had not given its imprimatur to inter-Korean economic cooperation through the Kumgang Mountain project, North Korean authorities maintained that the NECF, the North Korean partner in the venture, was simply a "civic" organization, rather than a North Korean governmental body.[5]

In June 2000, the North Korean government finally crossed the Rubicon, and offered explicit support for inter-Korean economic cooperation from the very highest level, inaugurating the so-called Sunshine era. At the landmark Pyongyang summit between ROK President Kim Dae Jung and Kim Jong Il, Chairman of the DPRK National Defense Commission (NDC), the two leaders ratified a "North-South Joint Declaration," the fourth point of which affirmed that "The North and the South agreed to promote the balanced development of the national economy through economic cooperation. . . ."[6]

In the months following the Pyongyang summit, North Korean authorities repeatedly reaffirmed and expanded upon their new commitment to the principle of inter-Korean economic cooperation. In mid-September, WPK Central Committee Secretary Kim Yong Sun—often regarded by "North Korea watchers" as a Kim Jong Il confidant—traveled to Seoul to meet with Lim Dong Won, an architect of the current ROK Sunshine policy, and chief of the ROK's intelligence service. Following this meeting, a "Joint Communiqué on Kim Yong Sun's Visit" declared, among other things, that the two sides would "open a working-level contact for . . . the ensuring of investment and the prevention of double taxation . . . and strike a deal at an early date in order to promote economic cooperation between the North and the South."[7] A few days later, the first North-South "working level" governmental meeting on economic cooperation was convened in Seoul. The two-day gathering concluded with a communiqué stating that the two sides "agreed to arrange a systematic mechanism at an early date, including the guarantee of investments and the avoidance of double taxation,"[8] and indicated the group would meet the following month in Pyongyang to finalize details on this aspect of economic cooperation. (The meeting also featured an ROK verbal commitment to purchase internationally an additional 600,000 tons of grain as humanitarian food aid for the DPRK.[9]) And almost immediately thereafter, ministerial-level representatives of the DPRK and the ROK meeting in Cheju let it be known that the two sides had agreed to establish a new committee on inter-Korean economic cooperation. The new platform would deal with the re-linking of rail and road ties between the two countries, joint flood management activities, and "other issues of inter-Korean economic cooperation." According to one of the South Korean delegates at these talks, "representatives of the two sides also shared the understanding that cooperation and reconciliation is an irreversible trend."[10]

The sudden and apparently accelerating diplomatic momentum for inter-Korean economic cooperation generated excitement and high expectations not only in South Korea's government, but also in the ROK business community. In late September (2000), the Federation of Korean Industries (FKI), an association supported by the ROK's major business conglomerates, revealed that it was drawing up its own "master plan" for inter-Korean economic cooperation, and would "produce detailed guidelines for the most necessary and feasible inter-Korean projects by time and business sector."[11] Both the Hyundai group and the Samsung group had already outlined ambitious plans for industrial project development in the DPRK. Hyundai's research institute even published a "regional rating of investment conditions" within North Korea, awarding the Pyongyang-Nampo area "A's" for its "Industrial Base," "Openness," "Market

Scale and Prospects," and "Prospects for Development."[12] Illustrative of the business sector outlook on inter-Korean economic cooperation in 2000 was a published assessment by an analyst at the Korea Industrial Bank. According to his report, economic ties between the two Koreas would expand vigorously in the next few years. According to this view, by the following year inter-Korean economic cooperation would be so substantial that it would involve at least US$2 billion in annual hard-currency financing. And by the year 2005, it was expected to proceed on a scale of US$5 to US$10 billion a year.[13]

In the event, of course, these heady plans proved over-optimistic. The true volume of inter-Korean economic cooperation in 2005 was only a tiny fraction of that envisioned just five years earlier; the Pyongyang area remained completely off-limits to South Korean investors; and the joint agreements in 2000 that were to facilitate South Korean investment in the North did not begin to be implemented for an additional three and a half years.

Yet those same optimists might argue that they had only mistaken the departure date for the inter-Korean Sunshine era trade take-off—and they would have had evidence to adduce. In 2005, for example, South Korea announced the establishment a joint ROK-DPRK office, located in the North, to "support investment and direct trade links" between the two countries.[14] In 2005, moreover, work was well underway on the "Kaesong Industrial Complex" (KIC), an ambitious project to transform an area north of the DMZ into a huge economic zone managed by South Korean corporations and run according to international business standards. By early 2006, almost 7,000 North Korean workers and nearly 700 South Korean managers were already employed in "Stage 1" of KIC. By 2012, at the end of "Stage 3," KIC was scheduled to employ *350,000* North Korean workers.[15] In addition, travel (from the South to the North) was becoming a bit more routine. By year-end 2005, over one million South Korean visitors had come to the Kumgang area, and in 2005 alone over 80,000 South Koreans' visits to the North were recorded for non-touristic purposes.[16] Not insignificantly, North Korean leadership has explicitly praised both the Kumgang and the Kaesong projects in the domestic media, extolling them as "our proud successes showing the united power and patriotic will of our nation."[17]

Is inter-Korean economic cooperation really poised for an explosive take-off? Enthusiasts are confident this is the case, and defend their sanguine expectations about the future by pointing out that, a few years earlier, no one could have imagined the particulars of economic rapprochement between the two Koreas now being witnessed. Although their argument was not entirely without merit—it is never possible to conclusively refute today's predictions about tomorrow—in the following pages, I will offer a more skeptical assessment of the prospects for inter-Korean economic cooperation.

To borrow from a formulation recently popular in Washington, prospects for inter-Korean economic cooperation depend upon how one defines "economic cooperation." In the recent past, that term has come to conflate two distinct and very different concepts.

One definition of economic cooperation refers to mutually beneficial exchange between economizing entities, and connotes a process of broadening and deepening transactions that results in greater economic "integration" between the parties in question. But there is now another meaning of the phrase "economic cooperation," which has been embraced internationally as the latest euphemism for the unidirectional state-to-state concessional resource transfers, previously known as "development assistance," and originally called "foreign aid."

If "inter-Korean economic cooperation" is understood to mean unconditional grants and subsidies from Seoul to Pyongyang, then the prospects for inter-Korean economic cooperation look bright. After all, the ROK has shown itself quite willing to give—and with respect to untied aid from abroad, there has never been any question about the DPRK's willingness to receive. However, if "inter-Korean economic cooperation" is taken instead to mean a sturdy commercial relationship grounded in the pursuit of profit, I will argue that the prospects for such cooperation are far cloudier.

Even if the North Korean government were now genuinely committed to a lasting comity with the South, and to developing a business-like pattern of economic engagement across the divided peninsula—propositions which are hardly self-evident—the measures that would be required of the DPRK to sustain a mutually beneficial commerce with the ROK would entail a wrenching and utterly radical departure from the core policies and practices which have characterized the state's behavior for fully half a century. This would be a formidable challenge for any regime, much less a government so proudly defiant of norms beyond its borders and so unwilling in principle to adopt the customs of the outside world.

My argument will proceed through three sections. The first will analyze the current status of inter-Korean economic cooperation, examining its defining characteristics and inherent problems. The second will review the record of inter-German economic cooperation over the Cold War decades to identify parallels, lessons, or implications for the two Koreas. It will then look at another example of economic cooperation within a divided country: the "cross-strait trade" between China and Taiwan, in order to reflect upon what this burgeoning commerce may portend for commerce across the demilitarized zone (DMZ). The final section will discuss a few of the legal, institutional, and behavioral changes which will be required of the DPRK if it is to move toward cultivating a commercially viable and politically sustainable economic relationship with the ROK.

Patterns of Inter-Korean Economic Cooperation to Date

To trace the progress to date of economic relations between North and South Korea, we must rely almost exclusively upon data and information from the ROK. The reason for this one-sided reliance on South Korean materials, as explained in detail in Chapter 2, will be familiar to students of Korean affairs: Pyongyang remains under a self-imposed statistical blackout of extraordinary scope and duration.

For almost four decades, the DPRK has routinely and vigilantly suppressed official social and economic data that might permit outsiders to draw independent conclusions about the performance of the DPRK system. North Korea does not regularly publish data on its trade patterns, and the tidbits it has released on its international trade trends are seriously inconsistent with other, internationally available, information. In fact, as indicated earlier in Chapter 2, it is not even clear that DPRK statistical authorities are today capable of compiling accurate tabulations on this commerce.

But South Korea's official data on inter-Korean economic cooperation are not without their idiosyncrasies and limitations. The ROK maintains that trade between the two Koreas is *domestic* rather than *international* in nature. Consequently, the South Korean government does not compile information through the same ministries and administrative procedures, or in accordance with the same standards that are used for ROK international trade statistics.[18] Not only is the quality of the data on inter-Korean co-operation more problematic than that of ROK trade data, but Seoul also happens to be far less open in sharing the details of its inter-Korean trade with the outside world than one might expect from its ready dissemination of exacting information about its own international merchandise trade trends.[19]

In the Sunshine era, to be sure, inter-Korean economic cooperation is explicitly framed in some measure as an aid relationship, not simply a trade relationship. But the ROK has been a member of the OECD since 1994—and Seoul's exposition of its aid relationship with North Korea meets neither the standards of transparency, of accuracy, or of taxonomic coherence that are entirely routine for reports on aid commitments under the OECD's Development Assistance Committee (DAC).

Here, a single example may suffice. As is now publicly acknowledged, the South Korean government secretly arranged for the transfer of as much as $500 million—including $100 million in taxpayer funds—to the DPRK government in the run-up to the historic June 2000 Pyongyang summit as part of its campaign to induce Kim Jong Il to consent to hosting the Kim Dae Jung visit. President Kim Dae Jung eventually admitted to these transfers in early 2003 (days before he left office), and several of his aides were subsequently convicted in South Korean courts for the illegal use of public monies entailed.[20]

Although these inter-Korean financial transfers are thus by now a matter of public record (including court records), they have yet to show up in any form in MOU inter-Korean economic cooperation statistics.

Despite these shortcomings, South Korean data and information can be used to highlight the basic trends and characteristics that have defined inter-Korean economic cooperation to date.

Progress in inter-Korean economic cooperation since its formal inception is illustrated by Figure 6.1, which plots the growth in overall transaction volume between January 1989 and December 2005.

In cumulative terms, according to ROK figures, economic transactions between North and South have reportedly totaled $6 billion for the 1989–2006 period. This is not a large item in the trade ledgers of the ROK, a country whose exports averaged US$27 billion *per month* in 2005, but it is arguably a significant total for two countries that happen to be—at least officially—at war.

The reported volume of inter-Korean economic activity, furthermore, has been unmistakably rising over time. It is true that inter-Korean economic cooperation declined sharply in 1998—coinciding with the ROK's recession in the wake of its 1997 international liquidity crisis. It dipped again with the flare-up of tensions that followed the revelations of DPRK nuclear violations in late 2002. But the volume of transactions rebounded robustly each time, and has continued to grow to this writing: in 2005, in fact, officially reported North-South turnover exceeded $1 billion for the first time.

Figure 6.1

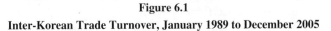

Inter-Korean Trade Turnover, January 1989 to December 2005

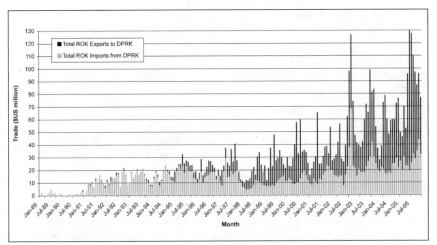

Source: ROK MOU, various years.

Superficially, these might have been promising forensics. A closer look, however, reveals troubling tendencies within this commerce.

As the Sunshine era commenced, the ROK government described its approach to inter-Korean economic cooperation as "separating business from politics."[21] It would be more accurate, unfortunately, to describe that approach—and indeed the approaches of Seoul's two previous, "pre-Sunshine" governments—as "separating trade from comparative advantage," and "separating inter-Korean commerce from the possibility of profit."

Owing to the "socialist calculation problem" identified by von Mises and his "Austrian School" colleagues eight decades ago,[22] there is no reason to expect that North Korean planners can determine the prospective comparative advantage of their national economy's international trade sectors. South Korea's economy is not similarly hobbled: its price system generates meaningful information about scarcity, which in turn provides a basis for economically rational interactions with the outside world. Indeed, South Korea's international trading patterns can be said to offer insight into the country's actual patterns of comparative advantage when contrasted with the patterns characterizing overall global commerce. As Balassa originally argued, the contrast between local and global trade composition offers information about "revealed comparative advantage (RCA)"[23] for the country in question—providing, of course, that the country in question has a market economy.

Given the lack of transparency that has characterized inter-Korean economic cooperation in the Sunshine era—Seoul, for example, has yet to publish detailed and internationally comparable data on the composition of its trade with the North for the period from 1998 onwards—it is impossible to measure South Korea's current patterns of inter-Korean commerce against its current revealed comparative advantage in international trade. We can, however, contrast these quantities for the pre-Sunshine era period, for which such data do exist.

Tables 6.1 through 6.3 juxtapose the composition of inter-Korean merchandise trade for the period 1989–97 with the composition of the ROK's international merchandise trade for the years 1992–95, and place both of these against the backdrop of the ROK's estimated RCA for the year 1995, broken down to the single-digit level under the standard international trade classification (SITC) schema. Though the periods of coverage differ slightly in each case, the differences should not strongly affect results or bias comparisons.

With respect to South Korean imports, RCA calculations indicate a comparative advantage in the categories of mineral fuels (SITC 3) and crude materials (SITC 2), and progressively increasing comparative disadvantage for food (SITC 0), miscellaneous manufacturing (SITC 8) and transactions not elsewhere specified (SITC 9). The composition of South Korea's imports from

Table 6.1
Estimates of Revealed Comparative Advantage (RCA)
in International Trade: Republic of Korea, 1995

SITC Code	Imports	Exports
0 Food, live animals	0.6094	0.2945
1 Beverages, tobacco	0.3841	0.1080
2 Crude materials, excl. fuels	1.9468	0.3469
3 Mineral fuels, etc.	2.0069	0.2780
4 Animal, vegetable oil, fat	0.5669	0.0316
5 Chemicals, related products, n.e.s.	0.9992	0.7659
6 Basic manufactured goods	0.9966	1.3694
7 Machinery, transport equipment	1.0130	1.3567
8 Misc. manufactured articles	0.5543	1.0092
9 Goods not by kind	0.1389	0.0142

Source: National Asia Pacific Economic and Scientific Database.

North Korea appear to be mismatched with the country's RCA, for by comparison with its overall merchandise purchases from abroad, the ROK's purchases from North Korea are significantly under-weighted in the mineral fuel and crude materials categories, and heavily over-represented when it comes to food, miscellaneous manufacturing, and transactions not elsewhere specified (i.e., gold).

The situation is, if anything, even more striking for ROK exports. According to Table 1, South Korea's comparative advantage here lies in the areas of basic manufacturing (SITC 6) and machinery and transport equipment (SITC 7). Significant comparative *disadvantage* is revealed (in ascending order) for crude materials (SITC 2), foodstuffs (SITC 0), mineral fuels (SITC 3), and beverages and tobacco (SITC 1). South Korea's exports to North Korea were heavily weighted toward one area in which the ROK appears to possess an international comparative advantage: namely, basic manufactured goods, more specifically, yarn and fabrics for inter-Korean processing on commission (POC) contracts. Yet machinery and transport equipment—a mainstay of contemporary ROK exports—is utterly under-represented in South Korean shipments to the North. On the other hand, crude materials, foodstuffs, mineral fuels, and beverages and tobacco are grossly over-represented. Such items accounted for less than 6 percent of ROK international merchandise exports in the early and mid 1990s, but they accounted for nearly 35 percent of South Korea's exports to the North between 1989 and 1997. In fact, over those years South Korea's principal reported export to North Korea, by commodity type, was crude oil!

Table 6.2

Composition of South Korean Imports from North Korea vs. ROK International Import Composition

1	2	3	4	5	6
SITC Code Broad Categories	Commodity	Inter-Korean Percentage	International Percentage	Absolute Difference (Columns 3–4)	Relative Difference (Columns 3/4)
0	Food, live animals	7.4	4.6	2.7	1.58
1	Beverages, tobacco	0	0.3	–0.3	*
2	Crude materials, excl. fuels	2.2	9.4	–7.2	0.23
3	Mineral fuels, etc.	2.2	16	–13.9	0.13
4	Animal, vegetable oil, fat	0.1	0.3	–0.2	*
5	Chemicals, related products n.e.s.	0.4	9.4	–9	0.04
6	Basic manufactured goods	46.1	15.5	30.6	2.98
7	Machinery, transport equipment	0.4	35.8	–35.4	0.01
8	Misc. manufactured articles	10	6.1	3.8	1.62
Selected categories					
0–3	Fish and preparations	3	0.6	2.4	4.92
0–4	Cereals and preparations	1.3	1.6	–0.3	0.79
65	Textiles, yarn, fabrics, etc.	1.9	3.2	–1.3	0.6
66	Non-metal mineral manufactures n.e.s.	1.6	1.2	0.5	1.63
67	Iron and steel	7.4	4.4	3	1.69
68	Non-ferrous metals	31.8	3	28.8	10.73
84	Clothing	9.3	0.6	8.7	15.58
85	Footwear	0.1	0	0.1	**
Gold	Gold	31.4	1	30.4	31.55

Notes: Data for inter-Korean trade covers 1989–97; data for international trade covers 1992–95.
Composition of imports refers to the total nominal dollar value of products during that period.
Some apparent discrepancies in columns 5 and 6 result from rounding off in columns 3 and 4.

* = Less than 1 percent of both inter-Korean and international imports.
** = Negligible ROK imports of these products.

Source: Eberstadt, 1998.

Table 6.3

Composition of South Korean Exports to North Korea vs. ROK International Export Composition

1	2	3	4	5	6
SITC Code Broad Categories	Commodity	Inter-Korean Percentage	International Percentage	Absolute Difference (Columns 3–4)	Relative Difference (Columns 3/4)
0	Food, live animals	7.1	2.3	4.8	3.09
1	Beverages, tobacco	1.5	0	1.5	**
2	Crude materials, excl. fuels	7.4	1.4	6	5.42
3	Mineral fuels, etc.	18.6	2	16.6	9.47
4	Animal, vegetable oil, fat	0.4	0	0.4	*
5	Chemicals, related products n.e.s.	6.5	6.1	0.3	1.06
6	Basic manufactured goods	38.2	22.8	15.4	1.67
7	Machinery, transport equipment	12.9	45.8	−32.9	0.28
8	Misc. manufactured articles	7.6	14.1	−6.5	0.54
Selected Categories					
0–3	Fish and preparations	0.2	1.4	−1.2	0.16
0–4	Cereals and preparations	2.5	0	2.5	**
65	Textile, yarn, fabrics, etc.	35.9	10.1	25.8	3.55
66	Non-metal mineral manufactures n.e.s.	0.7	0.7	0	*
67	Iron and steel	1	5	−4.1	0.19
68	Non-ferrous metals	0.3	0.7	−0.5	*
84	Clothing	4.7	6	−1.2	0.79
85	Footwear	1	2	−1	0.5
Gold	Gold	0	0.9	−0.9	*

Notes: Data for inter-Korean trade covers 1989–97; data for international trade covers 1992–95; composition of exports refers to the total nominal dollar value of products during that period; some apparent discrepancies in columns 5 and 6 result from rounding off in columns 3 and 4.

* = Less than 1 percent of both inter-Korean and international exports.

** = Negligible ROK exports of these products.

Source: Eberstadt, 1998.

Suffice it to say that while there are many factors that might possibly explain the composition of inter-Korean economic transactions during the years under consideration, anticipated ROK gains from trade does not look like a strong contender among them. Nor is there reason to expect that the divorce between South Korea's international comparative advantage and its profile in inter-Korean economic cooperation should be less pronounced today than it was a few years ago. On the contrary, with the growing importance of Seoul-to-Pyongyang shipments within this overall commerce, and the increasing weight of food and energy products within Seoul-to-Pyongyang shipments, the schism in the patterns of comparative advantage and patterns of trade between South and North may be even more extreme today than it was before the Sunshine era.

Under the right cost structures and pricing conditions, of course, cross-border transactions can fly in the face of comparative advantage and still result in profit for both sides of the deal. But it is hardly apparent that such anomalous cases figure prominently in Seoul's commerce with Pyongyang. Information about profits and losses on their trade with the North is typically regarded as proprietary information by the South Korean companies engaged in this trade, and tends to be tightly held. Even so, though inter-Korean economic cooperation by now has entailed many thousands of specific transactions, it is not clear that the South Korean partner has made money on a single one of them. Quite the contrary, as for South Korean concerns, trading with the North is understood, at least to date, to be a money-losing proposition.

Emblematic of the indifference to financial loss manifest by ROK businesses dealing with the North is the Hyundai Kumgang Mountain tourism venture— the largest North-South project to date and the flagship of all Sunshine era initiatives in inter-Korean economic cooperation. The Kumgangsan venture commits the Hyundai group to a minimum of US$942 million in payments to the DPRK over the course of the six-year contract. Frontloaded with such exorbitant costs, it is difficult to imagine how the project could ever have hoped to generate a profit. Independent South Korean assessments concluded early on that Hyundai would lose vast sums on the project—at least US$750 million, by some initial estimates. And those assessments might have been *optimistic*, since in the first 11 months of operation alone, the Hyundai cruise tours reportedly lost US$258 million.[24]

Why this equanimity in the face of major losses? Marcus Noland may offer the answer:

Hyundai . . . is in weak financial condition, and it is highly questionable whether it was in any condition to commit nearly US$1 billion to North Korea as is called for in the agreement with the North. When questioned about this, Hyundai officials have indicated that the government would "make it up to us," a claim that was verified in private conversations with government officials.[25]

It seems that the project was recognized as inherently unbankable, and was apparently predicated on the presumption of an eventual governmental assumption of associated risks. Sure enough: in Fall 2001 the ROK National Tourism Organization intervened with public funding to prop up the failing Hyundai Asan Corporation (the Hyundai affiliate responsible for the Kumgang tours),[26] and ever since then has doled out, on a monthly or quarterly basis, as much ROK taxpayer money as was deemed necessary to keep the tour project alive.

It is true that state subvention, or even wholesale bailout, for major business groupings agreeing to undertake government-favored projects is something of a tradition in South Korea.[27] In that respect, the unbankability of Hyundai's North Korean venture is arguably nothing new. But there are inescapable consequences for fashioning business with North Korea as a perpetual loss-leader.

One of them is to deter those businesses that are unable or unwilling to sustain unending losses from entering into or staying involved in inter-Korean economic cooperation. In concrete terms, this means that doing business with North Korea is prohibitive for smaller- and medium-sized South Korean corporations—that is to say, for concerns with relatively limited resources of their own, and without the political clout to draw on state resources to cover risky enterprises. Smaller companies simply cannot afford inter-Korean economic cooperation as it exists today; and those that have already attempted to pursue the North Korean market have mostly given up the quest. As *Business Korea* noted at the time of the Pyongyang summit: "Although about 500 companies have crossed the border over the past ten years, only 30 of them remain in the North."[28] Those remaining firms are, not surprisingly, principally *chaebol* subsidiaries—whose North Korean activities are supported by cross-subsidies from their respective mother-conglomerates.[29] By 2005, the ROK Unification Ministry was estimating that 1,000 South Korean ventures had gone bankrupt in the North, or had curtailed their business there due to losses.[30] To put that figure in perspective: as of late 2004, South Korea's Export-Import bank, the ROK Korea Export Insurance Corporation (KEIC) was estimating that only 40 small and medium size South Korean enterprises (SMEs) were operating in North Korea.[31] South Korea's official response to the unattractive "business environment" facing its country's SMEs in the North: more public guarantees for taking the risk of setting up ventures there. Starting in 2004, KEIC began to draw on a special line of funding from the Unification Ministry's "North-South Economic Cooperation Fund" to indemnify smaller firms against up to 90% of any losses they might incur in doing business with the North.[32]

A second implication of this money-losing strategy is that North-South trade cannot be expected to expand spontaneously, on the strength of its own fundamentals. Despite the South Korean government's willingness to subsidize *chaebol* involvement in inter-Korean economic cooperation, the business environment in the North is sufficiently harsh as to have prevented any expansion of commercial interactions between the two Koreas under the Sunshine era.

This fact is disguised by summary ROK statistics on inter-Korean cooperation, which lump commercial transactions together with non-commercial ones (such as food aid, KEDO-related shipments of oil, and light water reactor components). If ostensibly commercial transactions are disaggregated from this overall traffic, as they are in Figure 6.2, it is apparent that their volume has been stagnating, or worse, since 1995.

In nominal dollar terms, for example, the value of *commercial* turnover in North-South trade was 25 percent lower in the first half of the year 2000 than it had been in the first half of 1995. And for all the ambitious talk of possible joint ventures between North and South Korea, actual ROK investments in North Korean projects reportedly totaled a negligible US$15.4 million as of July 2000—i.e., at the time of the historic North-South Pyongyang summit.[33] ROK policies at that juncture were subsidizing trade with North Korea, but evidently were not yet adequate to subsidize sunken investment in that country.

Figure 6.2
Inter-Korean Commercial Trade, January 1989 to December 2005

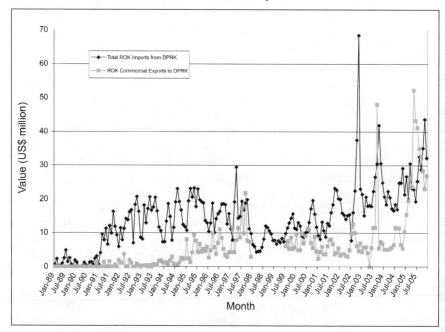

Source: ROK MOU, various years.

The situation did arguably improve after the Pyongyang summit—but not appreciably. For the three year period from July 2000 through June 2003, for example, the level of officially designated North-South "commercial trade turnover" was only barely greater, in nominal dollar terms, than it had been for 1995–97, the three last years of the pre-Sunshine period ($857 million vs. $848 million). Officially designated "commercial exports" from South to North, moreover, averaged under $84 million a year from July 2000 through June 2004—a level below the $92 million a year average for the pre-"Sunshine" period 1996–97, even in nominal terms. Placing the picture in context makes these lackluster results look even more dismal. Between 1995 and 2004, producer prices in the United States (the index against which nominal dollar international trade values arguably should be deflated) rose by about 16%[34]; over that same period, the nominal dollar value of ROK international trade turnover rose by nearly 85%.[35]

It would thus appear by these soundings that commercial North-South trade during most of the Sunshine era had declined in real terms by comparison with the pre-Sunshine years—that North-South commerce accounted for a substantially *smaller* share of South Korea's trade volume in 2004 than it had in 1995, almost a decade earlier (and well before Seoul had made the regular expansion of economic ties with Pyongyang an official policy objective).

In the year 2005, according to Figure 6.2, North-South "commercial" trade enjoyed a dramatic upswing, with ROK "commercial" exports to DPRK more than tripling over the previous year. But these impressive results seem to have been "achieved" through definitional sleight-of-hand. For 2005, the ROK Unification Ministry included as "commercial exports" activities that it described as "economic cooperation projects"—meaning expenditures for developing the Kaesong Industrial Complex, including road and rail links between Kaesong and the South. Much—perhaps most, as MOU presentations are not forthcoming on this point—of these activities were financed by the MOU "North-South Economic Cooperation Fund" and thus by definition public rather than private in nature. Excluding "economic cooperation projects" from the tally, South Korea's "commercial" exports to the North in 2005 would have totaled $119 million—only a marginal improvement, even in nominal terms, over the $115 registered in the pre-Sunshine year 1997.

Although the North-South economic relationship began in the late 1980s on purely commercial terms, inter-Korean "economic cooperation" did entail aid transfers even before the Sunshine era: South Korean government shipments of food aid to the North, for example, began in 1995,[36] during the North Korean famine. Since the advent of the Sunshine era, however, official aid has come to rival and sometimes even displace subsidized trade as the primary vehicle for inter-Korean "economic cooperation." In the second quarter of the year 2000—the period leading up the historic North-South summit—officially reported commercial turnover between North and South reportedly totaled US$54 million, while non-commercial shipments of goods from Seoul to Pyongyang amounted to US$73 million—a first, according to Seoul's statistics on inter-Korean "economic cooperation" and since two successive ROK administrations indicated their receptiveness to a greatly expanded aid program for Pyongyang in the wake of the amicable Pyongyang summit, the prospects were that aid flows would increasingly dominate and define "inter-Korean economic cooperation." Sure enough: by 2004, official Unification Ministry tabulations indicated that non-commercial transactions had edged out ostensibly commercial transactions within overall inter-Korean "economic cooperation"—and the same would be true for the year 2005 if spending on "economic cooperation projects" were counted in the non-commercial rather than the commercial ledger. Even if "economic cooperation projects" are treated as for-profit commerce, however, South Korea's non-commercial shipments of goods to the North over the years 2000–2006 would have been over twice as great as its "commercial" exports to the DPRK—while the trend of ostensibly commercial imports from the North over those same years, more than for any other region from which the ROK purchases goods and services, would reflect the influence of import subventions (Figure 6.3).

The scope for subsidized trade, for its part, will depend in some direct measure upon the depth of the South Korean government's "South-North Economic

Figure 6.3

Inter-Korean Economic Cooperation: Total Commercial Turnover vs. ROK Non-Commercial Shipments to the North, January 2000–December 2005

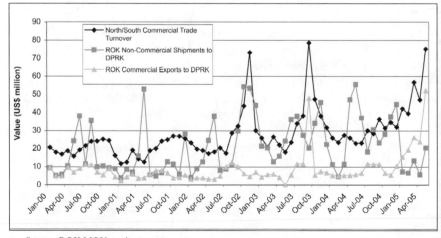

Source: ROK MOU, various years.

Cooperation Fund," and upon the generosity of its terms.[37] Official ROK largesse has been on a generally ascending course over the Sunshine era—and Sunshine proponents are eager to make this ascent steeper. Indeed: in mid-year 2005, MOU officials reported that the government had nearly run through full year's "North-South cooperation fund," which had been allocated over $600 million in the country's 2005 budget; MOU officials proposed a replenishment to the fund at a level of over $850 million (at prevailing exchange rates) for the following year.[38] Whether the ROK administration can continue to convince the public and its representatives to be as generous toward Pyongyang as its Sunshine policymakers would wish, of course, remains an open question. But in any case, for the time being and over the foreseeable future, "inter-Korean economic cooperation" is a venture whose scope is essentially defined by, and ultimately limited to, the providence of the South Korean taxpayer.

Economic Cooperation between Other Divided Nations: Indications and Implications

In assessing the prospects for inter-Korean economic cooperation, it may be useful to review the nations that were split between hostile and ideologically contending states. In the following pages, we will provide a thumbnail summary of some of the facets of inter-German and inter-Chinese economic relations that may prove worthy of consideration in contemplating prospective economic relations between the two Koreas.

Inter-German Economic Relations

Like the two Koreas, West Germany (Federal Republic of Germany, or FRG) and East Germany (German Democratic Republic, or GDR) were sundered through the settlements of World War II.[39] In all, however, commercial relations between communist and non-communist Germany were set on a much more advantageous footing than the one presented to the two Koreas in 1988.

As with divided Korea, the capitalist German state asserted that its commerce with the socialist portion of the country was domestic trade, subject to neither international tariff schedules nor local value-added taxes. Such tax treatment encouraged commerce. But intra-German trade was also supported by a number of historical and institutional factors. For one thing, inter-German trade was never really fully interrupted. Whereas commerce between the two Koreas essentially ceased for almost four decades, between 1950 and 1988, inter-German trade was dislocated for only eleven months, during the Berlin blockade of 1948–49. For another, the German Democratic Republic was programmatically supportive of "economic integration" with external trading partners—in the main, admittedly, its CMEA allies—whereas the DPRK stubbornly foreswore economic integration and upheld the doctrine of *juche* (usually rendered as "self-reliance"). Lastly, the functionaries charged with inter-German commerce, by dint of their particular life-memories and personal experiences, had a reservoir of understanding about the pedestrian requisites of international commerce that is manifestly lacking among North Korean economic functionaries today.

After a fashion, inter-German economic cooperation eventually blossomed. Unlike the DMZ, the Berlin membrane that separated the two Germanys was semi-permeable from 1950 until 1961—hence the loss of over a million GDR citizens over that interim, and the 1961 imposition by the GDR of the infamous "Berlin Wall." With *Ostpolitik,* the West German government by the 1970s had committed itself to "*Annaeherung durch Wandel*," or "rapprochement through change." And inter-German commerce was integral to this vision. Total trade turnover during the 1970s and early 1980s swelled to volumes as yet only imagined for inter-Korean economic cooperation. By 1980, for example, the commerce reportedly topped 10 billion *deutschmarks*—the equivalent today of over US$10 billion. With a smaller population than present-day North Korea, East Germany maintained a trade volume with its counterpart over 20 times greater than today's volume of inter-Korean economic cooperation.

In these particulars, the prospects for the inter-German economic cooperation of yesteryear would appear more favorable than that of inter-Korean economic cooperation today. And yet in the event, inter-German commerce proved to be a self-limiting phenomenon. For West Germany, sales and purchases with the GDR never amounted to even as much as 2 percent of its foreign trade, and the share gradually declined over the course of the 1980s, as inter-German commerce stagnated and the global commerce of the FRG burgeoned.

Why did inter-German commerce stall? Many reasons may be adduced, but perhaps the most important of them was that East German leadership had no interest in economic integration with West Germany. On the contrary, the hierarchy of the East German Socialist Unity Party (SED) judged that while commercial interdependence with its richer and more productive neighbor might offer tangible economic benefits, it would be politically destabilizing for their system.[40] East Germany's leadership opted instead for subsidy in the service of stability—and never permitted inter-German trade to exceed boundaries set by West German aid flows, concessional FRG sales opportunities, and unrepaid debt.

Unlike other Eastern European communist states in the era of détente, East Germany vigilantly eschewed joint ventures with Western partners, and never tolerated more than a handful of such projects with West German partners. Rather than produce Western-quality goods, the SED determined it would import them—at the politically tolerable minimum level. Between 1972 and

1989, the West German government provided East Germany with 14 billion DM in state-to-state aid.[41] These funds helped to finance East Germany's consumer import program. A steady accumulation of hard currency debt—much of it contracted from offshore West German banks which were able to circumvent Bank for International Settlements (BIS) reporting requirements in that manner, provided additional resources for Western, particularly West German, goods purchases. For East Berlin, inter-German trade was thus a means of augmenting resources under the careful control of the state—not a mechanism for initiating unplanned and undirected economic change. Inter-German trade only served a purpose to the extent that it promoted the former and minimized the latter.

Thus inter-German trade was regarded and utilized as an instrument for *preventing* economic reform, *avoiding* economic integration with Western countries, and *concentrating* the power of a command police state. Timothy Garton Ash describes the East German government's strategy lucidly, and is worth quoting at length:

> [T]he economic growth to underpin [East Germany's] welfare and consumer provision was not to be achieved by further market-oriented economic reforms . . . [but] first, by making the existing system (and people) work as hard as possible; second, by technological innovation—Honecker himself was particularly keen on microelectronics; and, last but not least, by opening to the West.
>
> . . . One might describe this political strategy as one of "reform substitution." Social benefits and consumer goods were offered to the people not as complements to a reform of the system but as substitutes for a reform of the system which the Party leadership considered . . . too dangerous . . . and one of the main substitutes for reform was—imports. Imports of Western technology, whether obtained legally or illegally, . . . [i]mports of goods . . . [and] of DM . . .
>
> Honecker was able to sustain this strategy virtually unchanged into the second half of the 1980s, thanks partly to (East) German good housekeeping, efficiency, hard work and so forth, but also crucially, and increasingly, to the financial and economic advantages of the relationship with West Germany. . . .
>
> From the outset . . . the opening to the West was accompanied by redoubled efforts to maintain the Party's political control and ideological rigor. . . . [T]here was also an ideological escalation of what was officially called *Abgrenzung* (with the connotations of "drawing the line" and "fencing off"). The escalation of *Abgrenzung* was the ugly twin sister of the opening to West Germany . . . "Defense education" was stepped up, with verses exalting a soldier's readiness to shoot his West German counterpart . . .
>
> In sum, one has to conclude that after some fifteen years of Honecker's rule and West German "GDR policy," there had been a significant, though still fragile, stabilization of the party-state, but no significant liberalization. If the West German hope had been liberalization through stabilization, the interim balance was stabilization without liberalization.[42]

To repeat the point, "stabilization without liberalization" set strict limits on the scope of possible inter-German economic cooperation. The implications of the experience for inter-Korean economic cooperation would seem direct, and to merit careful consideration.

There is a final aspect of the German experience that is worth mentioning. Militant as the East German communist project was, and omnipresent though its security apparatus may have been, inter-German economic cooperation and exchange nevertheless resulted in a real and increasingly significant loss of economic control by the GDR leadership. The SED recognized the problem early on. In December 1974, SED Secretary Erich Honecker complained to USSR President Leonid Brezhnev that, due to the 1972 "Basic Treaty" (*Grundvertrag*) between the two Germanys, which Brezhnev had supported, the annual number of West German visitors to the GDR had already tripled. Honecker explained:

> Under conditions of mass visitation to the GDR by citizens of the FRG, we believe it is necessary to solve a whole range of social problems (increasing pensions, raising the minimum wage, promoting families, help in child care, speeding up the construction of apartments, hospitals, schools).[43]

The inter-German opening, limited though it was, had unleashed material expectations and consumerist forces with which the East German government now had to contend. Those expectations and forces diverted the state from its preferred economic plan and implicitly challenged the authority of the state to make fundamental decisions about economic life for its subjects. From a Marxist-Leninist perspective, these expectations and forces were fundamentally anti-socialist and counter-revolutionary. Ultimately, as we know, East German leadership was unable to cope with the anti-socialist and counter-revolutionary pressures confronting it from without and within.

This aspect of East German history has not gone unnoticed and unremarked upon by North Korean authorities. In fact, no less a theoretician than Kim Jong Il has analyzed the role of consumerism in contributing to the downfall of Soviet and Eastern European communism. In his 1993 treatise on "Renegades of Socialism," he wrote that those governments acquiesced in

> . . . [t]endencies to rouse people's enthusiasm by means of such material levers as economic incentives . . . If . . . emphasis is put merely on material incentives, this will reduce people to egoists . . . In those societies . . . the building of socialist economy became stagnant . . . [T]hey went so far as to deny the leadership of the working-class party and state over the socialist economy.[44]

North Korean leadership has emphasized repeatedly that they do not intend to repeat Soviet and Eastern European mistakes. Their posture would suggest that for the North Korean state to survive, Pyongyang's approach to economic cooperation with capitalist compatriots must be even stricter, and even more ideological, than that of the former East German government.

Cross-Strait Economic Relations

A very different example of economic cooperation within the framework of a divided nation is provided by contemporary China (People's Republic of China, or PRC) and Taiwan (Republic of China, or ROC).[45] Despite continuing political tension between Beijing and Taipei, and the still-appreciable contrasts between their economic systems, PRC-ROC commerce has boomed since 1988, when Taipei formally permitted indirect cross-strait trade.

The precise volume of this commerce has remained a matter of some uncertainty—fairly significant discrepancies separate some of the data about these transactions officially compiled by the PRC and ROC. Accurate measurement of the commercial and financial linkages across the Taiwan Strait, furthermore, continues to be obscured by a number of practical complications. But the overall picture is clear enough: the scale of commerce across the Taiwan Strait is major, even by the standards of the contemporary world economy—and it has been expanding vigorously, practically year by year.

In the period of 1989–93—the first five full years in which Taipei sanctioned indirect trade with the Mainland—ROC figures tally a cumulative turnover totaling about US$45 billion. Over the next five years (1994–98), according to both Beijing and Taipei, cross-strait trade roughly doubled. In Taipei's estimate, cross-strait trade exceeded US$25 billion in the year 1999. Just six years later— in 2005—total China-Taiwan trade had reached US$76 billion, according to the ROC's Mainland Affairs Council, while the PRC's customs statistics placed the turnover for that same year at over US$90 billion.[46]

As for the investment, Chinese sources put accumulated Taiwanese investment on the Mainland by the year 2000 at nearly US$25 billion—a number so large as to imply that half of all Taiwanese overseas investment in the 1980s and the 1990s might have gone into China.[47] In 2001, according to Taiwan's own figures, one sixth of *all* new investment projects for the ROC were based in China[48]—and in 2005, Taipei calculated that fully 70 percent of all overseas ROC investment was in the Mainland.[49] By year-end 2005, the ROC Ministry of Economic Affairs had approved a cumulative total of about US$47 billion in proposed projects in China (not all subsequently consummated), while the Chinese government identified Taiwanese projects in China with US$90 billion in contracted capital and about US$42 billion in actualized investment.[50] Yet the higher Chinese figure may understate the actual magnitude of Taiwanese investment in China today.[51] Some business sources believe that the true level of Taiwanese capital investment in China had exceeded US$100 billion by 2005.[52]

In sum, despite their acute and unresolved diplomatic frictions, the two Chinas manage to conduct an economic relationship whose turnover volume is almost a hundred times larger than that of the two Koreas.[53] The absolute volume of Taiwanese investment in China, moreover, may be nearly a thousand times greater than South Korea's current total in North Korea.[54] The second point deserves special attention: although China's commercial codes and business laws have been gradually evolving in the direction of international norms since the 1978 opening,[55] these investments enjoy no fixed and inviolable legal protections. Yet Taiwanese businesses have felt confident enough to expose their capital in such an environment because of the security they perceive in their *guanxi* with local Chinese partners.[56] Thanks to this "Asian way of doing business," the risks posed by a socialist system with an ambiguous commitment to property rights and the rule of law have apparently been radically reduced, thereby making China a highly attractive investment environment for Taiwanese compatriots and establishing PRC-ROC economic relations as a model of successful economic cooperation within a divided country.

It is naturally the inter-Chinese model of economic cooperation that South Korean policymakers and businessmen hope to emulate in their dealings with the North. Although this particular expectation is not always spelled out explicitly, many South Koreans seem to feel that their "Asian-ness" will permit them to emulate it; just as the "Asian way of doing business" prevailed for the Taiwanese in socialist China, so the ROK's entrepreneurs will be able to thread the seemingly impenetrable maze of obstacles to doing business in North Korea through cultural approaches that Westerners cannot comprehend.

It is certainly true that South Koreans appreciate the "Korean-ness" of the DPRK and its residents with a sophistication non-Koreans cannot hope to match. At the same time, one may raise questions about the relevance, much less the replicability, of the cross-strait experience for "real existing inter-Korean economic cooperation."

We may begin by recalling the significance in not just the aggregate amount of estimated Taiwanese investment in China, but the total number of projects underway. According to the Chinese government, over 45,000 Taiwanese funded enterprises were operating on the mainland around the turn of the century[57]—around the time, we will recall, that Beijing was estimating overall capitalization of Taiwanese projects in the country at about $25 billion. As a practical matter, this means that most Taiwanese ventures on the mainland are rather small. Their average capitalization, after all, would have been about half a million U.S. dollars, and in most projects undertaken would have been considerably smaller than that. In 1991, according to Chin,[58] the mean capitalization of Taiwanese funded China ventures in the toy sector was US$91,000, but for pearl and jewelry ventures just US$59,000. While the scale of Taiwanese businesses in China has been trending steadily upwards, as of year-end 2005, the average size of all Taiwanese projects approved to date by Beijing remained well below $1.5 million, in the PRC's own official estimate.[59]

Cross-strait economic cooperation, in short, has been built through micro-projects, not mega-deals. The Taiwanese entrepreneurs who have cultivated the cross-strait economic relationship, correlatively, are proprietors of small- and medium-sized businesses, not tycoons. These small business owners did not move their money to China out of kindness for their poorer compatriots or for reasons of patriotism. They were seeking profits on their own hard-earned resources, and were not typically inclined toward throwing their personal wealth away. By available indications, investing in China has made good business sense for most of these concerns. For example, Hsing indicates that gross profit on production on Taiwanese funded shoe-making enterprises in China was about 24 percent, as against 15 percent for shoe firms in Taiwan itself.[60]

Unlike South Korea's economic relations with North Korea, Taiwan does not offer subsidies and concessional aid to China today, and never did. The cross-strait economic relationship has arisen entirely as a consequence of the Taiwanese pursuit of profit—and a reciprocal Chinese capacity for, and assent to, the local generation of profits for these Taiwanese entrepreneurs. For similar conditions to obtain in inter-Korean economic relations, the entire legacy of existing precedents in economic cooperation would have to be repudiated.

Then there is the matter of the actual business practices that make possible today's inter-Chinese economic cooperation. Hsing describes these in some detail, and it is well to keep some of the particulars in mind. Taiwanese employers, he writes, rely upon a "strategy of 'people sea'" in their enterprises in Southern China. They depend upon "free hiring and firing, low wages and very intensive work," drawing upon "the abundant supply of cheap and unprotected migrant workers in [the region]."[61] The preferred hires in this commerce come from the "floating population"—people who have left their officially registered areas of domicile and have no administrative approval for locating in the jurisdiction where they are employed. Business dealings have been facilitated by unimpeded direct communication with the outside world, "By the late 1980s, telephone calls between Hong Kong and Guangzhou could be dialed directly."[62] They have also been signally assisted by what Hsing terms "reform coalitions" between Taiwanese entrepreneurs and local Chinese officials, alliances in which the Chinese cadres assist in redrawing or ignoring state strictures to mutual advantage, deliberately competing against other potential investment venues within mainland China to create a more favorable investment climate by overlooking burdensome official statues.[63] Hsing highlights the emergence of a cohort of "bureaucratic entrepreneurs" as pivotal to the success of inter-Chinese economic cooperation: "A competent cadre," he explains, "is expected to find markets and funds, arrange transport, and obtain materials, new technologies, and expertise for local enterprises,"[64] with the criterion of competence being measured in terms of success in subverting existing state procedures and regulations.[65] Finally, and not least importantly for the success of cross-strait commerce:

> The shared language and culture between the Taiwanese employers and the Chinese employees have facilitated a more effective transfer of managerial skills and the capitalist ideology of efficiency . . . As a Taiwanese investor pointed out, the most evident impact of overseas Chinese investors in China has been the "change of mind" of local Chinese employees and partners.[66]

Margaret Pearson's study of China's "new business elite" probes these new attitudes in greater depth. She finds that among "foreign-sector managers" (FSMs) in Chinese joint ventures (JVs) or wholly owned foreign enterprises (WFOEs), "the views of the business elite toward economic reform and politics are fiercely pro-market and, to a large extent, anti-regime and anti-communist."[67] While she avers that "there is reason to be skeptical that the business elite in the PRC will . . . be at the center of a more progressive form of state-society relations,"[68] she reports:

> [FSM's] views about economic reform in important ways are independent from the dominant ideology and policy of the reformist [Chinese] state. Their views are more market-oriented—and they favor change that goes further—than the policies of [Beijing in] the early and mid 1990s.[69]

Pearson further describes the manner in which these "anti-authoritarian" "economic liberals"[70] have succeeded in "clearly [breaking] the 'organized dependence'"[71] upon which Communist Party control of economic life in a socialist society is predicated. "In joint ventures," she writes,

> the Party presence has not been eliminated completely, but is quite weak. . . . Interference by Party members has come to be seen as an illegitimate intrusion . . . Chinese managers in wholly foreign owned enterprises and representative offices all along have been quite unrestricted by Party reins. Because there is no Chinese state participation in these businesses, they need reserve no role, either open or clandestine, for the Party.[72]

She further reports that the political file or dossier—the instrument through which Marxist-Leninist states have traditionally collected information about and exercised control over their subjects—has fallen into virtual disuse in state relations with parts of China's business elite. In WFOEs, political dossiers are "held in Chinese organizations located outside the foreign company. These managers have thus become remote from the power the Party-state wields through the dossier system."[73]

One further feature of cross-strait intercourse merits mention in the inter-Korean context: this is the dimensions of the human contacts that take place between the societies linked in this successful economic relationship. As of 2005, Taiwan's population (23 million) was somewhat less than half as large as South Korea's (48 million). In that year alone, however, the ROC counted over 4 million Taiwanese visits to the Mainland.[74] Unlike the typical South Korean Sunshine era visit to the North—which involves sealed vehicle or vessel transit to the beautiful but virtually uninhabited Kumgang Mountain area for a brief but memorable tour of the scenery—many of the Taiwanese visitors have become fairly deeply embedded within China.

It is currently thought, for instance, that as many as one million Taiwanese were living in China as of 2005—working there on a regular basis.[75] (That would amount to as much as one tenth of the entire Taiwanese labor force.) In Shanghai alone, received wisdom puts the Taiwanese population at 450,000 to 600,000—and these residents are becoming firmly rooted to the area. One recent survey, indeed, indicated that 30 percent of the Taiwanese businessmen in Shanghai had already bought a home there—and another 40 percent were intending to do so in the coming year.[76]

There is also an enormous sphere of more casual and spontaneous contact among individuals between Taiwan and China, as indicated by some of the data on communications. In the year 2005, according to ROC authorities, a total of over two billion minutes of telephone time—and over six hundred million calls—linked Taiwan and China. That works out to an average of over one and a half million calls a day.[77] Such figures betoken an enormous flow of uncontrolled information cascading into the Mainland: for not all of these were business calls between China-based Taiwanese businessman and their respective home offices.

Will the North Korean government tread down this "Chinese path"? A growing number of foreign analysts speculate that it might well do so. For evidence to corroborate their supposition, some have highlighted Kim Jong Il's repeated unofficial visits to China, where—they say—the Dear Leader embraced the prospect of China-style economic reform for his regime.

We would do well to read North Korea's official accounts of these visits, for according to the North Korean version of events, Kim Jong Il—in the seat of power of Pyongyang's Chinese benefactors—agreed to no such thing.

Consider this formulation, from the official North Korean description of Kim's May 2000 China visit:

> At the talks and meetings the great successes the Communist Party of China has made in the socialist modernization drive with Chinese characteristics by pursuing the policy of reform and opening to suit the specific conditions of the country were hailed *and the signal successes the Worker's Party of Korea has made in socialist construction by leading the Korean people to overcome manifold hardships and difficulties in the revolutionary spirit of self-reliance were highly appreciated.* (Emphasis added.)[78]

Similarly, from the DPRK press on Kim's January 2001 travels to Beijing and Shanghai:

> Jiang Zemin [CCP General Secretary] was delighted to see substantial progress and new achievements made by the Korean people in economic construction . . . and in other fields under the leadership of the the WPK headed by Kim Jong Il. . . . Zhu Rongji [PC premier] in his speech said that in recent years the Korean people have made such remarkable progress and achievements in various domains including socialist construction, national reunification and foreign relations as to attract the world's attention . . . He said that the Chinese people are rejoiced over this [sic] and warmly congratulate the Korean people on their successes.[79]

And this on Kim's next officially depicted China visit, in April 2004:

> Hu [e.g., Hu Jintao, CCP General Secretary] noted that the Party and the people of the DPRK have achieved great successes in the building of a great prosperous powerful nation overcoming manifold difficulties in the spirit of self-reliance and fortitude and made steady and fresh achievements . . . under the leadership of Kim Jong Il, adding China sincerely rejoiced over them.[80]

DPRK resistance to emulating Beijing's "socialist modernization drive with Chinese characteristics" is rooted not in chauvinistic pride or in Pyongyang's exasperating stubbornness, but rather derives from national security concerns. If the DPRK's leadership regards the cross-strait-style economic relationship as fundamentally inconsistent with the preservation of their "own style of socialism" (*urisk sahoejuii*)—a point of view that might not, as we have just seen, look wholly unreasonable—it is difficult to see why Pyongyang would consent to inter-Chinese-style economic cooperation.

Selected Issues in Inter-Korean Economic Cooperation

Having reviewed the current status of inter-Korean economic cooperation and the experiences of economic relations within other nations with divided systems, we may now touch upon some of the issues that must be satisfactorily resolved before inter-Korean economic cooperation can shift to a self-sustaining commercial footing. Many items could be mentioned here. In the interest of brevity, we will simply touch here upon three very general questions.

Pre-legal and Opportunistic Behavior in External Economic Relations

Although "socialist legality" has always been something of a contradiction in terms, the North Korean interpretation of socialism probably represents the most extreme instance of this contradiction. Even the system's most basic written laws, codes, and regulations correspond only problematically with the actual operations of state. The ruling party's congresses and the legislative assembly's elections, for example, have *never* occurred in accordance with the timetables specified in their respective authorizing documents. And as of September 1998, the DPRK had a constitution which did not specify whether the country has a head of state!

In the economic realm, the DPRK is ostensibly a planned economy. Yet for different periods—including the years 1994 to the present—Pyongyang has promulgated no specific economic plan. Kimura has described the DPRK as "a planned economy without planning," a critique North Korean leadership seemed implicitly to acknowledge with the promulgation of a new Law on People's Economic Plans.[81] Even at the highest levels, fixed, pre-existing rules seem to play a surprisingly small role in the operations of state.

Perhaps more than any spot on the face of the earth today, the DPRK lacks a tradition consonant with the observation of the specified parameters, contractual obligations, and enforceable duties presupposed by international business law, and on which it depends. A weak or opaque legal system, to be sure, is not necessarily an insuperable obstacle to mutually beneficial economic cooperation (as the contemporary Chinese experience attests). But when formal legal rules are weak or notional, business dealings require a strong and credible sense that reciprocal obligations do indeed exist, and that the spirit of reciprocal obligation will be honored in the business relationship. In the case of the DPRK, unfortunately, longstanding patterns of international behavior underscore a deeply embedded mentality of situational opportunism in economic relations, in which regime norms support whatever given action or outcome is deemed to be in Pyongyang's immediate advantage at the moment.

Emblematic of the North Korean government's opportunistic view of economic relations is its stance on the repayment of foreign loans. Simply put, North Korea seems to believe it should not have to do so—ever. Thus, North Korea has been in *de facto* default for almost a quarter century on loans contracted with Western banks back in the 1970s. Lest one suspect that this default impasse might have been a consequence of prickly interactions with capitalist financiers, one may note that even when, in earlier periods, North Korea's loans came exclusively from socialist governments, Pyongyang still did not repay its debts. As Soviet sources noted with exasperation, the DPRK was quite willing to reschedule its debts—but never to repay them.[82]

Situational opportunism is further evident in a "hit and run" approach to contracted commercial deals. In the early 1990s, for example, North Korea arranged through an American firm to import US$76 million in grain. The shipment arrived, but Pyongyang never provided payment for it.[83] Later, in the mid-1990s, North Korea entered into a grain-for-zinc barter agreement with the American firm Cargill. Ultimately, the deal fell through when North Korean authorities reported that they did not have the requisite zinc for the swap. It was later learned that the North Korean side had realized that the spot price of zinc had risen US$100 a ton above the Cargill contract price—and had simply sold the allotment to another buyer.[84] These two incidents merit special consideration since the firms in question were American—and establishing an economic relationship with the United States was a high regime priority at that very time. Important as cultivating better economic relations with the United States may have been, short-term thinking and predatory predilections won out.

The DPRK's lack of binding legal structures, together with its "hunter-gatherer" approach to commercial transactions with external parties, raises serious doubts about the prospects for dispute resolution in inter-Korean economic dealings. In 1994, the DPRK passed the "External Economic Arbitration Law," which established a "Korea International Trade Arbitration Committee" to adjudicate commercial disputes involving foreigners. However, the law specified that the body was to be composed entirely of DPRK cadres. Is it possible to imagine any circumstances in any case under its review in which this "external" panel could rule in favor of a foreign party and against the DPRK side?

For the DPRK, today as in the past, a disadvantageous financial outcome in any transaction between the North Korean state and an outside party seems to be regarded as something very close to an infringement upon national sovereignty. Thus, acquiescence in a disadvantageous deal constitutes something very close to treason. It will be necessary to change this outlook before mutually beneficial commerce between the two Koreas can proceed.

The Problem of Profit for the Non-DPRK Side

Can the DPRK condone *any* economic arrangement with an outside party that results in a profit for its partners? The answer to this question is not at all clear.

Under North Korean civil law (when such laws were being written and published), making a profit of any sort was flatly illegal for any DPRK citizen.[85]

The only entity authorized to profit on economic transactions within the DPRK was the North Korean state.

Whether Pyongyang is, by analogy, also categorically opposed to the accruing of profits in North Korea by outsiders is an issue of deepest import for the future of inter-Korean economic cooperation. While the evidence is ambiguous on this point, indications are not reassuring.

The North Korean government seems to hold a peculiarly political view of international trade and finance, a perspective in which these transactions, far from promising mutual gains from trade, entail zero-sum struggle in which one party's gain must be the other's loss. More than one foreign concern has emerged from deliberations with the DPRK under the impression that their counterparts regarded a deal in which the non-DPRK side had a chance at making money as a failure of North Korean negotiating skills.

These attitudes are in keeping with the pre-modern, tribute-seeking strategies that have so strongly defined North Korean international economic behavior. By that worldview, North Korea's role is to receive, and it is the duty of others to give. Inter-Korean economic cooperation has been strongly shaped by this worldview. As a South Korean business magazine opined in the year of the historic North-South summit, "North Korea does not recognize inter-Korean trade officially, but just accepts it as a kind of 'charity' that successful South Korean tycoons act out of patriotism to help their North Korean countrymen."[86] Pronouncements by North Korean media since that summit seemingly continue to validate this assessment. Consider, for example, the following from Pyongyang's official press agency, KCNA from year-end 2005:

> . . . the South Korean authorities are openly revealing their attempt to change the system in the North whenever they are talking about "investment in the North". . . . "Aid to the North," "investment in the North" and "economic exchange and cooperation" touted by the South Korean authorities once again brought to light their intention to extend their "liberal democratic system" to the North. . . . The South Korean authorities seek to destabilize the North through cooperation and exchange but it is nothing but a foolish day-dream.[87]

Discarding this worldview will not be a sufficient condition for a mutually beneficial economic relationship with the South, but it is surely a necessary one.

Transfer of Skills and Managerial Know-how

The transfer of technical and managerial skills will presumably be necessary if inter-Korean economic integration is to proceed, and if South Korean ventures in the North are to earn profits from their activities there. The DPRK government, however, seems to regard just such transfers as inherently risky, and potentially subversive.

Ever since the collapse of the Soviet bloc, the danger of "cultural and ideological infiltration" has been an abiding preoccupation of North Korean leadership, and in its pronouncements. In Pyongyang's assessment, "ideological and cultural infiltration" figured centrally in the downfall of Soviet and Eastern European socialism. Through such infiltration, Pyongyang warns, international imperialism will always "try to spread bourgeois reactionary ideology and corrupt bourgeois culture and way of life."[88] The invocation against "ideological and cultural infiltration" has remained steady fare in the North Korean media throughout the Sunshine era. Indeed: the DPRK's most recent New Year's Day joint editorial—the government's most important regular policy pronouncement—specifically instructed:

> Everybody should resolutely crush the enemies' mean ideological and cultural infiltration and psychological warfare with revolutionary offensive of ideology, and absolutely keep all kinds of alien elements that gnaw away the socialist system from infiltrating.[89]

But what exactly *is* "ideological and cultural infiltration," and how does it occur? North Korea's leadership has described the methods quite precisely:

> First, they infiltrate the bourgeois idea and culture into other countries through economic "exchanges" . . . The imperialists use these exchanges to spread their bourgeois reactionary ideology and rotten bourgeois culture and lifestyle. Technical cooperation, joint ventures, and joint management are frequently used in developing economic relations between countries. . . . Waiting for this critical moment, the imperialists have slyly placed impure elements in delegations, groups of visitors, inspecting teams, tourists entering other countries, and manipulated them in order to use them to infiltrate ideological culture. These people cunningly maneuver to create a fantasy about capitalism through contacts with the people in a given country.[90]

Unfortunately, the DPRK's definition of what "cultural and ideological infiltration" entails is not readily distinguishable from what outsiders would call education or training. Under such circumstances, the scope for training and educating the North Korean workforce or North Korean managers involved in inter-Korean economic cooperation would seem to be distinctly limited. Yet there clearly remains room for improvement in the technical skills and managerial know-how of the North Korean populace—and even of those at high levels, entrusted with weighty responsibilities.[91]

To conclude: in 2000, North-South relations seemed to be on the threshold of a new and very different era—one in which both governments might support and explore avenues for inter-Korean cooperation. For better or worse, the same may still be said six years later.

By all means let us hope the promise of those new tendencies in North-South relations will eventually be realized. Progress in inter-Korean economic cooperation, however, will require unflinching realism about where things stand today, and about how much remains to be done before *mutually beneficial* economic interactions can be routinized. Heartening as it may be to see the deliberations of the two Korean governments over a treaty to avoid the double taxation of profits generated by a future inter-Korean commerce, we must recognize that there are rather more immediate issues which must resolved before a sound commercial relationship between the two Koreas can ripen.

Notes

1. The full text of "North-South Joint Agreement on Reconciliation, Non-aggression, and Cooperation and Exchange" is available electronically on the website of *People's Korea* at: http://www.korea-p.co.jp/pk.
2. *Choson Nodongdang*, or WPK.
3. The 1980 Charter (or Rules) of the WPK is translated in Yang (1994), pp. 905–931; citation at p. 907.
4. Ibid., p. 907.
5. For background on the NECF, see *FBIS*-EAS-2000-0926a.
6. *KCNA*, 2000, accessed on the website of *People's Korea*.
7. *People's Korea*, 2000.
8. *FBIS*-EAS-2000-0926b.
9. *FBIS*-EAS-2000-0928a.
10. *FBIS*-EAS-2000-0928b.
11. *FBIS*-EAS-2000-0928c.
12. Hyundai Research Institute, 2000, p. 12.
13. Kim, 2000, pp. 138–147.
14. *China Daily*, 2005.
15. For more details, see ROK MOU, 2006.
16. Derived from ROK MOU, various years.
17. *BBC Monitoring International Reports*, 2006 (13 January).
18. Inter-Korean trade statistics are collected by the ROK Ministry of Unification (ROK MOU); the MOU has released only one publication which describes inter-Korean trade in accordance with the conventional international trade taxonomies (HS and SITC), and at that, only for the years 1989–1997; see Republic of Korea Ministry of Unification, 1998; thus, as of this writing, internationally comparable data on the composition of inter-Korean trade are apparently unavailable for the entire Sunshine era!
19. Furthermore, ROK official data on inter-Korean trade and economic exchange, are marked by some inconsistencies of coverage and definition, and include some highly questionable implicit prices for a number of major transactions.
20. Marquand, 2003, p. 8; Ward, 2003, p. 11; *Korea Times*, 2004.
21. *Korea Times*, 1998.

22. See von Mises, 1951 (English language version), and Hayek, 1935.
23. Balassa, 1965.
24. For more details, see Kim and Yoon, 1999, and *FBIS*-EAS-1999-1217.
25. Noland, 2000, p. 116.
26. *AFX News Ltd.*, 2001.
27. See ibid., and Clifford, 1997; it is also true that such arrangements nicely exemplify the concept of "moral hazard" which contributed so directly to South Korea's 1997 financial crisis—but that is another story.
28. *Business Korea*, 2000, pp. 24–25.
29. Some sources offer somewhat different totals: a news report in 2005, for example, wrote that "immediately after the June 2000 North-South summit between Kim Jong Il and Kim Dae Jung, 670 companies had some form of trading link with the North, but 15 months later only 171 remained involved"; while exact numbers may be a matter of dispute, there is no ambiguity about the trend; Alford, 2005.
30. Faiola and Cho, 2005, p. A. 23.
31. *Korea Times*, 2004 (25 September).
32. *Asia Pulse,* 2005 (22 August).
33. Lee, 2000.
34. United States Census Bureau (USCB) 2005. Table 705, p. 481.
35. Derived from World Trade Organization (WTO) "Statistics Database."
36. *Associated Press*, 1995.
37. Korea Institute for National Reunification (KINR), 2000, p. 133; "the guideline stipulates that the financial support (loans with annual interest of 6 percent for up to 7 years) will be provided within 50 percent of the total budget of a program in [South] Korean currency under condition that the loan should not exceed the amount after deducting funds raised by itself or received from North Korea or financial organizations in a third country in loans"; in sum, the grant component of these loans is appreciable.
38. *Yonhap*, 2005.
39. For background, see Holbik and Myers (1964), Jacobsen (1985 and 1987), and Plock (1993).
40. East German state and party archives reveal the extent to which the hierarchy in East Berlin deliberated explicitly about such matters; see, for example, Kopstein, 1997.
41. Garton Ash, 1993, p. 158.
42. Ibid., pp. 187–194.
43. Kopstein, op. cit., p. 86.
44. *FBIS*-EAS 1993-0305.
45. For background, see Chen and Kan (1997), Chin (1994), Freund (1997), Hsing (1998), Leng (1998), Sutter (2002), Susuga (2004), Chase et al. (2004), and Ash (2005).
46. ROC, 2005; Table 5.
47. *BBC,* 2000.
48. Chase et al., 2004, p. 51.
49. Hille, 2006.
50. ROC, 2005, Table 10.
51. For example, Ash (2005) asserts that the overwhelming majority of investments in China from the Cayman Island and British Virgin Island venues are in fact

Taiwanese in origin; such flows had reached an annual US dollar volume in the billions by the turn of the century.

52. Chen, 2005, p. 21.
53. This generalization holds despite the spike in North-South "economic cooperation" in 2005, the most recent year for which data are yet available.
54. Depending upon just what one counts as "investment"—and who happens to be doing the counting.
55 See Guo (1999), Potter (1999), and Zhang (1997); China's post-Mao economic policy shift can be dated to the December 1978 3rd Plenum of the 12th Chinese Communist Party Congress.
56. "*Guanxi*" is probably untranslatable into English, but may be approximated by the concepts of "special relationship" and "network"; for discussions of the role of personal relationships in cross-strait business, and in East Asian business more generally, see Chen and Chen (1998), Hsing (1996), Hsing (1998), La Croix and Xu (1994), Lee (1997), Luo (1998), Perkins (2000), and Redding (1995).
57. *The People's Daily*, 2000.
58. Chin, 1994, pp. 218–219.
59. ROC, 2005, Table 10.
60. Hsing, 1998, p. 18.
61. Ibid., p. 79.
62. Ibid., p. 20.
63. Ibid., p. 130.
64. Ibid., p. 127.
65. "Bureaucratic entrepreneurs" are also rewarded for their efforts by gifts and payments from grateful outside partners—precisely the arrangements that reportedly led to the disappearance of the DPRK's Kim Jong U, mastermind of North Korea's ill-fated Rajin-Sonbong "Free Economic Trade Zone."
66. Hsing, 1998, p. 106.
67. Pearson, 1997, p. 4.
68. Ibid., p. 164.
69. Ibid., p. 88.
70. Ibid., p. 95.
71. Ibid., p. 86.
72. Ibid., pp. 69–71.
73. bid., pp. 73–74.
74. ROC, 2005.
75. *Agence France Presse*, 2005
76. *Asia Pulse*, 2005 (11 August).
77. ROC, 2005.
78. *KCNA*, 2000 (1 June).
79. *KCNA*, 2001.
80. *KCNA*, 2004.
81. Kimura, 1994; the law was adopted in April 1999; for the text of the law, see the *People's Korea* website http://www.korea-np.co.jp/pk/; the quality of North Korea's published statistical materials raises the question of whether the DPRK statistical apparatus is currently capable of providing decision makers with the data they would need to frame and implement economic plans.
82. See van Ree, 1989.
83. Quinones, 1997.

84. *Washington Times*, 1997, p. A19.
85. Roh, 2000.
86. *Business Korea*, 2000, p. 25.
87. *KCNA*, 2005.
88. See *BBC* Summary, 1996; *FBIS*-EAS-2000-0630; *FBIS*-EAS-2000-0823.
89. *BBC Worldwide Monitoring*, 1 January.
90. *FBIS*-EAS-1997-0626.
91. Two vignettes may illustrate the point:

In early 1998, an official from the World Bank visited Pyongyang to explain the purpose and functions of the World Bank and other international financial institutions; at the DPRK's Central Bank, his presentation was interrupted by the bank's director, who asked for a brief explanation of the difference between "macroeconomics" and "microeconomics"; Claire Topal, (2005) "Brinkmanship or Engagement? The Koreas in 2005," *Tufts-Fletcher-News*, available at: http://fletcher.tufts.edu/news/2005/03/korea-conf.shtml.

And in late 2005, over seven years later, the DPRK's leading economic journal *Kyongje Yongu* saw fit to give prominent placement to an article that explained for its audience in the most general of terms the concept of double-entry bookkeeping; *FBIS*, 2006.

References

AFX News Ltd. 2001. "Hyundai Asan calls on government to pay out 45 billion *won* of pledged 90 billion aid." 26 October.
Agence France Presse. 2005. "China, Taiwan agree to direct flights during 2006 Lunar New Year." 18 November.
Asia Pulse. 2005 (11 August). "Taiwan Investors Looking North to China's Yangtze Delta." Hong Kong. 11 August.
———. 2005 (22 August). "S. Korean State Insurer to Help Resource Development in N. Korea."
Ash, Robert F. 2005. "China's Regional Economies and the Asian Region: Building Independent Linkages." In David Shambaugh, ed. *Power Shift: China and Asia's New Dynamics*. Berkely, CA: University of California Press. 96–131.
Associated Press. 1995. "First Batch of Emergency Food Aid Arrives in North Korea." 26 June.
Balassa, B. 1965. "Trade Liberalization and 'Revealed' Comparative Advantage." The Manchester School 33(2):99–123.
British Broadcasting Corporation (BBC) Summary of World Broadcasts. 1996. Rebroadcast from *KCNA* (Pyongyang) 5 September as "Party daily warns against 'cultural infiltration.'" FE/D2710/D.
———. 2000 (20 September). Rebroadcast from Xinhua News Service (Beijing, 13 September "Trade Between Taiwan, Mainland Growing." FE/W0658/WG.
BBC Worldwide Monitoring International Reports. 2006. "Full text of North Korean new year editorial." 1 January.
———. 2006 (13 January). Rebroadcast from *Nodong Sinmun*, 3 January as "North Korean Paper Stresses Nation's Patriotic Spirit." A200601132F-FBDD-GNW.
Business Korea. 2000. "To Good to Be True?" 24–25 July.

Chase, Michael P., Kevin L. Pollpeter, and James C. Mulvenon. 2004. *Shanghaied? The Economic and Political Implications of Information Technology and Investment across the Taiwan Strait.* Santa Monica, CA: RAND Corporation. TR-133.

Chen, Homin and Tain-Jy Chen. 1998. "Network Linkage and Location Choice in Foreign Direct Investment." *Journal of International Business Studies* 29(3):445–68.

Chen, Shiyin. 2005. "Poll result adds gloss to shares in Taiwan." *International Herald Tribune.* 15 December.

Chen, Pochih and Chak-yuen Kan. 1997. "Taiwan's Trade and Investment in China." Kui-wai Li, ed. *Financing China Trade and Investment.* Westport, CT: Praeger. 121–37.

Chin, Chung. 1994. "Taiwan's DFI in Mainland China: Impact on the Domestic and Host Economies." Thomas P. Lyons and Victor Nee, eds. *The Economic Transformation of South China: Reform and Development in the Post-Mao Era.* Ithaca, NY: Cornell University Press. 215–42.

China Daily. 2005. "ROK and DPRK to open historic joint trade office." Beijing. 28 October.

Clifford, Mark. 1997. *Troubled Tiger: Businessmen, Bureaucrats and Generals in South Korea* (rev. ed.). Armonk, NY: M.E. Sharpe.

Eberstadt, Nicholas. 1998. "Inter-Korean Trade, 1989–1997: Decomposition In Accordance With SITC, Rev. 1" Seattle, WA: National Bureau of Asian Research, December. Unpublished.

Faiola, Anthony and Joohee Cho. 2005. "Perils of Investing in N. Korea Become Clear to a Pioneer." *Washington Post.* 24 November.

———. 2000. "Prospects for Inter-Korean Economic Cooperation in the "Sunshine" Era." *Korea and World Affairs* XXIV(4). Winter. pp. 537–572.

FBIS-EAS-1993-0305 (5 March 1993) Reprinted from *KCNA Radio* (Pyongyang): "Kim Chong-il Rejects 'Renegades' of Socialism."

——— -1997-0626 (26 June 1997). Reprinted from *Nodong Sinmun* (24 May 1997): "North Korea: Daily Warns against Ideological 'Infiltration'."

——— -1999-1217 (17 December 1999). Reprinted from *Yonhap* as "Naval Clash 'Biggest Headline."

——— -2000-0630 (30 June 2000). Reprinted from *Nodong Sinmun* as "DPRK: Party Principle of Giving Priority to Ideological Work Discussed."

——— -2000-0823 (23 August 2000). Reprinted from *Minju Choson* (10 August 2000) and *Nodong Sinmun* (22 August 2000) as "DPRK: US Ideo-Cultural Infiltration Viewed."

——— -2000-0926a (26 September 2000). Reprinted from *Yonhap* as "Role of DPRK National Eco-Cooperation Fed in N-S Korean Economic Talks Noted."

——— -2000-0926b (26 September 2000). Reprinted from *Yonhap* as "ROK's Yonhap Reports on Full Text of Joint Communiqué on N-S Economic Cooperation."

——— -2000-0928a (28 September 2000).Reprinted from *Yonhap* as "ROK's Yonhap: Seoul to Offer 600,000 Tons of Rice, Corn by Year-End."

——— -2000-0928b (28 September 2000). Reprinted from *Yonhap* as "ROK, DPRK Agree To Launch Economic Cooperation Committee."

——— -2000-0928c (28 September 2000). Reprinted from *Yonhap* as "ROK's Yonhap: FKI to Draw up Master Plan for Inter-Korean Business.

——— -2006. Reprinted from *Kyongje Yongu, no. 4, 2005,* as "DPRK Economic Journal Explains Workings of Double-Entry Bookkeeping, Urges Methodology." 18 February 2006, document no. 200602181477.1_7b27056f7c27f3a8.

Freund, Elizabeth M. 1997. "Growing Interdependence: Economic Relations between China and Taiwan." Christopher Hudson, ed. 1997. *The China Handbook*. Chicago: Fitzroy Dearborn Publishing. 59–68.

Garton Ash, Timothy. 1993. *In Europe's Name: Germany and the Divided Continent*. New York: Random House.

Guo, Rongxing. 1999, *How the Chinese Economy Works*. New York: St. Martin's Press.

Hayek, F.A., ed. 1935. *Collectivist Economic Planning*. London: George Routledge & Sons, Ltd.

Hille, Kathrin. 2006. "China ire as Taiwan curbs business deals." *Financial Times*. 11 April.

Holbik, Karel and Henry Myers. 1964. *Postwar Trade in Divided Germany*. Baltimore, MD: Johns Hopkins University Press.

Hsing, You-tien. 1996. "Blood, thicker than water: Interpersonal relations and Taiwanese investment in Southern China." *Environment and Planning A* 28:2241–61.

———. 1998. *Making Capitalism in China: The Taiwan Connection*. New York: Oxford University Press.

Hyundai Research Institute. 2000. "Strategies for Investing in North Korea." VIP Milennium Report 2000. Seoul. 8 August

Jacobsen, Hanns-D. 1985. "The Special Case of Inter-German Relations." Reinhard Rode and Hanns-D. Jacobsen, eds. *Economic Warfare or Détente: An Assessment of East-West Economic Relations in the 1980s*. Boulder, CO: Westview Press. 120–27.

———. 1987. "The Foreign Trade and Payments of the GDR in a Changing World Economy." Ian Jeffries and Manfred Melzer, eds. *The East German Economy*. London: Croom Helm. 235–60.

Korea Central News Agency (KCNA). 2000 (1 June). "Kim Jong Il pays unofficial visit to China." Available at: http://www.korea-np.co.jp/pk

———. 2000 (15 June). "Joint North-South Declaration." Pyongyang.

———. 2001. "Kim Jong Il pays unofficial visit to China." 21 January. Available at: http://www.kcna.co.jp

———. 2004. "Kim Jong Il Pays Unofficial Visit To China." 23 April. Available at: http://www.kcna.co.jp

———. 2005. "S. Korean Authorities' Scheme to Undermine North Assailed." 2 December. Available at: http://www.kcna.co.jp

Kim, Ki-Jung and Deok Ryong Yoon. 1999. "Beyond Mt. Kumgang: Social and Economic Implications." Chung-in Moon and David I. Steinberg, eds. *Kim Dae-jung Government and Sunshine Policy: Promises and Challenges*. Seoul: Yonsei University Press. 105–34.

Kim, Myung-shik. 2000. "Financing Methods for North Korean Development." *The Economics of Korean Reunification* (Seoul), vol. 5, no. 1 (2000), pp. 138–47.

Kimura, Mitsuhiko. 1994. "A planned economy without planning: Su-ryong's North Korea." Discussion Paper F-081, Faculty of Economics, Tezukayama University (Japan).

Kopstein, Jeffrey. 1997. *The Politics of Economic Decline in East Germany, 1945–1989*. Chapel Hill, NC: University of North Carolina Press.

Korea Times. 1998. "Kim Pledges to Pursue Unification Policy Backed by Both Progressives, Conservatives." 19 August.

———. 2004 (29 March). "Supreme Court Conforms Guilt Verdict in 'Cash-for-Summit' Scandal."

———. 2004 (25 September). "Exim Bank to Finance Investors in Korea."

Korea Institute for National Reunification (KINU). 2000. *The Unification Environment and Relations between South and North Korea.* Seoul: KINU.

La Croix, Sumner J. and Yibo Xu. 1994. "Political Uncertainty and Taiwan's Investment in Xiamen Special Economic Zone." Sumner J. La Croix, Michael Plummer, and Keun Lee, eds. *Emerging Patterns of East Asian Investment in China.* Armonk, NY: M. E. Sharpe. 23–142.

Lee, Charles. 2000. "Koreas Discuss Investing in the North." *United Press International.* 25 September.

Lee, Tahirih V., ed. 1997. *Contract, Guanxi and Dispute Resolution in China.* New York: Garland Publishers.

Leng, Tse-Kang. 1998. "Dynamic Taiwan-Mainland China Economic Relations." *Asian Survey* 38(5):494–509.

Luo, Yadong. 1998. *International Investment Strategies in the People's Republic of China.* Brookfield, VT: Ashfield.

Marquand, Robert. 2003. "Summit Scandal Rocks South Korea." *Christian Science Monitor.* 20 March.

Mises, Ludwig von. 1951. *Socialism.* New Haven, CT: Yale University Press.

National Asia and Pacific Economic and Scientific Database (NAPES). Available electronically at: http://napes.anv.edu.av/nph/reademo.html

Noland, Marcus. 2000. *Avoiding the Apocalypse: The Future of the Two Koreas.* Washington: Institute for International Economics.

Pearson, Margaret M. 1997. *China's New Business Elite: The Political Consequences of Economic Reform.* Berkeley, CA: University of California Press.

The People's Daily (online). 2000. "Cross Straits Trade Rising." 13 September. Available at: http://english.people.com.cn/english/200009/13/eng20000913_50452.html

People's Korea. 2000a. "Joint Communiqué on Kim Yong Sun's Visit." 22 September.

———. 2000b. "Kim Jong Il pays unofficial visit to China." 1 June. KCNA (Pyongyang); available at: http://www.korea-np.co.jp/pk

Perkins, Dwight H. 2000. "Law, Family Ties, and the East Asian Way of Business." Lawrence E. Harrison and Samuel P. Huntington, eds. *Culture Matters: How Values Shape Human Progress.* New York: Basic Books. 232–43.

Alford, Peter. 2005. "N.Korea turns on its savior." *The Australian.* 26 October.

Plock, Ernest D. 1993. *East German-West German Relations and the Fall of the GDR.* Boulder, CO: Westview Press.

Potter, Pitman B. 1999. "The Chinese Legal System: Continuing Commitment to the Primacy of the State." *China Quarterly* 159:673–83.

Quinones, C. Kenneth. 1997. "Food and Political Stability in North Korea." Korea Economic Institute of America. *Korea's Economy* 13:97–103.

Roh, Jeong-Ho. 2000. "Making Sense of the DPRK Domestic Legal Regime: Mechanisms or Control." Paper presented at the Workshop on the North Korean System in The Post Cold-War Era. Columbia University. East Asian Institute. 19–20 May.

Redding, Gordon. 1995. "Overseas Chinese Networks: Understanding the Enigma." *Long Range Planning* 28(1):61–9.

Republic of China (ROC). 2005. *Cross-Strait Economic Statistics Monthly, No. 157.* Taipei: Mainland Affairs Council. December. Available at: http://www.mac.gov.tw/index.htm

Republic of Korea Ministry of Unification (ROK MOU). English Language Website. Available electronically at http://www.unikorea.go.kr/eg

———. 1998, Nambuk Kyoyoek Tonggye Charyo 1989–1997 (Tr. North-South Trade Statistical Compilation). Seoul: MOU.

———. 2006. "Introduction to and Implications of Gaesong Industrial Complex." April. Available at: http://www.keia.org/3-Programs/kaesong.final.presentation.pdf

———. Various years. "Inter-Korean Cooperation: Overview of Intra-Korean Exchanges and Cooperation." Available at: http://www.unikorea.go.kr

Susuga, Katsuhiro. 2004. *Microregionalism and Governance in East Asia.* London: Routledge.

Sutter, Karen M. 2002. "Business Dynamism across the Taiwan Strait: The Implications for Cross-Strait Relations." *Asian Survey* 41(3): 522–540.

Topal, Claire. 2005. "Brinkmanship or Engagement? The Koreas in 2005." *Tufts-Fletcher-News.* Available at: http://fletcher.tufts.edu/news/2005/03/korea-conf.shtml

United States Bureau of the Census. 2005. *Statistical Abstract of the United States: 2006.* Washington, D.C.: Government Printing Office.

Van Ree, Erik. 1989. "The Limits of Juche: North Korea's Dependence on Soviet Industrial Aid, 1953–1976." *Journal of Communist Studies* 5(1):50–73.

Ward, Andrew. 2003. "S. Korea 'Did Pay for Summit': Prosecutor's Findings." *Financial Times.* 26 June.

Washington Times. 1997. "Pyongyang voids swap to cash in on zinc." 19 June 1997.

World Trade Organization (WTO). "Statistics Database." Available at: http://www.wto.org/english/res_e/statis_e/statis_e.htm

Yang, Sang Chul. 1994. *The North and South Korean Political Systems: A Comparative Analysis.* Boulder, CO: Westview Press.

Yang, Ya-huei, Tzong-ta Yen and Ying-yi Tu. 1996. "The Financial Aspects of Taiwanese Investment in South China." Chung-Hua Institution for Economic Research Discussion Paper Series (Taipei), No. 9602.

Yonhap. 2005. "Ruling camp seeks more money for inter-Korean economic projects." Seoul. 22 July.

Zhang, Zhaoyang. 1997. "China's Foreign Trade Reform and Export Performance." *Asian Profile* (Hong Kong) 25(3):177–92.

7

Economic Recovery in the DPRK: Status and Prospects*

Early in September 2000, a front page story in the *Washington Post* nicely captured the newly prevailing view among international "North Korea watchers" concerning the Democratic People's Republic of Korea (DPRK, or North Korea) economy's current condition and immediate outlook. The article, titled "North Korea Back from the Brink," reported that "[visitors and other analysts] say the North Korean economy is growing for the first time in nine years, the mass starvation is over. . . ." It remarked upon "nascent signs of recovery—more traffic on the roads, more livestock in the fields, peasants who look healthy." The story further noted that the Republic of Korea's Bank of Korea (BOK) recently "concluded, with some surprise, that the North's economy grew last year by a sustainable 6.2 percent, the first growth since 1990" and quoted the Republic of Korea's (ROK, or South Korea) central bank as stating that "it's reasonable to predict that the worst is over for the North Korean economy."[1]

Did the North Korean economy indeed turn the corner at the end of the Twentieth Century? Is it now rebounding from the tribulations of the 1990s and poised for recovery and development in the years ahead?

Stabilization and improvement of the North Korean economic situation, of course, is an outcome that diverse contingents within the international community have long been hoping for. In humanitarian circles, economic revitalization is correctly regarded as the only means by which the DPRK can manage to feed its own populace, and bring the country's food crisis—which has

*This chapter appeared in 2000 in the *International Journal of Korean Studies* IV(1), Fall/ Winter; an earlier version was presented at "The Korean Peninsula in the 21st Century: Prospects for Stability and Cooperation," a symposium cosponsored by the Korea Institute for International Economic Policy (KIEP) the Korea Economic Institute of America (KEI), and the Paul H. Nitze School of Advanced International Studies (SAIS), at Johns Hopkins University, Washington D.C., 18–19 September 2000; the chapter has been slightly revised and updated for publication here.

already claimed a still-unknown toll of life, and occasioned an international food relief effort now entering its twelfth consecutive year—to a decisive close. To many stewards of security policy, North Korea's economic recovery and rehabilitation is taken to be a necessary step along the path that would lead to the ultimate success of the present U.S.-ROK-Japan policy of "engagement" with Pyongyang. According to this reasoning, North Korean leadership cannot be expected to accept the far-reaching changes in international behavior that the "Perry Process" or "Sunshine Policy" would envision for it, so long as its system verges on economic collapse. And for proponents of Korean reunification, revitalization of the DPRK economy offers the possibility that the socio-economic chasm between the North and the South—a gap that has been widening for at least a generation—may at last begin to narrow, so that an eventual reintegration of the two Koreas might prove a less wrenching and expensive proposition than it looks to be today.

For a multiplicity of responsible and respectable reasons, then, many specialists and policymakers who concern themselves with North Korean affairs today are wishing for an upturn in the North Korean economy, and therefore tend to be especially alert to those indications and emanations that would seem to corroborate and validate their hopes. Such an approach to problems is entirely human and completely understandable. Yet whatever else may be said about such an approach, it cannot provide a sound basis for objective economic analysis.

In the following pages, I will attempt to make the case that it is premature to speak of the stabilization of the North Korean economy, much less its recovery. Analysis of the DPRK economic situation, I will argue, must draw the crucial distinction between artificial improvements in living standards due to foreign subventions on the one hand, and augmentation of value added due to increased domestic productivity or resource mobilization, on the other. Empirical evidence of the latter is still extremely limited. Evidence of an economic stabilization or recovery, moreover, is counterbalanced by other evidence—some of it quantitative and relatively reliable—which bears directly on the development of the DPRK national economy, but which appears to be inconsistent with the vision of an economic turnaround. Finally, I will argue that the scope for an economic revival in the DPRK in the years immediately ahead will be constrained by a problem that North Korea watchers do not seem to have fully considered: degradation of the country's human resources. By some quantitative indications, North Korea would appear to have suffered a severe depletion of human capital during its prolonged economic crisis—a depletion perhaps most acute among its young and rising cohorts. Even if the DPRK were to embrace a more pragmatic economic regimen, the productivity improvements elicited by such a shift might be limited for a number of years by the reduced capacities of the North Korean population.

Perceptions and Evidence of a North Korean Economic Revival

As informed students of North Korea will readily appreciate, it is a more problematic challenge to assess the economic performance of the DPRK than that of any other country on the face of the earth today. The difficulty does not derive primarily from the distinctive and idiosyncratic structural characteristics of North Korea's "own style of socialism," although these assuredly complicate the analysis. The central problem, as I have described in detail in Chapters 2, 3, and 4, is that the DPRK has waged a four-decade long campaign against the release to the outside world of any information which might permit observers to draw independent conclusions about the performance of the North Korean system. It is a campaign the government has prosecuted with remarkable success. As a consequence of this campaign, vastly less quantitative economic information is available about North Korea than for any contemporary country in Asia—very possibly, indeed, less than for any other modern-day low income country. Certainly no other urbanized and literate society has ever experienced an enforced statistical blackout of such intensity and duration. Moreover, in the wake of this prolonged suppression of official data and Pyongyang's extreme politicization of economic life, the DPRK's own capability to compile reliable numbers for its own internal use is open to question. It is not self-evident that North Korea's statistical organs can present an accurate picture of socio-economic conditions and trends to the country's own leadership.

Thanks to Pyongyang's relentless war against official statistics, analysis of the DPRK economy must rely to an extraordinary degree upon intuition, perception, anecdote, and inductive reasoning—that is to say, exercises in logic supported by a presumed array of "stylized facts." Under such circumstances, what the DPRK leadership says and indicates about the condition of its national economy weighs heavily as evidence. And the North Korean government has been talking as if its economy were stabilizing, and recovering, since 1998.

Pyongyang's tone of economic confidence can be dated to the September 1998 Supreme People's Assembly (SPA), when Kim Jong Il formally acceded to the DPRK's "top position of state."[2] At that gathering, the era of the "Arduous March"—as the time of troubles following Kim Il Sung's death had been designated—was officially declared to be over. With Kim Jong Il's public elevation to supreme leadership, the country had embarked on the path to becoming a "rich and powerful state" (*kangsong taeguk*)—the slogan adopted to describe the epoch ahead.

Over the following two years, North Korean officialdom and their media outlets repeatedly asserted that the worst of the economic crisis is over, and that the national economy is on the upswing. A few illustrations will suffice. In April 1999, at the annual SPA gathering, the DPRK Finance Minister announced that state budget totals for 1998 exceeded those for 1997. She proclaimed that "the finance of the country took a new road of advance last year. . . [T]he forced march of socialism [has been brought] to a successful end."[3] Some months later, in its authoritative annual Joint New Year's Day editorial, the North Korean government acknowledged that "Our economy is still in a difficult condition," but announced that 1999 was a

> historic year in which a great turn was made in the building of a powerful nation. . . . Over the last couple of months, we have ridden out the unprecedented hill of trials. . . . Under the torch of Songgang, we waged vigorous struggles to bring about a product-upsurge in various fields of the people's economy. . . . Last year [i.e., 1999] the solid foundation for a powerful nation was made and we grew strong enough to make a quicker advance in the future.[4]

At the April 2000 SPA meeting, the DPRK Finance Minister reported the budget results for 1999, and declared they were "evidence that the economy has begun to recover."[5] And by summer 2000, the DPRK's Kim Jong Il had personally informed Hyundai group founder Chung Ju-yung that the North Korean economy grew by 6 percent in 1999—and could grow 20 percent a year "if inter-Korean cooperation is further activated."[6]

In the outside world, the interpretation that current events signaled a North Korean economic turnaround began to gather in the middle of 1999. Again, a few illustrative examples must suffice. In May 1999, Ambassador Charles Kartman, U.S. Special Envoy for the Korean Peace Talks, presumably drawing upon the intelligence sources at his disposal, told an audience at the Korea Society that "the DPRK economy hit its trough months ago."[7] In August 1999, the ROK Korea Trade and Investment Promotion Agency (KOTRA) noted that the DPRK had, for several months, ceased denuding its forestland to sell logs to China in exchange for foodstuffs—a development taken to suggest that North Korea's "serious food shortage has been mitigated."[8] In December 1999, *Yonhap* news agency reported that Kim Jong Il appeared to be pleased with his country's economic performance in 1999 because he conducted more "on the spot guidance" visits in economic sectors than in the previous year— and was filmed smiling on several of those occasions.[9] That same month, the Korea Development Institute (KDI) noted that a commentator for pro-DPRK publications in Japan had written that the North Korean economy had "bottomed out between October and November 1998, [and] has now entered a rapid recovery phase."[10] In January 2000, the ROK Ministry of Unification released a paper concluding that the North Korean economy turned around and grew "a little bit" in 1999.[11] In March 2000, the *New York Times* stated that "[l]ast year, the [North Korean] economy is believed to have grown slightly, for the first time in a decade."[12] That same month, a survey of research institutes in Seoul by the *Korean Economic Daily* suggested that "North Korea's gross domestic product (GDP) grew by up to three percent least year."[13] And in June 2000, as already mentioned, the ROK Bank of Korea (BOK) put North Korea's 1999 GDP growth at 6.2 percent.

The Bank of Korea's 1999 GDP Estimates for the DPRK

Since the BOK annual report on the North Korean GDP constitutes the most detailed and painstaking quantitative estimate of the economic performance of the DPRK currently published, we should review its results and the method by which they were derived.[14]

The BOK has never laid out all the particular points of its methodology, but it has described the approach in general terms. Using classified information from the ROK intelligence service, the BOK assembles several dozen separate physical production (and demographic) indicators which are meant to represent performance in various sectors of the DPRK national economy.[15] The BOK then applies the ROK relative prices to these vectors to obtain implicit cost structures, thereby to calculate value added (in ROK *won*). These computations thus offer not only an estimate for value added in the economy as a whole, but also for the level and trend of value-added in the economy's major subsidiary components.

Table 7.1 presents the results of the BOK's June 2000 study.

By the BOK's reckoning, output in North Korea's service and government sectors slumped in 1999, but value-added in agriculture, manufacturing and mining, and construction were up sharply over 1998, with especially pronounced gains in construction (over 24 percent) and agriculture (over 9 percent).

Table 7.1
Bank of Korea Estimates of North Korea's GDP Growth Rates
(Percent Pear Year)

Sector	1994	1995	1996	1997	1998	1999
Agriculture, forestry, and fishing	2.7	−10.4	0.5	−3.8	4.1	9.2
Manufacturing	−3.7	−5.2	−8.9	−16.8	−3.1	8.5
Construction	−26.9	−3.2	−11.8	−9.9	−11.4	24.3
Services	2.4	1.7	1.1	1.3	−0.5	−1.9
Government	−3.3	2.8	1.8	2.2	−0.3	−4.5
Overall GDP growth rate	−2.1	−4.1	−3.6	−6.3	−1.1	6.2

Source: ROK BOK, June 2000.

Elaborating upon its results, the study explains that North Korea's sharp rise in GDP over 1998 "was mainly thanks to an increase in grain production and the expanded support by South Korea and the international community."

Since neither the finer points of the BOK's methodology nor the detailed physical indicators utilized are in the public domain, it is impossible to attempt to reproduce these results. One may, nevertheless, highlight three important issues in the BOK's approach, each of which could strongly affect calculated GDP totals.

The first is the particular choice of physical production data series. In a society as closed as the DPRK, the exact levels of annual output for various commodities are far from obvious. Even for primary and homogeneous North Korean commodities, output estimates differ appreciably among ostensibly informed outside sources. In attributing a major increase in cereal production to the DPRK in 1999, the BOK used a grain harvest number of 4.22 million tons. That figure happens to be very close to the 4.28 million ton claim for 1999 by the DPRK's Assistant Minister of Agriculture (tendered to the FAO in Rome in November 1999).[16] It would be distinctly higher, however, than the estimate of South Korea's own Rural Development Administration, which was expecting the DPRK to produce 3.9 million tons of grain in 1999[17]—and it would be far above the 3.4 million tons that the UN Office for Coordination of Humanitarian Affairs believes the DPRK harvested that year.[18] Incidentally, the UN Food and Agriculture Organization (FAO) reports that North Korean cereal production *fell* by over 9 percent in 1999 (to 4.0 million tons from 4.4 million tons in 1998).[19] Although precise figures cannot be calculated without access to the BOK model, it would appear that entering those FAO estimates in the place of the ROK intelligence service numbers for grain output could virtually eliminate the BOK's entire calculated increase in North Korean GDP for 1999.

A second issue concerns the use of the ROK price and cost structure in computing value-added within the North Korean national economy. By embracing the South Korean relative price structure, the BOK approach also implicitly posits for the DPRK the same relationship between gross output, intermediate output, and net value-added as obtained within the various sectors of the ROK economy. Unfortunately, there is little reason to expect this presumption to hold up in practice. Among other problems, socialist centrally-planned economies are famously less adept at economizing the use of inputs than their market-oriented sisters. Indeed, for any given branch of the economy, *ceteris paribus*, the ratio of value-added to gross output would be expected to be characteristically lower in the communist system. Even if the BOK's physical production estimates accurately tracked changes in commodity output, the risk of biasing upwards consequent estimates of sectoral value-added would loom large. (Examination of these potential biases might seem especially a propos for the DPRK construction sector—a branch of the economy evidently deemed severely inefficient even by North Korea's own leadership, but accorded a 20-plus percentage point leap in annual output in 1999 under the BOK methodology.)

The third, and possibly most vexatious, issue concerns the treatment of the external economy—including transfers from abroad—in the calculation of DPRK gross domestic product.

In the national accounts framework, "gross domestic product" has a very specific conceptual meaning. In their classic text on national accounts and national income analysis, Ruggles and Ruggles spell this out:

> [GDP] takes for its frame of reference the production occurring within a geographic area, irrespective of whether the productive resources in question are owned by the nationals of that area or not. . . . *[T]he focus of gross domestic product is the productive activity taking place within designated boundaries. . . .* From a statistical point of view the shift in coverage from gross national product to gross domestic product will . . . affect exports and property income received . . . and imports and property income paid. . . . *In measuring gross domestic product, property income received from and paid to abroad must be excluded from consideration,* so that only imports and exports will appear on the sources side of what will now be the Gross Domestic Income and Product Account.[20] (Emphasis added.)

To arrive at gross domestic product, in other words, one must adjust local product not only to reflect the net balance of trade, but also to accord for the net international flow of "property income"—or, as we would say today, factor income. Yet for North Korea, this is no easy task. To accomplish those very calculations, we would require 1) reliable estimates of the DPRK's net balance of trade; 2) reliable figures on North Korea's net factor income from abroad; and 3) a reliable exchange rate at which to convert these foreign balances into domestic resource values.

With regard to the net balance of trade, a formal calculation of GDP for the DPRK presupposes that local product be reduced by the amount of North Korea's perennial balance of trade deficit—however accurately that annual sum can be reckoned. The BOK indicates that it attempts a national accounts tally for North Korea within the framework of the United Nations' System of National Accounts (SNA)—an approach which posits that the various accounting identities be linked, with accounting linkages which include transactions with the rest of the world. Whether the BOK actually computes those full identities, and attempts to incorporate North Korea's net trade balances into these national accounts calculations is not at all clear from the published materials the BOK has circulated to date.

Then there is the question of "net factor income from abroad." For example, exactly how the United States' 1999 commitment of 600,000 tons of food aid to the DPRK should be treated in the national accounting framework is not entirely clear. The United States maintains that transfer was a humanitarian gift, whereas the DPRK has always insisted that it was a "fee" for the privilege of visiting the underground Kumchang-ri facility.[21] If the North Korean position is accepted, those payments—and others generated by extortive diplomacy—might arguably be akin to "net factor income from abroad," and thus would be subtracted from output in determining GDP. On the other hand, if the inflows of aid that North Korea has absorbed over the past years are categorized as gifts, the logic of GDP calculations would suggest that they still be subtracted from total product precisely to the degree that they finance imports.[22] Either way, the foreign exchange value of transfers from abroad must be deducted from local production totals if the level of gross domestic product is to be established.

But exactly how should they be deducted? By calculating North Korean GDP in ROK *won*, the Bank of Korea attempts to circumvent the medium of exchange question for the North Korean economy. While the approach may solve the immediate computation problem, it only finesses the underlying conceptual problem. With the US dollar reportedly trading against the DPRK *won* for 50 to 100 times the officially fixed rate in Najin-Sonbong and other areas of the country in recent years,[23] it is apparent that the domestic resource value of foreign exchange in North Korea is vastly higher than is implied by officially-established exchange rates that link the dollar, the ROK *won*, and the DPRK *won*. Thus, a full adjustment to factor out foreign aid, "property income from abroad," and other components of the country's balance of trade deficit could have an even greater impact in reducing calculated gross value-added in the DPRK than the BOK's ostensible approach would indicate.

Net infusion of foreign resources into the DPRK system on a significant scale, indeed, may constitute the main conceptual rub against the current attempt to calculate accurate trends for the North Korean GDP. Unless those infusions are accounted and corrected for, calculated GDP will be exaggerated—possibly quite significantly. If external transfers are on the increase—as they apparently have been for the DPRK during the past few years—trends could be biased upward correspondingly. The BOK analysts indicate that they recognize this problem when they identify "expanded support by South Korea and the international community" as one of the two principal factors accounting for their computed increase in 1999 GDP for the DPRK. But it is by no means clear that their effort distinguishes between increased domestic generation of economic output and the elevation of local (individual and governmental) consumption levels due to foreign aid—or can even manage to do so.

Additional Indicators of Performance in the DPRK Macroeconomy

As we have just seen, the proposition that North Korea's GDP is in the process of stabilization and recovery is built upon fragile evidence and a somewhat tenuous methodology. But additional empirical evidence on the performance of the DPRK is also available. This evidence includes the two most reliable quantitative sources of data about the North Korean economy. There is an inescapable measure of ambiguity in any interpretation of these data and reports. On their face, however, the trends reflected by these additional indicators would not appear to square with economic stabilization and recovery. On the contrary, they could be read more easily as signs of continuing macroeconomic weakness and decline.

Trade Performance

Although North Korea does not release trade data, North Korean export and import performance can be reconstructed, after a fashion, by compiling reports by its trading partners on their sales to and purchases from the DPRK.[24] As discussed in Chapters 2 and 3, such "mirror statistics" are used by KOTRA and the Government of Japan's Japan External Trade Organization (JETRO) to estimate global export and import trends for the DPRK. (For a variety of technical reasons, these trade trends are calculated in current US dollars, since a constant long-term trade series for the DPRK is not available. Their estimates for North Korean trade trends over the years 1989–99 are presented in Figures 7.1 and 7.2.)

As may be seen, JETRO and KOTRA estimates of North Korea's trade trends track very closely. Both series indicate a severe deterioration of North Korean trade performance during the decade under consideration. Between 1990 and 1999, according to both series, total DPRK trade turnover plummeted by an estimated 62 percent or more.

However, according to both series a consequential portion of this trade collapse occurred in the last couple of years under consideration. Between 1997 and 1999, according to both KOTRA and JETRO estimates, DPRK trade turnover fell by well over 25 percent.[25] By virtually any definition, a sudden contraction of trade volume on such a scale would qualify as a "trade shock"— and a severe one.

A severe trade shock does not automatically preclude the possibility of stabilization and growth of a national economy—as the economic histories of the major combatant powers in World War II clearly attest.[26] In those cases, however, output growth depended upon a shift to a wartime economic footing and a militant mobilization of theretofore unutilized or underutilized factors of pro-

Figure 7.1
Estimated DPRK Exports, 1989–1999

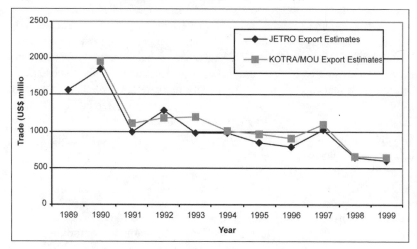

Sources: KOTRA, various years; ROK MOU, various years; JETRO, various years.

Figure 7.2
Estimated DPRK Imports: 1989–1999

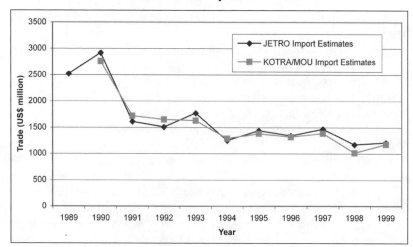

Sources: KOTRA, various years; ROK MOU, various years, JETRO, various years.

duction—an option not obviously open to the already hyper-militarized North Korean command economy in 1997.

Between 1997 and 1999, according to KOTRA's estimates, the nominal dollar volume of North Korea's imports fell by over 15 percent; by JETRO's reckoning, imports declined by over 17 percent. That drop in estimated import levels, we should note, took place despite an evident rise in Western aid (i.e., import finance) during those same years. All other things being equal, a sharp drop in measured imports would be expected to create supply constraints in a national economy, and thus to constrain output, rather than stabilizing or stimulating it.

Export performance should also provide some insight into the state of the macroeconomy. For the DPRK, indeed, export trends may be especially informative. Their level and direction depend rather less upon external subsidies and supports than those of imports. According to both JETRO and KOTRA estimates, the nominal dollar value of North Korean global exports dropped by about three-eighths between 1997 and 1998, and then dropped still further in 1999. KOTRA and JETRO both estimate the nominal drop in DPRK exports over the 1997–99 period at about 42 percent.

State Budget

The returns from the DPRK state budget are, by its own custom, the *only* official economic data that the North Korean government has released on a regular basis since the early 1960s.[27] On the basis of those reports, it is possible to calculate the annual growth in total state expenditures in nominal DPRK *won*—a number that reflects, in some fashion, changes in the national economy.

Reported annual changes in state expenditures for the 1980–2000 period are presented in Figure 7.3.

Between 1980 and 1985, North Korea's nominal state expenditures rose at a pace of 8.6 percent per year. The tempo was 5.4 percent a year for 1985–90, and 3.8 percent a year for the years 1990–94.

For 1998, Pyongyang announced a total increase in expenditures of just 0.4 percent over 1997. In April 1999, the DPRK Minister of Finance projected a 1.8 percent increase over 1998 in state budget expenditures.[28] However, the final report on the 1999 budget indicated that expenditures in this 20 billion *won* account had increased by just three million *won*—that is to say, by 0.015 percent.

In April 2001, the DPRK Finance Minister reported state budget expenditures for the year 2000 at 20.955 billion *won*, an increase of 4.7 percent over the previous year.[29] It should be noted that this represents the highest reported annual increment since 1992. But the "recovery" indicated by the budgetary

Figure 7.3

Annual Change in Reported DPRK State Budget Expenditures, 1980–2000

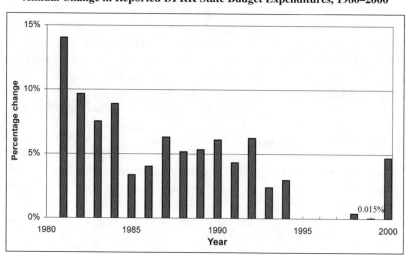

Sources: BBC, 1994 and 1999 (9 April); Hwang, 1993; IMF, 1997.

returns of 1999–2000 must be put in perspective. Reported nominal increases in state expenditure for those two years averaged less than 24 percent per annum. By way of comparison, state budgetary expenditures grew by over 5 percent a year in the late 1980s—a period widely believed to be one of near-stagnation in the DPRK economy—and by almost 4 percent a year in the early 1990s—a time when the economy was in sharp decline, even by Pyongyang's admission. What then does it mean for the macroeconomy when the DPRK state budget is recording an expenditure rise of less than 2.5 percent per year?

Again, we should stress that slow growth in the DPRK's nominal state expenditures would not necessarily be antithetical to stabilization and growth for the North Korean macroeconomy. For example, it is possible to hypothesize conditions under which those two trends could be consistent with a decline in overall domestic price levels, or with sharp differential growth between the country's market economy and its state economy.

In the DPRK's shortage-and-requisition system, however, price levels—if this term can be used meaningfully under such conditions—are most unlikely to be in decline, owing to the perpetual imbalance between supplies and demand. We cannot dismiss out of hand the possibility that non-state sectors of the North Korean economy are growing rapidly even though the "people's economy" is not. (A recent BOK study in the year 2000, for example, reportedly concluded that underground and other market-style economic activities had by then come to account for 27 percent of North Korea's Gross National Income.[30]) But when DPRK leadership (and Bank of Korea national accounts analysts) talk of the stabilization and recovery of the North Korean economy, it is the formal "people's economy" to which they refer. On the contrary, with its April 1999 "Law of People's Economic Plans," Pyongyang strictly reaffirmed that "the DPRK economy is a planned one based on socialist ownership of the means of production," and that "it is the consistent policy of the DPRK to manage and operate the people's economy under centralized and unified guidance."[31]

How the extremely slow growth in reported state expenditures—a fact officially acknowledged by Pyongyang—is to be reconciled with the vision of a stabilizing or recovering national economy is not immediately obvious.[32]

Energy Shortages

The third indicator of economic performance to be considered is not quantitative in nature, but it has been officially mentioned by the North Korean government. These are the recurrent reports during the past year of severe power shortages in the national economy.

Once again, a few citations will illustrate the many. In January of 2000, *Nodong Sinmun* wrote of the need to solve the country's "acute power shortages," a problem the editorial ranked alongside the country's food shortages.[33] In February, Pyongyang's *Korean Central News Agency* (KCNA) declaimed that "Never before in the history of Korea has there been such power shortage as today. This is adversely affecting the overall economic life in the DPRK."[34] In March, the vice Minister of the DPRK Power and Coal Industries "revealed"

> that electricity is not being sent sufficiently to mines, metal, chemical, and railways sectors and electricity for residents are not being supplied appropriately. Vice-Minister O Kwang-hum said that hydroelectric power stations are not being operated due to small amount of rain and thermoelectric power stations are not being operated appropriately due to lack of coal.[35]

Then, in April 2000, ROK Prime Minister Park Tae-joon reported that North Korean officials had urged the United States to pressure South Korea to provide the DPRK with electricity.[36]

As with so many other things North Korean, there is no single straightforward explanation for these external soundings. Official lamentations about "power shortages" could simply be part of a paper trail that would bolster the North Korean government's brief pressing the United States and KEDO for additional "compensation" for purportedly forgone energy supplies from its currently shelved graphite-modulated nuclear reactors at Yongbyon. And it was clear that North Korean authorities had planned to demand additional aid from the United States and the KEDO consortium, should Washington and KEDO fail to provide the operating light water nuclear reactors that the Agreed Framework had initially envisioned as functioning on DPRK soil by the year 2003.[37] On the other hand, much of the North Korean commentary about energy shortages has focused upon failures due to hydroelectric and coal-industry shortages—*pace* the BOK's imagined surge in North Korea's mining industries!—problems for which neither the United States nor the KEDO consortium could plausibly be held liable.

Perhaps more pertinently, "energy shortages" could also signify a resurgence of (unfulfilled) demand by revitalized North Korean industrial sectors, and thus augur a recovery of the DPRK national economy. But insofar as anecdotal accounts by foreigners have pointed to an increasing frequency of "blackouts" in the privileged sectors of the country in which they are permitted to reside or travel,[38] and given the inevitable loss of transmission efficiency that might be expected in any national energy grid poorly maintained over long periods of time, it is by no means self-evident that the current alleged "energy shortage" in North Korea is a demand-side problem alone.

By themselves, the data on trade performance or state outlay growth—or the reports of increasing energy shortages in the national economy—might be dismissed as all-too-familiar inconsistencies in an always-confusing North Korean tableau, which, nevertheless, pointed on balance toward stabilization and upturn in the DPRK's gross domestic product. Taken together, they are not so easily discounted. The seeming contradiction between these poor macro-economic soundings and the many more optimistic reports by "North Korea watchers" on current economic conditions in the DPRK can be resolved only if one considers the role of external assistance in raising living standards and government consumption. A little-noticed KOTRA report in January 2000 may have grasped the essence of this contradiction, warning that "despite signs of recovery after bottoming out last year, [N]orth [K]orea's economy will fare badly or worsen this year without assistance from [S]outh [K]orea and other countries . . ." and that "the likelihood still exists of a relapse if international assistance decreases."[39]

Human Resources and the Prospects for Economic Growth in DPRK

The analysis presented thus far has attempted to raise questions about the soundness of the consensus among informed students of North Korean affairs that the DPRK economy had "bottomed out" and had entered a period of recovery by the time of the historic Pyongyang summit between ROK President Kim Dae Jung and DPRK chief Kim Jong Il, that is, 2000.

It is of course possible that genuine stabilization and recovery for the DPRK economy could be achieved—if North Korean leadership could acquiesce in the policies that could bring about such a revitalization.[40] What may not have been adequately considered by outside observers in contemplating such a prospect, however, is the enduring toll that North Korea's years of extreme economic crisis may exact on its future workforce, even under a more auspicious policy environment than can be imagined in the country today. For, as explained in detail in Chapter 5, disturbing indications have already emerged to suggest that North Korea's long-standing food crisis, its dire famine of the late 1990s, and the government's disregard of the social welfare of the non-privileged majority of its populace may have had a severe impact on the country's human resource base—and in particular, upon the surviving children who will be the workers of tomorrow.

Just how disastrous in human terms the DPRK's recent crises may have been is impossible to say—for all the cruelly familiar reasons noted earlier. Results of nutrition studies by the UN World Food Programme, in conjunction with UNICEF and the European Union indicate that North Korean boys in the late 1990s were far smaller than South Korean boys were in the mid-1960s, four decades ago. In fact, to go by those survey results, and earlier anthropometric surveys from the Korea, North Korean boys today would not only be littler than boys from then-impoverished South Korea at the time of the Korean War (1953), but even smaller and slighter than their forebears in the Korean War in 1913–22, almost eight decades ago, during the era of Japanese colonialism.[41]

By such indications, it would appear that not only has the youngest generation in North Korea failed to thrive, but it has actually suffered a terrible physiological retrogression. We must wonder whether this reported maiming of North Korea's youth may not also be a proxy for the reduction in its human capital, and consequently its economic capabilities.

To be sure, we have long known that it is possible to be "small but healthy," to borrow a phrase from David Seckler,[42] but in large populations, what concerns us is not individual cases, but rather the odds. For North Korea's younger generation, the odds against human capital formation appear to have been worsened not only by undernutrition, but by educational neglect. Data on the DPRK educational system are of course all but unavailable to outsiders. In August 2000, however, Matsuura Koichiro, the head of UNESCO, visited the DPRK and reported at the conclusion of his visit that up to 40 percent of the country's elementary-school-age children currently were not receiving an education.[43]

Today's elementary school children will be tomorrow's working age population. Figure 7.4 illustrates this inexorable progression.

In the year 2000, according to U.S. Bureau of the Census data, the cohort aged 15–24 constituted 22.8 percent of the total population of "working age," conventionally, arbitrarily, and not unreasonably defined as ages 15–64. In 2010, the 15–24 group is anticipated to account for a slightly larger portion of North Korea's "working age" population. The 15 to 24-year-olds of 2010, however, were the babies born between 1986 and 1995. This means that the eldest of that grouping were year nine years old when Pyongyang first officially acknowledged its hunger emergency in 1995, and the youngest in that cohort were born into the food emergency, and knew nothing but that emergency as infants, toddlers and young children.

We can only wonder about the economic potential of this vulnerable group in the North Korean population. It bears repeating that while policies can change—and sometimes do—even radically, human capabilities, unfortunately, are typically less prone to sudden melioration. As we look for a brighter economic future for North Korea, we should not forget that the DPRK's grim past may continue to punish future populations for years after the regime's most destructive economic policies are abandoned.

Figure 7.4
North Korean Population, 2000 and 2010

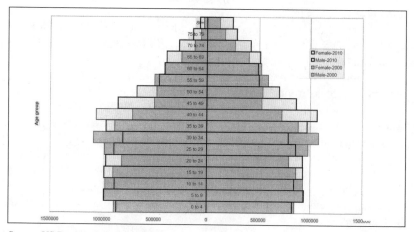

Source: US Bureau of the Census, 2005.

Update 2006: A North Korean Economic Recovery at Last?

Now that six years have elapsed since the preceding analysis was prepared, it may be time for a second look at the issue of economic recovery in the DPRK. Does North Korean economic performance suggest that the country has now embarked upon a path of self-sustaining economic growth? Does it demonstrate signs of production-led economic upswing? At the very least, has it finally achieved macroeconomic stabilization?

Surprising as it may seem, the weight of empirical evidence does not, as yet, afford an affirmative answer to any of those questions.

To be sure: by all external indications, living standards in North Korea are not so fearsomely desperate in the first years of the new century as they were in the mid-1990s. Data on actual living standards are still astonishingly limited and sketchy, but at a minimum, one may safely note that reports of mass starvation of North Koreans no longer circulate these days in the international media, or among international humanitarian relief agencies.

Yet as we have already noted, in a state that is heavily dependent upon concessional resource transfers from abroad, local living standards may be a poor proxy for trends in domestic value-added. Indeed, given sufficient and continuing inflows of foreign resources, it is, in theory, possible for those two trends to move in opposite directions for years on end.

As we will see in subsequent chapters, Pyongyang seems to have managed in recent years to extract more resources from abroad with almost every passing year. Mirror statistics for merchandise trade attest to this success: whereas these foreign trade reports indicate that North Korea's surfeit of commercial commodity imports over exports averaged less than US$600 million a year for the dire "Arduous March" years of 1995–98, the imbalance tilted up to an average of about US$950 million a year for 1999–2000, and averaged close to US$1.5 billion a year for the period 2003–2005.

What these trends portend for domestic consumption levels is one thing; what they may tell us—or conceal from us—about local productivity is something else again. There is scant reason to believe, for example, that the Bank of Korea's estimates of North Korean national accounts are any more adept today than they were half a decade ago at parsing the distinction between consumption and value added in the DPRK economy. BOK calculations, for example, imply that North Korea's GNI was nearly 18 percent higher in 2004 than it had been in 1998—with per capita GNI roughly 12 percent higher in 2004 than it had been six years earlier.

But that same BOK series would have us believe that the overall value of agricultural produce in North Korea in 2003 and 2004 was actually *higher* than it had been in 1990[44]—that is, before the end of Soviet bloc aid and trade, and before North Korea's sickening economic downward slide. Such an assessment beggars credibility.

Consider: *FAOSTAT*, the statistical database of UN Food and Agriculture Organization (FAO), estimates that per capita caloric supplies were 18 percent lower for the DPRK in 2003–04 than in 1990, a drop from about 2,640 calories per person per day to 2,170 calories per person per day. Yet despite that envisioned slump, net cereal imports were estimated to have more than tripled over the same period, making for a net shift in foodgrain balances of about 1.2 million tons annually for the years under consideration.[45] (The FAO's estimated increase in foreign cereal supplies, incidentally, would amount to an addition of over 500 calories per person per day in the North Korean diet— equivalent, in fact, to over a quarter of the presumed daily calorie supply for the North Korean populace in 2003–04.) As for population growth—the final factor in this arithmetic tableau regarding local food production—North Korea's population may have increased between 1990 and 2003–04, but growth would have been marginal.

It is flatly impossible to reconcile the international assessment of North Korea's agricultural performance over these years (as represented in the FAO estimates) with the portrait BOK numbers present for that same interval. And if the basic estimates for agricultural performance are so obviously askew in the BOK national accounts, we need not linger over the rest of the series which purportedly traces a North Korean economic recovery from 1998 onwards.

Other potentially corroborating indicators of economic upturn are obscure or ambiguous for current interpretation. For example, nominal DPRK merchandise exports do appear to have increased significantly between 1998 and 2005,[46] but the entirety of this export upswing is accounted for by purchases from China and South Korea, governments both committed to subsidized trade with the North. North Korea's state budget numbers since 2002 cannot be deconstructed—for reasons discussed in Chapter 2—and for the 1998–2001 period, the returns cannot easily be interpreted to signify macroeconomic stabilization, much less brisk economic progress.

As for the DPRK's energy situation: official media pronouncements suggest that the North Korean leadership regards power shortages as a less critical constraint in recent years than they did in 1999 or 2000—this despite the shutoff, in late 2002, of the 500,000 tons a year in free fuel oil that had been flowing to Pyongyang since 1995 under the terms of the Agreed Framework. In 2005 and again in 2006, North Korea's annual New Year's Day policy pronouncements identified agriculture and food production rather than energy as the pressing domestic economic concern.[47] Does it augur well for macroeconomic stabilization and growth that North Korea should now regard food shortages as a more immediate issue than energy shortages? One can argue the case either way—but neither will look terribly conclusive.

Finally, there is the matter of human resource constraints on North Korean growth prospects—if and when an auspicious "environment" for material advance is established in Northern Korea. Although the international community has spent billions of dollars over the past decade attending to the humanitarian tragedy in the DPRK, it is still impossible for outsiders to know just how nutritionally and educationally disadvantaged North Korea's rising generations may be at present.

For reasons already noted in Chapter 2, we can have no confidence in the DPRK's own recent "surveys" on local nutritional conditions. But judging from the UN World Food Programme (WFP) official, who asserted in early 2004 that "thousands" of persons in North Korea were still suffering from hunger at that time,[48] the DPRK's food crisis is far from over. As to education and school attendance, the DPRK Ministry of Education and the DPRK National Commission for UNESCO asserted in 2003 that "the enrollment rate of educational institutions up to secondary level is 100 percent."[49] On the other hand, in 2002 a newly arrived North Korean defector to South Korea claimed that actual school attendance in parts of North Korea was only 20 percent or lower.[50] And in 2006, an NGO active in North Korean relief declared that "due to the enduring economic and food crisis, the term 'free education' has long been forgotten," and estimated that "the level of attendance for most secondary schools[51] nation-wide is only about 70 percent."[52] All in all, it may be safe to say that the human capital constraints pressing North Korea's rising generation of workers are more severe than those faced by their parents—possibly even their grandparents.

A little-noticed KOTRA report in January 2000 may have grasped the essence of this contradiction, warning that "despite signs of recovery after bottoming out last year, North Korea's economy will fare badly or worsen this year without assistance from South Korea and other countries . . ." and that "the likelihood still exists of a relapse if international assistance decreases."[53] Sadly, little has occurred over the past six years to alter such an assessment for the DPRK economy.

Notes

1. Struck, 2000.
2. According to the revised 1998 DPRK Constitution, Kim Il Sung, though dead, remains the country's "eternal President"; Kim Jong Il's highest state post is Chairman of the DPRK National Defense Commission (NDC)—an institution whose

authority within the overall state structure is constitutionally ambiguous; however, in nominating Kim Jong Il for Chairmanship of the NDC, SPA Presidium President Kim Yong Nam declared that Chairmanship to be the "highest post of the state"; thus, Kim Jong Il may be said to rank as North Korea's highest *living* functionary.

3. *BBC*, 1999 (9 April).
4. *People's Korea*, 1 January 2000.
5. *Agence France Presse*, 1999.
6. *FBIS*-EAS-2000-0706.
7. Hong Sun-chik, 2000.
8. *FBIS*-EAS-1999-0830.
9. *FBIS*-EAS-1999-1228a.
10. *FBIS*-EAS-1999-1229.
11. *Associated Press*, 2000.
12. French, 2000.
13. *Agence France Presse*, 22 March 2000.
14. For the purposes of this study, we used the BOK 1999 estimates.
15. Demographic indicators are used to estimate output of the government and service sectors, since the approach presumes output per worker in these two branches of the economy to be fixed and invariable.
16. *BBC*, 1999 (19 November).
17. *FBIS*-EAS-1999-1228b.
18. Kim Ji-ho, 2000.
19. FAO, 2000.
20. Ruggles and Ruggles, 1956.
21. For the DPRK's position, see *People's Korea*, 18 March 1999.
22. OECD, 1958, p. 75; in its original guidelines regarding the organization of national accounts, the OECD specifically stipulated that the export ledger should include "the value of gifts in kind"; conversely, this would mean the receipt of in-kind gifts should be tallied in the import ledger. KEDO transfers (including heavy fuel oil and other materials) and humanitarian relief supplies (food, medicines) are among the items which would presumably qualify for inclusion under "imports" according to this line of reasoning.
23. *FBIS*-EAS-1998-0721, 21 July 1998.
24. Because the South Korean government maintains that its commerce with North Korea is "domestic" rather than international trade, North-South trade is excluded from the KOTRA figures; to make the KOTRA figures comparable with the JETO numbers we must therefore add the data on "Inter-Korean Cooperation" compiled separately by the ROK MOU; thus, the following discussion of "KOTRA" estimates should, technically, be considered KOTRA/MOU estimates.
25. The trend for DPRK trade turnover for 1998/99 is unclear; KOTRA data show an increase, while JETO data suggest a slight but continuing decrease.
26. See Milward, 1977.
27. Although even the release of these numbers, traditionally announced at the country's spring SPA gathering, was interrupted with the more than four-year suspension of the SPA in the wake of Kim Il Sung's death.
28. Kang, 2000.
29. *BBC*, 2001.
30. *FBIS*-EAS-2000-0807.
31. *People's Korea*, 21 April 1999.

32. The economic implications of these trends, in fact, could be even more inauspicious than a cursory inspection of budget totals might initially suggest; traditionally, the DPRK's consolidated state budget treated aid from abroad as an item on the revenue side of the ledger; such aid thus directly supported state budgetary expenditures; see, for example, Goto, 1990; we cannot yet know whether the DPRK has implemented any major unannounced changes in its budget accounting procedures in recent years; if it has not, however, the slow growth of reported expenditures, in tandem with the relatively rapid growth of aid from abroad, would seem to have ominous implications for the performance of the state economy.

33. *BBC*, 2000 (26 January).

34. *AFP*, 2000, (23 February/a).

35. *BBC*, 2000 (18 March).

36. *FBIS*-EAS-2000-0412.

37. For information regarding Pyongyang's take on the year 2000 energy shortage, see, inter alia, *Xinhua*, 2000.

The light water reactors (LWR) originally envisioned as coming online in 2003 under the term of the Agreed Framework were never actually completed; with the revelations in late 2002 of a covert North Korean program for uranium enrichment, the KEDO consortium first suspended heavy fuel oil shipments to Pyongyang and then, in 2003, formally suspended construction on the LWRs, which had already fallen far behind schedule; in late 2005, KEDO's Executive Board began deliberations for the official termination of the LWR project; as of this writing, those details are still being hammered out; for background, see KEDO, "About Us: Our History," available at: http://kedo.org/au_history.asp.

38. For example, *AFP*, 2000 (23 February/b).

39. *FBIS*-EAS-2000-0118.

40. For a penetrating overview of the issues involved, see Noland, 2000.

41. See Chapter 5, Figures 1 and 2.

42. Seckler, 1980.

43. *Kyodo News Service*, 2000.

44. Bank of Korea, 2005; value-added in constant 1995 *won*; available at: http://210.104.132.11/contents_admin/info_admin/eng/home/press/pressre/info/timeseriesnk1.xls.

45. Food and Agriculture Organization, 2006; available at: http://faostat.fao.org/faostat/collections?version=ext&hasbulk=0.

46. Albeit from a pitifully low 1998 base level.

47. *BBC*, 2006 and 2005.

48. *Inter Press Service*, 2004.

49. DPRK Ministry of Education and DPRK National Commission for UNESCO. 2003. *Democratic People's Republic of Korea: National Plan of Action on Education for All.* Pyongyang: Ministry of Education. Cite at p. 4. Available on UNESCO website at: http://portal.unesco.org/education/en/file_download.php/3290d6261627a2fd5c3ce8df79b7cbecEFAPlanE-PRK1.doc.

50. *Korea Herald.* 2002. "Food crisis causes low school attendance in N.K.: defectors." (13 July).

51. 5th to 10th grade in the DPRK school system.

52. Research Institute for the North Korean Society (sic). 2006.

53. *FBIS*-EAS-2000-0118.

References

Agence France Presse (AFP). 1999. "N. Korea budget deficit in 1999." 4 April.
———. 2000. (23 February/a) "N. Korean economy crippled by worst power shortage: state media."
———. 2000. (23 February/b) "N. Korean winter conditions severe this year: UN report."
———. 2000. (22 March) Reprinted from the *Korean Economic Daily.* "N. Korea rebounds from 10-year contraction: economists."
Associated Press. 2000. (20 January) "North Korea expected to try to join international fund groups."
British Broadcasting Corporation (BBC) Summary of World Broadcasts. 1994. (9 April) Rebroadcast from *Korea Central News Agency* (Pyongyang) as "Budget outcome for 1993 and allocations for 1994." FE/1967/D.
———. 1999. (9 April). Rebroadcast from *Korean Central News Agency* (Pyongyang). "North Korean finance minister reports on state budget." FE/D3504/D.
———. 1999. (19 November). Rebroadcast from *Yonhap News Agency.* "South agency says grain harvests up 40 percent on last year." FE/D3696/D.
———. 2000. (26 January). Rebroadcast from *Korea Central News Agency* (Pyongyang). "Economic policy to solve 'acute' power shortage and 'food problem.'" FE/W0624/WD2.
———. 2000. (18 March). Rebroadcast from *KBS Radio* (Seoul). "Official reportedly reveals power shortages." FE/D3792/S1.
———. 2001. (5 April) Rebroadcast from *Korea Central News Agency* "North Korea: Finance minister presents budget to Supreme People's Assembly."
———. 2005. (1 January). Rebroadcast from *Korea Central Broadcasting Station* (Pyongyang) as "North Korean Joint New Year Editorial—Text."
———. 2006. (1 January) Rebroadcast from Korea Central Broadcasting Station (Pyongyang) as "Full Text of North Korean New Year Editorial." A20060101F-F9D9-GNW.
DPRK Ministry of Education and DPRK National Commission for UNESCO. 2003. *Democratic People's Republic of Korea: National Plan of Action on Education for All.* Pyongyang: Ministry of Education. Available on UNESCO website at: http://portal.unesco.org/education/en/file_download.php/3290d6261627a2fd5c3ce8df79b7cbecEFAPlanE-PRK1.doc
Eberstadt, Nicholas. 2000. "Economic Recovery in the DPRK." *International Journal of Korean Studies* IV(1), Fall/Winter. 15–35.
FBIS-EAS-1998-0721 (21 July) Reprinted from *Korea Times* (Internet version). "South Korea; Foreign Currencies Reportedly Circulating In DPRK."
——— -1999-0830. (30 August). Reprinted from *Chungang Ilbo* (Internet version). "KOTRA: DPRK Restricts Exports of Logs to PRC.
——— -1999-1228a. (28 December). Reprinted from *Chungang Ilbo:* "Kim Chong-il Said Happy About Signs of Economic Recovery."
——— -1999-1228b. (28 December). Reprinted from *Korea Times* (Internet version). "DPRK Grain Production Up, Still Short Of Need."
——— -1999-1229. (29 December). Reprinted from *Yonhap* (Internet version). "DPRK Entering Recovery Phase."
——— -2000-0706. (6 July). Reprinted from *Yonhap News Agency* (Seoul): "ROK Hyundai Official: DPRK Leader Kim Says DPRK Economy Grew 6 Percent."

———— -2000-0807. (8 August). Reprinted from *Korea Herald* (Internet version). "'Market Economy' in DPRK Accounts for 27 percent of GNI."

———— -2000-0118. (12 September). Reprinted from *Yonhap News Agency.* 18 January. "ROK Group Says Recovery Depends on Aid."

———— -2000-0412. (10 September). Reprinted from *Yonhap News Agency* (12 April). "DPRK Said to Demand U.S. Pressure Seoul for Electricity."

Food and Agriculture Organization (FAO). 2000. Statistical Database. New York: United Nations. Available at: http://apps.fao.org

————. 2006. *FAOSTAT Database Collections.* Available at: http://faostat.fao.org/faostat/collections?version=ext&hasbulk=0

French, Howard W. 2000. "Suddenly, Reclusive North Korea Reaches Out to the World." *New York Times.* 17 March. A8.

Goto, Fujio. 1990. *Estimates of the North Korean Gross Domestic Product, 1956–1959.* Kyoto: Kyoto Sangyo University Press.

Hong Sun-chik, 2000. "Outlook on DPRK's economic policy and North-South economic cooperation." Rebroadcast from *Tongil Kyongje* by *BBC Summary of World Broadcasts.* FE/W0629/S1.

Hwang, Ei-Gak. 1993. The Korean Economies: A Comparison of North and South. New York, Oxford University Press.

International Monetary Fund. 1997. "Democratic People's Republic of Korea: Fact Finding Report." 12 November 1997. Unpublished.

Inter Press Service (IPS). 2004. "Development: North Korea Faces Food Crisis." 30 April.

Japan External Trade Organization (JETRO) Various years. Kita Chosen no keizai to boeki no tenbo [North Korea's Economy and Trade Outlook]. Tokyo: Nihon Boeiki Shinkokai.

Kang, Il Chon. 2000. "Recent Economic Tendency in DPRK." *People's Korea* (Internet version). Available at: http://www1.korea-np.co.jp/pk/157th_issue/099th_issue/99061604.htm

Kim, Ji-ho. 2000. "U.N. report shows no improvement in North Korean food situation." *Korea Herald* (Internet version). 21 July.

Korea Central News Agency (KCNA). 2000.

Korea Herald. 2002. "Food crisis causes low school attendance in N.K.: Defectors." 13 July.

Korea Trade Investment Promotion Agency (KOTRA). Various years. *Pukhan ui Muyok Hoesa* (*North Korea's Trade*) Seoul: Taehan Muyok Chinhung Kongsa.

Korean Peninsula Energy Development Organization (KEDO). 2006. "About Us: Our History." New York: KEDO. Available at: http://kedo.org/au_history.asp

Kyodo News Service. 2000. "N. Korea School Enrollment Has Plummeted: UNESCO Chief," August 22.

Milward, Alan S. 1977. *War, Economy and Society 1939–1945.* Berkeley, CA: University of California Press.

Noland, Marcus. 2000. *Avoiding the Apocalypse: the Future of the Two Koreas* Washington, DC: International Institute for Economics.

Organization for Economic Cooperation and Development. 1958. *A Standardized System of National Accounts.* Paris: OECD.

People's Korea. 1999. (18 March). "4th DPRK-U.S. underground facility negotiations." Korean Central News Agency (Pyongyang). Available at: http://www.korea-np.co.jp/item/1999/9903/990318.htm.

————. 1999. (21 April). "DPRK Law on People's Economic Plans." Available at http://www.korea-np.co.jp/pk

————. 2000. (1 January). "Glorify This Year Greeting the 55th Anniversary of the Party Foundation as a Year of Proud Victory in the Frame of Great Chollima Upsurge." Joint editorial. *Nodong Sinmun, Choson Inking,* and *Choson Jonwi.* Available at: http://www.korea-np.co.jp/pk

————. 2000. (18 April). "SPA Adopts New State Budget for the Year 2000." Available at: http://www.korea-np.co.jp/pk.

Research Institute for the North Korean Society. 2006. *North Korea Today(20).* Seoul: Goodfriends Center for Peace, Human Rights, and Refugees.

Republic of Korea Bank of Korea (BOK). 2000. "Gross Domestic Product of North Korea in 1999. June. Available at: http://210.104.132.11/content/old/attach/00000013/060631NORTH-GDP(1999).doc

————. 2005. "GDP of North Korea in 2004." Seoul: Hanguk Unhaeng. Available at: http://210.104.132.11/contents_admin/info_admin/eng/home/press/pressre/info/time seriesnk1.xls

————. Ministry of Unification (ROK MOU). Various years. Inter-Korean Cooperation. Seoul: Tongilbu. Available at: http://www.unikorea.go.kr/en/EPA/EPA0401L.jsp

————. Various years. *Wolgan Nambuk Kyoryu Hyomnyok Tonghyang* (Monthly North-South Exchange and Co-operation Trends), Seoul: Tongilbu.

Ruggles, Richard and Nancy D. Ruggles. 1956. *National Income Accounts and National Income Analysis.* New York: McGraw-Hill Co.

Seckler, David. 1980. "Malnutrition: An Intellectual Odyssey." *Western Journal of Agricultural Economics* 5:219–227.

Struck, Doug. 2000. "N. Korea Back from the Brink: Aid Helps End Mass Starvation." *Washington Post.* 5 September.

United States Bureau of the Census. 2005. International Data Base. Available at: www.census.gov/ipc/www/idbagg.html

Xinhua News Agency (Beijing). 2000. "DPRK Holds U.S. Responsible for Power Shortage." 3 February.

8

If North Korea Were Really "Reforming" How Could We Tell and What Would We See?*

[*Author's note: The content of this chapter essay was initially drafted in late summer 2001—roughly five years ago.*

A number of dramatic developments in North Korean affairs, dealt with elsewhere in this book, have taken place in the interim. To mention only the most obvious of these on the promising side of the ledger, note Pyongyang's enactment of "economic management improvement measures" in July 2002 and its ongoing development of economic relations with the Republic of Korea (ROK, or South Korea) highlighted by the gradual progress of the ambitious "Kaesong Industrial Complex". And on the other side of the ledger, the brief and disastrous September 2002 experiment with the special economic zone in Sinuiju under the ill-fated Yang Bin,[1] and the still-ongoing international drama that commenced in late 2002 with the revelations that Pyongyang was violating its non-proliferation promises and commitments—a drama that has resulted among other things in the termination of the "Agreed Framework" LWR project for North Korea, and the dissolution of the KEDO consortium charged with facilitating it.[2]

Momentous as those developments may have been, they do not negate the thrust of the analysis presented below. Indeed, for better or worse, the basic arguments and analysis offered here in 2001 about the prospects for DPRK economic reform are still current in 2006. The essay is therefore offered for the reader's consideration with only minor revisions of the original text.]

Few items on the Northeast Asian agenda are as pressing, or so potentially important, as the matter of systemic reform in the Democratic People's Republic of Korea (DPRK, or North Korea).

---

*This chapter is slightly adapted from the original paper presented at the 16th Annual Conference of the Council on U.S.-Korea Security Studies, Washington, D.C., October 18–20, 2001, and subsequently published in *Korea and World Affairs* 26(1), Spring 2002; it also draws upon a longer study by the author in Ellings and Friedberg, 2001.

From the humanitarian standpoint, improving the efficiency and performance of the North Korean economy could have an extraordinarily important impact on the well-being of North Korea's 20-odd million people; for perhaps hundreds of thousands of them, it could literally mean the difference between life and death. From the standpoint of the Korean question, a more open and flexible North Korean system would surely facilitate the reintegration and eventual reunification of the peninsula for which so many Korean patriots yearn. From the standpoint of regional security, systemic reform in North Korea would constitute a significant and highly promising development, for the embrace of a less ideological and more pragmatic external policy by Pyongyang would temper the regime's bellicosity and reduce the tensions that have typically characterized North Korea's relations with the outside world.

Given the evident desirability of North Korean reform, then, we may well ask: if North Korea really were "reforming," how could we tell—and what would we see?

Structural Problems in the Study of the DPRK

The question is not meant to be mischievous. Rather, it is intended to highlight some enduring problems in the study of the DPRK. To put the matter plainly: North Korean external behavior is unfortunately not easily understood by foreign analysts—nor is it typically anticipated by them.

The reasons are readily explicable. As a socialist dictatorship that simultaneously embraces hereditary succession, the basic precepts of North Korean governance are intuitively alien to viewers of a liberal, Western sensibility. Furthermore, for over four decades Pyongyang has striven assiduously—and with extraordinary success—to suppress any and all information that might permit an independent assessment of the regime's performance. No less important, North Korea is a state that cleaves unremittingly to a policy of strategic deception (in bygone Soviet terminology, *maskirovka*).

Indeed, misleading potential adversaries about its intentions and capabilities seems to lie at the very heart of North Korea's statecraft. As we now know, the preparations for North Korea's surprise attack against South Korea in June 1950 were carefully kept secret, and Pyongyang even used diplomacy to help keep its target off-guard, offering Seoul a new peace and unification initiative just a week before it launched its assault.[3]

The outbreak of the Korean War, however, is only the most famous of the DPRK's exercises in strategic deception, a mainstay in North Korean external policy during the Cold War, and an integral part of its foreign policy since the end of the Cold War. For example, in early 1992, as the "Joint Declaration on the Denuclearization of the Korean Peninsula"[4] that Pyongyang had just signed with Seoul was supposed to be coming into force, the DPRK submitted falsi-fied data to the UN International Atomic Energy Agency (IAEA) about the sta-tus of its nuclear development program.[5] It was the discovery and exposure of these falsifications that triggered the international community's North Korean nuclear crisis of 1993–4. North Korea's reputation for "unpredictability," then, is in no small measure a testimony to the success of official government policy.

North Korea: Gathering Signs of Change

For all the difficulties in divining the significance of developments in North Korea, signs of change on the North Korean stage have been gathering since Kim Jong Il's accession to the DPRK's "highest post of the state" in Septem-ber 1998.[6] We can surely all agree that the Kim Dae Jung—Kim Jong Il Pyongyang parleys of June 2000 marked a momentous departure from North Korea's previous posture toward inter-Korean summitry.[7] Other noteworthy, and intriguing, divergences from past practices or policies have been gradu-ally accumulating. A partial inventory of these would include:

North-South relations. Pyongyang's November 1998 six-year, US$942 million deal with the Hyundai business group for tourism in the Kumgang Mountain area, under whose terms over 400,000 outsiders have already visited the scenic North Korean site[8]; the commerce-oriented November 2000 ROK-DPRK agreements on investment protection, prevention of double taxation, resolution of commercial disputes, and clearing settlement;[9] and the now-unfolding pro-ject (reportedly approved directly by Kim Jong Il) for a multi-billion dollar, 66-square-kilometer, Hyundai-built industrial park and residential develop-ment in the vicinity of Kaesong, just above the DMZ[10];

Relations with the United States. The unprecedented and cordial high-level meetings between Kim Jong Il and former Secretary of State Albright in Pyongyang, and in Washington between former President Clinton and Kim's emissary NDC Vice Chairman Jo Myong Rok, in 2000; no less unprecedented, the repeated reports that Kim Jong Il had informed South Korean and Ameri-can leaders that he was reconciled to a continuing U.S. troop presence in the Korean peninsula, even after reunification[11];

International diplomacy. The establishment, between early 2000 and summer 2001, of diplomatic relations with 11 OECD countries and the European Union (and with most of its erstwhile Korean War military opponents as well!)[12]—punctuated by DPRK declarations that "there is no reason to hesitate about improving relations with capitalist countries"[13] and that "North Korea seeks friendly relations with all countries"[14];

International security policy. The DPRK's accession, in the year 2000 to membership in the ASEAN Regional Forum (ARF), the first such multilateral security dialogue that Pyongyang had ever entered; and North Korea's presentation at the 2001 ARF of an official paper titled "Annual Report on Security Prospects": a small but highly symbolic step toward making the regime's security calculations more transparent;

Economic policy. In January 2001, came the striking pronouncement in *Nodong Sinmun*, the DPRK's party paper, that "Things are not what they used to be in the 1960s. . . . With the start of the new age of the 2000s, an all-around re-examination should be given to outworn patterns and practices. . . . We should bring about technical modernization by boldly doing away with what needs to be abolished, instead of being shackled by ready-made ideas or hanging on to the old and outdated conceptions."[15] Following this call for "a new way of thinking," the DPRK revealed that Chairman Kim Jong Il made an "unofficial" six-day trip to China in 2001.[16] During their stay in Shanghai, Kim Jong Il and his delegation apparently devoted much of their time to inspecting profit-oriented, Chinese-, Japanese-, and American-owned factories and reportedly twice toured the Shanghai stock exchange.[17] Shortly thereafter, the DPRK formally requested the United Nations Industrial Development Organization (UNIDO) to teach some North Korean college students about market systems and management,[18] while North Korean officials publicly voiced the hope that the DPRK might join the World Bank and the International Monetary Fund.[19] Another sign of "a new way of thinking" on the ground was the appearance of North Korea's first commercial billboard[20] in spring 2001, and its first ever fashion show to exhibit South Korean haute couture;[21] perhaps more importantly, rumors were circulating that the DPRK was poised to enact a China-style contract-farming arrangement on a nationwide scale[22] and to develop a domestic internet infrastructure.[23]

Indispensable Facets of a Meaningful DPRK "Reform"

Not so long ago, any and all of the markers listed above might have seemed unthinkable for North Korea. Clearly, the country *is* changing. But to appreciate the *actual significance* of these changes, we must ask: how profound are the changes now underway, what accounts for them, and what do they augur for the DPRK's habitually adversarial relations with its neighbors and the rest of the outside world?

The answers to all of these questions, of course, turn on the intentions of North Korean leadership. Unfortunately, that critical quantity remains obscure—for, at least as yet, ruling circles in Pyongyang are no more inclined now than ever in the past to disclose their true thinking about the tactical and strategic issues they face. Consequently, deductions abroad about the regime's outlook, motivations, and estimations are unavoidably based upon inferences drawn from critically incomplete and often inconsistent evidence.

Be that as it may, and despite Pyongyang's preternatural secrecy, we can be reasonably confident that we already know what sorts of changes in regime outlook would be necessary for a fundamental recasting of the country's international policy to be regarded as feasible or desirable. That knowledge provides us with the rudiments of a decryption key with which to decode the diverse signs of change in North Korea today, so that we might distinguish the meaningful from the epiphenomenal.

As a necessary precondition for a more peaceable *modus vivendi* with the international community, we may submit, the DPRK would have to embrace bold new answers to three old problems bearing centrally upon the identity and character of the state:

The problem of "ideological and cultural infiltration." North Korean authorities coined the term "ideological and cultural infiltration" to describe their perception of the impact on their country of exchanges of people, ideas, and goods with the outside, "imperialist"-dominated world. In the aftermath of the Soviet collapse, North Korean ideologists argued that the downfall of socialism in Eastern Europe and the USSR was due in large measure to "cultural and ideological infiltration," and DPRK leadership vowed to protect their system from this menace.[24] If North Korean authorities decided, however, that "ideological and cultural infiltration" were a manageable difficulty rather than a regime-threatening menace, then experimentation with more pragmatic economic policies—including some sort of economic opening toward the outside world—would be a viable rather than a subversive proposition. An opening to the world economy, for its part, would raise the possibility that the DPRK could finance the operations of its system from the sale of conventional goods and services—rather than depend upon international military extortion for financial survival.

The problem of WMD and regime survival. North Korea's prolonged, unfathomable investment in its WMD programs, and its accomplished recourse to nuclear diplomacy over the past decade, strongly suggest that DPRK leadership regards mass destruction weaponry not only as an invaluable asset, but perhaps also as an indispensable tool for guaranteeing regime survival. (Official declarations in the past have hinted as much.[25]) An independent state will never willingly trade away an instrument it regards as vital to its survival—but if DPRK leadership regarded its WMD as valuable but not vital, it would presumably be possible to negotiate an end to those programs in exchange for some particular package of benefits.

The problem of South Korea's legitimacy. From its earliest days, North Korea has insisted that the DPRK was the sole legitimate government on the Korean peninsula. Pyongyang, further, has exacted terrible sacrifices from its people in its long and dogged quest for unification of the peninsula on its own and its terms alone. The quest for unconditional unification with the South, one might argue, is deeply and inextricably fused into the constituting rationale of the DPRK system that we know today. If, however, DPRK leadership convinced itself that the North Korean system could survive indefinitely next to the Republic of Korea, and that purposes of state were served by recognizing the legitimacy of the ROK, then a revolution in inter-Korean relations would be possible—a genuine Seoul-Pyongyang peace agreement (and presumably, a correlative official declaration of some kind of "one nation, two states" policy by which to justify the pact for the DPRK), a *detente* worthy of the name, and a massive demobilization of military forces on the Korean peninsula could all then be theoretically within grasp.

It will be evident upon reflection, incidentally, that arriving at new answers to every one of these problems is contingent upon, and reinforced by, arriving at new answers to each of the others.

Assessing Change in North Korea

From the perspective of systemic reform, signs of change in North Korea may thus be deemed important and meaningful insofar as they portend internal regime movement on three scores: economic opening, WMD proliferation, and the North-South struggle. Consequently, we must ask: what would meaningful movement on these issues look like to us, given the limited apertures that outsiders have for peering into North Korea? And does available evidence suggest that such movement is currently taking place?

Economic Opening. We must bear in mind the simple fact that even serious adjustments in official economic policies and practices may not necessarily be driven by "new thinking." Such adjustments can also be forced upon a regime by sheer exigency—and official claims of "turning the corner" and "completing the Forced March" notwithstanding, the DPRK remains in dire economic straits. According to one assessment by the UN Food and Agriculture Organization (FAO) and the World Food Programme (WFP), for example, cereal production for the DPRK for 2000–01 is expected to be fully a third below the level of 1995–96[26]—when Pyongyang first launched its international appeal for emergency food aid. The country's export capabilities are likewise in a state of virtual collapse: according to the ROK Unification Ministry, North Korea's export earnings in the first half of the year 2001 amounted to barely US$350 million[27]—a sum equivalent to well under US$20 per capita.

Under such circumstances, tactical and opportunistic improvisations may well be imperative for the survival of what Pyongyang terms "our own style of socialism." From an analytic standpoint, attributing the DPRK's observed economic improvisations to a postulated change in outlook on the part of North Korean leadership is to violate the very logic underlying "Ockham's razor," that is, "what can be done with fewer [assumptions] is done in vain with more."

It is perfectly true that North Korean party journals have recently averred that DPRK policy "by no means" insists upon a strategy of "economic construction with the door closed."[28] But as those same articles patiently emphasize, North Korea's "door" is officially open to "the accomplishments of modern science and technology"[29]—nothing else. In particular, North Korean policy still categorically opposes what it brands "ideological and cultural infiltration": including "international, regional, and global cooperation and exchanges." "Lessons of history," according to an article in the July 2001 *Nodong Sinmun*, "show that once the door is open to the imperialists' ideological and cultural infiltration, the revolution can be destroyed at one stroke"; accordingly, "it is mandatory to completely block the route through which their ideology and culture infiltrate."[30] So deep is North Korea's doctrinal antagonism to these tendencies, that the DPRK Constitution specifically enjoins the state to combat "cultural infiltration" (Article 41). And since international economic integration is a prime vector for just such "cultural infiltration," North Korean doctrine remains implacably hostile to "globalization," a tendency Pyongyang continues to describe as "a nefarious crime against humanity."[31]

As of today (2006), North Korean economic praxis has faithfully followed published doctrine regarding "ideological and cultural infiltration." The 1998 Mt. Kumgang tourism deal—the largest commercial venture Pyongyang has ever undertaken with a foreign partner—entails almost no exposure to the outside world, since the tourists in question are ferried to the site, cordoned within a remote military area, with cash payments for the visits wired directly to North Korean bank accounts. More recently, North Korea's posture on "ideological and cultural infiltration" has been revealed by its behavior on the light water nuclear reactor project underway in the country under the auspices of the Korean Peninsula Energy Development Organization (KEDO), the multilateral institution created under the 1994 "Agreed Framework." In 1997, that project had hired 200 North Korean workers to assist in construction activities, alongside 700 South Korean engineers. Even this tiny amount of contact with outsiders proved to be unacceptable to the regime; in 2000, under the pretext of a "labor dispute," the DPRK withdrew half of its local workers from the construction site, and in 2001 had KEDO replace them with Uzbek nationals.[32] By 2001, KEDO was poised to replace the North Korean workforce in its entirety,[33] but as noted in Chapter 4, KEDO's end in 2006 clearly shows this was not to be the case.

Evocative as Kim Jong Il's 2001 tour of Shanghai has been to many students of North Korean affairs, there are reasons to doubt that the visit portends a North Korean effort to replicate a China-style economic opening.

First, the visit served clearly identifiable North Korean interests entirely separate from any possible urge to emulate China. For one thing, as a longstanding recipient of Chinese foreign aid, it would certainly be in Pyongyang's interest to make a symbolic gesture sure to please its sponsors. For another, Pyongyang is fervently committed to defense modernization, and the tour of diverse high-tech plants and facilities by Kim Jong Il's predominantly military delegation[34] self-evidently served pre-existing martial objectives. Foreign visits by high-level North Korean delegations typically serve military purposes. Recall that NDC Vice Chairman Cho Myong Rok began his October 2000 visit to the United States with a visit to Lucent Technologies[35] and other "IT" concerns— information technologies are the basis of today's emerging "revolution in military affairs" (RMA)—and that Kim Jong Il inspected a tank factory and a former Soviet ICBM development facility on his July–August 2001 visit to Russia. North Korea's interest in a country's military or dual-use technology does not necessarily imply a corresponding interest in its economic system.

Second, Kim Jong Il's reported Shanghai-tour comments concerning China's achievements were actually quite circumspect and noncommittal.[36] In the Chinese press, Kim was quoted as "stress[ing] that the big changes that had taken place . . . since . . . China began the reform and opening up drive, proved that the policies of reform and opening up adopted by the [Chinese Communist Party] are correct"[37]—for China. North Korea's policies, by contrast, were held to be correct for the DPRK, and the North Korean press pointedly emphasized that China's leadership had congratulated "the Korean people" for "remarkable progress and achievements in various domains including socialist construction . . . successfully surmounting manifold difficulties under the leadership of . . . Kim Jong Il."[38] Third, the particulars of China's post-1978 economic policy would seem poorly suited for the contemporary DPRK. The mismatch involves both initial conditions and policy priorities:[39]

- Post-Maoist China was a predominantly rural, agricultural society, whereas North Korea is already urbanized and (mis)industrialized;

- China's economy in the late 1970s enjoyed a measure of macroeconomic stability obviously absent from North Korea's today;

- Though the *renminbi* in the late 1970s was a non-convertible currency, its role as a medium of economic exchange was vastly greater than that permitted the DPRK *won* today;

- China's reallocation of resources included massive (if temporary) demobilizations of military manpower and cutbacks in the defense industries, while North Korea continues to enshrine "military-first politics"; and

- China relied heavily upon ethnic Chinese from the diaspora for the capital, technology, and entrepreneurship that stimulated Chinese linkages with the world economy; any call today for a similar reliance by the DPRK on outside Koreans would be labeled counter-revolutionary in Pyongyang.

Given these nontrivial discrepancies and contradistinctions, an attempt to implement China-style economic policies could easily have economic and political repercussions which the North Korean leadership would regard as highly adverse. *Choson Sinbo*, the paper of the pro-DPRK Korean community in Japan (*Chochongnyon* or *Chosen Soren*), was therefore most likely correct when it asserted, in the aftermath of Kim's Shanghai tour, that "[H]is inspection was aimed at seeking 'reference,' not at following a Chinese-style reform and opening."[40]

If North Korea *were* to experiment deliberately with a new economic direction, one might expect the chosen path to comport less with the recent "China model" than with a "military-as-modernizer" template familiar from the political economies of pre-WW II Japan and Park Chung Hee's South Korea.[41] Both of those "models," it may be recalled, relied upon an "economic opening," and indeed depended upon growing integration with outside economics for their success.[42]

If Pyongyang were to embark upon a genuine move toward an economic opening, what initial signs would outsiders be able to see? Some of these might include: 1) meaningful departure from old "economic" themes, and new dialogue about economic issues, in DPRK propaganda and guidance organs; 2) doctrinal reorientation regarding the treatment of profit-generating transactions in official DPRK pronouncements—and especially profits involving transactions with foreign concerns; 3) an attempt on the part of the DPRK to settle its longstanding international "debt default" problems[43]; 4) a parallel effort to remonetize the domestic North Korean economy; 5) a move toward greater economic transparency, i.e., the publication of economic and social statistics describing the North Korean domestic situation; and 6) serious attempts to promulgate a legal framework for potential foreign investors that might assist in attracting profit-seeking overseas entrepreneurs to North Korean soil. As yet, for better or worse, none of those "indicator lights" appears to be flashing.

WMD Development. Hopes that the DPRK's commitment to its decades-old drive for WMD might be wavering—and that Pyongyang might ultimately be convinced to forswear the project altogether—are buoyed by the following facts:

- On the nuclear front, the "Agreed Framework" has resulted in a shutdown of North Korea's only identified reactor/reprocessing facility, and the United States has not confirmed any suspicious nuclear activities in the DPRK since the signing of the document in 1994.

- On the missile front, in September 1999 the DPRK acquiesced in the previously mentioned rocket-launch moratorium in talks with the United States; in July 2000 Kim Jong Il privately advised visiting Russian President Vladimir Putin that North Korea would scrap its missile program if other countries would launch DPRK satellites into space[44]; in October 2000, Kim Jong Il personally assured visiting US Secretary of State Albright that there would be no more North Korean "satellite" launches[45]; in late 2000, Clinton Administration officials engaged in extensive missile talks with North Korean counterparts, and the US point person in the discussions concluded that "an agreement was within reach"[46]; in May 2001, Kim Jong Il told a visiting European Union delegation headed by Swedish Prime Minister Goran Persson that North Korea's missile-launch moratorium would be extended to the year 2003[47]; and in August 2001, in a visit to Moscow, Kim Jong Il issued a joint declaration with President Putin in which North Korea reaffirmed its pledge to refrain from missile tests until 2003.[48]

Weighing against these promising signs, however, are a host of indications that the DPRK continues to place an extraordinarily high value on its present capabilities and future potential as a producer of weapons of mass destruction. While it may not be possible for outsiders to determine categorically whether North Korea's posture in its international diplomacy concerning DPRK WMD programs reflects deep strategic design or instead mere tactical bargaining, Pyongyang has been stubbornly unwilling to date to provide the international community with credible assurances that it has abandoned the path toward proliferation.

On the nuclear issue, to begin, North Korea has, for nearly seven years and under a succession of objections and excuses, adamantly refused to permit the unrestricted inspections of its Yongbyon facilities by the IAEA specifically envisioned in the "Agreed Framework"[49] document. (Those inspections are supposed to determine how much bomb-quality plutonium North Korea generated before the "Agreed Framework"—and by extension, whether the DPRK may already possess nuclear weaponry.) Further, Pyongyang has, in the course of its wide-ranging negotiations with the United States, repeatedly threatened to restart its frozen Yongbyon nuclear program.[50] Despite America's certification that Washington has not detected any illicit DPRK nuclear activities, North Korea has also deliberately encouraged, and skillfully profited from, the international perception that it could not be trusted to abide by its promised freeze of its nuclear program: in March 1999, it extracted what it called a "visit fee" of over 500,000 tons of cereals from the United States for permission for a US team to inspect an enormous underground facility at Kumchang-ri whose construction suggested surreptitious nuclear development efforts were underway, and whose purpose Pyongyang would not forthrightly explain.[51]

Finally, there is the unanswered question of why the DPRK has insisted, in the crafting of the "Agreed Framework" and ever since, in the replacement of its plutonium-generating Yongbyon plant with new, KEDO-supplied, plutonium-generating light-water nuclear reactors. Pyongyang officially acknowledges that it is suffering from pervasive electricity shortages,[52] and the new reactors, which will not be completed for at least seven more years,[53] will not be able to provide power to the North Korean economy until the DPRK's electrical grid is renovated and upgraded.[54] Why a project incapable of meeting the country's pressing and immediate economic needs, but potentially capable of eventually supplying fissile material to the regime, should meet Pyongyang's strategic objectives has yet to be explained by the North Korean leadership.

On the missile issue, North Korea's pledge of a launch moratorium until the year 2003 offers rather less than meets the eye. In the five years between May 1993 and August 1998, it will be recalled that the DPRK launched no rockets—yet thanks to clandestine development projects, Pyongyang successfully leapfrogged from its single stage, liquid-fuel No Dong missile to the improved multi-stage, solid-fuel, ballistic Taepo Dong model.[55]

Since September 1999—in the period of the self-declared DPRK moratorium on test-launches—Pyongyang has carefully underscored that it is not bound to halt rocket and satellite research and development (since these are "sovereign rights"[56]); and indeed, in July 2001, American intelligence reportedly detected tests of new North Korean rocket engines.[57] North Korea has also consistently reaffirmed as its sovereign prerogative the right to sell abroad any missiles that it might be able to manufacture, and through 2001 was reportedly exporting missile components and technology to Iran and other interested buyers.[58]

As for the claims by former Clinton administration officials at the end of their tenure that "a deal was within reach" on North Korean missiles, the then-new Bush administration (which is now privy to the confidential details of those past Pyongyang-Washington deliberations) has publicly demurred. In the words of one Bush administration National Security Council (NSC) official, "We've looked at the [record] . . . There was nothing close to an agreement. There was no verification element in anything the previous administration had discussed."[59]

Finally, there is the curious detail of North Korea's relentless denunciation of America's proposed national missile defense (NMD) plan.[60] It is true that Washington's prospective program for NMD has been sharply criticized by both Moscow and Beijing—but both Russia and China are countries with acknowledged nuclear and ballistic inventories, whose credibility would be directly affected by the success of the envisioned American program. Wherefore, then, Pyongyang's bitter opposition to American missile defense?

To this date, there is little evidence that North Korea has, at any point in its more than five decades of existence, ever voluntarily abjured any new instrument of military force that might possibly lie within its grasp. (Today, indeed, such a renunciation would seem fundamentally inconsistent with the state's established policies of "strong and prosperous state" (*kangsong taeguk*) and "military-first politics" (*songun chongchi*). Moreover, North Korea's commitment to developing weapons of mass destruction was implicitly reaffirmed in June 2001 in a full front-page *Nodong Sinmun* editorial, which exhorted that "We should hold fast to the military-first politics *and build up our military strength in every possible way*"[61] [emphasis added].

If North Korea *were* to head on a different road regarding proliferation, the first clear sign of a change in attitude would be a new stance toward outside verification of North Korean WMD activities. For the time being, however, Pyongyang maintains that U.S. calls for verification conceal "a dark ulterior motive to thoroughly investigate our national defense and military bases . . . [a plot to] completely dig out our interior organs [*sic*] . . ."[62] and that "the issue [of verification] can never be on the agenda for DPRK-U.S. talks."[63]

North-South Relations. The DPRK's diplomatic behavior toward Seoul since early 2000—the Pyongyang Summit and North-South Declaration; the subsequent high-level deliberations between the two sides; Kim Jong Il's promise to visit the South "at the appropriate time;" the North's willingness to accept food aid and economic subsidies from the South Korean government—all may seem to suggest that Pyongyang implicitly has come to recognize the ROK's right to exist as a state. Unfortunately, other evidence suggests the matter is not so straightforward.

Although the North Korean government unarguably toned down its anti-Seoul invective in the wake of the Pyongyang summit, the DPRK's longstanding official estimate of the legitimacy of the South Korean state remained unaltered. This fact was underscored by the pronouncements of the National Democratic Front of South Korea (NDFSK)—the only entity representing the South to be accorded a mission in Pyongyang at that time.[64]

Two months after the Pyongyang summit, a statement by the NDFSK explained the group's purpose: "to put an end to the U.S. colonial rule over South Korea and establish a regime based on national independence and . . .

democracy . . ."[65] That formulation unmistakably characterized the ROK as an American colony, possessed of neither national independence or a democratic system. The assessment has since been reinforced and clarified by NDFSK calls for South Korea's "emancipation" from "the 50-odd year U.S. colonial rule"[66] and admonitions that South Koreans "will forever undergo disgrace as colonial slaves of foreign forces" if they do not "rise in anti-U.S. resistance" and "abolish pro-U.S. submissive diplomacy."[67]

The NDFSK is ostensibly unconnected to the North Korean government. But official statements by the DPRK media convey the very same message. A February 2001, KCNA report, for example, referred to South Korea's legislature as the "national assembly"—with sneer quotes and lower case letters in the original.[68] And in August 2001, *Minju Choson*, the DPRK's party journal, made Pyongyang's view of the ROK crystal clear. The essay decried the present ROK government as the descendant of "the Korean government-general of the Japanese imperialists," which "the U.S. imperialists . . . renamed the 'U.S. military government;'" it further intoned that the United states "enforced a 'military rule' in South Korea" and "illegally . . . set up a pro-American 'separate government' there"[69]; that is, the state currently governed by the Roh Moo-hyun administration.[70]

Is it possible that these media pronouncements misstate official DPRK policy? While this contingency cannot be dismissed, the chances of such a media error are exceedingly unlikely. More than possibly any other Communist state, the DPRK has made a fetish of subjecting its media outlets to party discipline. Kim Jong Il's own extensive background in propaganda and "guidance" underscores the attention that is devoted by Pyongyang to every word it prints or broadcasts. That recent reading of the South Korean system, furthermore, is consistent with both North Korea's basic ideological documents and the present declarations of the DPRK's top officials. The current preamble of the Workers' Party of Korea (WPK) charter, for example, states that "The present task of the WPK is to ensure . . . the accomplishment of the revolutionary goals of national liberation and the people's democracy in the entire area of the country,"[71] that is, in South Korea.[72]

Korean "Reform" and the U.S.-ROK Military Alliance

The corollary of the DPRK's estimate of the legitimacy of the South Korean state is Pyongyang's posture toward the ROK's military alliance with the United States. According to former President Kim Dae Jung, at the Pyongyang summit "North Korea has consented to the South's view that U.S. troops should continue to stay on the Korean peninsula."[73] Former President Kim has recounted his June 2000 conversation with Kim Jong Il over the future of

American forces in the peninsula on a number of occasions; his account seems to be corroborated by China's *Beijing Review*, which has intimated that North Korean officials told Chinese sources that Pyongyang might reconcile itself to a long-term U.S. troop presence under certain specific conditions.[74] Yet these fascinating emanations are to date wholly at odds with the stated position of the North Korean government, and indeed with Kim Jong Il's own published post-Pyongyang summit comments, all of which maintain that the United States is responsible for the division of Korea, that the U.S. alliance with South Korea is totally unacceptable, and that U.S. troops should withdraw from the ROK and the Korean peninsula.

In the months since the Pyongyang summit, Kim Jong Il has given two interviews in which he discussed American forces on the Korean peninsula: one to a Korean-American reporter (June 2000), the other to Moscow's *Itar-Tass* news agency (July 2001). In the former, he is quoted as saying:

> [Former] President Kim Dae Jung's image had not been so good among our people. For instance, he has advocated continued U.S. military presence in our country even after the unification has been realized. . . . We have urged U.S. forces to leave Korea. However, I don't expect them to leave soon. The Americans, more than anybody else . . . are responsible for the partitioning of Korea into two halves. They are accordingly obligated to facilitate its reunification.[75]

In the *Itar-Tass* interview, Kim's view is more succinct: "the whole world knows that the United States has forcibly occupied half of our country's land and is constantly threatening us."[76] Neither of these pronouncements sounds like an invitation to American forces for an indefinite stay on the Korean peninsula.

The DPRK's post-Pyongyang summit declamations about U.S. forces in Korea are entirely consonant with Kim's words, and elaborate upon his expressed viewpoint. Especially interesting is the sounding of *Nodong Sinmun* on June 16, 2000—the day after the Pyongyang summit concluded. In that presentation, it is emphasized that

> Korea's division is what outside forces imposed upon the country. If they had not occupied Korea, there would have been no division of the county. . . The major outside power responsible for the division of the country is the United States. . . . U.S. imperialists [are] the mastermind of national division and the key obstructer of national unification. . . . Withdrawal of U.S. troops—that should be the first step for the United States to take to help Korea's reunification. . ."[77]

In the following months, the drumbeat of criticism against a U.S. military alliance with South Korea continued to reverberate. Thus, in various pronouncements, the U.S. troop pullout was held to be a "stumbling block to reunification"[78]; a "prerequisite for disarmament"[79]; "a precondition for arms reduction"[80]; and even "the master key to reconciliation, cooperation, and lasting peace on the Korean peninsula."[81] In March 2001, *Pyongyang Central Broadcasting Station* insisted "the United States . . . give up its domination and invasive policy over the South."[82] In July 2001, *Nodong Sinmun* demanded "the unconditional withdrawal of the U.S. imperialist aggression troops from South Korea."[83]

Any lingering doubts about the DPRK's official position on U.S. troops in South Korea should have been satisfied by the joint declaration with the Russian government on the occasion of Kim Jong Il's August 2001 meeting with Vladimir Putin in Moscow. In that document, the DPRK avowed, "The pullout of the US forces from South Korea is a pressing issue which brooks no delay."[84]

Pyongyang has indicated, incidentally, that it would not be satisfied simply with a U.S. military withdrawal from South Korea: since it holds that "the U.S. insistence on its military presence in the region is designed to establish military domination over the Asia-pacific" and "is aimed to use Japan as a shock brigade in Asian aggression,"[85] a U.S. military pullout from Japan is also a required for peace and stability in the region.

In the North Korean lexicon, an "independent" South Korea is defined as a South Korea no longer stationing American forces, or bound to the United States by a military alliance. It is therefore highly significant that the first point in the June 15, 2000 "North-South Declaration" signed by Kim Dae Jung and Kim Jong Il in Pyongyang should read, "The North and the South agreed to solve the question of the country's reunification independently by the concerted efforts of the Korean nation responsible for it."[86]

After the Pyongyang summit, it became known that President Kim had not consulted the United States about this particular linguistic innovation in his "Sunshine Policy."[87] Former President Kim Dae Jung further revealed that he "had agreed to include the North Korean phrase [in the declaration] in return for Kim Jong Il's agreement to a new government framework [for eventual reunification'],"[88] and gamely explained that his own interpretation of the phrase "independent" was that "the two Koreas will work together maintaining friendly relations with surrounding nations."[89]

In the context of the joint declaration, however, what mattered was not President Kim's personal definition of the word "independent." The meaning of the joint summit declaration, Pyongyang stressed, was that "reunification will be realized only when the two Koreas gather together to resolve matters without any other foreign powers involved in the process."[90] North Korean officials have further explained that the key obstacle to the progress of the North-South declaration is the United States, which is "refusing the North-South Joint Declaration and hindering its implementation."[91] For although (as North Korean media phrases it) the "North-South relationship . . . has entered the track of harmony . . . with the historic . . . announcement of June 15 North-South Joint Declaration . . . [the U.S.] block[s] our nation's independent reunification."[92]

By Pyongyang's particular construction, of course, any American effort to preserve or uphold the U.S.-ROK military alliance would amount to hindering the implementation of the joint declaration.

If North Korea were to evidence a new attitude toward the legitimacy of the ROK, the indications of this change would be direct and unmistakable: its highest figures and its official media would simply disclose that they were prepared to accept the existence of the South Korean state, that they recognized the ROK's right to conduct its own foreign policy, and they respected (while respectfully disagreeing with) Seoul's decision to maintain a military alliance with the United States. No such disclosures, of course, have been offered to date. On the contrary, Pyongyang has steadily attempted to use the South's Sunshine Policy to drive a wedge between the United States and the ROK.

Those of us who would favor a turn in Pyongyang toward a more open, flexible and pragmatic policy can, of course, still live in hope of systemic North Korean reform. My point here is simply that outside observers have not yet detected the sorts of emanations from the DPRK that might be expected to register on our all-too-limited faculties if a pronounced shift toward "reform" were indeed underway in North Korea.

If this analysis is correct, furthermore, one important but perhaps unanticipated marker of gathering systemic reform in the DPRK would be a pronounced moderation of Pyongyang's hostile posture toward the U.S.-ROK military alliance. Unlike so many other aspects of North Korean policy, that feature of official statecraft would seem not at all opaque. If this "signal light" should suddenly begin flashing, outside observers will be able to tell.

Notes

1. See *Yonhap*, 2002; Kynge, 2002, p. 6; *BBC Worldwide Monitoring*, 2002.
2. See *Yonhap*, 2006.
3. Merrill, 1989, p. 176.
4. The text of the Declaration is available electronically at the ROK Unification Ministry's website at: http://www.unikorea.go.kr/index.jsp.
5. Oberdorfer, 1997, pp. 268–271.
6. As with so many things North Korean, there is ambiguity today about what exactly the top slot in the government happens to be; according to the 1998 revision of the DPRK Constitution, Kim Il Sung (who died in 1994) is the "eternal President of the Republic." The full text of the Socialist Constitution of the DPRK is available electronically at *People's Korea* website at: http://www1.korea-np.co.jp/pk/061st_issue/98091708.htm.

    The Constitution itself does not indicate the top position of state for living officeholders, but in nominating Kim Jong Il for National Defense Commission (NDC) Chairman, Kim Yong Nam, head of the Presidium of the DPRK Supreme People's Assembly (SPA), declared that "the NDC chairmanship is the highest post of state; see *KCNA* website, at: http://www.kcna.co.jp/index-e.htm.

7. It is true that North Korea had previously invited South Korean leaders to Pyongyang; but the earlier invitation to President Roh Tae Woo would have cast him as a celebrant—and supplicant—at Kim Il Sung's colossal national birthday party, and these would have been terms of reference no ROK President could have accepted; again, in 1994, Kim Il Sung invited Roh's successor, President Kim Young Sam, to a meeting in Pyongyang in 1994, but Marshal Kim died just after extending the invitation, and before any arrangements for that summit had been negotiated.

8. By late May 2001, a total of 396,000 tourists—almost all of them South Korean—had visited Kumgangsan through Hyundai Asan Corp; see *Korea Times*, 2001.

9. ROK Ministry of Unification, 2001, pp. 2–3.

10. See Hyundai Asan Corporation website, available at: http://www.hyundai-asan.com/english/news1/list.asp ; Hong, 2001, pp. 15–19.

11. See, for instance, *Korea Times*, 2000; Yuasa, 2000; *Financial Times*, 2000; Struck, 2000, p. A1; Perlez, 2000, p. A3; Lee (Young-jong), 2001.

12. Between January 2000 and August 2001 the DPRK normalized diplomatic relations with Australia, Italy, the United Kingdom, the Netherlands, Belgium, Luxembourg, Canada, New Zealand, Germany, Spain, Greece, and the European Union; eight of those countries (Australia, Belgium, Canada, Greece, Luxembourg, Netherlands, New Zealand, and the UK) had shed blood in the Korean War, under the aegis of the UN Command; over this same period, North Korea also forged diplomatic ties with two other former United Nations Command enemies: the Philippines and Turkey; as of August 2001, only two of the 17 countries which had fought against North Korea in the Korean War had not yet established diplomatic relations with the DPRK: South Korea and the United States.

13. *FBIS*-EAS-2001-0112.

14. *BBC World Monitoring*, 2001 (4 May).

15. *People's Korea*, 2001a.

16. *KCNA*, 2001 (20 January).

17. *FBIS*-CHI-2001-0120; *FBIS*-EAS-2001-0118.

18. *FBIS*-EAS-2001-0301; according to the ROK Ministry of Unification, nearly 400 North Korean officials had received overseas training since 1998; Ko, 2001.

19. *FBIS*-EAS-2001-0311.

20. *BBC World Monitoring*, 2001 (4 June).

21. *Choson Ilbo*, 2001 (30 May).

22. *Chosun Ilbo*, 2001 (4 March).

23. *Korea Times*, 2001 (13 February).

24. For example: "The former East European socialist countries opened their door to the imperialists' ideological and cultural infiltration. . . As a result, . . . they were ruined after all. . . . The fact that these countries collapsed without firing even a single shot clearly exhibits how dangerous the imperialists' ideological and cultural infiltration is"; *FBIS*-EAS-2001-0220.

25. For example: in December 1998 a spokesman for the General Staff of the North Korean People's Army (KPA) pointedly asserted that "It must be clearly known that there is no limit to the strike of our people's army and that on this planet there is no room for escaping the strike"; more recently, the DPRK media intoned that "The nation's flourishing and the country's prosperity entirely depend upon the barrel of the gun. . . When the barrel of the gun rusts, the country and the nation collapses. . . . [O]ur people will become slaves and the party and the revolution will all perish when the barrel of the gun bec[omes] rusty . . ."; *FBIS*-EAS-2001-0725.

26. Food and Agriculture Organization and World Food Programme, 2000.
27. *English JoongAng Ilbo*, 2001; that report placed North Korea's "international" exports for the first half of 2001 at US$290 million; the South Korean government does not count North-South commerce as "international" trade—but North Korea only exported US$63 million in goods to the ROK during that same period, according to the Unification Ministry; taken together, the Unification Ministry's estimates imply global commodity export revenues of US$353 million; assuming a North Korean population in the range of 20 to 25 million would imply per capita export revenues of US$14–$18 for the first half of the year 2001.
28. *FBIS*-EAS-2001-0316.
29. Ibid.
30. *FBIS*-EAS-2001-0727.
31. *FBIS*-EAS-2001-0629.
32. *BBC Summary*, 2001(16 February).
33. *FBIS*-EAS-2001-0524.
34. *FBIS*-EAS-2001-0121.
35. Chapman, 2000.
36. Kim Jong Il has only once been quoted as evidencing personal interest in another country's economic system; during Secretary of State Albright's October 2000 visit to Pyongyang, Kim reported told her that he was looking to Sweden as a model for national development (see *BBC Summary of World Broadcasts*, 2000); Sweden, of course, is an export-oriented, high-tax capitalist economy with solid commercial codes and firm property laws, and with a convertible currency; Kim's curious comment may or may not have been intended to test his guests; that comment should be kept in mind, however, in judging the credibility of other confidential revelations that he has personally offered to outsiders.
37. *BBC Summary*, 2001 (20 January).
38. KCNA, Website, available at: http://www.kncna.co.jp/item/2001/200101/news01/21.htm#1.
39. For background on the Chinese experience, see Bennett, 1978; Yun, 1991; Shirk, 1994; Lardy, 1998; and Hsing, 1998.
40. *FBIS*-EAS-2001-0211.
41. It was no coincidence, in 1998, that Kim Jong Il adopted for his formal accession the slogan *kangsong taeguk* [rich and powerful nation], one strikingly similar to the prewar Japanese *Fukoku Kyohei*.
42. For background, see Allen et al., 1940; Barnhart, 1987; Woo, 1991.
43. For the past quarter century, the DPRK has been in effective default on roughly US$1 billion in European, Japanese and Australian loans contracted in the early 1970s; for more detail, see Eberstadt, 1995, Chapter 1.
44. Gordon, 2000, p. A6; Chen, 2000, p. A14.
45. Lakshmanan, 2000, p. A1.
46. Gordon, 2001, p. A1.
47. Kirk, 2001, p. 1.
48. Besserglik, 2001.
49. Shin, 2000; *Agence France Presse*, 2000 (11 September); Choe, 2001; Kim, 2001.
50. *FBIS*-EAS-2000-0702; *FBIS*-EAS-2000-0712; *FBIS*-EAS-2001-0606.
51. For Pyongyang's official statement on the Kumchang-ri affair, see KCNA, 1999.
52. Lee (Charles), 2001.
53. *Kyodo News Service*, 2001.
54. Nonproliferation Policy Education Center, 2001.

55. For information on the specifications and capabilities of North Korean rockets, see Federation of American Scientists website, at: http://www.fas.org/nuke/guide/dprk/index.html.

56. In the July 2001 ASEAN Regional Forum (ARF), North Korea's "Annual Report on Security Prospects" stated that the "test of missile belongs thoroughly to the sovereignty of each country, that is why nobody has right to interfere with it" (p. 37). (I am indebted to Ms. Joy Yamamoto of the U.S. State Department for making this DPRK document available to me); almost simultaneously, in an interview with Itar-Tass, Kim Jong Il declared that "[p]ursuing a peaceful missile program is our legitimate, independent, right"; see *FBIS*-EAS-2001-0727.

57. Gertz, 2001b, p. A1.

58. Gertz, 2001a, p. A1.

59. Torkel L. Patterson, Special Assistant to the President and Senior Adviser for Asian Affairs, National Security Council, in address to the Institute for Corean-American Studies (sic), see, Patterson, 2001.

60. *FBIS*-EAS-2001-0714.

61. *FBIS*-EAS-2001-0629.

62. *BBC Worldwide Monitoring*, 2001 (8 July).

63. *FBIS*-EAS-2001-0801.

64. The NDFSK is purportedly a South Korea-based organization, but is actually a creation of the DPRK, operating in and broadcasting for North Korea.

65. *FBIS*-EAS-2000-0825.

66. *FBIS*-EAS-2001-0505.

67. *BBC Worldwide Monitoring*, 2001 (8 June).

68. *KCNA*, 2001 (25 February).

69. *KCNA*, 2001 (1 August).

70. It may seem paradoxical for Pyongyang to accept aid and financial transfers from the ROK if it does indeed regard Seoul as an illicit political entity; to the DPRK's leadership, however, such transactions pose no contradiction; in Pyongyang's well-rehearsed formulation, "those with strength should devote strength, those with knowledge give knowledge, and those with money give money" to the "struggle for national reunification"; *BBC Summary of World Broadcasts*, 1996.

71. Sixth revision of the charter of the Workers' Party of Korea (WPK), 13 October 1980; cited in Yang, 1994, p. 907.

72. Kim Jong Il reportedly indicated to both Kim Dae Jung in June 2000 and to a visiting group of South Korean newspaper editors in August 2000 that the preamble of the WPK charter would be changed in the fall of 2000 (*Agence France Presse*, 2000 (20 June) and *FBIS*-EAS-2000-0813); as of yet, however, no emendations of the preamble have been promulgated.

73. Kim 2000, p. 9.

74. *Agence France Presse*, 2000 (26 July).

75. *People's Korea*, 2001b.

76. Ibid., 2001c.

77. *FBIS*-EAS-2000-0630.

78. *FBIS*-EAS-2001-0317.

79. *Agence France Presse*, 2001 (29 April).

80. *FBIS*-EAS-2001-0528.

81. *KCNA*, 2001 (22 April).

82. *FBIS*-EAS-2001-0326.

83. *FBIS*-EAS-2001-0718.

84. *KCNA*, 2001 (5 August).
85. *KCNA*, 2001 (23 February).
86. *People's Korea*, website at: http://www.korea-np.co.jp/pk/.
87. *The Korea Herald*, 2001.
88. *BBC Worldwide Monitoring*, June 15, 2000.
89. *FBIS*-2000-0616.
90. Kim, 2001.
91. *FBIS*-CHI-2001-0802.
92. *FBIS*-EAS-2001-0730.

References

Agence France Presse. 2000 (20 June). "North Korea to alter goal of making South communist: report."
————. 2000 (26 July). See "North Korea could accept long-term US military presence: Chinese report."
————. 2000 (11 September). "IAEA says North Korea not allowing nuclear access."
———— *Agence France Presse*. 2001 (29 April). "N. Korea demands US troop pullout as 'prerequisite' for disarmament."
ASEAN Regional Forum. 2001. "North Korea: Annual Report on Security Prospects." Pyongyang. July.
Barnhart, Michael A. 1987. *Japan Prepares For Total War: The Search for Economic Security*. Ithaca, NY: Cornell University Press.
Bennett, Gordon, ed., 1978. *China's Finance and Trade: A Policy Reader*. Armonk, NY: M.E.Sharpe.
Besserglik, Bernard. 2001. "N. Korean leader Kim pledges 'peaceful' use of missile programme." *Agence France Presse*. 4 August.
British Broadcasting Corporation (BBC) Summary of World Broadcasts. 1996. Rebroadcast from *KCNA*, 15 August as "Pan-national meeting for peace and reunification help in Pyongyang." FE/D2692/D.
————. 2000. Rebroadcast from *Yonhap News Agency*, 25 October as "North Korea said adopting Swedish economy as development model." FE/W0664/S1. 1 November.
————. 2001 (20 January). Rebroadcast from *Xinhua* as "North Korean leader pays 'unofficial' visit." FE/D4050/G. 22 January.
————. 2001 (16 February). Rebroadcast from *Choson Ilbo* February as "Nuclear group refuses North Korean wage demand, to use Uzbek workers." FE/D4075/S1. 19 February.
BBC Worldwide Monitoring. 2000. Rebroadcast from *Yonhap* News Service, 15 June as "Korea: South President gives details behind summit declaration."
————. 2001 (4 May). Rebroadcast from *Pyongyang Central Broadcasting Station* as "North Korean radio reviews developments in relations with EU."
————. 2001 (4 June). Rebroadcast from *Yonhap News Agency* as "South Korean agency reports North approves first billboard ads."
————. 2001 (8 June). Rebroadcast from *Pyongyang Central Broadcasting Station* as "North Korean radio broadcasts 'letter of appeal' by pro-North radio station in Seoul."
————. 2001 (8 July). Rebroadcast from *Pyongyang Central Broadcasting Station* as "North Korea demands compensation from USA for delay to reactor project."

————. 2002. Rebroadcast from *Hong Kong Economic Journal*, 13 December 2002 as "Case of arrested Chinese tycoon with North Korea links reported by HK daily." 20 December.

Chapman, Glen. 2000. "North Korean Envoy Arrives in US." *Agence France Presse*. 9 October.

Chen, Edwin. 2000. "Clinton, Putin Discuss N. Korea." *Los Angeles Times*. 22 July.

Choe, Sang-hun. 2001. "North Korea again rejects inspection of its nuclear program." *Associated Press*. 21 June.

Choson Ilbo. 2001 (30 May). "South Korean Designer to Hold Fashion Show in Pyongyang." Available at: http://nk.chosun.com/english/news/news.html?ACT= detail&res_id=4298

————. 2001 (4 March). "North Korea to Introduce Farmers' Contract." Available at: http://www.chosun.com/w21data/html/news/200103/200103040310.html

Eberstadt, Nicholas. 1995. *Korea Approaches Reunification*. Armonk, NY: M.E. Sharpe.

Ellings, Richard J. and Aaron Friedberg, eds. 2001. *Strategic Asia 2001–2002: Power and Purpose*. Seattle: National Bureau of Asian Research.

English JoongAng Ilbo. 2001. "N.K. Overseas Trade Estimated as 1.51 billion for First Half." 27 July. Available at: http://service.joins.com/news_asp/narticle.asp?aid= 1892688

FBIS-EAS-2000-0616. Reprinted from *Yonhap News Service* as "ROK President Provides Further Details of Summit at Cabinet."

———— -2000-0630. Reprinted from *Nodong Sinmun*, 16 June as "DPRK: Journal Urges US to Change Korea Policy." 3 July.

———— -2000-0813. Reprinted from *Choson Ilbo* as "Excerpts of DPRK Leader's Dialogue with ROK Media Heads." 13 September.

———— -2000-0702. Reprinted from *Korea Herald*, 3 July as "DPRK Threatens to Restart Nuclear Program."

———— -2000-0712. Reprinted from *KCNA* as "DPRK's KCNA: KCNA on compensation for loss of electricity." 13 July.

———— -2000-0825. Reprinted from *KCNA* as "DPRK's KCNA: More vigorous movement for national reconciliation and unity called for." 28 August.

———— -2001-0112. Reprinted from *KCNA* as "DPRK's KCNA: Respect for independence called for."

———— -2001-0118. Reprinted from *Joongang Ilbo*, 19 January as "Kim Chong-Il Confers With PRC President Jiang Zemin, Visits Stock Market Twice."

———— -2001-0121. Reprinted from *Choson Ilbo* as "Further on Nine Figures Who Accompanied DPRK Leader on Visit to PRC." 24 January.

———— -2001-0211. Reprinted from *Yonhap News Service* as "DPRK Said Not Planning to Adopt Chinese-Style Economy." 13 February.

———— -2001-0220. Reprinted from *Nodong Sinmun*, 6 February as "DPRK Daily Urges 'Imperialists' Ideological, Cultural Infiltration' Be Blocked." 26 February.

———— -2001-0301. Reprinted from *Korea Herald*, 2 March as "DPRK Asks UN to Teach Students Market Systems."

———— -2001-0311. Reprinted from *Korea Herald* 12 March as "DPRK Officials Said Hoping for P'yongyang to Join World Bank."

———— -2001-0316. Reprinted from *Nodong Sinmun*, 18 February as "DPRK Daily: Self-Reliance Des Not Mean Keeping 'Door Closed Up' To S&T." 21 March.

———— -2001-0317. Reprinted from *Yonhap News Service* as "ROK's Yonhap: North Korea Renews Its Call for U.S. Troop Withdrawal." 20 March.

————-2001-0326. Reprinted from *Yonhap News Service* as "ROK's Yonhap: N.K. Demands Withdrawal of U.S. Troops, Nuclear Weapons." 27 March.

————-2001-0505. Reprinted from *KCNA* as "DPRK's KCNA: Anti-U.S. resistance called for." 7 May.

————-2001-0524. Reprinted from *Yonhap News Agency* as "ROK's Yonhap: Seoul, Tokyo Already Fund $510 Mln Into KEDO Project." 29 May.

————-2001-0528. Reprinted from *Pyongyang Central Broadcasting Station* as "DPRK's Nodong Sinmun Demands Withdrawal of US Forces Stationed in South." 30 May.

————-2001-0606. Reprinted from *KCNA* as "DPRK's KCNA: U.S. Urged To Compensate for DPRK's 'Loss of Electricity' Due to Delay in LWR Project." 7 June.

————-2001-0629. Reprinted from *Nodong Sinmun*, 1 June as "DPRK Daily Full Front-Page Article Discusses 'National Pride.'" 3 July.

————-2001-0714. Reprinted from *Pyongyang Central Broadcasting Station* as "US Plan To Build Test Facility for WMD System Criticized." 16 July.

————-2001-0718. Reprinted from *KCNA* as "DPRK's KCNA: U.S. forces' pullback from S. Korea urgently demanded by times and nation (sic)." 19 July.

————-2001-0725. Reprinted from *Pyongyang Central Broadcasting Station*, 24 July as "DPRK Stresses Leader's 'Invincible' Military-First Politics."

————-2001-0727a. Reprinted from *Nodong Sinmun*, 20 July as "DPRK Daily Urges Prevention of 'Imperialists' Ideological, Cultural Infiltration." 2 August.

————-2001-0727b. Reprinted from *Pyongyang Central Broadcasting Station* as "DPRK Radio Carries Kim Chong-Il's Interview With Tass-Itar." 30 July.

————-2001-0730. Reprinted from *Pyongyang Central Broadcasting Station* as "DPRK Radio Decries U.S. as 'Vicious Enemy' to Reunification." 31 July.

————-2001-0801. Reprinted from *Yonhap News Service* as "ROK's Yonhap: N.K. Says U.S. Demands for Verification Ruse to Disarm It." 2 August.

————-2001-0802. Reprinted from *Xinhua* as "*Xinhua* Cites DPRK Condemning U.S. for Refusal of North-South Joint Declaration." 3 August.

FBIS-CHI-2001-0120. Reprinted from *Xinhua* as "Kim Chong-Il Visits China 15–20 January; Holds Talks with Jiang Zemin, Others."

Federation of American Scientists website, http://www.fas.org/nuke/guide/dprk/index.html.

Financial Times. 2000. "North Korean Leader Okays US Forces on Peninsula." 10 August.

Food and Agriculture Organization and World Food Programme. 2001. "FAO/WFP Crop and Food Supply Assessment Mission to the Democratic People's Republic of Korea." 27 July. Available at: http://www.wfp.org/english/?ModuleID=137&Key=10 2004 version available at: http://documents.wfp.org/stellent/groups/public/documents/ena/wfp042118.pdf

Gertz, Bill. 2001a. "North Korea Sends Missile Components, Technology to Iran." *Washington Times*. 18 April.

————. 2001b. "N.Korea tests its missile engine." *Washington Times*. 3 July.

Gordon, Michael R. 2000. "North Korea Reported Open to Halting Missile Program." *New York Times*. 20 July.

————. 2001. "How Politics Sank Accord on Missiles With North Korea." *New York Times*. 6 March.

Hong, Soon-jick. 2001. "Developing the Kaesong Industrial Area: Economic Effects and Future Tasks." *VIP Millennium Report*. Seoul: Hyundai Research Institute.

Hsing, You-tien. 1998. *Making Capitalism Work in China: The Taiwan Connection.* New York: Oxford University Press.

Hyundai Asan Corporation. 2000. "Kaesong to be designated as special economic zone to host Hyundai's industrial complex (2000.8.10)." Available at: http://www .hyundai-asan.com/english/news1/list.asp

KCNA. 1999. "4th DPRK-U.S. underground facility negotiations." 18 March. Available at: http://www.kcna.co.jp/index-e.htm

———. 2001 (20 January). "Kim Jong Il pay unofficial visit to China." Available at: http://www.kcna.co.jp/item/2001/200101/news01/21.htm

———. 2001 (23 February). "Utterances of US ambassador to Japan blasted." Available at: http://www.kcna.co.jp/item/2001/200102/news02/23.htm#5

———. 2001 (25 February). "Revocation of proposed revision of 'Labour Law' demanded." Available at: http://www.kcna.co.jp/index-e.htm

———. 2001 (22 April). "U.S. military presence in South Korea, source of war." Available at: http://www.kcna.co.jp/item/2001/200104/news04/22.htm#8

———. 2001 (1 August). "Minju Joson on scientific exposition of root cause of Koreas division." Available at: http://www.kcna.co.jp/index-e.htm

———. 2001 (5 August). "DPRK-Russia Moscow Declaration." Available at: http://www.kcna.co.jp/index-e.htm

———. Website: "Kim Jong Il's election as NDC chairman proposed." Available at: http://www.kcna.co.jp/index-e.htm

———. Website: "Kim Jong Il pays unofficial visit to China." Available at: http://www .kncna.co.jp/item/2001/200101/news01/21.htm#1

Kim, Dae Jung. 2000. "North and South Korea Find Common Ground." *International Herald Tribune.* 28 November.

Kim, Hee-sung. 2001a. "Foreign Forces Must be Driven out, Pyongyang News Reports." *JoongAng Ilbo.* 7 June.

———. 2001b. "Pyongyang Refuses IAEA Inspection." *English Joongang Ilbo*, 18 July.

Kirk, Don. "North Korea Pledges to Extend Its Missile-Test Ban." *International Herald Tribune.* 4 May.

Ko, Soo-kuk. 2001. "Nearly 400 N.K. Officials Out to Study Capitalism Abroad." *English JoongAng Ilbo.* 4 June.

Korea Herald. 2001 (15 March). "Sunshine Policy at Stake." *The Korea Herald.* 15 March.

Korea Times. 2000. "Kim Says He Struck Unexpected Accord with Kim Jong Il on Unification Issue." *Korea Times.* 17 June.

———. 2001 (13 February). "North Korea Online This Year." Available at: http://search.hankooki.com/times/times_view.php?term=north++korea++onlinethisyear ++&path=hankooki1/times/200102/t2001021317385540111114.htm&media=kt

———. 2001 (28 May). "Hyundai Finds No Breakthrough In Mt. Kumgang Project." 28 May.

Kynge, James. 2002. "China arrests North Korea's first free trade zone chief." *Financial Times*, 28 November.

Kyodo News Service. "U.S. provides $20 million for heavy oil for N. Korea." 6 July.

Lakshmanan, Indira A.R. 2000. "N. Korea Pledges to End Rockets Trust an Issue Despite Overture." *Boston Globe.* 25 October.

Lardy, Nicholas R. 1998. *China's Unfinished Economic Revolution.* Washington, DC: The Brookings Institution.

Lee Young-jong. 2001. "North 'Understands' Troops." *English JoongAng Ilbo* (Internet). 21 February.

Lee, Charles. 2001. "Koreas conduct survey of North's energy shortage." *Associated Press.* 3 February.

Merrill, John. 1989. *Korea: The Peninsular Origins of the War.* Newark, DE: University of Delaware Press.

Nonproliferation Policy Education Center. 2001. "NPEC Releases Trip Report and Recommendation on 1994 Agreed Framework." Nonproliferation Policy Education Center. 14 March. Available at: http://www.wizard.net/~npec/announce.htm#trip

Oberdorfer, Don. 1997. *The Two Koreas: A Contemporary History.* Reading, MA: Addison Wesley.

Patterson, Torkel L. 2001. Address to the Institute for Corean-American Studies, 21 June. Available at: http://www.icasinc.org/2001/2001s/2001stlp.html

People's Korea. "North-South Joint Declaration." Available at: http://www.korea-np .co.jp/pk/

———. 1998. "DPRK's Military Warns of 'Annihilating Blow' to U.S." *KCNA,* 2 December. Available at: http://www.korea-np.co.jp/pk/

———. 2001a. From *Nodong Sinmun*, 4 January, "21st Century Is Century of Great Change and Creation." Available at: http://www1.korea-np.co.jp/pk/154th_issue/2001012503.htm

———. 2001b. "Interview with General Secretary Kim Jong Il." 30 June. Available at: http://www1.korea-np.co.jp/pk/157th_issue/144th_issue/2000072502.htm

———. 2001c. "General Secretary Kim Jong Il Answers Questions Raised by Itar-Tass." 1 August. Available at: http://www.korea-np.co.jp/pk/

Perlez, Jane. 2000. "South Says North Agrees US Troops Should Stay." *New York Times.* 11 September.

Republic of Korea Ministry of Unification (ROK MOU). Website: From *English JoongAng Ilbo* "Inter-Korean Trade Decreased by 2.7% for First Half." Available at: http://service.joins.com/news_asp/narticle.asp?aid=1892574

———. 2001. "Economic Agreements between South and North Korea." *Korean Unification Bulletin* 31. May.

———. 2006. Website at: http://www.unikorea.go.kr/index.jsp

Schumpeter, E.B. ed. 1940. *Industrialization of Japan and Manchukuo, 1930–1940.* New York: Macmillan.

Shin, Yong-bae. 2000. "Japanese demand inspections of North Korean reactors." *The Korea Herald.* 9 September.

Shirk, Susan L. 1994. *How China Opened Its Door: The Political Success of the PRC's Foreign Trade and Investment Reform.* Washington, D.C.: The Brookings Institution.

Struck, Doug. 2000. "South Korean Says North Wants US Troops to Stay." *Washington Post.* 30 August.

Woo, Jung-en. 1991. *Race to the Swift: State and Finance in Korean Industrialization.* New York: Columbia University Press.

Yang, Sang Chul. 1994. *The North and South Korean Political Systems.* Boulder, CO: Westview Press.

Yonhap News Agency. 2002. "North Korea, China said to suffer 'severe' diplomatic 'friction' over SAR chief." Seoul. 11 October.

———. 2006. "Demise of Reactor Project." 5 June.

Yuasa, Shino. 2000. "North Korean leader Okays US forces on Peninsula: Report." *Agence France Presse.* 9 August.

Yun, Wing Sung. 1991. The China-Hong Kong Connection: The Key to China's Open-Door Policy. New York: Cambridge University Press.

9

Economic Implications of a
"Bold Switchover" in DPRK Security Policy*

We now turn to an examination of the potential economic ramifications of a DPRK shift to something like "defense sufficiency," from its current "military-first politics" posture, positing that the DPRK would remain as an independent socialist state on the Korean peninsula. The study points to three basic findings: 1) North Korea's recent dismal economic performance cannot be explained in terms of the generic inefficiencies of communist economies, but rather must be understood as the consequence of Pyongyang's particular and peculiar interpretation of "socialism with Korean characteristics," in which hyper-militarization of the economy and international extortion based on military menace figure centrally; 2) considerable new sources of Western aid would be available to Pyongyang for a genuine "bold switchover" in DPRK security policy, and even more could be found to support a shift to market-oriented economic reforms; and 3) to judge by "structural growth equations" of international economic patterns, North Korea's economic performance would likely be much better than today after a bold switchover in security policy, even if Pyongyang continued to embrace communist central economic planning.

Ever since its founding in 1948, the Democratic People's Republic of Korea (DPRK, or North Korea) has maintained an aggressive and bellicose international security posture. Today, a decade and a half after the end of the Cold War, North Korea's external defense and security policies look arguably more

---

*The material in this chapter first appeared in *The Korean Journal of Defense Analysis* XVII (1), Spring, 2005; I would like to thank Ms. Assia Dosseva of the American Enterprise Institute for her research assistance and her data analysis in preparation of this paper; thanks are also due to David Asher, William Newcomb, Marcus Noland, Charles Wolf Jr., Benjamin Zycher, and an anonymous reviewer for penetrating comments and constructive criticisms on an earlier draft; any remaining errors are those of the author.

extreme and anomalous than ever, in the sense of being more distant from evolving international security norms than they have been until now.

The particulars of DPRK "extreme" security policies and practices are well known, including:

Hyper-militarization of society, economy, and policy. This reality is reflected in the regime's current top political slogan, "military-first politics" (*songun chongchi*). But the astonishingly high priority that the defense sector now enjoys is nothing new. Although reliable statistics on the modern DPRK military are indeed scant, there are strong indications that the DPRK has been running its society and economy on something like a full war footing since the early 1970s, or even earlier.[1] Pyongyang's own data suggest that the government was fielding a military force of over 1.2 million in the late 1980s—proportionately, a mobilization level parallel to that of the United States in 1943.[2]

Maintenance and augmentation of chemical and biological weapons capabilities. At a time when almost all of the world's government have renounced biological and chemical warfare—and when most of the governments with bio-chemical war-fighting capabilities have dramatically reduced or entirely eliminated those arsenals—Pyongyang appears to be adding to its stockpiles, and perfecting its bio-chemical delivery systems.[3]

Ballistic missile development. Despite its dire economic straits since the end of the Cold War, North Korea has been deeply committed to developing and improving its ballistic missile program. Its launch of the Taepo Dong in August 1998 signified that North Korea was one of only six states with demonstrated multi-stage ballistic missile capabilities. Although there is as yet no conclusive evidence that Pyongyang has launched a multi-stage rocket since that 1998 test, published reports suggest, at a minimum, that research and development work on the DPRK's long-range missile program continue robustly.[4]

Relentless overt and covert nuclear weapon development programs. Pyongyang's persistent drive to acquire the means of producing nuclear weaponry, irrespective of treaty obligations or other promises is, of course, the matter at the heart of the ongoing North Korean nuclear drama. Today, having withdrawn from the Nuclear Nonproliferation Treaty (the only state ever to do so), the DPRK is apparently pressing forward with plutonium reprocessing for what it terms a "war deterrent." It is also evidently pushing forward with a now-notorious "second-track" HEU program for producing weapons-grade nuclear materials.

Bared-fang, white-knuckle international confrontation diplomacy. Pyongyang adopts a singularly vicious language of threat in its dealings with its neighbors and their allies. Pyongyang's diplomats first warned of turning Seoul into "a sea of fire" in 1994, but the warning has subsequently been repeated on numerous occasions. Japan has likewise been warned it might suffer a "catastrophe from which it would not soon recover"; and since 1998, Washington has repeatedly heard variations on that same theme.[5]

Continuing unconditional stance on unification with South Korea. Unlike the example of China's unification policy—where a "one country/two systems" formula is still represented in the stark differences between political and economic rules in Hong Kong and on the Mainland—the North Korean government shows no indication that it would ever accept anything less than a complete absorption of Republic of Korea (ROK, or South Korea) under Kim family rule and DPRK-style socialism. The North Korean official press and "unofficial" media of the National Democratic Front of South Korea (NDFSK) continue to imply, or sometimes to insist, that the ROK government—even under the present constitutional democratic structure, with its current progressive President Roh Moo-hyun—is an illegitimate colonial police state that must be thoroughly extirpated so that the suppressed population of the South can join under the government in the North that it adores.[6]

The DPRK's provocative and extraordinarily militarized external policies have alarmed all its neighbors. Yet while "exporting" strategic insecurity, these have also apparently "imported" economic failure. The DPRK economy, alone among the economies of East Asia, has suffered prolonged economic retrogression since the end of the Cold War.

The most vivid sign of that failure, of course, was the North Korean famine of the 1990s—the only-ever famine to be visited upon a literate, urbanized population in peacetime. North Korea's economic performance has also been miserable by the metric of commercial exports (one of the few economic indicators that can be traced with relative confidence). Between 1990 and 2003, reported world exports of merchandise more than doubled (in current U.S. dollars)—but DPRK commercial merchandise exports are estimated to have *dropped* by about 50 percent.[7] North Korea's confrontational external posture, in short, has been coincident with a regimen of decreasing economic self-sufficiency, that is, a declining ability to finance state operations and state survival as "normal" nations do.

Given all this, we may ask: what would be the economic implications of a "bold switchover" in North Korean security policy, to echo language Pyongyang has used in a call for a redirected U.S. policy toward Pyongyang?

Let us specify the question: let us first assume that the DPRK remains an independent socialist polity, committed to central economic planning and dictatorship of the proletariat and to a continuing partition of the Korean peninsula between DPRK and ROK. Let us further stipulate that Leninist governance continues to prevail in the DPRK—i.e., Western criticisms concerning human rights abuses, political prisons, et alia, remain unaddressed or unresolved. Finally, let us for the moment maintain an agnostic stance on the question of whether the bold switchover is implemented by Kim Jong Il and his lineage, or some alternative leadership faction. Thus, at least for the moment, let us simply assume a change in "regime behavior" without stipulating a necessary concomitant change in "regime personnel."

What would such a "switchover" augur for the new-thinking—but still independent and socialist—regime's economic polices, for its prospects of attracting economic support from the outside world, and for its chances of embarking on a path of economically self-sustaining growth?

In the following obviously hypothetical exercise, we will assume that the DPRK bold switchover amounts to adoption of a doctrine of "defense self-sufficiency." Broadly speaking, this would mean that North Korea would maintain a significant (but not grotesque) conventional army, and would hold on to its artillery positions near the demilitarized zone (DMZ), but that it would:

- relinquish its nuclear ambitions in a credible and permanent manner;
- scrap its biological, chemical, and ballistic programs in a likewise convincing and transparent fashion;
- substantially demobilize its conventional military forces and the allied defense industries which sustain it;
- resolve the existing obstacles blocking the improvement of DPRK-Japanese relations, such as, Pyongyang's involvement in abduction of Japanese citizens, international narcotics trafficking, and Weapons of Mass destruction (WMD);
- move toward a position of genuine "co-existence" with South Korea, recognizing the legitimacy and the right to exist of the Republic of Korea and the right of the ROK to conduct its own defensive security policies, including defensive security alliances; and
- correlatively, acknowledge the legitimacy of the ROK government's right to enter into a defensive military alliance with the United States (and Japan).

In the next few pages, we will argue that the hypothetical economic implications of such a bold switchover would:

- make possible the redress of many of the policies that have accounted for North Korea's dismal economic performance over the past generation;
- set the stage for an upsurge of external aid for the DPRK from Western governmental and NGO sources;
- offer the potential for a substantial improvement in North Korea's capacity for export revenue generation (a key element of state financial sustainability) and also in per capita output levels; and

- be consonant with a package of "reform socialist" measures, possibly resulting in the sorts of enhanced economic productivity indicated in the previous conjecture.

Why has the DPRK Economy Performed so Badly over the Past Generation?

As was pointed out earlier, the DPRK has not always been an economic basket case. Though not everyone may recall this, North Korea's level of per capita exports was apparently higher than South Korea's until about 1970, and per capita GNP in the two Koreas as of 1975 was judged to be almost exactly the same by, among other assessments, a CIA study released in 1978.[8] Between 1975 and 2003, South Korea's per capita output nearly quintupled, and its volume of merchandise exports (adjusting for inflation) rose by a factor of 16.[9] By contrast, North Korea's inflation-adjusted commercial merchandise exports actually *declined* between 1975 and 2003, and its per capita level of real commercial merchandise exports may have fallen by nearly *two-thirds*.[10] It is anyone's guess how DPRK per capita GDP for 2003 compares to 1975. Reliable and widely accepted estimates of the quantities are simply not available today, despite some attempts by outsiders to offer up figures for North Korean output. We cannot discount the possibility that North Korea's per capita GDP is actually lower today than it was a generation ago.

These discrepant results from divided Korea cannot be attributed to differences in culture, history, or ethnic background for the two populations in question—for the very same people inhabit both sides of the DMZ. The strikingly discordant performance of the North and South Korean economies over the past generation should prompt us to ask just how a people so obviously capable of economic success were organized and managed into "achieving" catastrophic economic failure in the DPRK.

One immediate hypothesis might be that North Korea was subject to communist central economic planning, and that central economic planning always fails. Such an answer might seem plausible in the aftermath of the collapse of the Soviet empire, but the suggestion is challenged by both theory and fact.

In terms of theory, Nobel Economics Laureate Friedrich Hayek and his mentor Ludwig von Mises demonstrated in the 1920s and 1930s that central planning systems suffered from an irresolvable "socialist calculation problem," that is, an inability to determine scarcity relationships for the purpose of allocating resources efficiently.[11] But this insight by the Austrian school merely criticized centrally planned systems for mounting inefficiencies and unnecessarily heightened costs, rather than for sharp and prolonged economic decline.

From the empirical standpoint, estimates by eminent Western economic historians suggest that the Soviet bloc economies and Mao-era China did in fact experience considerable and long-term material advances,[12] even if their "total factor productivity" suffered, and their command mobilization and technical innovation forced output up for many successive decades.

North Korea's conspicuous economic failure, then, must be explained not in the failings of the Korean population, or even in terms of the generic economic shortcomings of command socialism, but instead in terms of the particularities of "socialism with Korean characteristics" as it evolved in the DPRK over the past generation—what North Korean officialdom terms "our own style of socialism" (*urisik sahoejuui*).

What are the particular factors contributing to modern North Korea's disastrous economic record? We can identify some of the more obvious elements succinctly:

Breakdown of the DPRK statistical system. Since the early 1970s, there have been continuing signs that the DPRK statistical apparatus was becoming increasingly incapable of transmitting accurate and comprehensive information to the country's decision-makers—a critical danger for any centrally planned system.[13]

Breakdown of the DPRK central planning apparatus. The North Korean economic planning system remains opaque to outsiders, but there are indications that the process has become increasingly compartmentalized, irregular, and ad hoc since the early 1970s, and that it may have ceased to function in a systematic, long-range manner altogether, after the end of the last announced plan (1993). Professor Mitsuhiko Kimura (now of Kobe University) terms the current North Korean approach "planning without plans."[14]

Hyper-militarization of the national economy. If North Korea is operating on something like a total-war footing, it is allocating an enormous share of its resources to the defense sector and the allied defense industries. Under such circumstances, there is likely to be an extraordinary and continuing drain of potentially productive resources into activities that produce little or no economic "value added." A total-war footing may have limited long-term economic consequences if the mobilization is for relatively short period periods of time,[15] but North Korea's hyper-militarization has been in progress for over three decades.

Relentless war against the consumer sector. All Soviet-type economies have unnaturally small consumer sectors, but North Korea's tiny consumer sector is strangely compressed, even by the standards of Stalinist planning. (Even before the hyper-militarization of the 1970s, the estimated share of the consumer sector within the DPRK economy was much lower than for counterpart economies within the Soviet bloc.[16]) Extreme suppression of the consumer sector inhibits productivity and growth by reducing the consumption of goods and services contributing to "human capital," and by eliminating the sort of "inducement goods" whose attractiveness would otherwise be motivating workers to earn and save money.

Demonetization of the national economy. Complex modern economies cannot function efficiently on a barter basis. Nevertheless, money has played an amazingly limited role in the DPRK's economic activities over the past generation. In the late 1980s, the DPRK's wage bill apparently amounted to only a third of its "net material product," and therefore, to far less than a third of its GNP.[17] Even for a communist economy, this was a remarkably low ratio—one which presumably declined still further over the 1990s. With the July 2002 economic measures, Pyongyang effectively re-introduced money into its consumer sector—a welcome event—but that sector accounts for only a small share of the overall national economy.

Lack of financial intermediation. As has by now been well established in the economics literature, financial intermediation (banking, credit markets, etc.) plays a direct and positive role in the growth and development of national economies. North Korea has virtually no officially approved mechanisms for such intermediation in its domestic economy.

Defiant nonpayment of international debts. The DPRK has been in virtual default on its Western loans since the mid-1970s. Although many other debtor governments from low-income areas have experienced performance problems on their loans over the past generation, Pyongyang has adopted an almost uniquely pugnacious and hostile posture of non-repayment toward its creditors. Consequently, the DPRK's international credit rating is approximately zero.

Allergy to trade with "imperialist" countries. Despite the huge and steadily expanding opportunities to earn export revenues from the import markets of the world's most advanced economies, North Korea has exerted virtually no effort toward penetrating these lucrative markets, and, consequently, made little headway. In fact, inflation adjusted exports to the advanced Western economies were *lower* in 2000 than in 1980 (even including inter-Korean trade in the tally).[18] This strikingly poor record of performance reflects the content of North Korea's trade policies—an approach largely informed by Pyongyang's continuing apprehension about what it terms "ideological and cultural infiltration."

Exceptionally inhospitable institutional landscape. Although Soviet-type economies are always characterized by a problematic "business climate," the North Korean setting is perhaps uniquely unfavorable for spontaneous economic activity or independent enterprise. Some of the factors worth mentioning: 1) pervasive restrictions against and penalties on private initiative for both individuals and enterprise—recent "reforms" notwithstanding; 2) highly opaque and unpredictable application of existing economic measures, regulations, and laws toward DPRK citizens; 3) often severe extra-legal intervention in business activities of the domestic population; 4) unattractive economic legislation governing foreign enterprises; 5) lack of consistency between existing legislation and actual government decisions concerning foreign business activities; and 6) pervasive government opposition to the generation and/or repatriation of profits by foreign businesses.

When one considers this imposing array of economically wasteful—or positively destructive—policies and practices, the explanation for North Korea's prolonged and severe economic decline becomes clear enough. North Korea's political economy is the proximate explanation for the country's current, precarious economic straits—no additional external or internal factors need be adduced to explain this dismal record.[19]

The converse of this proposition, of course, is that *relief from Pyongyang's current regimen of wasteful and destructive economic policies and practices* would be the key to prompting an economic revitalization in North Korea. And when one considers the means by which this straitjacket of economically suffocating policies might be relaxed, while still positing the preservation of an independent socialist state in North Korea, one will see that a most parsimonious way to affect such a broad change would be to enact a bold switchover in DPRK security policies and practices.

A bold switchover would have the following both immediate and indirect domestic and international economic implications for the DPRK, the net impact of which would be to enhance the productive potential, the trade performance, and the financial stability of the North Korean state over the short run and the longer term:

- A bold switchover in DPRK security policy, to begin, would permit an enormous reallocation of resources—manpower and capital—from military purposes to potentially productive civilian enterprises. Given the scale of the possible redirection of resources in North Korea under a "defense sufficiency" doctrine, one could imagine a truly significant initial "supply side" stimulus.

- The bold switchover would generate pressures which inevitably militate for relaxation of the other constraints of perverse policies and practices currently shackling the DPRK economy. Most important of all of these would be the consequences of the end of North Korea's "international military extortion" approach to international fundraising. Without the instruments of international military menace that Pyongyang uses for extracting aid and/or appeasement payments from the international community, Pyongyang would perforce be obliged to move toward a more internationally open economic orientation, with all that such a change would imply.

- There would of course be a lag between the bold switchover and the economic supply-side responses that such a shift in security policy would set in motion. In economic terms, that lag-period would be the time of maximum vulnerability for the domestic economy, and as far as economic pressures were concerned, the time of maximum pressure on the "new direction" DPRK government. But these economic pressures could be mitigated by new inflows of external aid—and as we shall indicate in the next pages, there is reason to expect that a bold switchover in DPRK security policy would meet with a major response from the international aid-giving community, at least for the politically critical transitional years.

Foreign Aid for a Bold Switchover in North Korea: Potential Sources and Magnitudes

In considering the magnitude of the international community's potential financial response to a bold switchover of DPRK security policy, the appropriate metric is arguably the amount of official aid and public loans necessary to maintain current North Korean levels of imports from the outside world. That is to say, maintaining, and increasing, North Korea's capacity for procuring goods and services from abroad for both consumption and investment would be the critical purpose of foreign monies in the years during and immediately after a bold switchover.

Figure 9.1 presents estimates of North Korean import levels over the period 1989–2003. These numbers are, once again, "mirror statistics", derived from

Figure 9.1
North Korean Merchandise Imports, 1989–2005

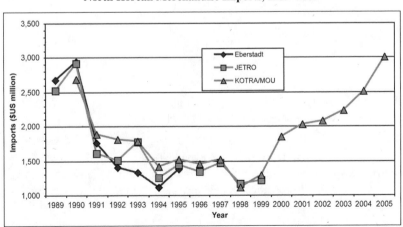

Sources: Eberstadt, 2000; JETRO, various years; KOTRA, various years; ROK MOU, various years.

reports of North Korea's trade partners, adjusted to account for c.i.f. expenses[20] and converted into current U.S. dollars at current official exchange rates. Since some of the DPRK's purchases and imports may have gone undetected, the estimates in Figure 9.1 will probably underestimate North Korean import levels somewhat. Nevertheless, we expect the estimates to be fairly close to true levels, and we believe the trends indicated are also probably roughly accurate.

As may be seen in Figure 9.1, the absolute estimated level of North Korean imports varied between about US$3 billion and US$1.2 billion a year over the period 1989–2003 (valued in current U.S. dollars). As may also be seen, the level of estimated imports tracks quite closely with the DPRK's state of economic well-being, as perceived abroad. As explained in earlier chapters, the drop in import levels associated with the end of the Soviet bloc, for example, coincides with North Korea's well-known economic tailspin in the 1990–93 period, and the announced failure of the third Seven-Year Plan that ended in 1993. The exceptionally low level of imports in the 1994–98 period coincides with the time now officially termed the "Arduous March" (and with the worst days of the North Korean famine of the 1990s). And the estimated upsurge in reported import levels in the 1998–2005 period is consistent with the timing of the "strong and prosperous country" (*kangsong taeguk*) campaign, and with a general perception (discussed at some length in Chapter 7) that economic conditions in the DPRK are on an upswing.

Bearing these North Korean import trends in mind, we can contemplate the prospects for renewed foreign official financial assistance for the DPRK once it satisfies the international community's major security concerns.[21]

Two distinct types of international government funding could be available to a post-bold switchover DPRK: political aid and development aid. The former would be contingent upon a credible switchover in DPRK security policy; the latter would be conditioned upon additional changes and reforms in North Korean economic policy.

Political Aid

The major likely sources of new politically-conditioned aid for "post-switchover" North Korea would be:

Republic of Korea. In the wake of a genuine switchover, the South Korean public's disposition to supply North Korea with massive aid would likely be strong, and such a disposition would likely span South Korea's otherwise quite polarized political spectrum. While it might be hazardous to assign particular numbers to a South Korean political aid response, it does not seem fanciful to imagine that South Korea's political leadership and voting public could easily approve an additional US$2 billion a year for the DPRK, simply on the basis of the "security switchover"—that is to say, with additional sums possibly forthcoming if credible economic reform strategies were embraced.

The US$2 billion figure adduced here is admittedly arbitrary, but it is offered as an arbitrary likely *minimum* for such political aid. ROK aid calculations would be framed in part against the expected defense savings a bold switchover would permit. Since the ROK's 2004 defense budget was slightly over US$16 billion, a bold switchover in DPRK security policy would presumably permit much more than US$2 billion a year in defense savings for the South Korean taxpaying public.

Japan. With a resolution of Japan's security concerns regarding the DPRK, the stage would be set for DPRK-Japan normalization; and with such a normalization of diplomatic relations could come an award by Japan of grants, aid, and trade credits, fashioned on the formula that was used in the ROK-Japan normalization of 1965.

The 1965 "Agreement on the Settlement of Problems Concerning Property and Claims" between Seoul and Tokyo established that Japan would provide US$300 million in grants (over a ten-year period), US$200 million in government-to-government loans (at an annual interest rate of 3.5 percent, 20-year terms, seven-year grace period), and up to US$300 million in commercial credits over ten years, with all grants and credits to be paid in Japanese goods and services.[22]

If an analogous settlement were offered to the DPRK, the question of how to adjust the 1965 South Korean terms to current North Korea would have to be answered. The answers are not self-evident, as, in addition to the straightforward pro-rating for population size, adjustments would have to be made to reflect changes in price levels, yen-dollar exchange rates, and accrued interest (if any) over the intervening period—and all of these could be very substantial. As of the year 2000—the last time DPRK-Japan normalization talks were being seriously bruited—the calculated range of hypothetical adjustments ran from about US$4 billion to about US$20 billion, with Japanese officials reportedly considering a US$9 billion package.[23]

Given this background, and the intervening passage of years and changes in the yen-dollar exchange rate, it might not seem implausible to suggest that Japan would be offering North Korea a package of roughly US$12 billion on the occasion of normalized relations. If it were structured like the 1965 package, this would make for approximately US$1.2 billion a year in additional grants, aid and credits over a 10-year period.[24]

United States. It is difficult to imagine any American government's providing new political aid to a DPRK headed by Kim Jong Il, given his lack of credibility in all political circles within Washington today, Republican and Democratic alike. With a new and credible leadership configuration in Pyongyang, however, the notion of a new U.S. security assistance program for North Korea would not necessarily be unthinkable. With a credible "switchover" in DPRK security policy, a highly tailored program on the order of a few hundred million dollars a year might be politically imaginable, if it were offered in conjunction with conditioned political aid from America's Japanese and South Korean allies.[25]

European Union. Given the EU's relatively recent expressed interest in the Korean peninsula and its security situation, it is not entirely implausible to imagine an EU commitment of security assistance. Any such commitment, however, would likely be mainly symbolic.

Russian Federation. Moscow would be a major financial beneficiary from a bold switchover in DPRK security policy, insofar as such a change would make possible the long-envisioned "Korean spur" for the trans-Siberian railway, and the oil and gas pipelines to link Russian fields to South Korean and Japan. Those projects could generate considerable revenues for the Russian government as well as for the DPRK government. Neither quantity will be considered here, however.

At the moment, Russia itself behaves more like an aid-seeking than an aid-giving state. As best can be told, Russia has been a negligible aid donor to DPRK since the end of the Cold War. We might expect this pattern to continue even after any bold switchover by the DPRK.

China. In the post-Cold War era, China has emerged as North Korea's aid giver of last resort, as Figure 9.2 underscores.

Between 1990 and 2004, implicit Chinese aid to North Korea, as measured by Pyongyang's balance of trade deficit with Beijing rather than formal aid program announcements, has varied inversely with the DPRK's balance of trade deficit with the rest of the world. China seems to have increased its implicit aid for North Korea when Pyongyang's balance of trade deficit with the rest of the world was being squeezed, and has cut back on implicit aid to North Korea when the DPRK's balance of trade with the rest of the world was on the rise. In any case, until 2005, China's implicit post-Cold War aid to North Korea has varied within fixed and rather modest boundaries, ranging only between about US$250 million and about US$500 million a year.

Just what China's aid determinations would look like in the wake of a bold switchover in North Korea is, of course, an open question. It is possible that Beijing might decide to increase its aid commitments. What is important to emphasize here, however, is that there is no obvious reason to *assume* China

Figure 9.2

North Korea's Merchandise Trade Deficit with

China and Rest of World, 1990–2005

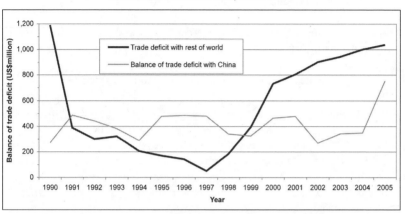

Sources: Figures 9.1 and 9.3; People's Republic of China (PRC), various years.

would increase its commitments of political aid to the DPRK—and given past Chinese behavior, in fact, a *reduction* in aid to DPRK would seem the more likely impulse.

Development Aid

New flows of development-assistance aid for North Korea would depend upon DPRK willingness to meet a variety of conditions according to which development funds are customarily allocated. For example, any regular aid from the International Financial Institutions (IFI), such as the World Bank, Asian Development Bank, etc., is contingent upon gaining membership in those organizations, which, in turn, requires membership in the International Monetary Fund. The volume of development aid which might be considered by donors would depend upon the credibility of the particular programs and projects that were proposed.[26] Given the magnitude, focus, and geographical distribution of their existing programs, however, some of the likely candidates for official development assistance (ODA) for a reform socialist DPRK would be:

- World Bank Family (IBRD, IDA, IFC, etc.)
- Asian Development Bank (ADB)
- United Nations Family (UNDP, etc.)[27]

- Government of Japan
- EU area ODA programs
- Other OECD country bilateral ODA programs[28]

The above thumbnail survey is perforce sketchy and speculative. Even so, it illustrates an important potentiality for a bold switchover in North Korean security policy.

With a bold switchover, Pyongyang could plausibly expect a major inflow of political aid from outside donors—even as a communist state still uncommitted to far-reaching economic reforms. The magnitude of such funding might plausibly be imagined in the range of US$4 billion or more in the initial years after such a switchover. Even if some of these resources were replacing current illicit North Korean earnings (i.e., drug trafficking, military sales, etc.), North Korean import levels could be increased by at least US$3 billion a year on the basis of political aid alone. That would amount to more than doubling the DPRK's current estimated import levels.

Furthermore, if the DPRK were to move toward "reform socialism," akin to the Asian model as viewed in Vietnam or China, still more development assistance would be available.[29]

None of this is to suggest that the outside world would necessarily view a proclaimed bold switchover under a regime still headed by Kim Jong Il as credible. Nor is it to make a judgment about the inescapably political question of whether North Korean leadership could maintain authority in a post-bold-switchover DPRK.

Rather, what this conspectus should make clear is that *economic resource* constraints would not be the limiting constraint for such a future North Korean regime. Quite the contrary, the North Korean economy could expect to enjoy a higher level of imports, on both an absolute and a per capita basis, than it has ever before experienced in the regime's history. Even without reform socialism, North Korea's economy would be in a better position to grow and develop than at any time in decades, arguably, at any time since the 1960s.

Potential Economic Performance in a Communist Bold Switchover North Korea: Quantitative Indications from International and Historic Patterns

What sort of economic stimulus might the DPRK enjoy if it were able to maintain political order after a bold switchover, and at the same time to adhere more closely to the performance patterns exemplified in traditional communist—or reform socialist—or post-communist states?

While the question is in some sense fundamentally speculative, we can throw intriguing light upon it by examining international patterns of development.

At this point, there exists a wellspring of quantitative data on development patterns in communist and non-communist countries over the entire post-World War II era. We can use these data to describe the sorts of trade and economic performance a country like North Korea could be predicted to exhibit under a traditional Soviet-type communist economy, and under a reform socialist or post-communist regimen.

The approach we use here is known in the contemporary economics literature as "structural growth equations," which try to predict variations in output on the basis of other cross-sectional economic and social relationships across countries.[30]

In the following exercise, we use the World Bank's *World Development Indicators 2003* (WDI) as our database for estimating the relationships that a more "normal" DPRK might exhibit.

Because economic data concerning the DPRK are so scarce, we will not even attempt to construct structural growth equations that require any estimates of North Korean income levels, capital stock accumulations, ratios of imports and exports to GNP, average years of schooling attained, etc.—the conventional sorts of variables used on the "x" side of such equations. Instead, we build our structural growth equations on the basis of data that we can be more confident about in the case of North Korea, namely, the following independent variables: illiteracy rates; urbanization rates; life expectancy levels; and a government's status as a never-communist, traditional communist, reform socialist, or post-communist regime.

Through other research, we have indicated the likely bounds of DPRK levels of illiteracy, urbanization, and life expectancy.[31] As it happens, all of these quantities are directly related to economic productivity—and all of them provide a good predictive base for estimating any unknown country's level of exports per capita or economic output per capita.[32]

In the following regressions, we specified the relationship between the independent variables identified above (illiteracy, urbanization, life expectancy and communist governance status), and our dependent variables: per capita exports (current U.S. dollars) and per capita GNP (PPP adjusted current dollars), as a "semi-logarithmic" relationship. That is to say, we compared absolute differences in reported illiteracy (for example) against the natural logarithm of per capita exports (for example) to attempt to trace out a relationship (through "ordinary least squares" regressions).[33]

In our regression analysis, we traced the international relationship in 1980 and 2000 between the following variables:

ln_percapexp:	Per capita exports in current dollars (in natural log)
ln_percapgni:	Per capita gross national product ppp current (in natural log)
ILLIT:	Illiteracy rate
URBANIZATION RATE:	Urbanization rate
LIFEEXPBIRTH:	Life expectancy at birth
ILLIT*URBAN:[34]	Illiteracy rate multiplied by urbanization rate
LE*ILLIT*URB:	Illiteracy rate times urbanization rate times life expectancy
COMMUNIST:	Communist government variable (a "dummy variable"—"0" for no, "1" for yes)

Since we were measuring international relationships in both 1980 and 2000, the COMMUNIST variable was actually measuring several different sorts of communist governance. Given the nature of international communism in 1980, the 1980 soundings would have been examining more or less traditional communist states—i.e., communist governments before reform socialist tendencies had progressed far in any of the Marxist-Leninist economies. By 2000, on the other hand, virtually all the governments denoted as communist were actually reform socialist (China, Vietnam) or post-communist (like the states of the former Soviet bloc). This distinction allows us to look at the impact on economic performance of traditional communism, on the one hand, and reform socialist or post-communist governance on the other.

All in all, we present results for sixteen regressions: eight equations each for the years 1980 and 2000, half of which examine per capita exports and half per capita GNP. The regressions, which we drew from the World Bank's data in *World Development Indicators 2003*, compare 92 countries in the year 1980, and 118 countries in 2000.

The results of our regression analysis are presented in Tables 9.1 through 9.4. These numbers may call for a bit of interpretation and explication.

All in all, the results of our regressions are quite robust—meaning that the relationships they describe tend to be strong and stable, with a fair degree of statistical significance, i.e., unlikely to have been generated by pure chance. The structural growth equations for predicting per capita exports generated R-squareds of 0.54 to 0.60 for 1980 and 0.69 to 0.72 for 2000, meaning that our

Table 9.1
The International Relationship between Per Capita Exports and Other Developmental Indicators for the Year 1980 as Revealed by Structural Equations

	Dependent Variable = ln_percapexp 1980			
	Equation 1	Equation 2	Equation 3	Equation 4
N	92	92	92	92
ADJUSTED R-SQUARED	0.54	0.54	0.58	0.60
CONSTANT	4.20	4.33	5.21	2.37
	(8.68)***	(8.80)***	(9.43)***	(1.19)
ILLIT. RATE	−0.01	−0.01	−0.04	−0.02
	(−1.80)	(−2.04)*	(−3.71)**	(−1.60)
URBANIZATION RATE	0.05	0.04	0.02	0.02
	(6.68)***	(6.53)***	(2.45)*	(1.72)
COMMUNIST	N/A	−0.88	−0.72	−0.84
		(−1.30)	(−1.11)	(−1.30)
ILLIT.*URBAN	N/A	N/A	0.0008	N/A
			(3.04)**	
LIFEEXPBIRTH	N/A	N/A	N/A	0.04
				(1.51)
LE*ILLIT*URB	N/A	N/A	N/A	0.00001
				(2.90)**

Notes: ln = Natural logarithm; numbers in parenthesis are "t-statistics;" * = significant at $p < 0.05$; ** = significant at $p < 0.01$; *** = significant at $p < 0.001$
Source: WDI, 2003.

selected variables could trace over half of the observed difference between countries in per capita export in 1980, and over two-thirds of the observed per capita export differences in 2000. For our equations predicting per capita GNP (i.e., gross national income), the corresponding range of R-squareds was 0.68 to 0.72 for 1980 and 0.64 to 0.71 for 2000—meaning that our selected dependent variables could account for about two-thirds of the observed differences between countries in per capita GNP in both years.

As might have been expected, life expectancy levels and urbanization rates tracked positively with per capita exports and per capita income, while illiteracy rates correlated negatively with these measures of economic performance. Generally speaking, these relationships were highly significant in a statistical sense—meaning that they were extremely unlikely to have been achieved by pure chance.[35] The dummy variable for communist governance

Table 9.2

The International Relationship between Per Capita Exports and Other Developmental Indicators for the Year 2000 as Revealed by Structural Equations

	Equation 9	Equation 10	Equation 11	Equation 12
Dependent Variable = ln_percapexp 2000				
N	118	118	118	118
ADJUSTED R-SQUARED	0.69	0.70	0.70	0.72
CONSTANT	4.55	4.86	4.81	2.36
	$(13.66)^{***}$	$(13.68)^{***}$	$(12.03)^{***}$	$(3.09)^{**}$
ILLIT. RATE	−0.03	−0.04	−0.03	−0.02
	$(-6.15)^{***}$	$(-6.62)^{***}$	$(-3.17)^{**}$	$(-2.42)^{*}$
URBANIZATION RATE	0.04	0.04	0.04	0.03
	$(9.07)^{***}$	$(8.65)^{***}$	$(6.72)^{***}$	$(5.33)^{***}$
COMMUNIST	N/A	−0.58	−0.59	−0.65
		$(-2.22)^{*}$	$(-2.22)^{*}$	$(-2.56)^{*}$
ILLIT.*URBAN	N/A	N/A	−0.00006	N/A
			(-0.24)	
LIFEEXPBIRTH	N/A	N/A	N/A	0.04
				$(3.86)^{**}$
LE*ILLIT*URB	N/A	N/A	N/A	NEGL.
				(-0.35)

Notes: ln = Natural logarithm; numbers in parenthesis are "t-statistics;" * = significant at $p <$ 0.05; ** = significant at $p < 0.01$; *** = significant at $p < 0.001$
Source: WDI, 2003.

only met the test of significance some of the time (three out of 11 equations in which it appeared). Nevertheless, these results demonstrated a notable consistency.

In our various equations for per capita exports, a 1-point increase in illiteracy corresponded with about a 1 percent reduction in per capita exports in 1980, and about a 3 percent reduction in 2000. A 1-point increase in urbanization, on the other hand, tracked with a 2 percent to 4 percent increase in per capita exports in 1980, and with a 3 to 4 percent increase in 2000. A year's increase in life expectancy tracked with a 4 percent increase in per capita exports in both 1980 and 2000. Communist governance, for its part, was associated with a dramatic diminution of per capita exports—51 to 59 percent less than for comparable never-communist countries as of 1980, and 45 to 48 percent less than in comparable never-communist countries in 2000. These numbers speak to the "export allergy" characteristic of central economic planning

Table 9.3
The International Relationship between Per Capita
Gross National Income and Other Developmental Indicators
for the Year 1980 as Revealed by Structural Equations

		Dependent Variable = ln_percapgni 1980		
	Equation 5	**Equation 6**	**Equation 7**	**Equation 8**
N	92	92	92	92
ADJUSTED R-SQUARED	0.68	0.68	0.69	0.72
CONSTANT	6.82	6.91	7.17	4.51
	(28.96)***	(28.67)***	(25.64)***	(4.67)***
ILLIT. RATE	−0.01	−0.01	−0.02	−0.01
	(−3.62)**	(−3.81)**	(−3.68)**	(−0.96)
URBANIZATION RATE	0.03	0.03	0.02	0.01
	(7.94)***	(7.78)***	(4.10)***	(2.97)**
COMMUNIST	N/A	−0.41	−0.37	−0.49
		(−1.24)	(−1.12)	(−1.57)
ILLIT.*URBAN	N/A	N/A	−0.0002	N/A
			(−1.74)	
LIFEEXPBIRTH	N/A	N/A	N/A	0.04
				(2.95)**
LE*ILLIT*URB	N/A	N/A	N/A	NEGL.
				(1.61)

Notes: ln = Natural logarithm; numbers in parenthesis are "t-statistics;" * = significant at $p <$ 0.05; ** = significant at $p < 0.01$; *** = significant at $p < 0.001$
Source: WDI, 2003.

systems. By 2000, the impact of communist government status on export performance was less severe than it had been 20 years earlier—but reform socialist and post-communist countries nevertheless continued to export less than would have otherwise been predicted.

As for per capita GNP, a 1-point increase in illiteracy generally reduced per capita GNP by 1 to 2 percent in 1980 and 2000. A 1-point increase in urbanization tracked with a 1.4 to 2.7 percent increase in per capita GNP in our analyses, while a one-year rise in life expectancy tended to correspond with a 4 percent increase in per capita output. Communist status reduced predicted economic performance substantially: by 31 to 34 percent in 1980, and by 16 to 23 percent in 2000, all other things being equal. (Here again, the values or the COMMUNIST dummy variable were consistent with the proposition that reform-socialist or post-communist governance is less economically costly than traditional communist rule—but as yet by no means entirely cost-free.)

Table 9.4
The International Relationship between Per Capita
Gross National Income and Other Developmental Indicators
for the Year 2000 as Revealed by Structural Equations

	Dependent Variable = ln_percapgni 2000			
	Equation 13	Equation 14	Equation 15	Equation 16
N	118	118	118	118
ADJUSTED R-SQUARED	0.64	0.64	0.64	0.71
CONSTANT	7.47	7.57	7.41	5.46
	(36.66)***	(34.32)***	(30.08)***	(12.12)***
ILLIT. RATE	−0.02	−0.02	−0.01	−0.01
	(−5.96)***	(−5.94)***	(−1.91)	(−1.34)
URBANIZATION RATE	0.02	0.02	0.03	0.02
	(7.78)***	(7.44)***	(6.55)***	(4.47)***
COMMUNIST	N/A	−0.18	−0.22	−0.26
		(−1.14)	(−1.37)	(−1.75)
ILLIT.*URBAN	N/A	N/A	−0.0002	N/A
			(−1.34)	
LIFEEXPBIRTH	N/A	N/A	N/A	0.04
				(5.42)***
LE*ILLIT*URB	N/A	N/A	N/A	NEGL.
				(−0.95)

Notes: ln = Natural logarithm; numbers in parenthesis are "t-statistics;" * = significant at $p <$ = significant at $p < 0.01$; *** = significant at $p < 0.001$
Source: WDI, 2003.

Given the relatively high degree of consistency of these structural estimates, we can use them to illustrate the sorts of export performance and per capita income levels a country with North Korea's development characteristics might be expected to display, even under a communist government—if only the peculiar deformities associated with the DPRK's present approach to policy were decisively abandoned.[36]

Admittedly, we cannot be certain about North Korea's precise current illiteracy rate—or its exact levels of urbanization and life expectancy. We are, however, in a position to suggest a reasonable lower and upper boundary for each set of variables. For adult illiteracy, a reasonable range might be 5 to 10 percent; for urbanization, 40 to 60 percent; for life expectancy at birth, 60 years to 70 years. If we use these lower and upper boundaries, what do our structural growth equations suggest about North Korea's potential economic performance?

Tables 9.5 and 9.6 lay out the results.

Table 9.5
Predicted Levels of Annual Per Capita Exports for DPRK Based on International Patterns for Communist, Reform Socialist, and Post-Communist Societies and Assumptions about Current DRPK Illiteracy, Urbanization, and Life Expectancy at Birth

	Predicted Annual Per Capita Exports (US$)	
Predictive Relationship	Lower DPRK Levels (US$)	Higher DPRK Levels (US$)
Equation 2 (1980)	168	441
Equation 3 (1980)	216	385
Equation 6 (2000)	260	707
Equation 7 (2000)	253	700
Equation 8 (2000)	275	691

Notes: Estimated DPRK per capita merchandise exports in 2003: US$42; Lower DPRK levels = Illiteracy rate: 10 percent; urbanization rate: 40 percent; life expectancy at birth: 60 years; Higher DPRK levels = Illiteracy rate: 5 percent; urbanization rate: 60 percent; life expectancy at birth: 70 years.

Source: WDI, 2003.

Table 9.6
Predicted Levels of Gross National Product for DPRK Based on International Patterns for Communist, Reform Socialist, and Post-Communist Societies and Assumptions about Current DRPK Illiteracy, Urbanization, and Life Expectancy at Birth

	Predicted GNI Per Capita (US$)	
Predictive Relationship	Lower DPRK Levels (US$)	Higher DPRK Levels (US$)
Equation 10 (1980)	1,698	3,023
Equation 11 (1980)	1,808	2,919
Equation 14 (2000)	2,928	5,372
Equation 15 (2000)	2,934	5,203
Equation 16 (2000)	2,547	5,110

Notes: Lower DPRK levels = Illiteracy rate 10 percent; urbanization rate 40 percent; life expectancy at birth 60 years; Higher DPRK levels = Illiteracy rate 5 percent; urbanization rate 60 percent; life expectancy at birth = 70 years.

Source: WDI, 2003.

On a traditional communist polity performance trajectory, the DPRK would be predicted to earn a low of US$170–220 per year through commercial exports, and a high of US$390–440 per capita. On the patterns characteristic of reform socialist or post-communist countries, the corresponding estimates would range from a low of US$250–280 to a high of US$690–710. While these numbers may look rather low in the abstract, it should be remembered that the DPRK's level of estimated per capita export earnings through legitimate commercial merchandise in 2003 was under US$45. Thus these figures point to a potentially major increase in North Korean export earnings. Using a national population estimate of 23 million for the contemporary DPRK, these equations would predict export earnings for a more normal communist DPRK in the range of US$4–6 billion if literacy, urbanization and life expectancy were on the lower end of our assumptions—and annual export revenues of US$9–16 billion if the higher estimates were right. These sums should be compared to North Korea's recent performance in legitimate commercial exports—where commercial merchandise earnings have never exceeded an estimated US$2 billion, and currently are estimated to total not much more than US$1 billion.

As for GNP per capita, our structural growth equations indicate that a country with North Korea's assumed literacy, urbanization, and life expectancy levels would report a GNP per capita of about US$1,700–3,000 under traditional communist polity, and US$2,500–5,400 under reform socialism or post-communist polity. That is to say, our regressions predict that a country with North Korea's assumed range of literacy, urbanization, and life expectancy

Figure 9.3
North Korean Merchandise Exports, 1989–2005

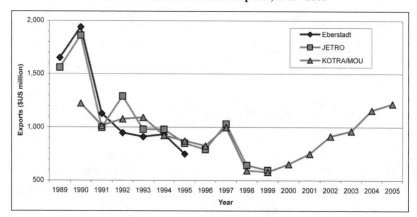

Sources: Eberstadt, 2000; JETRO various years; KOTRA various years; ROK MOU various years.

levels would generate a GNP of US$39–69 billion under a "traditional" Communist polity, and US$58–123 billion under reform socialism or post-communist polity. We do not have a reliable set of estimates for current GNP in the DPRK. By way of comparison, however, the ROK Bank of Korea estimates DPRK for 2003 at US$18.1 billion.[37]

This analysis of international development patterns points consistently toward a single proposition: namely, that the DPRK, even under its current weakened circumstances, is capable of performing very much better than it has been doing over the past generation, even if its polity remains communist, and even if that government abjures reform socialism. For reasons we have already touched upon, it is reasonable to suggest that a bold switchover in security policy would be the first step in capitalizing upon the unreaped potential for economic improvement that lies fallow today in the North Korean political economy.

There are of course qualifications that could be lodged to the analysis in the preceding pages. The effect on North Korea's productive capacity of the prolonged famine may well be unexpectedly strong—certainly none of the countries with which the DPRK is being compared suffered a similar fate. In 1980, furthermore, most of the traditional communist states were trading primarily with one another, and since our analysis estimates their trade in dollar terms at official exchange rates, we may be systematically overestimating their trade performance.[38] Be all that as it may, when all is said and done, international structural growth equations nevertheless indicate that there would be enormous scope for economic improvement in the DPRK today—even as an independent and still communist state—if its government were simply to embrace a more "normal" Communist polity.

Concluding Observations and Cautionary Comments

The analysis above has made three basic points:

First, North Korea's appalling economic performance over the past generation is mainly explained by the government's perverse mesh of economic policies and practices—and most of these destructive policies and practices are posited or abetted by the government's peculiar and extremist approach to external security.

Second, very substantial amounts of foreign aid could be expected if North Korea were to relinquish this exceptional military posture, and these sums would be adequate to support a major infusion of consumer goods and capital during a post-bold switchover transition period in the DPRK, thus stabilizing living standards and productive potential.

Third, international comparisons through structural growth equations hint that a country with North Korea's general level of human capital and complexity characteristics—i.e., literacy, urbanization, and life expectancy levels—could expect to attain much higher levels of export performance and per capita output than are thought to prevail in North Korea today. Strikingly, these predicted results imply that substantially enhanced export and GNP levels could prevail under a *communist government*—that is to say, under a Marxist-Leninist state characterized by more ordinary Stalinism—to say nothing of the further enhanced potentialities of reform socialism.

There are a number of obvious and important points not addressed in this chapter. To begin with, we have not offered a schema for a program of economic rejuvenation in a socialist DPRK. Numerous suggestions of this sort are already available.[39] And we have not argued that the connection between a switchover and economic upsurge is determinative. Rather, we have talked about a change in the realm of the possible, not what can be asserted with certainty about an inherently unpredictable future.

We have not dealt with the question of whether outside governments would judge a promised bold switchover by a government led by Kim Jong Il credible under any circumstances, although this is a legitimate and perhaps pressing issue. And we have not engaged the issue of whether a post-bold-switchover DPRK would be politically viable, although we recognize this to be a matter of more than academic interest.[40]

What we have attempted to show here is that a bold switchover in security policy would decisively improve—rather than prejudicially complicate—the prospects for economic growth and development in North Korea, even under a continued independent socialist government. The other questions noted but not addressed here are clearly important. Any broad fears about necessarily negative economic ramifications for the DPRK devolving from a bold switchover in security policy, however, are clearly unfounded.

Notes

1. For an analysis of these data, see Eberstadt, 1995, Chapter 1.
2. Eberstadt and Banister, 1991, pp. 1095–115.
3. For more details on the DPRK program and other past or present programs, see the website of the Monterey Institute for International Studies, Center for Nonproliferation Studies, Chemical and Biological Weapons Resource Page, available at: http://cns.miis.edu/research/cbw/possess.html.
4. Bermudez, 2004; see also Wisconsin Project on Nuclear Arms Control, 2005, available at: http://www.wisconsinproject.org/countries/nkorea/north-korea-miles.html.
5. For example, *Korean Central News Agency* (KCNA), 1998.
6. *KCNA*, 2003; thus, for example, the following pronouncements from the NDFSK's "Chief of Pyongyang Mission" in June 2003:

   Reverence for Kim Jong Il is daily mounting in South Korea because [of] the South Korean people's attraction and worship for him. . . .

The vigorous anti-U.S. struggle of the South Korean people is an eruption of national self-respect. . . .

[W]e should follow the road of Songun [military first politics] indicated by Kim Jong Il. . . . Songun might is a powerful war deterrent force . . . enough to decisively overpower the U.S. in a showdown with the U.S.:

7. For data on global export trends, see WTO, Statistical Database at: http://stat.wto.org/StatisticalProgram/WSDBStatProgramHome.aspx?Language=E; for DPRK export trends, see Figure 3.

8. USCIA, 1978.

9. Calculations derived from WTO statistics databases, World Development Indicators 2003 database, and US Bureau of the Census.

10. Eberstadt, 2004.

11. See von Mises (1951) and Hayek, (1989).

12. See Maddison, 1995; by Maddison's estimates, for example, per capita output in the USSR rose from US$1,386 (in 1990 Geary-Khamis dollars) in 1929 to US$7032 in 1989—a fivefold increase over six decades, implying an average growth rate of 2.7 percent per year over that period; by Maddison's estimates, even Maoist China managed to double its per capita output between 1950 and 1975, rising from US$614 to US$1250, implying a long-term per capita growth rate of nearly 3 percent per annum.

13. Pyongyang's 1999 "Law on Socialist Economic Planning" can be seen as an implicit acknowledgement that the statistical apparatus necessary for centrally planning had effectively broken down; for details of earlier signs of trouble in the DPRK statistical system, see Eberstadt, 1995, Chapter 1.

14. Kimura, 1994.

15. See Milward, 1977.

16. Eberstadt, 1996.

17. Ibid.

18. Eberstadt, 2004.

19. For additional analysis and quantitative assessments regarding the failure of the North Korean economy, see the important work by Marcus Noland of the Institute for International Economics, especially 2000.

20. For an explanation of "c.i.f." and f.o.b." see Chapter 3, footnote 38; in the figures cited here we *assume* that the DPRK's c.i.f. costs add a flat 10 percent to reported purchase prices for merchandise; this 10 percent markup is standard practice by the IMF and other organizations in cases where actual c.i.f. charges are unknown.

21. Note that we are examining *only* public sources of finance here; the potential for private finance could be an additional and possibly very important source of international revenue for a more "normal" DPRK, but that issue should be left for a different discussion.

22. See Kwan, 1971, p. 57.

23. Manyin, 2001, available at: http://www.fcnl.org/pdfs/01june13_nkjapan.pdf.

24. If the package were somewhat "front-loaded," as might also possibly be arranged, it might be structured to provide more during the first five years of the agreement, with less in the out-years; for example, US$1.6 billion annually for the initial period, US$800 million for the out-years.

25. We have explicitly avoided consideration of a possible resurrection of KEDO or a KEDO-like vehicle for political aid here; such an institution might—if, of course, it had not been disbanded—figure in the transfer of political aid to a "post bold switchover" DPRK.

26. For further discussion of those conditions and general guidelines, see Babson and Yoon (2004), pp. 65–96, and also Babson and Lancaster (2004).
27. Presumably any new UN commitments would also be countered by reduction or termination of "emergency" humanitarian food aid from the World Food Programme.
28. E.g., Canada, Australia, New Zealand, and the United States.
29. It is worth noting that Vietnam was the recipient of about US$2.4 billion in ODA commitments in 2002; to be sure, Vietnam's population is nearly four times as large as that of North Korea; yet such a figure may nevertheless suggest an upper boundary of plausible ODA commitments to a reforming DPRK, considering the scale of potential reconstruction that might be required in the initial years after a bold switchover.
30. This approach is associated today most closely with the work of Robert J. Barro of Harvard University; see Barro, 1991, pp. 407–43; earlier research on international structural development patterns would include the work of Hollis B. Chenery; see in particular Chenery and Syrquin, 1975.
31. See Chapter 5, Eberstadt and Banister (1992) and Eberstadt (1996).
32. Literacy levels, for example, bear upon a population's capabilities in productive employment; urbanization levels tell us about the proportion of population that lives in non-rural areas—a broad indication of the level of productivity that has been attained by local agriculture, and, more generally, about the level of complexity and differentiation in a population's labor force; life expectancy levels tell us about the health and thus the productive potential ("human capital") in a population.
33. The reason for the "semi-log" specification is that the semi-log curve happens, more or less, to match the patterns observed internationally between illiteracy, urbanization, and life expectancy levels, on the one hand, and per capita output levels, on the other; our semi-log functions also allow us to estimate particular elasticities, such as the predicted percentage impact on per capita or per capita GNP for a point change in literacy, urbanization, etc.
34. ILLIT*URBAN and LE*ILLIT*URB were introduced to determine whether additive effects occurred from the interaction of those variables.
35. The only exception to this generalization concerned the statistical significance of the illiteracy rate when life expectancy levels were also being examined; in three out of four such equations the coefficient for the illiteracy rate did not meet the basic 5 percent confidence test; this seems to be due to the strong evident collinearity between illiteracy and life expectancy.
36. Our use of these structural equations to predict the economic performance of an ordinary Communist DPRK raises a number of technical econometric questions, the most acute of these perhaps bearing on the issue of *heteroskedacity* in our regression results; *heteroskedacity*, one may recall, is the non-random distribution of errors in predicted OLS results—a phenomenon often especially characteristic in the sort of cross-sectional regressions we have just computed here; examination of the regression results in Tables 9.1 to 9.4 does indeed reveal some *heteroskedacity* in these structural equations; more specifically, our residuals showed a slight positive association with the reported value of a country's per capita exports or its per capita GNI; this means that our equations have some tendency to overpredict true per capita exports or per capita GNI when those quantities are low, and to underpredict them when those quantities are high; fortunately, those biases were rather limited, as the relatively high R-squared values in our OLS equations might in themselves suggest in the range of predicted values for per capita exports and per capita

GNI most relevant to the DPRK in our equations, moreover, the distribution of errors generated by our equations did not deviate appreciably from zero.

37. ROK Bank of Korea, 2004, available at: http://www.bok.or.kr/contents_admin/ info_admin/eng/home/press/pressre/info/timeseriesnk.xls

38. Another qualification to be noted is that the estimates generated by our 1980 equations would be in current 1980 dollars, while our 2000 equations generate estimates in 2000 dollars; full standardization would require a deflator to link the two; we should note that, in an effort at sensitivity analysis, we replaced the export and GNI series from Tables 9.1–9.4 above with other export and per capita GNI or per capita GDP series available through the WDI dataset. All of the alternatives we tested revealed similar general relationships, and on the whole similar levels of statistical significance, to the equations presented in Tables 9.1–9.4—although the particular beta-coefficients for the independent variables naturally differed from one exercise to the next.

39. See, for example, Åslund (2004) and Babson and Bradley O. Babson and William J. Newcomb *Economic Perspectives On Demise Scenarios For DPRK*, a paper presented for the USIP Seminar, January 2, 2004.

40. In particular, the question of voluntary migration from DPRK to ROK—for economic or non-economic reasons—must be examined closely, especially in light of the ROK's constitutional guarantee to accept people from North Korea as ROK citizens; this relevance of this issue is acknowledged, but discussion of it is beyond the scope of this book.

References

Åslund, Anders. 2004. "Prospects and Preconditions for Market Economic Transformation in North Korea." Choong Yong Ahn, Nicholas Eberstadt, and Young Sun Lee, eds. *A New International Engagement Framework for North Korea? Contending Perspectives.* Washington DC: Korea Economic Institute of America.

Babson, Bradley O. and William J. Newcomb. 2004. *Economic Perspectives on Demise Scenarios for DPRK."* Paper presented for the United States Institute of Peace Seminar. Washington DC: USIP. 2 January.

Babson, Bradley O. and Yoon Deok Ryong. 2004. "How to Finance North Korea's Capital Requirements for Economic Recovery." *East Asian Review* 16(2): 65–96. Summer.

Barro, Robert J. 1991. "Economic Growth in a Cross Section of Countries." *Quarterly Journal of Economics* 106(2):407–43.

Bermudez, Joseph Jr. 2004. "North Korea deploys new missiles." *Jane's Defense Weekly.* 2 August 2004.

Chenery, Hollis B. and Moises Syrquin. 1975. *Patterns of Development: 1950–1970.* New York: Oxford University Press.

Eberstadt, Nicholas. 1995. *Korea Approaches Reunification.* Armonk, NY: M.E. Sharpe & Co.

———. 1996. *Policy and Economic Performance in Divided Korea, 1945–1995.* Unpublished Ph.D. dissertation. Harvard University.

———. 2000. "Economic Recovery in the DPRK: Status and Prospect." *International Journal of Korean Studies* IV(1). Fall/Winter.

———. 2004. "The Persistence of North Korea." *Policy Review* 127. October/November.

————. 2005. "Economic Implications of a "Bold Switchover" in DPRK Security Policy." Korean Journal of Defense Analysis XVII(1):53–84. Spring.

Eberstadt, Nicholas and Judith Banister. 1991. "Military Buildup in the DPRK: Some New Indications from North Korean Data." *Asian Survey* 31(11):1095–115. November.

————. 1992. *The Population of North Korea.* Berkeley, CA: University of California at Berkeley Press.

Hayek, Friedrich A. 1989. *The Fatal Conceit.* Chicago: University of Chicago Press.

Japanese External Trade Organization (JETRO). Various years; Kita Chōsen no keizai to bōeki no tenbō. (North Korea's Economy and Trade Outlook) Tokyo: Nihon Bōeki Shinkōkai.

Kimura, Mitsuhiko. 1994. *A Planned Economy without Planning: Su-ryong's North Korea.* Discussion Paper F-081. Faculty of Economics. Tezukayama University.

Korean Central News Agency (KCNA). 1998. "KPA will answer U.S. aggression forces' challenge with annihilating blow (Statement of KPA general staff spokesman)." 2 December. Available at: http://www.kcna.co.jp

————. 2003. "Chief of Pyongyang Mission of NDFSK interviewed by reporters." 14 June. Available at: http://www.kcna.co.jp, January 13, 2005.

Korea Trade Investment Promotion Agency (KOTRA), various editions; *Pukhan ui Muyok Hoesa* (Tr. North Korea's Trade) Seoul: Taehan Muyok Chinhung Kongsa.

Kwan, Bong Kim. 1971. *The Korea-Japan Treaty Crisis and the Instability of the Korean Political System.* New York: Praeger Publisher.

Maddison, Angus. 1995. *Monitoring the World Economy: 1820–1992.* Paris: OECD.

Manyin, Mark E. 2001. "North Korea/Japan Relations: The Normalization Talks and the Compensation/Reparations Issue." *Congressional Reports for Congress.* Congressional Research Service. 13 June. Available at: http://www.fcnl.org/pdfs/01june13_nkjapan.pdf

Milward, Alan S. 1977. *War, Economy, Society: 1939–1945.* Berkeley, CA: University of California Press.

Monterey Institute for International Studies. 2004. Chemical and Biological Weapons Resource Page. Center for Nonproliferation Studies. Available at: http://cns.miis.edu/research/cbw/possess.htm

Noland, Marcus. 2000. *Avoiding the Apocalypse: The Future of the Two Koreas.* Washington, DC: IIE.

People's Republic of China (PRC). Various years. *China's Customs Statistics.* Beijing: General Administration of Customs.

Republic of Korea Bank of Korea (ROK BOK). 2004. "GDP of North Korea in 2003." 8 June. Available at: http://www.bok.or.kr/contents_admin/info_admin/eng/home/press/pressre/info/timeseriesnk.xls

————. Ministry of Unification (ROK MOU). Various years. Inter-Korean Cooperation. Seoul: Tongilbu, available at: http://www.unikorea.go.kr/en/EPA/EPA0401L.jsp.

————. Various years. *Wolgan Nambuk Kyoryu Hyomnyok Tonghyang.* [Monthly North-South Exchange and Cooperation Trends] Seoul: Tongilbu.

United States Bureau of the Census. 2005. *International Trade Database.* Washington, D.C.: USBC.

United States Central Intelligence Agency (CIA). 1978. *Korea: The Economic Race between the North and the South.* Washington, DC: National Foreign Assessment Center. 19 January. ER 78-10078.

Von Mises, Ludwig. 1951. *Socialism.* New Haven, CT: Yale University Press.

Wisconsin Project on Nuclear Arms Control. 2005. "North Korea Missile Milestones: 1969–2005." *The Risk Report* 11(5). September–October 2005. Available at: http://www.wisconsinproject.org/countries/nkorea/north-korea-miles.html

World Bank. 2003. *World Development Indicators 2003*. Washington, D.C.: World Bank.

World Trade Organization. 2006. Statistical Database. Available at: http://stat.wto.org/StatisticalProgram/WSDBStatProgramHome.aspx?Language=E

10

North Korea's Survival Game: Understanding the Recent Past, Thinking about the Future*

Can the Democratic People's Republic of Korea (DPRK, or North Korea) survive as a distinct regime, an autonomous state, a specific political-economic system, and a sovereign country?

Can it continue to function in the manner in which it has been performing since the end of 1991—that is to say, since the final collapse of the Soviet empire? Or is it doomed to join the Warsaw Pact's failed communist experiments in the dustbin of history? Or might it, instead, adapt and evolve—that is, survive by maintaining its political authority and power to rule, but transforming its defining functional characteristics and systemic identity?

Back in 1994, I would not have expected to be writing on this particular theme more than a decade hence. My own work on the North Korean economy has generally been associated with what others have termed the "collapsist"[1] school of thought, and not unfairly. As far back as June 1990, I published an op-ed essay titled "The Coming Collapse of North Korea."[2] Since then, my analyses have recurrently questioned the viability of the DPRK economy and system.[3]

It is perhaps especially fitting, then, having imagined the odds of the DPRK's post-Soviet survival to be very low, that I should be charged with explaining just how the North Korean system *has* managed to survive these past sixteen or so years, and to speculate about the possibility of sustainable

*This chapter, updated for inclusion here, is based on a presentation made to the conference "Peaceful Resolution with North Korea: Towards a New International Engagement Framework," sponsored by the Korea Institute for International Economic Policy, the Korea Economic Institute, and the American Enterprise Institute, held in Washington, D.C., 12–13 February 2004; portions of that presentation were previously published under the same title in Ahn Choong-yong et al. 2004a, and under the title "The Persistence of North Korea" in Ahn Choong-yong et al. 2004b.

pathways which might permit regime, state, and system to endure that far, or further, into the future.

This chapter proceeds through four sections. The first discusses the epistemology of state collapse, focusing on a particular historical example of potential relevance. The second focuses on some of the factors which may have abetted state survival in the DPRK case in recent years. The third will discuss the sustainability of North Korea's current economic *modus operandi*. The fourth will examine some of the questions pertaining to a DPRK transition to a more pragmatic variant of a planned socialist economy.

The Epistemology of State Collapse: A Cautionary Ottoman Tale

Although major efforts have been undertaken in the hope of systematizing the study of state failure,[4] the simple fact is that the modern world lacks anything like a corpus of science by which to offer robust predictions about impending episodes of social revolution, systemic breakdown, or state collapse. At the very best, the anticipation of such dramatic political events might aspire to *art* rather than *science*[5]—just as the technique of successful stock-picking (or short-selling) has always been, and still remains, an art and not a science.[6] A common set of factors, furthermore, consigns both of these endeavors to the realm of art: first, the extraordinary complexity of the phenomena under consideration; second, the independent and unpredictable nature of the human agency at their center; and third, the ultimately irresolvable problem of asymmetries of information.

All of this is to say there is no reason to expect that students and analysts should be able to predict in advance the breakdown of political systems with any degree of accuracy, on the basis of any regular and methodical model. Indeed, predicting the breakdown of communist systems is arguably even more difficult than for open societies, insofar as the problem of asymmetries of information is—by systemic regime design—that much more extreme.[7]

If anticipating state collapse is, at best, a matter of art, it is an art whose most obvious failures might be classified into two categories of error. First, there are the failures to predict events which actually took place. The 1989–91 collapse of all the Warsaw Pact states—an upheaval which caught almost all informed Western observers unawares[8]—is certainly the most memorable recent example of this type of error. Second, there is the error of predicting upheaval and abrupt demise for states or systems which do *not* end up suffering from such paroxysms. This category of error would encompass, inter alia, the past century of Marxist-Leninist prognoses for Western Europe, the apocalyptic assessments from the 1970s and 1980s on the future of South Africa,[9] the premature predictions of the fall of Soviet communism[10]—and, of course, at least to date, the presentiments of the collapse of the DPRK.

This particular type of mistake may be likened to "Type I" and "Type II" errors in statistical inference. But for our purposes here we should emphasize that the family of analytical errors that can attend assessments of state failure or collapse is *not* dichotomous. Other types of errors can also occur. Among these, and the one I wish to draw our attention to for the moment, is the *failure to recognize imminent, but averted, collapse.*

The notion that a state might be on the verge of collapse without interested outsiders fully understanding that this was in fact the case is not merely an abstract theoretical possibility. With the situation of North Korea in the back of our minds, I would ask the reader's indulgence to make a digression, in order to examine a real-life incident as an "existence proof" that such things do indeed happen—sometimes with serious historical consequences.

In fact, history is replete with examples of this phenomenon. One particular example worth recalling involves the collapse of the Ottoman Empire, and the battle of Gallipoli. As early as the 1853,[11] the Ottoman Empire had been dubbed "the sick man of Europe" by those other Great Powers engaged in the struggle for mastery of the continent. Saddled with a sclerotic and corrupt Byzantine administrative system and an overtaxed, under-innovating economy,[12] Constantinople was set on a course of steady relative decline.[13]

As it turned out, however, the Ottoman invalid survived for almost 70 years after that diplomatic diagnosis of its poor political health, and the Empire was finally laid to rest only in 1922/23, with Mustapha Kemal Ataturk's revolution and the founding of the modern Turkish state. What is less well known, however, is that the Ottoman Empire very nearly came to an end in 1915—in the World War I campaign that came to be known as Gallipoli.

The Gallipoli campaign of 1915–16 is remembered as a military debacle for the forces of France and, more particularly, of the British Empire. In a bold and risky bid to capture Constantinople by naval attack and amphibious invasion, the Allied troops were instead trapped on their own beachheads on the Gallipoli peninsula, unable to displace the Ottoman forces from their fortified positions on the high grounds above. For months, the soldiers of the British Commonwealth—quite a few of them Australian and New Zealand regulars— were slaughtered in futile attempts to break the Ottoman line. (The plight of these unfortunates is vividly portrayed in Peter Weir's 1982 movie, *Gallipoli*.) At the end of 1915, the British began a total evacuation of the surviving continents, a total of over 100,000 Commonwealth casualties having been sustained in the campaign. In the course of the Gallipoli campaign, Ottoman General Mustapha Kemal secured his reputation as a brilliant and heroic military leader, while Winston Churchill, the then-young Lord Admiral of the British Navy, was obliged to resign his post in humiliation.

Gallipoli is considered a classic military blunder today—literally a textbook case. Recently the campaign was even included in an influential treatise on great military mistakes,[14] having been studied for decades in military academies around the world. But what is not commonly appreciated, however, is that the Franco-British naval assault that was to become Gallipoli very nearly *did* succeed, and indeed came within an ace of toppling the Ottoman Empire.

In early March 1915, a Franco-British flotilla that included sixteen capital ships (battleships, cruisers, and destroyers) commenced Churchill's plan to "force" the Dardanelles Strait. Artillery fire from the Turkish gun emplacements proved ineffectual against these mighty warships. On March 18, 1915, the flotilla prepared to advance through the Dardanelles Strait and into the Sea of Marmora—from whence they would steam on to Constantinople. Over the course of a day-long battle between big guns, the Allied fleet slowly moved forward against the Ottoman emplacements. Then, in the late afternoon, three British ships—one of them a battleship—unexpectedly struck mines and sank. The British commander of the operation, rear admiral John de Roebeck, was severely shaken by this setback, as he was apparently certain that he would be sacked for the loss of those ships.[15] At the end of the day, the Allied fleet regrouped, but did not pursue its assault the next day, or indeed in the weeks that immediately followed. As David Fromkin notes, "only a few hundred casualties had been suffered, but the Admiralty's Dardanelles campaign was over."[16]

De Roebeck could not have known at the time about the circumstances on the other side of the barricades. With the benefit of Ottoman and German records and memoirs, historians have revealed that the Ottoman administration and its German military advisers were grimly convinced the Allied assault would spell doom for Constantinople, for they had no hope of putting up a successful resistance.

As chronicler Alan Moorehead recounts, Ottoman Minister of the Interior Talaat was himself

> . . . utterly despondent. As early as January he had called a conference (with the top German military allies and advisers). All agreed that when the Allied Fleet attacked it would get through.[17]

In the days before the attempt to "force" the Dardanelles, indeed, Constantinople had begun to take on the smell of a defeated capital. David Fromkin writes:

> Morale in Constantinople disintegrated. Amidst rumors and panic, the evacuation of the city commenced. The state archives and the gold reserves of the banks were sent to safety. Special trains were prepared for the Sultan and for the foreign diplomatic colony. Talaat, the Minister of the Interior, requisitioned a powerful Mercedes for his personal use, and equipped it with extra petrol tanks for the long drive to a distant place of refuge. Placards denouncing the government began to appear

in the streets of the city. . . . The [German ship] *Goeben* made ready to escape to the Black Sea . . . [Ottoman War Minister] Enver bravely planned to remain and defend the city, but his military dispositions were so incompetent that—as [German military adviser General Otto] Liman von Sanders later recalled—any Turkish attempt at opposing an Allied landing at Constantinople would have been rendered impossible.[18]

Among the disadvantages weighing on the beleaguered Turks was the fact—unappreciated by de Roebeck—that the defenders were virtually out of artillery shells. As Moorehead commented:

[nothing] could alter the fact that they had so much ammunition and no more. . . . [I]f the battle went on and no unforeseen reinforcements arrived it was obvious to the commanders that the moment would come when they would be bound to order their men to fire off the last round and then to retire. After that they could do no more.[19]

As a historian who fought in Gallipoli would later note, the official records of Minister Enver's German advisers jotted the following entry on the fateful day of March 18, 1915:

Most of the Turkish ammunition has been expended; the medium howitzers and mine fields have fired more than half their supply. Particularly serious is the fact that the long rang high explosive shells, which alone are effective against British ship's armor are all used up. We stress the point that Fort Hamidieh has only seventeen shells and Kalid Bahr Fort only ten; there is also no reserve of mines; what will happen when the battle is resumed.[20]

The Ottoman government and its German advisers could not believe their good fortune when the Allied naval assault inexplicably (from their perspective) halted. Looking back later, Enver is reported to have commented:

If the English had only had the courage to rush more ships through the Dardanelles, they could have got to Constantinople; but their delay enabled us thoroughly to fortify the Peninsula, and in six weeks' time we had taken down there over 200 Austrian Skoda guns.[21]

General Liman von Sanders later commented tersely that the evacuation procedures underway in Constantinople in March 1915

were justified. . . . Had the [Allied landing] orders been carried out . . . the course of the world war would have been given such a turn in the spring of 1915 that Germany and Austria would have had to continue without Turkey.[22]

Fromkin stated the matter more plainly: "The Ottoman Empire, which had been sentenced to death, received an unexpected last-minute reprieve."[23]

Here we see another classic example of the role of asymmetries of information in the outsider's analytical failure—circumstances that tend to be most acute in times of hostility, with little regular communication between the actors in question, and with strategic deception being actively practiced in the quest for state survival.

From this Turkish parable, let us return to North Korea. The DPRK continues to function as a sovereign and independent state to this very writing. But is the North Korean state's recent survival a modern-day variant of the Gallipoli phenomenon—in other words, a case of imminent but averted collapse? In order to address this question, what information would we require that we presently lack?

Financing the Survival of the North Korean State

The speculative questions I have just posed are unfortunately unanswerable—and for now, quite untestable. We will probably have to await the eventual opening of the Pyongyang state archives to delve into those issues with any satisfaction—assuming that the DPRK's official files and data offer a sufficiently coherent and faithful record of events to aid such historical inquiries.

Available data do, however, shed light on one aspect of the DPRK's struggle to avoid collapse in the wake of the Soviet bloc's demise. These are the international data on North Korean trade patterns as reported by the DPRK's trade partners—the "mirror statistics" as they are known by their users, which we discussed in Chapters 3 and 4. Mirror statistics cannot tell us how close North Korea may have come to collapse in recent years, but they can help us explain how North Korea has managed to *finance* state survival.

Although the analysis of the modern North Korean economy has always been hampered by the extraordinarily paucity of reliable data that might facilitate independent assessments, it is not exactly a state secret that the DPRK national economy was in the grip of stagnation—or incipient decline—in the 1980s, and began to spiral downward once the aid and subsidized trade from the erstwhile Soviet bloc suddenly ceased in the early 1990s.

The steep and apparently unbroken decline in North Korean economic performance in the first half of the 1990s led to the outbreak of famine in the DPRK by the mid-1990s—the first and only instance of such mass hunger in an industrialized and literate society during peacetime. North Korea's patent economic dysfunction, and the seeming unwillingness or incapability of its leadership to address and correct it, seemed to me to raise the possibility of one very particular kind of systemic collapse: namely, *economic collapse*, a subject I discussed in some detail in my book, *The End of North Korea*.[24]

In discussing economic collapse, I was not, of course, venturing guesses about the possibility of some dramatic *political* event that might bring the

North Korean regime to an end—a coup at the top, say, or a revolt from below. (Then, as now, the sorts of information that might permit such a judgment were clearly unavailable to outside observers—especially to those with no access to confidential sources of intelligence.)

Economic collapse seemed an exceedingly elastic term, but I attempted to use it with some conceptual precision. In my analysis, economic collapse was *not* defined as an economic shock, or an economic dislocation, or a severe depression, or even a famine. Economic collapse instead was offered as a term to describe *the breakdown of the division of labor in the national economy,* that is, the process through which ordinary people in complex productive societies trade their labor for food.[25]

North Korea in the mid- to late-1990s, I argued, was set on a trajectory for economic collapse—for its domestic economy was incapable of producing the requisite goods necessary for the maintenance of a division of labor, and the regime seemed utterly unable to finance their purchase from abroad. Although it was impossible to determine from outside the precise breaking point at which the division of labor would unravel, events were bringing the DPRK system progressively closer to that point.

The situation in early 2006 admittedly looks somewhat different. The ordinary North Korean today, of course, does not exactly live in the lap of luxury. On the other hand, by most accounts the typical North Korean no longer suffers from the desperate privation that characterized the mid-to-late 1990s. As best can be told, the North Korean famine—which almost certainly claimed hundreds of thousands of victims, and may well have killed a million people between 1995 and 1998[26]—ceased raging seven years ago.

Officially, North Korean leadership indicated a new confidence in the DPRK's staying power back in September 1998, at the same Supreme People's Assembly which formally elevated Kim Jong Il to "the highest position of state." That convocation publicly declared the "Arduous March" of the previous several years to have been completed, and announced that the DPRK was then on the road to becoming a "powerful and prosperous state" (*kangsong taeguk*)."[27]

Whether or not the North Korean economy has enjoyed actual growth since 1998—a question that remains a matter of some contention—it is clear that the economic situation has in some meaningful sense stabilized, and improved, since the grim days of the "Arduous March." Chapters 3 and 4 describe, using mirror statistics, how this was accomplished.

We can begin by looking at reconstructions of North Korea's overall trends for merchandise imports. As Figure 10.1 shows, in 1990, the reported value of imports was nearly US$3 billion (in current dollars). By 1998, the reported level had dropped below US$1.2 billion—a catastrophic fall of over 60 percent. After 1998, however, North Korea's imports rebounded markedly. By 2001, the reported level exceeded US$2 billion—and appears to have risen still fur-

Figure 10.1
North Korean Merchandise Imports, 1989–2005

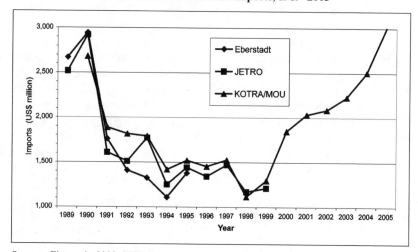

Sources: Eberstadt, 2000; JETRO, various years; KOTRA, various years; ROK MOU, various years.

ther since then. North Korea was apparently obtaining nearly 90 percent more in the way of supplies of goods from abroad in 2002 than it had in 1998. By 2004, DPRK import levels were almost 125 percent higher than in 1998. And by 2005, DPRK import levels may have passed an important symbolic and historical milestone: in nominal dollar terms, they may have re-attained or even exceeded their highest levels registered during the Cold War era, before the collapse of the Soviet Union.

And how did North Korea pay for this upsurge in imports? To judge by the mirror statistics, it did so *not* through any corresponding jump in reported export revenues. As we see in Figure 10.2, between 1990 and 1998, North Korea's reported merchandise exports collapsed, plummeting from about US$2 billion to under US$600 million. By 2002, these had recovered somewhat, to a reported level of just over US$900 million. Nevertheless, by any absolute measure, the DPRK's reported export level remained remarkably low in 2002—less than half as high as it had been in 1990, and even lower than it had been in the bitter "Arduous March" year of 1997. Though North Korean merchandise exports continued their rebound over the following years, DPRK export performance by 2005, in nominal dollar terms, was not clearly better—and may in fact have been poorer—than it had been in 1992.

Figure 10.2
North Korean Merchandise Exports, 1989–2005

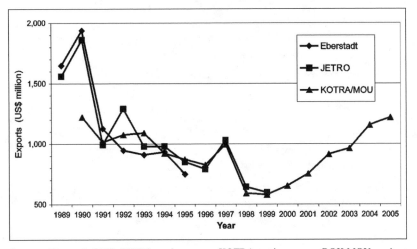

Sources: Eberstadt, 2000; JETRO, various years; KOTRA, various years; ROK MOU, various years.

In a purely arithmetic sense, North Korea succeeded in effecting a substantial increase of merchandise imports despite only modest improvements in its almost negligibly low levels of reported merchandise exports by managing to increase its reported balance of trade deficit appreciably. Figure 10.3 illustrates the situation during the "Arduous March" period—the famine years of 1995–98—when North Korea's reported surfeit of imports over exports averaged under US$600 million a year. By contrast, during the years 2000–2002—the *Kangsong Taeguk* era—the DPRK's reported trade deficit was over twice that high, averaging about US$1.2 billion annually. In the year 2002, North Korea's merchandise balance of trade deficit continued its upward ascent, and in 2005, this too passed a portentous threshold, when North Korea's nominal dollar-denominated balance of trade deficit exceeded all previously recorded levels, including the apex registered during the Cold War era. Though it is customary for economic analysts to regard a rising balance of trade deficit as a signal of impending economic difficulties and potentially unsustainable international economic policy regimes, for the DPRK regime this rising measured trade deficit constituted instead a representation of *successful* policy—for it suggested that a mounting net transfer of resources from abroad was being achieved from one year to the next.

Figure 10.3
North Korean Merchandise Trade Deficit, 1989–2005

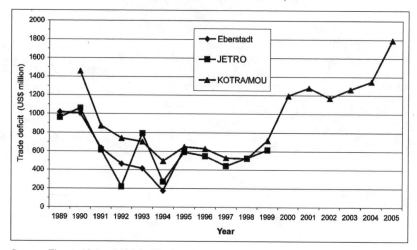

Sources: Figures 10.1 and 10.2 in this chapter.

But how was this reported trade deficit financed? The answer to the question is not self-evident. After all, North Korea is a state with a commercial credit-worthiness rating of approximately zero, having for a generation maintained its posture of defiant *de facto* default on the Western loans it contracted in the 1970s.

Historically, the DPRK relied upon aid from its communist allies—principally, the Soviet Union and China—to augment its imports. After the collapse of the USSR, China perforce emerged immediately as North Korea's principal foreign patron: and Beijing's largesse extended beyond its officially and episodically announced subventions for Pyongyang. The DPRK's seemingly permanent merchandise trade deficit with China actually constitutes a broader and perhaps more accurate measure of Beijing's true aid levels for Pyongyang (insofar as neither party seems to think the sums accumulated in that imbalance will ever be corrected or repaid).

Implicit Chinese aid, however, cannot account for North Korea's import upsurge of 1998–2002. To the contrary: China's implicit aid to North Korea—i.e., its reported balance of trade deficit—*fell* during these years, dropping from about US$340 million to about US$270 million. For the years 1992–2004—i.e., the period following the collapse of the USSR, and the end of Soviet bloc aid and subsidized trade for Pyongyang—the annual balance of trade deficit with Pyongyang that Beijing authorities would tolerate fluctuated within relatively bounded parameters. Chinese trade statistics suggest this implicit net transfer to the DPRK never fell below US$250 million a year, but never amounted to as much as US$500 million a year.[28]

By contrast with the somewhat cyclical but essentially static nature of the DPRK's balance of trade deficit with China over these years, however, North Korea's trade deficit with the rest of the world apparently soared upward. Whereas in 1997 the DPRK reportedly only managed to obtain a net of US$50 million more merchandise from abroad than its commercial exports would have paid for—after factoring out China—by 2002 the corresponding total was over US900 million. By 2004 and 2005, that sum looks to have reached, or exceeded, the billion-dollar mark. Indeed, if we remove China from the picture, the line describing North Korea's net imports of supplies from abroad rises steadily upward between 1997 and 2002. It is this graphic, seen in Figure 10.4, which captures the economic essence of North Korea's shift from its "Arduous March" period to its *Kangsong Taeguk* epoch.

And how was this jump in non-Chinese net imports financed? Unfortunately, we cannot be precise about this, since many of the sources of funds involve illicit transactions. North Korea's international counterfeiting, drug trafficking, and weapons/weapon technology sales all figure here, although the sums raised from those activities are a matter of some dispute.[29]

Figure 10.4
North Korea's Merchandise Trade Deficit, 1990–2005,
Excluding Trade with China

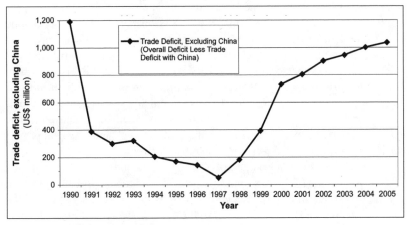

Sources: Figures 10.1 and 10.2 in this chapter; PRC, various years.

Nor do we yet know exactly how much of the South Korean taxpayers' money was furtively channeled from Seoul to Pyongyang during this period. One set of prosecutorial investigations has convicted former President Kim Dae Jung's national security adviser and several other aides of illegally transferring up to US$500 million to Kim Jong Il's "Bureau 39" on the eve of the historic June 2000 Pyongyang summit.[30] The possibility of other unreported official Seoul-to-Pyongyang payoffs during the 1998–2002 period cannot be ruled out as yet—nor of course can the potential volume of any such attendant funds be determined.

Broadly speaking, however, we can explain the timing and the magnitude of the 1998–2005 upswing in North Korea's non-Chinese net imports in terms of the North Korea policies which were embraced during those years by the United States and her Northeast Asian allies. The year 1998 heralded the inauguration of ROK President Kim Dae Jung and the advent of South Korea's "Sunshine Policy" for détente and reconciliation with the North. In 1999, the United States followed suit with unveiling of the "Perry Process"—the "grand bargain" approach to settling outstanding disputes with the DPRK, hailed by the ROK Foreign Minister in the year 2000 as "based on our engagement policy toward North Korea."[31] Japan and the EU both joined in the pursuit of "engagement" with North Korea during these years as well, although to differing degrees.

In their strict performance specifications and their defining actions—as opposed to their official rationales or stated intentions—the Sunshine and engagement policies effectively meant, and continue to mean, organized activity by Western governments to mobilize transfers of public resources to the North Korean state. If this formulation sounds provocative, reflection on some outstanding examples of those multilateral polices will show clearly that it is also functionally accurate: the Hyundai/ROK National Tourism Office payments for vacations to Mt. Kumgang; the U.S. "inspection fee"[32] of 500,000 tons of food aid granted in 1999 for permission to visit a suspect underground North Korean facility at Kumchang-ri; the continuing food and fertilizer shipments from Seoul; the occasional food transfers from Japan; the secret payment for the historic June 2000 Pyongyang summit; and the new, albeit modest, flows of aid from EU countries in the wake of the flurry of diplomatic normalizations between Pyongyang and EU states in 2000 and 2001. Thus, it is perhaps not surprising that North Korea's financial fortunes should have improved so markedly in 1998, and the years immediately following.

To some readers, it may sound perplexing and counterintuitive to hear the United States—the DPRK's longtime principal opponent and antagonist in the international arena—described as a major contemporary backer of the North Korean state. Yet, as we see from the detailed figures in Table 10.1, this is in fact the case.

Table 10.1
U.S. Assistance to North Korea, 1995–2004

Calendar or Fiscal Year	FOOD AID (PER FISCAL YEAR)		KEDO Assistance (Per Calendar Yr; US$ Million)	Medical Supplies (Per Fiscal Year, US$ Million)	Total (US$ Million)
	Metric Tons	Commodity Value (US$ Million)			
1995	0	$0.00	$9.50	$0.20	**$9.70**
1996	19,500	$8.30	$22.00	$0.00	**$30.30**
1997	177,000	$52.40	$25.00	$5.00	**$82.40**
1998	200,000	$72.90	$50.00	$0.00	**$122.90**
1999	695,194	$222.10	$65.10	$0.00	**$287.20**
2000	265,000	$74.30	$64.40	$0.00	**$138.70**
2001	350,000	$102.80	$74.90	$0.00	**$177.60**
2002	207,000	$82.40	$90.50	$0.00	**$172.90**
2003	40,200	$25.50	$2.30	$0.00	**$27.80**
2004	110,000	52.8	$0.00	$0.10	**$52.90**
Total	**2,086,694**	**$710.00**	**$403.70**	**$5.30**	**$1,102.40**

Source: Manyin, 2006.

During the 1996–2002 period, Washington provided Pyongyang with just over US$1 billion in food aid, concessional fuel oil, and medical supplies. (Interestingly enough, nearly US$350 million of these resources were transferred in the years 2001 and 2002—under the purportedly hostile aegis of the George W. Bush administration.)

By the second half of the 1990s, it may be noted, that North Korea's reliance on U.S. aid for financing its international purchases and supplies of goods was, in some quantifiable respect, more pronounced than for almost any other country for which Washington funded military, economic, and/or humanitarian assistance programs. This may be seen in Table 10.2.

Total American aid allocations to key recipients Israel and Egypt for the five years 1996–2000, for example, amounted to 34 percent and 67 percent of those states' respective export earnings for the year 2000. U.S. 1996–2000 assistance to North Korea, by contrast, actually exceeded the DPRK's reported year 2000 commercial export revenues. (Incidentally, since most of the American aid resources in Table 10.1 were not tallied in the international commercial ledgers upon which mirror statistics rely,[33] the DPRK's actual level of reliance upon non-Chinese net supplies from abroad was consistently higher for the years 1998–2002 than the graphic in Figure 10.4 suggests.) Ironic though it may seem, when considered in relation to the economy's evident capability to

Table 10.2
US Aid and National Exports, Selected Comparisons

a) Current comparison to selected countries		
Total military and economic aid, 1996–2000 (US$)	Exports of goods and services, 2000 (US$)	Total aid as percentage of exports
Pakistan	253,300,000	9,575,000,064	2.65
Ukraine	743,400,000	19,522,000,896	3.81
El Salvador	234,700,000	3,645,691,392	6.44
Nicaragua	206,600,000	962,200,000	21.47
Jordan	1,221,000,000	3,534,132,736	34.55
Israel	14,880,000,000	44,146,860,032	33.71
Egypt	10,595,200,000	15,931,033,600	66.51
Haiti	485,000,000	506,236,864	95.80
DPRK	663,600,000	653,100,000	101.61

b) Historical comparison to Taiwan and the ROK		
Total Military and Economic Aid (US$)[1]	Total Exports (US$)[2]	Total Aid as Percentage of Exports
DPRK	1,014,200,000	751,100,000	135.03
Taiwan	2,512,100,000	220,750,000	1137.98
ROK	4,346,200,000	56,000,000	7761.07

[1]For DPRK, figures represent total aid for 1995–2002; for Taiwan and ROK, total aid for 1955–1962.

[2]For DPRK, total exports for 2002; for Taiwan and ROK, total exports for 1962.

Sources: For DPRK total aid, 1995–2002: Manyin, 2006; for DPRK exports, 2002: Figure 10.2 in this chapter; for total military and economic aid for other recipients: USAID, 2006; for export revenues: IBRD, 2002 and IMF, various years.

finance its international needs from its own regular commercial exports, Washington's aid lifeline for the DPRK in recent years looks more consequential than any of the bilateral assistance relationships that Washington has arranged for treaty allies or friendly states in any spot on the globe.

This is not the first time, of course, that American aid has helped a state on the Korean Peninsula to survive. After the 1953 Korean Armistice, Washington devoted tremendous resources to propping up and strengthening the Syngman Rhee government in Seoul—a regime fascinated with "aid-maximizing stratagems"[34] and manifestly disinterested in improving its then-miserable export performance. To be sure, judged by the metric of US aid to recipient-country exports, the American Cold War project for preserving the ROK was *vastly* more intensive than Washington's post-Cold War programs sustaining the North Korean state. In the late 1950s, on the other hand, U.S. bilateral aid was just about the only game in town for states seeking Western largesse—in marked contrast to the situation today. And if we were able to consider all the aid packages, overt, covert, or semi-formal that were extended to the DPRK by Western governments in the *Kangsong Taeguk* period, we might well discover that the ratio of such outside assistance to local commercial earnings began to approach the scale of disproportion earlier witnessed in, say, the late-1950s U.S. project to preserve the independence of the Republic of China (ROC, or Taiwan). To be clear, that earlier Taiwan effort would have undoubtedly been the more aid-intensive by our selected metric. While lower, the aid-intensity of the recent DPRK arrangements would perhaps fall within the same approximate order of magnitude.

At the end of the day, we can never know what would have happened if the United States and her allies in Asia and Europe had refrained from underwriting the survival of the North Korean state in the late 1990s and the early years of the present decade. Such exercises in counterfactual speculation—"imaginary history," as they are known to their modern-day devotees[35]—can make for fascinating reading, but are ultimately inconclusive. We do not know, furthermore, just how close North Korea came to the critical breaking point of an economic collapse during the "Arduous March" period between Kim Il Sung's death and Kim Jong Il's formal appointment. What we do know—or think we know—can be stated succinctly (as shown in Figure 10.4): the DPRK was failing economically in the mid-1990s, that is, moving closer to the notional point of an economic collapse.

In the late 1990s and early years of the current decade, the prospect of economic collapse was diminished materially by an upsurge in provisions of goods from abroad—goods financed, in turn, in considerable measure by new flows of Western foreign aid.

Whether or not Western aid flows were the indispensable or instrumental factor in averting a North Korean collapse cannot, for now, be discussed with the sort of historical knowledge and texture that can be brought to bear in a discussion of the averted collapse of the Ottoman Empire in March 1915. What seems beyond dispute, however, is that the upsurge of Western aid for the DPRK under Sunshine and engagement policy played a role—possibly a very important role—in reducing the risk of economic collapse, and increasing the odds of survival—for the North Korean state.

Current Parameters in Financing State Survival for the DPRK

Although North Korea's flirtation with economic collapse did not commence until after the disintegration of the Soviet bloc, the DPRK's relative—and perhaps also its absolute—economic decline has been a long-term process, and by some indicators was already well underway in the Cold War era. The DPRK's long-term trade performance vividly describes this record of economic decline, and, since international trade bears more than incidentally upon the risk of the state's economic collapse, on systemic survival prospects as well. From our 21st century vantage point, we may not recall how steep and steady this long decline has been.

There was a time—within living memory—when the DPRK was *not* known for being an international trade basket-case. In 1970, the level of per capita exports in North and South Korea was roughly comparable (US$21 vs. US$27—in then-much-more-valuable dollars).[36] As late as 1980, in fact, North Korea's export profile, though hardly robust, was also not markedly disfigured. As we see in Table 10.3, in 1980, for example, the DPRK's level of reported per capita exports was just slightly higher than that of Turkey, and over five times higher than that of India.

That same year North Korea's reported imports exceeded reported export revenues, but by a margin that was in keeping with the performance of other developing economies, including quite successful ones. For example, as we see in Table 10.4, the DPRK's 1980 ratio of exports-to-imports was just slightly higher than Chile's—but it slightly lower than that of either Thailand or South Korea.

By 1990 the picture had worsened considerably, as seen in Tables 10.5 and 10.6. Despite a politically-determined surge in exports to the USSR under the terms of the 1985–1990 Soviet-DPRK Economic Cooperation accord, per capita exports now ranked in the lowest quartile of the world's economies—in a league with Equatorial Guinea and Kenya—and the ratio of exports to imports had risen, so that North Korea was among the quartile of states where this imbalance was greatest. (By 1990, the disproportion between North Korea's import and export revenues already placed it in the ranking next to such heavily aid-dependent economies as Jordan and Ghana.)

By 2000, as one might suspect, the DPRK was an outlier within the world system. That year, as shown in Tables 10.7 and 10.8, the DPRK's reported per capita export level would have ranked 158 among the 168 countries so tracked by the World Bank's *World Development Indicators*: below Chad, and at less than half of India's level. (Reported per capita exports in Turkey were now nearly 25 times as high as in the DPRK.)

Although the nominal level of per capita exports for the world was nearly 2.5 times higher in 2000 than in 1980,[37] North Korea's nominal reported per capita export level fell by almost two-thirds over those years. At the same time, North Korea's imbalance between reported imports and export earnings—former being 2.8 times as great as the latter—looked to be among the ten most extreme recorded that year. While a glaring discrepancy between imports and exports did not automatically betoken aid-dependence—several outliers in

Table 10.3
Per Capita Exports: DPRK Rank in World, 1980

Rank	Country	Exports (US$)	Population	Per Capita Exports (US$)
1	United Arab Emirates	23,086,758,915	1,043,000	22,134.96
2	Kuwait	22,438,280,854	1,375,000	16,318.75
3	Luxembourg	4,983,707,216	364,900	13,657.73
4	Saudi Arabia	110,748,188,896	9,372,000	11,816.92
5	Bahrain	3,813,478,376	334,000	11,417.60
6	Libya	23,522,973,568	3,043,000	7,730.19
7	Belgium	70,139,684,426	9,847,000	7,122.95
8	Norway	27,431,630,370	4,091,000	6,705.36
9	Netherlands	90,860,667,073	14,150,000	6,421.25
10	Switzerland	37,344,809,039	6,319,000	5,909.92
—	—	—	—	—
100	Bolivia	682,225,017	5,355,000	127.40
101	Kenya	2,030,403,493	16,632,000	122.08
102	Sao Tome and Principe	10,472,768	89,000	117.67
103	Kiribati	6,551,960	58,100	112.77
104	Niger	616,720,072	5,617,000	109.80
105	Sri Lanka	1,296,327,544	14,603,000	88.77
106	Congo, Dem. Rep.	2,371,496,686	26,908,000	88.13
107	Central African Republic	201,028,393	2,313,000	86.91
108	*DPRK*	*1,414,100,000*	*17,113,626*	*82.63*
109	Turkey	3,660,084,493	44,484,000	82.28
110	Sierra Leone	251,666,984	3,236,000	77.77
—	—	—	—	—
125	Mozambique	383,020,297	12,095,000	31.67
126	Somalia	200,271,012	6,487,000	30.87
127	Burkina Faso	172,600,568	6,962,000	24.79
128	Burundi	81,022,222	4,130,000	19.62
129	Uganda	242,000,000	12,806,900	18.90
130	Guinea-Bissau	14,039,310	763,000	18.40
131	India	11,249,000,000	687,332,000	16.37
132	Nepal	224,583,339	14,559,000	15.43
133	China	14,327,813,120	981,235,000	14.60
134	Bangladesh	995,270,012	85,438,000	11.65

Note: Data are for merchandise for DPRK, but for goods and services for all other countries.

Sources: IBRD, 2003; USCB, 2006; Figure 10.2 in this chapter.

Table 10.8, including Lesotho and West Bank/Gaza, speak to the importance of remittances in the local balance of payments—North Korea's ratio of reported commercial export revenues to reported imports was even lower in 2000 than in such all-but-permanent wards of the overseas development aid community as Haiti and Burkina Faso.

Table 10.4
Imports as a Percent of Exports: DPRK Rank in World, 1980

Rank	Country	Imports (US$)	Exports (US$)	Imports as a Percent of Exports
1	Kuwait	9,822,528,552	22,438,280,854	43.78
2	United Arab Emirates	10,215,784,647	23,086,758,915	44.25
3	Libya	11,166,994,610	23,522,973,568	47.47
4	Gabon	1,353,525,793	2,769,522,007	48.87
5	Indonesia	15,766,759,183	26,664,131,299	59.13
6	Oman	2,252,461,204	3,748,118,124	60.10
7	Nigeria	12,324,265,032	18,859,387,259	65.35
8	Venezuela, RB	15,142,691,030	19,965,055,658	75.85
9	South Africa	21,837,885,033	28,266,759,113	77.26
10	Trinidad and Tobago	2,430,708,170	3,145,833,262	77.27
—	—	—	—	—
60	Spain	37,942,881,948	32,740,267,959	115.89
61	Seychelles	116,615,430	100,141,584	116.45
62	Greece	13,560,731,209	11,526,621,528	117.65
63	Cote d'Ivoire	4,189,777,567	3,561,287,269	117.65
64	Chile	7,438,435,984	6,291,974,407	118.22
65	Philippines	9,253,067,162	7,661,066,650	120.78
66	Mexico	25,215,695,652	20,806,478,261	121.19
67	*DPRK*	*1,714,400,000*	*1,414,100,000*	*121.24*
68	Honduras	1,130,499,968	930,000,000	121.56
69	Mauritius	664,753,314	539,499,795	123.22
—	—	—	—	—
125	Maldives	24,569,536	7,748,344	317.09
126	Bangladesh	3,239,432,452	995,270,012	325.48
127	Burkina Faso	563,715,097	172,600,568	326.60
128	Guinea-Bissau	46,299,639	14,039,310	329.79
129	Dominica	54,703,703	13,000,000	420.80
130	Kiribati	30,807,885	6,551,960	470.21
131	Lesotho	475,069,333	90,648,365	524.08
132	Comoros	64,152,139	10,744,088	597.09

Note: Data are for merchandise for DPRK, but for goods and services for all other countries.

Sources: IBRD, 2003; USCB, 2006; Figure 10.2 in this chapter.

When it comes to trade performance and patterns of international finance, North Korea's downward trajectory and its current straits—so to speak, its structural descent from Turkey to Haiti in just one generation, at least in terms of the aforementioned particulars—represents in part the misfortune of circumstance. Clearly, the sudden and unexpected downfall of the Soviet bloc was

Table 10.5
Per Capita Exports: DPRK Rank in World, 1990

Rank	Country	Exports (US$)	Population	Per Capita Exports (US$)
1	Luxembourg	12,362,136,670	381,900	32,370.09
2	Singapore	67,490,758,621	3,047,000	22,149.90
3	Hong Kong, China	100,410,145,323	5,704,500	17,601.92
4	Belgium	139,596,575,589	9,967,400	14,005.31
5	Switzerland	82,819,232,945	6,712,000	12,338.98
6	United Arab Emirates	22,331,244,892	1,844,000	12,110.22
7	Norway	46,927,176,773	4,241,500	11,063.82
8	Netherlands	158,975,438,651	14,952,000	10,632.39
9	Bahrain	4,887,765,957	503,000	9,717.23
10	Denmark	47,781,564,820	5,140,000	9,296.02
—	—	—	—	—
120	Lebanon	511,008,107	3,635,000	140.58
121	Bhutan	80,434,166	600,110	134.03
122	Nigeria	12,365,872,842	96,203,000	128.54
123	Cape Verde	43,051,774	341,400	126.10
124	Equatorial Guinea	42,485,125	352,000	120.70
125	*DPRK*	*1,939,000,000*	*20,018,546*	*96.86*
126	Albania	312,500,000	3,277,000	95.36
127	Kenya	2,205,890,747	23,354,000	94.45
128	Comoros	35,635,055	432,000	82.49
129	Haiti	502,200,000	6,473,000	77.58
—	—	—	—	—
155	Rwanda	145,102,122	6,943,000	20.90
156	Uganda	311,673,602	16,330,000	19.09
157	Bangladesh	1,881,679,563	110,025,000	17.10
158	Burundi	89,130,244	5,456,000	16.34
159	Mozambique	201,346,835	14,151,000	14.23
160	Somalia	89,748,796	7,163,000	12.53
161	Ethiopia	534,884,615	51,180,000	10.45
162	Cambodia	68,528,864	9,145,000	7.49

Note: Data are for merchandise for DPRK, but for goods and services for all other countries.
Sources: IBRD, 2003; USCB, 2006; Figure 10.2 in this chapter.

a disaster for the North Korean economic system, a disaster from which the DPRK economy has not yet recovered.

But it would be a mistake for us to ignore the degree to which North Korea's aberrant and seemingly dysfunctional trade regimen today is actually a result of conscious purpose, deliberate design, and considered official effort. In other words, there is a deeply embedded *regime logic* in the DPRK's tangential and

Table 10.6
Imports as a Percent of Exports: DPRK Rank in World, 1990

Rank	Country	Imports (US$)	Exports (US$)	Imports as a Percent of Exports
1	Argentina	6,546,483,926	14,643,450,361	44.71
2	Venezuela, RB	9,808,102,070	19,168,442,360	51.17
3	Angola	2,147,299,976	3,992,499,897	53.78
4	Oman	3,224,967,490	5,555,266,580	58.05
5	United Arab Emirates	13,780,986,107	22,331,244,892	61.71
6	Trinidad and Tobago	1,448,894,118	2,299,011,765	63.02
7	Nigeria	8,202,785,667	12,365,872,842	66.33
8	Gabon	1,836,820,145	2,740,354,950	67.03
9	Macao, China	2,190,763,357	3,149,631,083	69.56
10	Colombia	5,969,031,672	8,282,579,458	72.07
—	—	—	—	—
110	Niger	544,691,917	372,432,639	146.25
111	Dominica	133,948,146	90,718,517	147.65
112	Grenada	138,799,998	93,796,295	147.98
113	Jordan	3,727,972,374	2,489,182,055	149.77
114	Pakistan	9,350,911,782	6,216,942,715	150.41
115	*DPRK*	*2,945,405,700*	*1,938,861,818*	*151.91*
116	Ghana	1,521,547,091	993,434,057	153.16
117	Greece	23,434,020,455	15,180,855,017	154.37
118	Solomon Islands	153,748,814	98,821,575	155.58
119	Albania	487,500,000	312,500,000	156.00
—	—	—	—	—
145	Cape Verde	148,025,383	43,051,774	343.83
146	Burundi	314,442,790	89,130,244	352.79
147	Guinea-Bissau	90,350,000	24,240,000	372.73
148	Somalia	346,105,365	89,748,796	385.64
149	Mozambique	888,444,767	201,346,835	441.25
150	Sao Tome and Principe	41,706,779	8,336,908	500.27
151	Lesotho	753,435,684	103,431,308	728.44
152	Marshall Islands	56,000,000	1,700,000	3294.12

Note: Data are for merchandise for DPRK, but for goods and services for all other countries.
Sources: IBRD, 2003; USCB, 2006; Figure 10.2 in this chapter.

precarious relationship with the world economy. And far from being irrational, it is based on careful and cool-headed calculations about regime survival.

Consider the DPRK's trade performance over the past generation with the 29 countries the IMF terms "advanced economies"[38]—designated in North Korean terminology as "capitalist" or "imperialist" countries. Between 1980

Table 10.7
Per Capita Exports: DPRK Rank in World, 2000

Rank	Country	Exports (US$)	Population	Per Capita Exports (US$)
1	Luxembourg	29,383,610,297	438,000	67,085.87
2	Singapore	165,812,183,176	4,018,000	41,267.34
3	Hong Kong, China	244,032,761,716	6,665,000	36,614.07
4	Ireland	90,440,955,002	3,794,000	23,837.89
5	Belgium	197,417,360,036	10,252,000	19,256.47
6	Norway	75,393,539,513	4,491,000	16,787.70
7	Netherlands	248,430,008,817	15,919,000	15,605.88
8	Switzerland	110,987,818,287	7,180,000	15,457.91
9	Macao, China	5,819,733,612	438,000	13,287.06
10	Denmark	70,193,357,431	5,340,000	13,144.82
—	—	—	—	—
150	Comoros	30,679,636	558,000	54.98
151	Benin	333,603,366	6,272,000	53.19
152	Bangladesh	6,611,000,000	131,050,000	50.45
153	Malawi	450,840,100	10,311,000	43.72
154	Tanzania	1,329,795,016	33,696,000	39.46
155	Timor-Leste	25,000,000	737,000	33.92
156	Central African Republic	125,250,709	3,717,000	33.70
157	Chad	233,152,617	7,694,000	30.30
158	*DPRK*	*653,100,000*	*21,647,682*	*30.17*
159	Niger	320,655,075	10,832,000	29.60
160	Uganda	656,000,000	22,210,000	29.54
161	Mozambique	469,194,516	17,691,000	26.52
162	Eritrea	97,489,583	4,097,000	23.80
163	Sierra Leone	110,005,233	5,031,000	21.87
164	Burkina Faso	236,804,405	11,274,000	21.00
165	Rwanda	149,602,258	7,709,000	19.41
166	Congo, Dem. Rep.	963,872,464	50,948,000	18.92
167	Ethiopia	984,250,978	64,298,000	15.31
168	Burundi	62,164,375	6,807,000	9.13

Note: Data are for merchandise for DPRK, but for goods and services for all other countries.
Sources: IBRD, 2003; USCB, 2006; Figure 10.2 in this chapter.

and 2000, the total size of the import market for this collectivity grew from about US$1.8 trillion to about US$6.1 trillion.

The DPRK, we recall, is precluded from exporting any appreciable volume of goods to the United States by Washington's thicket of sanctions and restrictions against U.S.-DPRK commerce, and America offers the world's largest single import market. But if we exclude the United States from the picture, the remain-

Table 10.8
Imports as a Percent of Exports: DPRK Rank in World, 2000

Rank	Country	Imports (US$)	Exports (US$)	Imports as a Percent of Exports
1	Libya	5,278,960,692	12,139,647,153	43.49
2	Algeria	11,371,246,346	22,715,918,150	50.06
3	Kuwait	11,370,823,146	21,300,733,496	53.38
4	Iran, Islamic Rep.	13,543,278,076	25,243,916,656	53.65
5	Russian Federation	62,466,000,000	115,540,000,000	54.06
6	Congo, Rep.	1,404,252,928	2,585,746,791	54.31
7	Saudi Arabia	46,987,983,979	82,368,491,322	57.05
8	Venezuela, RB	19,786,888,935	34,497,624,860	57.36
9	Botswana	1,936,345,996	3,119,408,836	62.07
10	Macao, China	3,642,719,197	5,819,733,612	62.59
—	—	—	—	—
147	Haiti	1,321,141,442	501,946,403	263.20
148	Cape Verde	344,211,362	130,517,532	263.73
149	Burkina Faso	657,602,742	236,804,405	277.70
150	*DPRK*	*1,847,800,000*	*653,100,000*	*282.93*
151	Rwanda	441,108,545	149,602,258	294.85
152	Mozambique	1,526,308,504	469,194,516	325.30
153	Lesotho	762,704,061	226,049,911	337.41
154	French Polynesia	952,020,780	192,401,162	494.81
155	West Bank and Gaza	3,085,316,244	603,791,679	510.99
156	Eritrea	498,593,750	97,489,583	511.43
157	Timor-Leste	160,000,000	25,000,000	640.00
158	Palau	127,100,000	11,500,000	1105.22

Note: Data are for merchandise for DPRK, but for goods and services for all other countries.
Sources: IBRD, 2003; USCB, 2006; Figure 10.2 in this chapter.

ing advanced economy market for foreign imports is nevertheless vast and, at least in nominal terms, rapidly expanding, growing from about US$1.5 billion in 1980 to US$4.6 billion in 2000. DPRK exports to this group, however, remained negligible and stagnant over these decades—even after the loss of Soviet bloc markets would seem to have made the need to cultivate new sources of commercial export revenue more urgent. In 1980 and 1990, North Korea's reported sales to this grouping totaled roughly US$430 million and roughly US$470 million, respectively. In 2000, the reported aggregate was about US$560 million, but that total may have been inflated somewhat by an unusual and perhaps questionable US$60 million in North Korean imports recorded that year by Spain. Yet even accepting that year's exceptional Spanish data, the real level of North Korean exports to these capitalist countries would have been substantially lower in 2000 than it had been two decades earlier.[39]

Ideological and Cultural Infiltration

Pyongyang's remarkably poor long-term performance in the advanced economies' huge markets is no accident. Rather, it is a direct consequence of official DPRK policy and doctrine, most particularly, Pyongyang's concept of "ideological and cultural infiltration." Official North Korean pronouncements relentlessly decry the dangers of this phenomenon, characterized as a technique by which outsiders attempt to undermine the foundations of established communist states. A recent declamation will give the flavor of the general argument:

> It is the imperialist's old trick to carry out ideological and cultural infiltration prior to their launching of an aggression openly. Their bourgeois ideology and culture are reactionary toxins to paralyze people's ideological consciousness. Through such infiltration, they try to paralyze the independent consciousness of other nations and make them spineless. At the same time, they work to create illusions about capitalism and promote lifestyles among them based on the law of the jungle, in an attempt to induce the collapse of socialist and progressive nations. The ideological and cultural infiltration is their silent, crafty and villainous method of aggression, intervention and domination. . . .
>
> Through "economic exchange" and personnel interchange programs too, the imperialists are pushing their infiltration. . . Exchange and cooperation activities in the economic and cultural fields have been on the rise since the beginning of the new century. The imperialists are making use of these activities as an important lever to push the infiltration of bourgeois ideology and culture. . . .
>
> The imperialists' ideological and cultural infiltration, if tolerated, will lead to the collapse and degeneration of society, to disorder and chaos, and even to the loss of the gains of the revolution. The collapse of socialism in the 20th Century—and the revival of capitalism in its place—in some countries gave us the serious lesson that social deterioration begins with ideological degeneration and confusion on the ideological front throws every other front of society into chaos and, consequently, all the gains of the revolution go down the drain eventually.[40]

DPRK party lecture notes published in South Korea late in 2002 put the point more succinctly:

> The capitalist's ideological and cultural infiltration will never cease, and the struggle against it will continue, as long as the imperialists continue to exist in the world . . .
>
> The great leader, Kim Jong Il, pointed out the following: "Today, the imperialist and reactionaries are tenaciously scheming to blow the wind of bourgeois liberalism into us". . . .
>
> People will ideologically degenerate and weaken; cracks will develop in our socialist ideological position; and, in the end, our socialism will helplessly collapse.

A case in point is the bitter lesson drawn from the miserable situations of the former Soviet Union and Eastern European countries.[41]

Economic exchange with the capitalist world, in other words, is explicitly and
officially regarded by Pyongyang as a process that unleashes powerful, unpredictable, and subversive forces—forces which ultimately erode the authority of
socialist states. Viewed from this perspective, North Korea's record of trade performance vis-à-vis the advanced market economies is not a record of failure—
i.e., failure to integrate into the world economy—but rather a mark of *success*—
i.e., effective containment of a potentially lethal security threat.

Moreover, it is worth recalling that the DPRK's public misgivings about
"ideological and cultural infiltration" are longstanding, almost precisely paral-
leling the state's record of minimal export outreach to advanced market
economies over the past generation. Although DPRK pronouncements about
ideological and cultural infiltration have attracted some attention abroad since
the downfall of Soviet bloc socialism, the slogan itself was *not* a response to
that defining historical event. On the contrary, North Korean leadership had
been highlighting the dangers of that tendency for at least a decade *before* the
final collapse of the Soviet Union. At the Sixth Congress of the Korean Workers' Party in 1980, for example, Kim Il Sung inveighed against the dangers of
"cultural infiltration." And by 1981, he was urging North Korea's "workers and
trade union members" to "combat the ideological and cultural infiltration of the
imperialists and their subversive moves and sabotage."[42]

It is true that official directives from Pyongyang have from time to time discussed the desirability of significantly increasing the DPRK's volume of international trade. Against such comments, North Korea's extraordinary and continuing weakness in export performance may seem especially curious, insofar
as it would be—at least in theory—so very easy to redress. But Pyongyang's
conspicuous neglect of the revenue potential from trade with advanced market
economies is not to be explained away as a prolonged fit of absent-mindedness.
Instead it speaks to fundamental and abiding calculations in Pyongyang's strategy for state survival.

Military-First Politics

If staying out of the poisonous embrace of the world economy is viewed as an
imperative for state survival by DPRK leadership, a corollary question about
state survival inevitably arises: how then to generate sufficient international
resources to forestall economic collapse? To date, Pyongyang's answer has
been to make non-market transactions. The DPRK has always pursued an "aid-
seeking" international economic strategy, but in the post-Soviet bloc era, the

particulars of that approach have perforce mutated. In the era of the "strong and prosperous state," North Korea's main tactics for generating international resources are viewed through the prism of the current state campaign for "military-first politics" (*songun chongchi*). Like the concept of ideological and cultural infiltration, the theory and recommended practice of military-first politics have received a tremendous amount of air-time in the North Korean media over the past five years. Two recent exegeses may clarify some of the economic implications of this doctrine.

As a long, official analysis in March 2003 instructed, it was a renewed emphasis on military development that enabled North Korea to conclude its "Arduous March" and to step onto the pathway to power and prosperity:

> Today, the peoples' struggle for their nation's independent development and prosperity is waged in an environment different from that of the last century.
>   . . . In building a state in our era, it is essential to beef up the main force of the nation and fortify the revolutionary base, and, in this regard, it is most important to build up powerful military might. In today's world, without powerful military might, no country can . . . achieve development and prosperity.
>   . . . During . . . "the Arduous March" in our history, great Comrade Kim Jong Il firmly believed that the destiny of the people and the future of the revolution hinged on the barrel of a gun, and that we could break through the difficulties and lead the revolution to victory only by depending on the Army. . . . Through the arduous practice in which the Army was put to the fore and the unheard-of trials were overcome, the revolutionary philosophy that the barrel of a gun was precisely the revolution and the barrel of a gun was precisely the victory of socialism was originated. . . .
>   Our theory on the construction of a powerful state . . . is the embodiment of the profound truth that the base of national strength is military might, and [that] the dignity and might of a country hinges on the barrel of a gun. . . . In a powerful state, the defense industry takes a leading and key position in the economy. . . .
>   Today, by firmly adhering to the principle of putting prime effort into the defense industry and, based on this, by developing the overall economy ceaselessly, our party is brilliantly resolving the issue of consolidating the national strength of a powerful state.[43]

And how exactly does military power conduce to prosperity? The answer was strongly hinted at in a statement the following month:

> A country's development and the placement of importance on the military are linked as one. . . .
>   Once we lay the foundations for a powerful *self-sustaining national defense industry*, we will be able to rejuvenate all economic fields, to include light industry and agriculture and enhance the quality of the people's lives.[44] (Emphasis added.)

This is a fascinating, and revealing, formulation. In most of the world today, a country's defense outlays are regarded as a weight that must be shouldered by the value-adding sectors of the national economy—hence the phrase "military burden." North Korean leadership, however, evidently entertains the concept of a "self-sustaining" defense sector, implying that Pyongyang views its military activities as *generating* resources, and not simply absorbing them. In effect, in the enunciated view of North Korean leadership, the DPRK's military sector is the key not only to unlocking the resources necessary to finance its own considerable needs, but to financing the recovery of the rest of the national economy as well.

It does not require a great deal of imagination to spell out the operational details of this approach. While forswearing any appreciable export revenues from legitimate commerce with advanced market economies, North Korean policy today seems to be banking on the possibility of financing state survival by exporting *strategic insecurity* to the rest of the world. In part, such dividends are derived from exports of merchandise, such as missile sales, or international transfer of WMD technology. But these revenues also depend heavily on what might be described as an export of services, or, in this case, military extortion services—might we better call them "revenue-sensitive threat-reduction services"?—based upon Pyongyang's nuclear development and ballistic missile programs.

The export of strategic insecurity, in its different components, can arguably be said to explain much of the upsurge in North Korea's unexplained surfeit of imports over commercial export revenues since 1998, especially to the extent that Western aid policies in recent years can be described as appeasement-motivated.[45] In an important tactical sense, that approach has enjoyed success, as it has facilitated state survival under imposing constraints. But the territory demarcated by ideological and cultural infiltration, on one side, and military-first politics, on the other, is also, quite clearly, a sort of no-man's land, an inherently unstable niche in which survival is utterly contingent, and sustained development utterly unlikely. In short, North Korea's current strategic policy may be deferring the question of economic collapse—but it has not yet answered it.

Avoiding Economic Collapse through Economic Reform Policies?

If the DPRK is currently sustaining its system through aid-seeking stratagems grounded in military menace, as I argue above, it would seem to have settled upon a particularly meager and highly uncertain mode of state finance. Even today, when this approach is "working," it is not clear that it generates sufficient funding to maintain, much less improve, the nation's aging and badly decayed industrial and transport infrastructure. Moreover, the stratagem may fail at any time for any number of reasons—donor "aid fatigue," DPRK miscalculation, or an external push for "regime change" in Pyongyang being but three of these.

Under these circumstances, as many foreign observers have argued, a more secure and ultimately satisfactory path for avoiding economic collapse and preserving the sovereignty of North Korean state might be a pragmatic reorientation of Pyongyang's policy in the name of promoting sustained growth. In some variants of this argument, it is said that China and Vietnam have already demonstrated that it is feasible for a Marxist-Leninist government in an Asian setting simultaneously to execute a shift to an outward-oriented economic regimen, to achieve rapid economic growth, and to maintain leadership authority and political stability.

Whether "reform" and "outward orientation" could be consonant with the preservation of unquestioned power for North Korea's leadership is a not a question to detain us here.[46] Nor will we be diverted by a discussion of the potential problems and preconditions of any "reform" worthy of the name under contemporary North Korean conditions.

North Korea's Economic Reforms to Date

Predictions that the DPRK would soon be embracing economic reform come from a family tree that is, if anything, even more prolific and older than the lineage of predictions about imminent or eventual DPRK collapse. Scholars and analysts have been detecting quiet signs of reform and opening in the North Korean system since at least the 1980s.[47] The intensity of these premonitions typically waxed and waned according to the current temperatures in Pyongyang's relations with Washington and/or Seoul.[48] In July 2002, however, Pyongyang enacted a package of macroeconomic policy changes which marked a notable departure from DPRK practices over the previous generation. Moreover, North Korean leadership now sometimes openly describes these measures as "economic reform"[49]—a term the DPRK had vigorously rejected heretofore, on the understanding that no reforms were needed for the real existing DPRK system.

The specifics of the July 2002 measures have been described in detail elsewhere.[50] Scholars and analysts have in addition offered some initial assessments of their significance and portent.[51]

It may be cheering, of course, to see *anything* self-described as "reform" emanating from the organs of power in the DPRK. And by comparison to North Korea's economic policy adjustments since, say, the late 1960s, these measures may be indeed described as bold and experimental steps. Yet in a sense this only attests to how impoverished our expectations for DPRK policy have become over the decades. Viewed for what they are—rather than for what we might hope they will prefigure—the July 2002 package of economic changes can best be described as modest: either by comparison to economic reforms undertaken in other troubled economies, or by comparison to the job that needs doing in the DPRK.

In practical terms, the July 2002 package—consumer price increases, wage hikes, currency devaluation, and ration system devolution—accomplished one important function: it remonetized a limited portion of the DPRK domestic economy. By the late 1980s, the DPRK was already a shockingly demonetized operation: back of the envelope calculations for the year 1987 suggest that the wage bill in that year would have amounted to less than a fifth of North Korea's official net material product. Over the following decade and a half, the role of the national currency in domestic economic activity was progressively diminished. By the turn of the century, North Korea was perhaps the modern world's most completely demonetized economy—excepting only *Khmer Rouge* Cambodia, where for a time by decree money was abolished altogether.

The reemergence of money in North Korean economic life—and with it, the reemergence of a limited measure of open market activity—mark an incontestable and important improvement for the DPRK's tiny consumer sector. But it is important also to recognize just what this July 2002 package does *not* signify. It does *not*, to begin, represent an unambiguous move toward market principles in the DPRK economy. On the contrary, remonetization of the domestic economy would likewise be a *sine qua non* for the resurrection of the DPRK's badly broken central planning mechanism ("a planned economy without planning," in Professor Mitsuhiko Kimura's apt phrase[52])—which has not managed to launch another multi-year national plan since the last one was concluded in 1993.

Limited remonetization of the domestic economy, furthermore, does not signify transformation of the DPRK's badly distorted production structure. On the contrary, the manifestly limited supply-response of the DPRK economy to the July 2002 measures is indicated, on the one hand, by the subsequent steep drop in the black market exchange rate for the DPRK *won*,[53] and, on the other, by Pyongyang's hurried introduction, barely 10 months after the July 2002 package, of new "people's life bonds"—worthless, utterly illiquid, and involuntarily assigned—in lieu of wages for workers or payments for enterprises.[54]

To be sure, the limited reintroduction of money in the DPRK domestic economy may elicit *some* supply response: a Leibenstein-style increase in "x-efficiency," for example.[55] But without the possibility of a reallocation of state resources in accordance with new demand conditions—and that possibility presently does not exist in the DPRK—the supply response must perforce be tepid and superficial. Thus, it should come as no surprise that the World Food Programme (WFP) has warned prospective donors that North Korea faces an imminent return to mass hunger, barring an influx of new food aid into the relief pipeline[56]—heartening signs of newly-sprouted "people's markets" notwithstanding. The contrast is not a contradiction, but rather a faithful reflection of the scope and limits of the July 2002 reforms.

The July 2002 reforms, in brief, do not in themselves stave off the specter of DPRK economic collapse. Nor do they have any obvious or direct bearing on the prospects for a shift to China-style or Vietnam-style export-led growth. One need only contrast North Korea's patterns of trade performance over the past generation with those of China and Vietnam to appreciate this, as we see in Figures 10.5 and 10.6. Vietnam began its push for export-orientation when its Soviet subsidies abruptly ended—whereas North Korea's export performance markedly worsened, and its aid dependence increased, after 1991. Though still predominantly agrarian societies, Vietnam and China both manage to export far more merchandise on a per capita basis today than does the ostensibly industrialized DPRK, precisely because of the linkages and supply-response mechanisms that the DPRK has assiduously prevented from taking root. At the risk of belaboring the obvious, the DPRK has not even begun to tinker with the macro-policies, or to promote the micro-institutions, which would permit a China- or

Figure 10.5
Imports as a Percent of Exports, 1977–2005

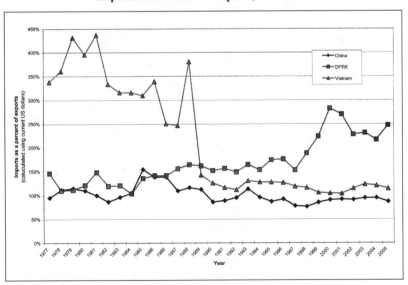

Notes: Estimates are for merchandise trade only.
Sources: Figures 10.1 and 10.2 in this chapter, WTO, 2006; USCB, 2006..

Figure 10.6
Per Capita Exports, 1977–2005

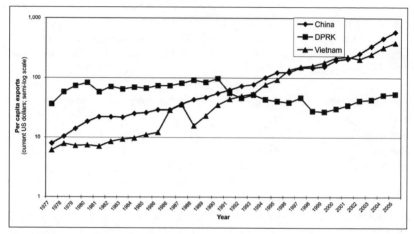

Notes: Estimates are for merchandise trade only.
Sources: Figures 10.1, 10.2 and 10.5 in this chapter, WTO, 2006; USCB, 2006..

Vietnam-style export response.[57] Thus for the time being, economic survival through export-orientation is simply not in the cards for North Korea.

What Would a Genuine Reform and Opening Look Like for North Korea?

Instead of sketching out the full contours of a DPRK transition to sustainable export-led growth, it may serve our purposes here to summarize and recapitulate our arguments from Chapter 8 on possible "indicators" of serious economic reform in North Korea—if and when that process is truly underway. In particular, we should dwell on three essential and inextricably linked features of any North Korean economy reform worthy of the name: the outward opening itself; military demobilization; and normalization of relations with the ROK.

Economic Opening. If Pyongyang were to embark upon a genuine move toward an economic opening, what initial signs would outsiders be able to see? Some of these might include: 1) meaningful departure from old economic themes, and new dialogue about economic issues, in DPRK propaganda and guidance organs; 2) doctrinal reorientation regarding the treatment of profit-generating transactions in official DPRK pronouncements—and especially profits involving transactions with foreign concerns; 3) an attempt on the part of the DPRK to settle its longstanding international debt default problems;[58] 4) a move toward greater economic transparency, i.e., the publication of economic and social statistics describing the North Korean domestic situation; and

5) serious attempts to promulgate a legal framework for potential foreign investors that might assist in attracting profit-seeking overseas entrepreneurs to North Korean soil. Although some observers may see glimmers of conditions 1) and 2), none of these "blinker lights" are flashing brightly and consistently in North Korea today.

Military Demobilization. Military demobilization would represent a critical aspect of a North Korean program for "reform" and "opening" insofar as 1) a dismantling of Pyongyang's WMD programs would indicate that North Korean leadership was committed to earning its living from activities other than international military extortion, and 2) reallocation of resources from the hypertrophied military to the civilian sectors would permit much more potentially productive economic activity in the DPRK.

As noted earlier, there is little evidence to date that North Korea has ever, at any point in its more than five decades of existence, voluntarily abjured any new instrument of military force that might possibly lie within its grasp. (Today, indeed, such a renunciation would seem fundamentally inconsistent with the state's established policies of *Kangsong Taeguk* and "military-first politics.") Moreover, North Korea's commitment to developing weapons of mass destruction was implicitly reaffirmed in the exhortation that "We should hold fast to the military-first politics *and build up our military strength in every possible way*"[59] [emphasis added].

Normalization of DPRK-ROK Relations. The DPRK cannot execute a successful economic opening unless it demobilizes, and it cannot demobilize unless it comes to terms with the right of the Republic to coexist with it on the Korean Peninsula. Consequently, one important and indeed indispensable marker of movement toward reform and opening would be a change in North Korea's official stance concerning the legitimacy of the ROK.

If North Korea were to evidence a new attitude toward the legitimacy of the ROK, the indications of this change would be direct and unmistakable: its highest figures and its official media would simply disclose that they were prepared to accept the existence of the South Korean state, that they recognized the ROK's right to conduct its own foreign policy, and they respected (while respectfully disagreeing with) Seoul's decision to maintain a military alliance with the United States. Suffice it so say that no such disclosures have been offered to date.

Concluding Remarks

In sum: there is little evidence that North Korea has yet embarked upon a path to "reform" and "opening," with all the transformations in polity this path would foreshadow. That oft-discussed strategy for economic survival appears, as yet, to be an option left unchosen by the DPRK's own leadership.

How long the DPRK can survive on its current trajectory is anyone's guess—and my dire predictions on this score have admittedly been off the mark, perhaps for reasons indicated above. But if the analysis in this chapter is correct, the specter of an economic collapse is a ghost that haunts the DPRK to this very day—and one that will not be exorcized unless or until North Korea's leadership agrees to undertake what, in a very different context, they have called "a bold switch-over." Whether Pyongyang accepts such a challenge remains to be seen. For the time being, however, North Korea is still wandering through an economic no-man's land bordered on one side by crisis and on the other by catastrophe.

Notes

1. See Noland, 2004.
2. Eberstadt, 1990.
3. Perhaps most memorably, including a statement in my 1995 study *Korea Approaches Reunification*, to the effect that "there is no reason at present to expect a reign by Kim Jong Il to be either stable or long."
4. Cf. the large interdisciplinary State Failure Task Force, the U.S. government-funded undertaking that spent six years attempting to devise econometric formulae by which to predict political upheaval and/or breakdown; the report from this project can be accessed electronically from the University of Maryland's Center for International Development and Conflict Management, at http://www.cidcm.umd .edu/inscr/stfail.
5. The distinction between art and science is elucidated in many places, but perhaps nowhere better and more clearly than in the writings of Michael Oakeshott (1991).
6. This is not to gainsay the utility of particular new mathematical or quantitative techniques used by contemporary stock-pickers and investors (e.g., Black-Sholes option-pricing models, etc); some principals have enjoyed fantastic success with these tools, and have amassed enormous personal wealth as a result; the point is that these successes are not *generalizable*, as scientific knowledge in principle always is; George Soros and Warren Buffett are practitioners of art, not science, as they themselves have said.
7. One scholar who has explored aspects of this asymmetry is Timur Kuran (1989, 1991a and 1991b, and 1995).
8. For an inventory and analysis, see Lipset and Bence, 1994.
9. For example, Johnson, 1977; seventeen years before the peace transition in the Republic of South Africa to pan-racial democracy, Johnson explained why this occurrence was an impossibility.
10. Cf. Amalrik, 1970; in a bitter historical irony, the USSR *did* last to 1984—but Amalrik did not.
11. de Bellaigue, 2001.
12. For some background on the long relative decline of the Ottoman economy, see Faroqhi et al., 1994.
13. An indication of that decline may be gleaned from estimates by the economic historian Angus Maddison; in 1870, by his reckoning, per capita GDP for modern-

day Turkey would have been US$825 (in 1990 international dollars)—or about 39 percent of the contemporary level for Western Europe; by 1913—on the eve of World War I—Turkey's per capita GDP had risen to an estimated US$1,213, but its relative standing had dropped to just 34 percent of the Western Europe level; derived from Maddison, 2003, pp. 61 and 156.

14. Cohen and Gooch, 1990.
15. Stephens, 1993, p. 74; Stephens has surmised that de Roebeck's "naval timidity" can be explained in part by "the high regard for battleships at that time; the loss of even one battleship was considered a national tragedy, more so than the loss of several thousand troops."
16. Fromkin, 1989, p. 154.
17. Moorehead, 1956, p. 72.
18. Fromkin, op. cit., p. 152.
19. Moorehead, op. cit., p. 77; in recent years a revisionist literature has challenged the notion that the Turkish and German defenders were critically short of ammunition; see for example Erickson, 2001, pp. 158–176; the literature does not account for, or explain, Ottoman and German military officers' own contemporary reports—and subsequent reminiscences—to the contrary.
20. Watson, 1982, p. 179.
21. Cited in Nevinson, 1929, p. 62.
22. Moorehead, op. cit., p. 74.
23. Fromkin, op. cit. p. 154.
24. Eberstadt, 1999.
25. To my knowledge, this conception of economic collapse was first developed and defined by Jack Hirshleifer of UCLA and RAND; see Hirshleifer, 1987.
26. See Goodkind and West, 2001, pp. 219–238; Goodkind and West's model posits a range of 600,000 to 1,000,000 deaths for the late 1990s.
27. Not too long thereafter, the ROK Bank of Korea (BOK) declared that North Korea's economy had resumed economic growth; in fact, BOK reports have suggested positive growth in the DPRK commencing in 1999, and continuing every subsequent year, although, as discussed earlier in Chapter 7, it is not self-evident that the BOK analysis can withstand scrutiny.
28. A new pattern, however, may have been developing in as of 2005; in that year, Chinese trade statistics indicated a dramatic increase in North Korea's merchandise trade deficit with Beijing; "mirror statistics" suggest the implicit transfer leapt from a little under US$350 million in 2004 to over US$750 million in 2005—by far the highest level ever recorded in the China-DPRK relationship; it remains to be seen whether this was a notable aberration in China-DPRK economic relations, or instead the start of a major new trend.
29. For an excellent summary and analysis of open-source evidence, see Chestnut, 2005.
30. For some of the details, see Ward, 2003, p. 9 and Lem, 2003, p. 2.
31. *Korea Times*, 2000.
32. Pyongyang's description of the transaction.
33. In theory, none of these American assistance resources should be included in "mirror statistics," but real-world practice is more haphazard; U.S. heavy fuel oil shipped to the DPRK in South Korean vessels, for example, has often been registered as "North-South trade" in the ROK Ministry of Unification's inter-Korean trade statistics.

34. In the felicitous phrase of Cole and Lyman (1971).
35. Interestingly, enough, a growing number of eminent historians and respected social scientists seem to be engaging in this pastime; see for example Polsby (1982), Ferguson, (1997) and Cowley (2003).
36. Eberstadt, 1995, Chapter 1.
37. Global calculations derived from IMF, 2003 and UN, 2003.
38. This grouping includes 24 of the current 30 OECD members (omitting Czech Republic, Hungary, Mexico, Poland, Slovak Republic, and Turkey) and five others: Cyprus, Hong Kong, Israel, Singapore, and Taiwan.
39. Between 1980 and 2000, the US producer price index—the more appropriate deflator for international tradables—rose by 51 percent; using that deflator, North Korea's inflation-adjusted export volume to this grouping of countries would have declined by about 16 percent between 1980 and 2000; note that the grouping includes South Korea, and figures in inter-Korean trade; we may note that the situation does not look appreciably different in 2005; although a breakdown of country-by-country exports by the DPRK is not yet available from conventional sources, summary calculations indicate that North Korea's non-China exports rose from US$620 million in 2000 to US$767 million in 2005, or by about 24 percent in current dollar-denominated terms; since the U.S. producer price index rose by a little over 12 percent during this same period, this suggests that North Korea's trade with all the rest of the world, including the "imperialist countries," rose by some 11 percent in real terms; without knowing the exact breakdown between exports to "imperialist countries" and the rest, such numbers may suggest that real exports to the "imperialist" group were sill lower in real terms in 2005 than they had been in 1980—a quarter century earlier.
40. *FBIS-EAS*, 2003b.
41. *FBIS*, 2002.
42. *BBC Summary*, 1981.
43. *Nodong Sinmun*, 2003a.
44. *Nodong Sinmun*, 2003b.
45. Even ostensibly humanitarian food aid transfers to North Korea are informed by the reality of military extortion; think, in particular, of the alleged underground nuclear site at Kumchang-ri, or, more generally, whether the opaque rules under which food relief is administered in the DPRK would be tolerated by the international donor community in any other setting.
46. Scalapino (1992) and Ezra Vogel, personal communications with the author, 1994–2004; we may note in passing that both Robert Scalapino and Ezra Vogel have suggested that North Korea might plausibly evolve from today's hermetic *juche* totalitarian system to a more familiar, Park Chung Hee-type authoritarian state, and the judgment of these two leading American authorities on modern Asia should be respectfully weighed in this consideration.
47. See, for example, Lee (1988), pp. 1264–79, Oh (1990), and Merrill (1991), pp. 139–53; each of these papers was written and initially presented in the 1980s.
48. The announcement of the Pyongyang North-South Summit occasioned an especially vigorous pulsation of such premonitions; thus, for example, Noland's statement in a *Washington Post* article (2000), to the effect that "the secret visit to Beijing last month by Kim Jong Il supports the argument that this is the real deal and that the North Koreans are serious about opening to the outside world" was written, of course, before the "outside world" had learned the true details of the "real deal" underpinning that historic summit.

49. Thus SPA President Kim Yong Nam in August 2002 in a conversation with UN officials: "We are reactivating the whole field of the national economy . . . we are reforming the economic system on the principle of profitability" cited in United Nations, 2002, p. 127.

  Note however that the term "reform" has not yet been embraced by the DPRK media, which still treats the concept as anathema; the March 2003 formulation from *Minju Choson* remains representative: "Even though the imperialists are trying to stile (sic) our economy by inducing it to 'reform' and 'opening,' our economic management is being improved without deviating even an inch from socialist principles"; *FBIS* 2003a.

50. See, for example, United Nations, 2002, pp. 127–32.

51. For cautiously optimistic analyses, see Noland, 2002; Ruediger, 2003a; for a more cautiously skeptical assessment, see Newcomb, 2003, pp. 57–60.

52. Kimura, 1994.

53. The initial July 2002 exchange rate was set at 153 *won* to the US dollar; by October 2003, DPRK government foreign exchange booths in Pyongyang were paying 900 *won* per dollar; *Yonhap*, 2003.

54. *BBC Worldwide Monitoring*, 2003.

55. Leibenstein, 1966, pp. 392–415.

56. Kim, 2004; McDonald, 2004; the WFP's own institutional interests, to be sure, coincide with an alarmist reading of the North Korean food situation—but that does not mean the WFP's latest warnings are wrong.

57. To date the only appreciable movement in these general areas would seem to be the events that found their denouement in the September-October 2002 Yang Bin fiasco.

58. For the past quarter century, the DPRK has been in effective default on roughly US$1 billion in European, Japanese, and Australian loans contracted in the early 1970s; for more detail, see Eberstadt, 1995, Chapter 1.

59. *FBIS*-EAS-2001-0629.

References

Ahn, Choong-yong, Nicholas Eberstadt, and Lee Young-sun, eds. 2004a. *A New International Engagement Framework for North Korea? Contending Perspectives.* Washington D.C.: Korea Economic Institute of America.

———. 2004b. "The Persistence of North Korea" in *Policy Review* 127, October/ November 2004, available at: http://www.policyreview.org/oct04/eberstadt.html

Amalrik, Andrei. 1970. *Will the Soviet Union Survive to 1984?* New York: Harper & Row.

British Broadcasting Corporation (BBC) Worldwide Monitoring. 2001. Rebroadcast from *Pyongyang Central Broadcasting Station* as "North Korea demands compensation from USA for delay to reactor project." 8 July.

———. 2003. Rebroadcast from *Korean Central News Agency* as "North Korea reports 'brisk' sale of public bonds." 8 May.

———. *Summary of World Broadcasts.* 1981. Rebroadcast from *Korean Central News Agency* as "Kim Il Sung's Speech to Trade Union Congress." 30 November. FE/ 6896/B/1.

Center for International Development and Conflict Management. University of Maryland. Available at: http://www.cidcm.umd.edu/inscr/stfail

Chestnut, Sheena E. 2005. "The 'Soprano' State'? North Korean Involvement in Criminal Activity and Implications for International Security." BA Thesis, Honors Program for International Security Studies. Stanford, CA: Stanford University. 20 May. Unpublished.

Cohen, Elliot and John Gooch. 1990. *Military Misfortunes: The Anatomy of Failure in War.* New York: Vintage Press.

Cole, David C. and Princeton Lyman. 1971. *Korean Development: The Interplay of Politics and Economics.* Cambridge, MA: Harvard University Press.

Cowley, Robert. 2003. *What Ifs? Of American History: Eminent Historians Imagine What Might Have Been.* New York: G.P. Putnam.

De Bellaigue, Christopher. 2001. "Turkey's Hidden Past." *New York Review of Books.* 8 March.

Eberstadt, Nicholas. 1990. "The Coming Collapse of North Korea." *Wall Street Journal.* 26 June.

———. 1995. *Korea Approaches Reunification.* Armonk, NY: M.E. Sharpe.

———. 1999. *The End of North Korea.* Washington, DC: AEI Press.

———. 2000. "Economic Recovery in the DPRK: Status and Prospect." *International Journal of Korean Studies* IV(1). Fall/Winter.

———. 2001. "Prospects for Economic Recovery: Perceptions and Evidence." *Joint US-Korean Academic Studies*:1–25.

———. 2004. "North Korea's Survival Game: Understanding the Recent Past, Thinking about the Future." Paper prepared for "Peaceful Resolution with North Korea: Towards a New International Engagement Framework." KIEP-KEI-AEI Conference, Washington, D.C. 12–13 February.

Erickson, Edward J. 2001. "One More Push: Forcing the Dardanelles in March 1915." *Journal of Strategic Studies* 24(3):158–176. September.

Faroqhi, Suraiya, Bruce McGowan, Donald Quataert, and Sevket Pamuk. 1994. *An Economic and Social History of the Ottoman Empire: Volume Two, 1600–1914.* New York: Cambridge University Press.

FBIS-EAS-2001-0629. Reprinted from *Nodong Sinmun* as "DPRK Daily Full Front-Page Article Discusses 'National Pride.'" 3 July.

——— -2001-0801. Reprinted from *Yonhap News Service* as "ROK's Yonhap: N.K. Says U.S. Demands for Verification Ruse to Disarm It." 1 August.

——— -2002. Reprinted from *Chosun Ilbo*, as "'Full Text' of DPRK Lecture Program in Capitalists' 'Ideological and Cultural Infiltration.'" AFS Document Number KPP20021222000016. 20 December.

——— -2003a. Reprinted from *Minju Choson* as "DPRK Cabinet Organ Discusses Improving Economic Management." AFS Document Number KPP 20030313000122. 6 March.

——— -2003b. Reprinted from *Nodong Sinmun* as "DPRK Organ Scores 'Imperialists' for Ideological, Cultural Infiltration Schemes." AFS Document Number KPP2003 0429000057. 20 April.

Ferguson, Niall, ed. 1997. *Virtual History: Alternatives and Counterfactuals.* London: Picador.

Fromkin, David. 1989. *A Peace To End All Peace: Creating the Modern Middle East 1914–1922.* New York: Henry Holt and Company.

Goodkind, Daniel and Loraine West. 2001. "The North Korean Famine and its Demographic Impact." *Population and Development Review* 27(2):219–38. June.

Hirshleifer, Jack. 1987. *Economic Behavior in Adversity.* Chicago: University of Chicago Press.

International Bank for Reconstruction and Development (IBRD). 2002. *World Development Indicators 2002*. Washington, D.C.: World Bank. CD-ROM.

———. 2003. World Development Indicators 2003. Washington, D.C.: World Bank. CD-ROM.

International Monetary Fund (IMF). 2003. World Economic Outlook Database (September 2003) http://www.imf.org/external/pubs/ft/2003/02/data/index.htm

———. Various years. International Financial Statistics. Washington, D.C.: IMF.

Japan External Trade Organization (JETRO). Various years. Kita Chōsen no keizai to bōeki no tenbō (North Korea's Economy and Trade Outlook). Tokyo: Nihon Bōeki Shinkōkai.

Johnson, R.W. 1977. *How Long Can South Africa Survive?* New York: Oxford University Press.

Kim, So-young. 2004. "WFP warns of N.K. food crisis." *Korea Herald.* 11 February.

Kimura, Mitsuhiko. 1994. "A Planned Economy Without Planning: *Su-ryong's* North Korea." *Discussion PaperF-081.* Faculty of Economics, Tezukayama University.

Korea Times. 2000. "Seoul Firmly Backs 'Perry Process'." 7 February.

Korea Trade Investment Promotion Agency (KOTRA). Various years; *Pukhan ui Muyok Hoesa* (North Korea's Trade) Seoul: Taehan Muyok Chinhung Kongsa.

Kuran, Timur. 1989. "Sparks and prairie fires: A theory of unanticipated political revolution." *Public Choice* 61(1-2): 41–78. April.

———. 1991a. "The East European Revolution of 1989: Is it surprising that we were surprised?" *American Economic Review* 81(1):121–25. May.

———. 1991b. "Now or never: The element of surprise in the East European revolutions of 1989." *World Politics* 44(1): 7–48. October.

———. 1995. "The inevitability of future revolutionary surprises." *American Journal of Sociology* 100(4):1528–51. March.

Lee, Hy-sang. 1988. "North Korea's Closed Economy: The Hidden Opening." *Asian Survey* 28(12):1264–79. December.

Leibenstein, Harvey. 1966. "Allocative Efficiency versus 'X-Efficiency." *American Economic Review* 56(3):392–415. June.

Lem, Samuel. 2003. "Seoul Court convicts 6 over summit funds." *International Herald Tribune.* 27 September.

Lipset, Seymour Martin, and Georgy Bence. 1994. "Anticipations of the failure of communism." *Theory and Society* 23(2):169–210. April.

Maddison, Angus. 2003. *The World Economy: Historical Statistics.* Paris: OECD Development Research Centre.

Manyin, Mark. 2006. "U.S. Aid to North Korea: Fact Sheet." Washington, D.C.: Library of Congress Congressional Research Service. 31 January. RS-21834.

McDonald, Joe. 2004. "WFP makes emergency food appeal for North Korea, saying supplies nearly exhausted." *Associated Press.* 9 February.

Merrill, John. 1991. North Korea's halting efforts at economic reform." Chong-Sik Lee and Se-Hee Yoo, eds. *North Korea in Transition.* Berkeley, CA: Institute of East Asian Studies. 139–53.

Moorehead, Alan. 1956. *Gallipoli.* London: Hamish Hamilton.

Nevinson, Henry W. *The Dardanelles Campaign.* London: Nisbet & Co.

Newcomb, William J. 2003. "Economic Development in North Korea: Reflections on North Korea's Economic Reform." *2003 Korea's Economy.* Washington, DC: Korea Economic Institute. May 2003.

Nodong Sinmun, 2003a. Translated text available at: http://www.nautilus.org/pub/ftp/napsnet/special_reports/MilitaryFirstDPRK.txt 21 March.

————. 2003b. Translated text available at: http://www.nautilus.org/pub/ftp/napsnet/ special_reports/MilitaryFirstDPRK.txt 3 April.

Noland, Marcus. 2000. "The Meaning in the Meeting of the Two Koreas: Out of Isolation," *Washington Post.* 12 June.

————. 2002. "West-Bound Train Leaving the Station: Pyongyang on the Reform Track." Available electronically at: http://www.iie.com/publications/papers/noland 1002.htm October.

————. 2004. *Korea After Kim Jong Il.* Policy Analyses in International Economics 71:12–19. Washington, DC: Institute for International Economics. January.

Oakeshott, Michael. 1991. *Rationalism in Politics and Other Essays.* Indianapolis, IN: Liberty Press.

Oh, Kongdan. 1990. "North Korea's response to the world: Is the door ajar?" *RAND Paper Series* P-7616.

People's Republic of China (PRC). Various years. *Chinese Customs Statistics.* Beijing: General Administration of Customs.

Polsby, Nelson W. ed. 1982. *What If? Explorations in Social-Science Fiction.* Lexington, MA: Lewis.

Republic of Korea Ministry of Unification (ROK MOU). Various years. Inter-Korean Cooperation. Seoul: Tongilbu. Available at: http://www.unikorea.go.kr/en/EPA/ EPA0401L.jsp

————. Various years. *Wolgan Nambuk Kyoryu Hyomnyok Tonghyang* (Monthly North-South Exchange and Co-operation Trends). Seoul: Tongilbu.

Ruediger Frank. 2003. "A Socialist Market Economy in North Korea? Systemic Restrictions and a Quantitative Analysis." Columbia University. Unpublished.

Scalapino, Robert. 1992. *The Last Leninists: The Uncertain Future of Asia's Communist States.* Washington, D.C.: CSIS.

Stephens, Lt. Col. Cortez D. 1993. "Gallipoli—What Went Right?" *Marine Corps Gazette.* 77 (10):73–77. October.

United Nations. 2002. *Consolidated Inter-Agency Appeal 2003: Democratic People's Republic of Korea.* Available at: http://www.reliefweb.nt/appeals/2003/files/dprk03.dpf November.

————. 2003. World Population Prospects Database. New York:. UN Population Division. Available at: http://esa.un.org/unpp

United States Agency for International Development (USAID). U.S. Overseas Loans and Grants, Obligations and Loan Authorizations: The Greenbook Data. Washington, D.C.: USAID. Available at: http://qesdb.cdie.org/gbk/index.html

————. Census Bureau (USCB). 2006. International Data Base. Washington, D.C.: USCB, International Programs Center. Available at: http://www.census.gov/ipc/ www/idbagg.html

Ward, Andrew. 2003. "Six convicted for Korea payments." *Financial Times.* 27 September.

Watson, Lieutenant Colonel S.H. 1982. "The Gallipoli Blunder." *The Army Quarterly and Defense Journal* 112(2):178–83. April.

World Trade Organization (WTO). 2006. *Statistics Database.* Geneva: WTO. Available at: http://www.wto.org/english/res_e/statis_e/statis_e.htm

Yonhap News Service. 2003. "N. Korea Depreciates Its Currency. Adopts Floating Rates: Asahi." Seoul. 4 October.

List of Abbreviations and Definitions
of Specific Korean Terms

ADB	Asian Development Bank
APES	(National) Asia Pacific Economic and Scientific Database
BEC	Broad Economic Categories (Classification by)
BIS	Bank for International Settlements
BOK	Bank of Korea (ROK)
CBS	Central Bureau of Statistics, or *Choson Chungang Tong-gye Kuk*
CDC	Centers for Disease Control
"chaebol"	Korean family-owned business association
CIA	Central Intelligence Agency (U.S.)
C.i.f.	Cost, insurance, and freight
CMEA	Council for Mutual Economic Assistance
DIA	Defense Intelligence Agency (U.S.)
DMZ	Demilitarized Zone
DPRK	Democratic People's Republic of Korea, or North Korea
EY	Executive Yuan
EAS	East Asia (region of FBIS reporting)
FAO	Food and Agriculture Organization
FBIS	Foreign Broadcasting Information Service (U.S.)
FSM	Foreign sector managers
F.o.b.	Free-on-board
FRG	Federal Republic of Germany
FY	Fiscal year
GDCF	Gross domestic capital formation
GDP	Gross domestic product
GDR	German Democratic Republic
GNI	Gross national income
GNP	Gross national product
HS	Harmonized System
IAEA	International Atomic Energy Agency

IBRD	International Bank for Reconstruction and Development
IDA	International Development Association
IFC	International Finance Corporation
IFI	International Financial Institutions
IIE	Institute for International Economics
IISS	International Institute of Strategic Studies
IMF	International Monetary Fund
ISIC	International Standard Industrial Classification of all Economic Activities (ISIC)
ILO	International Labour Organization
JETRO	Japanese External Trade Organization now JETO
"juche"	Roughly, "self-reliance"
JV	Joint venture
"kangsong taeguk"	"strong and prosperous state"
KCNA	*Korean Central News Agency* (DPRK)
KIEP	Korea Institute for International Economic Policy
KDI	Korea Development Institute
KEDO	Korean Peninsula Energy Development Organization
KINU	Korea Institute for National Reunification
KOTRA	Korea Trade Investment Promotion Agency
KPA	Korean People's Army (DPRK)
LWR	light water reactor
MOU	Ministry of Unification current English name of former Ministry of National Unification (MNU)
NDC	National Defense Commission
NDFSK	National Democratic Front of South Korea now
NECF	North Korean National Economic Cooperation Federation
N.e.s.	Not elsewhere specified
NPT	Non-Proliferation Treaty
NSO	National Statistics Office (ROK)
NUB	National Unification Board (ROK)
ODA	Overseas development aid
OECD	Organisation for Economic Co-operation and Development
OLS	Ordinary least squares regression
POC	Processing on commission
PPP	Purchasing power parity
PRC	People's Republic of China
RCA	Revealed comparative advantage
ROC	Republic of China
ROK	Republic of Korea

SED	Socialist Unity Party (East Germany)
SFTC	Standard Foreign Trade Classification
SITC	Standard International Trade Classification
SMPB	System of Material Product Balances
SNA	System of National Accounts
"songun chongchi"	"military-first politics"
SPA	Supreme People's Assembly (DPRK)
SPC	State Planning Commission (DPRK)
TFR	Total fertility rate
UNFPA	United Nations Population Fund
"urisik sahoejuui"	"our own style of socialism"
USAID	United States Agency for International Development
USDA	United States Department of Agriculture
USCB	United States Census Bureau
USCDC	United States Centers for Disease Control and Prevention
USCIA	United States Central Intelligence Agency
USDIA	United States Defense Intelligence Agency
WDI	World Development Indicators
WFP	World Food Programme
WFOE	Wholly foreign owned enterprises
WPK	Workers' Party of Korea (*Choson Nodongdang*) (DPRK)
WMD	Weapons of mass destruction
WTO	World Trade Organization

Index

317